SAMSUNG
SAMSUNG
SAMSUNG
CFC
9
12
17
11

OUT
OF THE
BLUE

GARY THACKER

OUT OF THE BLUE

Chelsea's Unlikely Champions League Triumph

pitch

First published by Pitch Publishing, 2022

Pitch Publishing
A2 Yeoman Gate
Yeoman Way
Worthing
Sussex
BN13 3QZ
www.pitchpublishing.co.uk
info@pitchpublishing.co.uk

A CIP catalogue record is available for this book from the British Library.

ISBN 978 1 80150 081 4

Typesetting and origination by Pitch Publishing

Printed and bound in India by Replika Press Pvt. Ltd.

Contents

This book is dedicated to my wife Sue, to Megan and Luke, Lydia and Gregory, and my beautiful granddaughters Eve and Polly.

* * *

It is also dedicated to all those who always supported and believed in me.
You are my strength.
And to those who only ever doubted me.
You are my inspiration.

Acknowledgements

MANY PEOPLE have assisted in the production of this book.

The following have generously agreed to be interviewed, and allowed me to use their wise words:

- Alan Addicott – assistant sports editor on *The Sun* between October 2010 and November 2014
- Kieran Allen – project manager at a promotions and events company; Chelsea fan and son of Danny Ridgeway
- Ryan Baldi – author, and sportswriter for the BBC, *The Guardian*, and *The Independent* as well as other magazines and websites
- Mike Collett – Reuters global soccer editor for 25 years until retiring in 2016
- John Helm – commentator for ITV on the 2008 Champions League Final
- Uli Hesse – German author, journalist and editor
- Seb Hutchinson – freelance sports commentator
- Luís Mateus – Portuguese journalist, football writer, analyst and pundit
- Jason Pettigrove – content editor at FC Barcelona

- Joe Ridgeway – manager at an electrical contractor; Chelsea fan and son of Danny Ridgeway
- Danny Ridgeway – retired college principal; lifelong Chelsea fan who saw his first match in February 1962
- Jonathan Northcroft – *Sunday Times* football correspondent
- Ian Ross – former journalist for *The Times*, *Daily Telegraph* and *The Guardian*
- Andy West – Spanish football correspondent for BBC Sport and commentator for La Liga TV
- Mark Worrall – author and long-time Chelsea fan

Special thanks also to:

- Sky UK Limited for supplying the author with access to archived television footage
- Stuart Horsfield, Steven Scragg, Aidan Williams and all colleagues at *These Football Times* for their help and unstinting encouragement.

Finally, thanks to all at Pitch Publishing for their professionalism and dedication.

Sincere thanks to one and all.

Introduction

AS ALMOST any football fan knows, the game can often be a strange mixture between the predictable and the unexpected, where the outcome is often teetering on a knife-edge, an eternal battle between a seemingly inevitable pathway and an invading element of chaos, keen to turn the expected into merely what might have been. On occasions, the fate of an individual game, or even a tournament, can appear to have been written in advance; conceived, predetermined and planned to the most minute detail by some celestial hand beyond our meagre human comprehension. At other times, events can suggest that such a thing is the case, only then to be harshly disavowed by an apparent quirk of fate, a twist of the knife, a malicious reality now revealed. All that seemed right is now wrong. All that seemed certain is imperilled. All that seemed to be coming together is now torn asunder.

In 2008, when Chelsea faced Manchester United in the Champions League Final, the latter was the case. The game took place in Moscow, and Chelsea owner Roman Abramovich was in the stand to watch the team his largesse has brought together deliver European club football's ultimate honour to him in the capital of his home country. It seemed to be written, as John Terry stepped up to convert the penalty that would take the trophy to Stamford Bridge, despite more than a few twists and turns on the way. Come the pivotal moment of the encounter though, chaos kicked down the door, and fate turned its face away from those wearing blue. The rain, a slip, a mishit and a few tears ended the story and denied what seemed to be the inevitable playing out of fate.

At other times, that celestial script is adhered to, and not even the coquettish caprices of chance dare to interfere. In such games, any human agency is just an unknowing, but obedient, adherent to a script, no matter how improbable the unfolding story appears to be. There are no genuine ad-libs, no improvisation, no off-the-cuff extemporisations. What is perceived as individuality is, in reality, mere slavish compliance to the preordained. At these times, there's one path and everyone is following it. No matter what may be seen to offer a detour from that path it will, it can only ever, be a deceptive diversion, leading eventually back to the inevitable. Sometimes, it's written. Sometimes.

Four years after Moscow, following a series of games that pointed the club to the door marked 'Exit' on numerous occasions, Chelsea once more had reached a Champions League Final. This time, the home advantage lay with their opponents. Facing the might of Bayern Munich in the Bavarian fortress of the Allianz Arena, all the smart money was on the German club winning the trophy. A huge banner behind one of the goals declared 'Our City. Our Stadium. Our Trophy' for any who might be clinging to a fantasy-like dream of an upset.

Overdrawn at the bank of good fortune following the epic and heroic backs-to-the-wall confrontations with Pep Guardiola's Barcelona in the semi-final, Chelsea surely could not go to the well again without the bucket coming up empty – could they? Well, sometimes, these things are indeed written. The tale of how Chelsea arrived at, and then won, the 2012 Champions League Final reads like a far-fetched tale, an outlandish yarn with interwoven threads that stretch boundaries of belief, but perhaps one that, putting it simply, was truly 'written'. 'If someone wrote a film about a football team who somehow managed to win the Champions League,' Frank Lampard said later, 'I think that was the year that we did it.'[1] Surely no Hollywood scriptwriter would ever consider such a story though, it's far too outlandish. Only reality can conjure up such events. It was a triumph that came out of the blue.

1 *Kings of Europe – The Chelsea Story*, Sky UK Limited, 16 September 2012.

1

Mourinho 1.0 to Mourinho 2.0?

'Of all the European finals I covered – Champions League, Cup Winners' Cup, UEFA Cup and even Inter-Cities Fairs Cup I think the devastation of defeat was more poignant in Chelsea's case than any other.'[2]

John Helm

THE RUN to Moscow had been taken over, midstream, by Avram Grant, when the tenure of José Mourinho had come to an end. As has been the case with many of the clubs managed by the Portuguese, the established pattern whereby early success is inevitably followed by discord, disagreement and dismissal applied at Stamford Bridge. After delivering back-to-back Premier League titles in 2004/05 and 2005/06, plus an FA Cup triumph the following year and two League Cups, by the 2007/08 season the downslope had definitely been reached.

---

2 Helm, John – commentator for ITV television on the 2008 Champions League Final, interview with the author.

That season's Champions League campaign had opened with a dispiriting 1-1 home draw against Norway's Rosenborg. It marked the end of the road. Mourinho left, with the club issuing that most universally inappropriate statement on 20 September 2007, announcing that the departure had been 'by mutual consent'. Rumoured to be a personal friend of Abramovich, Grant had been employed by the club as director of football since 8 July of the same year. Perhaps the owner had seen the writing on the wall with the incumbent coach, and was getting his ducks all lined up for when the inevitable parting of the ways happened. When Grant took over the manager's chair – in a move that was echoed some years later, when Roberto Di Matteo was brought in to work as assistant to André Villas-Boas – the club promoted Steve Clarke, former player and coach under Mourinho, to the position of Grant's assistant. Well known to the players, and respected, it was a shrewd decision that helped lubricate the wheels of change.

Whatever the case of that, Grant was shrewd enough to appreciate that there was precious little wrong with the squad that a little soothing of bruised egos and installing of a confidence that had wilted under the dog days of Mourinho's reign wouldn't solve. Adopting a 'steady as she goes' sort of philosophy, with Clarke very much seen as the training ground leader, Grant's calming hand on the tiller saw Chelsea recover from the stuttering start of their Champions League campaign to reach Moscow where, but for that slip by Terry, the Israeli may well have achieved legendary status at the club, and certainly retained his position.

As it was, the rain that had poured down on the Luzhniki Stadium pitch, slicking up the playing surface and leading to Terry's missed penalty, also washed away Grant's tenure as manager. Whether merely the victim of inclement weather and ill fortune or not, the Abramovich temptation to change managers was always on a hair-trigger setting.

With Grant gone, Chelsea cast their eyes over to South America, and their gaze alighted on Luiz Felipe Scolari. 'Big Phil' as he was widely known had been the scourge of England under Sven-Göran Eriksson, defeating the Three Lions with Brazil in the World Cup of 2002 when his *Selecao*, and Ronaldinho in particular, destroyed the myth of David Seaman having 'Safe Hands' during the quarter-final in Shizuoka. Two years later, now coaching Portugal as they hosted the 2004 European Championship, it was another last-eight elimination for England at the hands of Scolari as his team won through in a penalty shoot-out. Then, to round out the trilogy, at the 2006 World Cup another quarter-final, another penalty shoot-out saw Scolari prosper again, and England sent home as their spot kick nemesis struck again in Gelsenkirchen.

In typical Chelsea fashion it was both an ambitious appointment and an adventurous one. Although widely experienced in both South America and the Middle East, Scolari had never previously managed a European club, and there was plenty of controversy about the timing of the appointment's announcement. The Brazilian was still working with the Portugal team, strongly involved in the European Championship, when Chelsea broke the news. It's unclear how much disruption it caused in the Portugal ranks, but it can hardly have helped matters.

If the coach's departure was less than harmonious with his players, there was a not too dissimilar reaction from the squad he joined. The spine of the Chelsea team had several strong characters, not least Terry, but also Lampard, Petr Čech and Didier Drogba. Grant had succeeded – at least in part – by cajoling and encouraging, rather than challenging and contesting. Scolari wanted to bring in his own way of playing and expected the squad to adapt to it. In this particular club, it was a forlorn pursuit.

A difficult period in the Premier League radically weakened the Brazilian and, on 9 February 2009, following a 2-0 defeat at Liverpool and a dreary goalless draw at home to Hull City that left Chelsea in fourth place, seven points adrift of leaders Manchester United, Abramovich's trigger finger twitched again. Scolari was sacked. He had made a strong start to the campaign, going a dozen games without defeat, and had progressed through the group stages of the Champions League and reached the fifth round of the FA Cup. The club's form in the Premier League had fallen away badly, however, and just three wins in the last nine games had sounded the death knell. It was only the second time in a coaching career spanning 26 years that the Brazilian had been dismissed and, other than a brief period in Uzbekistan with Tashkent club FC Bunyodkor, he would not coach in Europe again.

In another of those so carefully worded statements that superficially says much, but means little, the club declared, 'Felipe has brought many positives to the club since he joined and we all feel a sense of sadness that our relationship has ended so soon. Unfortunately, the results and performances of the team appeared to be deteriorating at a key time in the season.'[3]

Old favourite Ray Wilkins was brought in on a brief caretaker basis, with rumours abounding of Chelsea seeking to poach former hero Gianfranco Zola away from West Ham United. Other names mentioned included another former player, Didier Deschamps, along with Eriksson,

---

3 'Chelsea sack Scolari after seven months at Stamford Bridge', *The Guardian*, 9 February 2009.

Frank Rijkaard and Roberto Mancini. When the decision was announced, however, Abramovich had gone back to his Russian connections for a temporary solution.

There had been stories circulating for a while that the salary of Guus Hiddink as the Russia national team manager was being met by Abramovich; some even suggested that the figure amounted to some £3.4m.[4] There was therefore some measure of effective persuasion when the Chelsea owner sought permission from the Russian FA to 'borrow' Hiddink for the remainder of the season.

The Dutchman's time in charge was brief, covering just a few months, but in that time he quickly became hugely popular with both players and fans at Stamford Bridge. Despite the poor form that cost Scolari his job, Hiddink was in an upbeat mood when interviewed by Chelsea TV on 12 February. '[The club] are in several races: the FA Cup is there, the Champions League and also the league. There is a ten-point difference [if United win their game in hand] but if you look in the past at this league, and other leagues as well, some things can happen during the final stages of the championship. All three roads are very important: the next game [in the FA Cup at] Watford, and then Aston Villa and Juventus, and then you go on the path of the Champions League and that is so attractive. The club has the experience to go to the final.

'When I was at Real Madrid, we did not win the league title. I haven't worked in England, which is considered the biggest league in the world, so [winning the title] would be a huge achievement. We try to go for this title, yes. I am not just here to add to my experience with the club

---

4 'As Chelsea feel pinch, Roman Abramovich dips into his pocket to pay Russia £3.4m for coach Hiddink's salary', *Daily Mail,* 4 December 2008.

and the Premier League. I want to see results as soon as possible.'[5]

That upbeat approach was precisely the tonic that the club had been looking for. Someone was needed to drag it from the pit of disillusion into which it had been gradually sinking, and the new man delivered the required dose of positivity. Hiddink would garner due reward. His first game in charge saw a 1-0 win at Villa Park, followed by a home victory over Juventus in the Champions League propelling Chelsea into a last-eight confrontation with their old adversaries, Liverpool.

The first leg visit to Anfield produced a 3-1 victory, with a brace from Branislav Ivanović and a strike by Drogba outweighing Steven Gerrard's early goal. In the return leg, a pulsating roller coaster of a game back in London saw an epic 4-4 draw, and Chelsea had qualified for the semi-finals of the Champions League. In the previous round, Liverpool had beaten the mighty Real Madrid in both home and away legs, accumulating a thumping 5-0 aggregate win. Defeating Rafa Benitez's Liverpool team was a huge psychological lift. Suddenly the sullen clouds enveloping Stamford Bridge were blown away. Was Hiddink the 'Golden Guus'?

For a while, it seemed there was little Hiddink could do wrong. Chelsea travelled to Barcelona and returned with a highly creditable goalless draw. Back at Stamford Bridge, a thumping volley by Michael Essien seemed to have paved the way to victory and a hasty return to the Champions League Final. A second-half red card for Eric Abidal only looked to confirm the flow of the game, but with no less than four worthy penalty claims denied by Norwegian referee Tom Henning Øvrebø, the single goal was a fragile lead and when

5 Chelsea TV, 12 February 2011.

Andres Iniesta fired home an injury-time equaliser, the full cost of what Chelsea fans considered to be Øvrebø's glaring errors of judgement was exposed.

Were they errors? Whatever the case, there was clearly no excuse for the abuse and threats the official received from a section of brutishly aggressive fans. A few years later, Øvrebø accepted he had made mistakes in the game. Interviewed by *Marca*, he confessed, 'It was not my best day, really, but those mistakes can be committed by a referee, and sometimes a player or a coach. Some days you are not at the level you should be. But no, I can't be proud of that performance.'[6] So many years after the event, it offered the coldest of comforts to Chelsea and their fans. The club was denied the opportunity to contest their second consecutive Champions League Final against Manchester United.

There was a measure of compensation as Hiddink guided Chelsea to an FA Cup Final against Everton and a 2-1 victory delivered some tangible reward for the Dutchman's brief tenure in the capital. The Premier League ended with Chelsea in third place and qualifying for the Champions League but, despite Hiddink suffering just one defeat in his reign – a 1-0 loss to Spurs – the gap to Manchester United, who won the title, remained stubbornly at seven points. In his time at Stamford Bridge, Hiddink would record an impressive win rate of 73 per cent. To put that into perspective, it was higher than that achieved by Mourinho despite his successes and trophies. At the club's final home game of the season, a 2-0 win over Blackburn Rovers, incessant chants from the crowd for Abramovich to 'sign him up' were both complimentary, but ultimately pointless. Hiddink was committed to returning full time to his job

6 'Øvrebø after Chelsea vs Barcelona: That night we had to change hotels', *Marca*, 18 February 2018.

with Russia, and Chelsea had already lined up the man to lead them into the following season.

The new man at the helm was Italian Carlo Ancelotti. The former AC Milan coach had led the *Rossoneri* to two Champions League triumphs, plus a brace of Serie A titles, and an Intercontinental Cup success. If Abramovich was looking for a coach with a winning continental pedigree, he'd found his man. Following the path taken with Steve Clarke and Avram Grant, the popular Ray Wilkins was installed as the Italian's assistant. It was a logical appointment as Wilkins had played alongside Ancelotti during his three-year spell with Milan. The new season would see the club achieve a success that had eluded them for their entire existence so far, but also endure a defeat that planted the seeds of doubt that would grow into full flowering with the coach's dismissal at the end of 2010/11.

Domestically, the 2009/10 season was a story of success, if not outright dominance. Aside from a League Cup fifth-round defeat on penalties against Blackburn Rovers in December, Chelsea scooped up all of the domestic trophies available to them. There was an early taste of what was to follow when, during the traditional curtain-raiser to the season, they overcame Manchester United on penalties to win the Community Shield at Wembley. It hardly compensated for the loss to the same club back in Moscow, but at least it got the season off to a good start, and set a trend that would see the club secure both the Premier League title and successfully retain the FA Cup, breaking records along the way.

In the league, Chelsea set a new mark for the most goals scored, netting 103 times across the 38-game programme. They also broke the record for the most home goals scored, with Stamford Bridge fans seeing their favourites hit the back of the net 68 times, and their final goal difference of +71 was also a record. The statistics are an empirical confirmation of a season that saw Chelsea redefined as a team playing ebullient, entertaining football with the ever-smiling Ancelotti, left eyebrow perpetually raised, offering up the image of a kindly, knowledgeable uncle and, at the same time, softening the hard-edged image of the club as one that had merely purchased success and had no true style or history.

The former accusation was something fans of opposing clubs, displaced by the new 'fastest gun in town', often threw at Chelsea fans. There was of course some measure of truth in Abramovich's largesse allowing Chelsea to elbow their way to the top table of English football, but it also ignored the fact that other clubs that had dominated in recent times – Manchester United, Arsenal and to some extent Liverpool and Blackburn – had done precisely the same thing. Under Ancelotti though, while it would be stretching things to say that Chelsea became liked, it's true that they became 'less disliked'.

On 3 April, Chelsea visited Old Trafford for, as the season played out, what proved to be a pivotal game in deciding the fate of the league title. Despite a late goal from Federico Macheda offering a glimmer of hope, earlier strikes from Joe Cole and Didier Drogba had given Chelsea a lead that Sir Alex Ferguson's team just failed to overhaul. On 9 May, the last games of the season saw Stoke City visit Old Trafford, and Wigan Athletic travel to Stamford Bridge with Chelsea holding a one-point advantage. United delivered on their requirement, defeating the Potteries side 4-0, but their efforts were rendered irrelevant by Chelsea rattling in eight goals to secure the title. Six days later, the Double was confirmed as the Blues overcame Portsmouth to retain the FA Cup.

If all seemed rosy in the Stamford Bridge garden, three months earlier a rare defeat had set forth a chain of events that would see the club hierarchy begin to doubt whether Ancelotti was the right man for the job. The loss of that Champions League Final of 2008 had seen the club come so close, so very close, to achieving Abramovich's stated dream and following that agonising defeat, it seemed that all coaches would be judged by success or failure in that competition. The Russian oligarch was a man used to getting what he wanted. He had laid out a sizeable measure of his personal fortune to provide different coaches with the means to achieve the desired end, and he expected, he demanded, results.

Ancelotti's Champions League campaign had begun well. Chelsea had skated through their initial stage undefeated and topped a group comprising Porto, Atlético Madrid and the Cypriot club, APOEL. As a group winner, they would play a runner-up in the round of 16 and, as the wild caprices of fate would have it, they were drawn against Internazionale who had finished second behind Barcelona in their group. Currently coaching Inter was none other than a certain José Mourinho, who had moved to the *Nerazzurri* after leaving Chelsea. The old saying is that revenge is a dish best served cold, and in this tournament Mourinho would enjoy exacting revenge on both Chelsea and Barcelona. The Catalans had scorned his approach to take control when they opted for Pep Guardiola instead, and then, for good measure, defeated the Portuguese's Italian club in the group games.

Chelsea visited Milan on 24 February 2010, and despite falling to an early goal from Diego Milito, Salomon Kalou equalised, before Esteban Cambiasso gave Inter a 2-1 lead to take to Stamford Bridge on 16 March. Despite having much of the attacking play in the return leg, Chelsea fell to a goal from Samuel Eto'o entering the final ten minutes of the game. They failed to find an adequate response in the remaining time and were eliminated. For the first time in four years they had failed to at least reach the quarter-final stage of the competition.

The higher cost to be paid, however, was that Ancelotti was perceived as having been out-thought by the man Chelsea had dismissed years earlier. Mourinho had exacted his revenge on the Stamford Bridge hierarchy and would take similar vengeance on Barcelona for shunning him. In the semi-final, Inter defeated Guardiola's team both home and away, before completing the perfect job interview by guiding his team to success in the final at the Estadio Santiago Bernabéu, before being appointed as coach to Real Madrid. Despite the fact that Mourinho's ultimate success in the Champions League would have caused envious angst at Stamford Bridge, given his domestic success, Ancelotti had banked sufficient goodwill to, at least temporarily, offset the doubts raised by the defeat to Inter, and Mourinho's triumph.

The new season began hopefully. A 6-0 win at home to West Bromwich Albion on the opening day was followed by another half-dozen without reply away to Wigan Athletic. Perhaps not the most challenging of opening fixtures, but 12 goals scored and none conceded was wildly encouraging. There then followed home wins against Stoke City and Blackpool, and away at West Ham United. Going into the sixth game of the season, Chelsea had garnered maximum points, having scored 21 times, and conceded a single goal. A 1-0 loss to Manchester City seemed to burst the balloon though and in the next 15 games, up to the middle of January 2011, they would record only five league victories.

On the day following the fourth of those five wins, on 11 November, Chelsea announced that Ray Wilkins's contract with the club would not be renewed and that he was leaving with immediate effect. Apparently, totally surprised by the decision, in a statement issued on his behalf by the League Managers' Association Wilkins initially claimed that he had been the victim of 'undoubtedly unfair dismissal' and would take legal advice in an attempt to reach 'an amicable solution'.[7] On the first day of December, however, *The Telegraph* reported that Wilkins announced that he had reached a 'harmonious conclusion' with the club. Whether that conclusion included a gagging clause on Wilkins was unclear, but the real reason for his dismissal has been shrouded in doubt ever since. It seemed a strange decision, and hardly helped matters on the pitch.

Chelsea had led the league table for most of the first half of the season, but once they lost top spot to Manchester United they would not redeem it again as results and performances tailed off badly. Three games from the middle of January brought hope with successive victories and, on the last day of the transfer window, reinforcements arrived. A British record-breaking transfer fee prised Fernando Torres from Liverpool, and he was joined by two signings from Benfica, David Luiz and Nemanja Matić.

Signing Torres, then widely regarded as the top striker in Europe, appeared to be a major coup, destined to reignite the club's ambitions. Sadly for Chelsea, the player who travelled down the M6 from Merseyside to London was a much-depleted talent from the one who Rafa Benitez had signed from Atlético Madrid and had scored 65 goals in a shade over a century of league appearances for the Anfield club. He wouldn't score his first goal for Chelsea until 24 April when, on a rain-sodden Stamford Bridge

7 'Ray Wilkins: I was unfairly sacked by Chelsea', *The Telegraph*, 20 November 2010.

pitch, he notched the middle goal in a 3-0 home win against West Ham.

A 1-0 defeat at home to Liverpool blunted the short run of success, but Chelsea then won eight of their next nine league games before rounding out the season with two losses and a draw. Success in Europe may have saved the Italian, but after a solid group stage and a less than impressive round of 16 win over FC Copenhagen, a quarter-final loss to Manchester United eliminated Chelsea. The final league game at Goodison Park brought a 1-0 defeat and the unseemly spectacle of Ancelotti apparently being dismissed in the corridors of the Everton stadium. After returning from the post-match press conference, the coach was met by chief executive Ron Gourlay outside of the media suite and told that he was being relieved of his position with immediate effect. It seemed to be an unnecessarily harsh and insensitive way to deliver the news. Typically, Ancelotti responded with grace and humility, 'I accept the decision and respect it. I am proud of the job I did but now I must think about my future. In my mind I would like to stay in the Premier League – that is my first choice.'[8]

Although it was in different circumstances, there was a similar feeling about the club when Ancelotti left as there had been after Hiddink's brief, but happy, tenure. What had been achieved initially should surely have been the catalyst for more success, but it wasn't to be, and Chelsea began the search for a new manager.

Unsurprisingly, one of the names bandied around in the press was Hiddink. A return to Stamford Bridge, on a full-time basis, looked an appetising prospect for Chelsea fans. Other names rumoured to be linked with the post included

---

8 'Chelsea sack Carlo Ancelotti within an hour of defeat by Everton', *The Guardian*, 23 May 2011.

Marco van Basten, Didier Deschamps – again, and Harry Redknapp. One name, far less well known than so many of the other contenders, began cropping up though with increasing regularity – André Villas-Boas.

When 16 years old, Villas-Boas happened to be living in the same apartment block occupied by Bobby Robson during his successful spell as coach of Porto. As football-obsessed as any teenage boy, the story goes that Robson's neighbour would surreptitiously slip notes through the letterbox of the coach's door, offering advice on tactics, team selection, and how the performance of the Porto team could be improved. At one stage, he even 'sought him out on the stairwell to protest against Domingos Paciencia's omission from the first team'.[9]

Unlike any number of coaches who would have given short shrift to such gauche approaches and, the typical gentleman that he was, Robson not only tolerated the over-enthusiastic teenager but also befriended him and encouraged his ambitions, eventually taking him on as a member of the club's coaching team working on player observation and analysis. Perhaps Robson had discerned something worthy in Villas-Boas's comments, or perhaps he recognised a nascent talent fuelled by enthusiasm for the game.

Villas-Boas's talent developed and Robson arranged for him to study for a UEFA coaching qualification in Scotland, and to supplement his studies by observing training and coaching sessions at his old English club, Ipswich Town. The assiduously committed Villas-Boas passed every test and progressed through the C Licence at just 17, the B Licence the following year, and the A Licence before his 20th birthday, before achieving the Pro Licence. At the

---

9 'José Mourinho and André Villas-Boas: how the inseparable duo grew apart', *The Guardian,* 26 September 2013.

tender age of just 21 years old, Villas-Boas was appointed to be head coach to the national team of the British Virgin Islands in the Caribbean.

Robson may have had a similar feel for the man who had been appointed as his interpreter when he joined his first Portuguese club, Sporting Lisbon, in 1992, later co-opting the young José Mourinho into his coaching setup, who then followed the former England manager to Barcelona. When Robson left the *Blaugrana* and moved briefly back to PSV Eindhoven, and then on to Newcastle United, Mourinho stayed in Catalonia, developing his education under new coach Louis van Gaal, before moving to Benfica as assistant to Jupp Heynckes and then taking over from the German.

In what would become a regular occurrence for Mourinho, a dispute with the club's directors led to him moving on and, after a brief stay with Uniao de Leiria, he was appointed to coach Porto, where he was reacquainted with Villas-Boas who was then working with the club's youth teams. The new coach recalled the successes of his former colleague and invited him to create an 'Observation' department at the club, scouting opposition teams and compiling dossiers on individual players. It was an offer the young and ambitious Villas-Boas readily accepted.

Villas-Boas's copious data fed into Mourinho's meticulous attention to detail and he became an integral part of Mourinho's team of assistants, often being referred to by his boss as 'my eyes and ears'.[10] Much as Mourinho had with Robson, Villas-Boas became a constant companion and valuable asset to the new head coach, following him on his travels to west London, and then on to Inter. As with so many of Mourinho's professional relationships though,

10 'José Mourinho and André Villas-Boas: how the inseparable duo grew apart', *The Guardian*, 26 September 2013.

what began as a successful collaboration, ended with a falling out.

Speaking in the Netherlands, at ASPIRE4SPORT and the Aspire Academy Global Summit in 2016, Villas-Boas recalled the early days and the success, ‘In my formative moments, working with José was the best time of my life. I was able to learn many things and working with him takes you to another level.’[11] He later added, ‘I wanted to be like him, know everything that he knew and absorb all the information he was giving.’[12]

It was while working together in Milan, however, that their relationship began to break down. The ambitious Villas-Boas was anxious to progress his career. For Mourinho, the value of his assistant was solely in the role to which he had been allotted. ‘Then you fall on the wrong side of José and that’s when things change and you realise that you’ve been blinded by someone,’[13] Villas-Boas explained.

While the post with Mourinho was an intensely useful finishing school for Villas-Boas, the younger man also saw it as a stepping stone to the things he wanted to achieve as a head coach himself. When he sought to expand his role on to the training field, there was resistance from Mourinho. Was a measure of Inter’s success attributable to the influence of Villas-Boas on the training field? The idea of moving Samuel Eto’o into a wider attacking position was a tactical stroke of genius but whose idea had it been? ‘The notion that it was [Villas-Boas’s] idea to play Samuel Eto’o wide at

---

11 ‘André Villas-Boas was “blinded by love” of José Mourinho’, skysports.com, 4 October 2016.

12 ‘André Villas-Boas was “blinded by love”’ of José Mourinho’, skysports.com, 4 October 2016.

13 ‘André Villas-Boas was “blinded by love” of José Mourinho’, skysports.com, 4 October 2016.

Inter, rather than Mourinho's, has been mooted in Italy,' [14] *The Guardian* reported. The problem was, of course, that in Team Mourinho, there's only room for a single Special One.

In early 2009, a chance for Villas-Boas to move on to the next stage of his rapidly developing career appeared to present itself. Back in Portugal, the directors of SC Braga were looking for a new coach as Jorge Jesus was leaving to take over at Benfica. Initial contact from the club led Villas-Boas to conclude that this was the role for him, and he informed Mourinho that he wanted to leave Inter. Unfortunately, no firm offer came from Braga, who appointed Domingos Paciencia – ironically the player who Villas-Boas had harangued Robson about omitting years earlier – instead.

A chastened Villas-Boas returned to Inter, frustrated, but hopeful that the events would convince Mourinho that he was worthy of an expanded role. Such hopes would be quickly dashed. Instead, if anything, his role was diminished. Perhaps it was Mourinho's way of exacting some kind of penitence for a perceived betrayal of loyalty. Those who perceive the Portuguese as arrogant and vindictive, and there are more than a few who acknowledge that they dwell in that camp, would readily believe that possibility. Alternatively, it may just have been a reorganisation that had little, if anything, to do with the apparent aspirations of a member of the coaching staff, and bore no malice at all. Whatever the case, it's difficult to see the relationship as anything other than now being on a one-way journey to divorce.

On 3 October of the same year, with his club struggling at the foot of Portugal's Primeira Liga, the Académica de Coimbra coach Rogério Gonçalves resigned. The club

14 'José Mourinho and André Villas-Boas: how the inseparable duo grew apart', *The Guardian*, 26 September 2013.

briefly installed Ze Nando as his temporary replacement, but would cast their eyes across to Lombardy for his permanent successor. Seeking a quick answer to their woes, they made a firm approach to Villas-Boas, offering him the position of head coach. The nature of football tends to be that opportunities to take over a club only occur in times of trouble, often deep trouble, but Villas-Boas was hardly put off by the enormity of the task of taking over a club yet to register a single win in the season, and approached Mourinho about moving on. This time, perhaps with the new support team structure in place following his earlier reshuffle, Mourinho wished his assistant well, and waved him on his way, with seemingly sincere good wishes. 'There was little hint of the subsequent animosity between the pair in the leaving of Italy,'[15] it was reported. Ten days after Gonçalves had resigned, Villas-Boas settled into the vacated chair. Four days short of his 32nd birthday, he was head coach of a top-tier football club. If the job was a test then it was one he would pass with distinction.

Just four days after Villas-Boas arrived, Académica enjoyed their first victory of the season, defeating Portimonense SC 2-1 in the Taça de Portugal. Although they would be eliminated in the next round, it set the tone for the remainder of the season. When the league programme was completed on 9 May 2010, the young coach had guided his club from the near certainty of relegation, and without a win in the first two months of the season, up to a comfortable mid-table 11th position, and ten points clear of the relegation zone. The amazing turnaround in fortunes had hardly been achieved by Mourinho-esque 'parking the bus' tactics, or

15 'José Mourinho and André Villas-Boas: how the inseparable duo grew apart', *The Guardian*, 26 September 2013.

as they say in Portugal by playing *antijogo*. Villas-Boas had introduced a fluid attacking style that had transformed the way Académica played. During the time he had been in charge, the 37 goals they scored was only bettered by the top five clubs in the league, and this was after their dreadful opening two months of the season. The stock of the young coach had rocketed, and bigger clubs began to cast covetous glances towards the Estádio Cidade de Coimbra.

In the same season, Porto had secured the domestic double and their coach Jesualdo Ferreira had been lured across the border to La Liga and Malaga. Ferreira had been hugely successful in his four years at the Estádio do Dragao, winning three Primeira Liga titles, and lifting the Taça de Portugal twice. His time in Spain would contrast dramatically. After nine games, with his team Malaga lying in 18th position and without a victory in half-a-dozen games, he was sacked. Back in Porto though, it meant there was a vacancy for a head coach to start the new season, and the young, enterprising manager of Académica de Coimbra was selected for the role.

If there had been doubts about Villas-Boas, perhaps being merely a big fish in a small pond while staving off relegation at Académica, they would be dispelled by the success he enjoyed at the Estádio do Dragao. Joining in June, within a couple of months he had netted his first trophy by overcoming Benfica 2-0 in Portugal's version of the Community Shield. As in many countries, these season-opening games are rarely seen as being particularly significant as an indicator for the campaign ahead. On this occasion though, that should very much have been the case.

There have been suggestions that it was this first season at Porto that led to the rift between Mourinho and Villas-Boas, with the former apparently resentful of the younger man's success and considering that it may even eclipse his own reputation with the club. Porto may have been the Dragons, with Benfica the Eagles, but with Mourinho, it may well have been a case of 'the ego has landed'. If the former Porto coach had expected, or even willed his former assistant to fail, he would be roundly disappointed. It's difficult to think how Porto's season could have been any more successful than it was.

The season opened with a home game against Paços de Ferreira and despite twice leading by two goals, it ended in a disappointing, although entertaining 3-3 draw. It would be the briefest of setbacks on a journey of glittering success. By the end of the 30-game league programme, Porto had finished no fewer than 21 points ahead of runners-up Benfica, having won 27 games, drawn three and not suffered a single defeat. It was only the second time in history that an entire Portuguese league programme had been completed without defeat and, at 33 years of age, Villas-Boas was the third-youngest man to land the Primeira Liga title and the youngest for more than 50 years.

Across those 30 league games, Porto scored 72 goals, a dozen more than the next best, and conceded a miserly 16, almost precisely half of the next best return, with both Benfica and Sporting Lisbon conceding 31. Unsurprisingly, they also had the league's top two goalscorers. The Brazilian forward, Hulk, scored 23 and Colombia's Radamel Falcao 16. The Taça de Portugal was added to complete the domestic double after a 6-2 romp in the final against Vitória de Guimarães. The success also spread into continental competition. The Europa League was won, with Porto defeating Braga – the club that had considered employing Villas-Boas a few years earlier, before looking elsewhere – 1-0 in the Dublin final.

There seemed to be a path of destiny laid out, wherein Villas-Boas would follow in the footsteps of Mourinho. He had not only emulated Mourinho's success at Porto, but as with the man who was now ensconced at the Estadio Santiago Bernabéu as Real Madrid coach, he had also followed his example of using success on a European, as well as domestic, stage to offer up the perfect job interview. His next position would keep that trend right on track. Before all the celebrations had died down at Porto, the next move on the apparent Villas-Boas inexorable march to success was being taken. On 21 June in Porto, he handed in his resignation and the following day, his new appointment was confirmed, as manager of Chelsea on a three-year contract.

Ryan Baldi is an author and sportswriter for the BBC, *The Guardian*, and *The Independent* as well as other magazines and websites. He recalls that the Chelsea motive appeared both obvious and perhaps a little naïve, 'It seemed pretty clear Chelsea were trying, in a less-than-subtle way, to recreate the magic they struck upon with José Mourinho's appointment seven years earlier. Young coach. Tremendous success with Porto. Looked suave in an expensive coat. But that was about where the similarities ended between these two very different characters.'[16]

The reception from the English football press was mixed at best. Ian Ross was a journalist at the time, writing for *The Times*, *Daily Telegraph* and *The Guardian*. He said, 'Despite his success at Porto it was generally a case of "who?" when Villas-Boas was appointed by Chelsea. Having worked under Mourinho it was inevitable that the two would be compared. I always had the feeling that despite his convivial nature

---

16 Baldi, Ryan, interview with the author.

there was a veneer of youthful arrogance simmering just below the surface – possibly the result of so many in England questioning his abilities.'[17]

There was certainly some doubt among pundits at the time. Alan Addicott, a Chelsea fan, was assistant sports editor at *The Sun*, and was less than convinced, 'I was never comfortable with the appointment of André Villas-Boas as Chelsea boss. He was brought in after the sacking of Carlo Ancelotti who had, in my opinion, been very well liked and proved that by winning a number of trophies. But as a Chelsea fan, you simply got used to Roman Abramovich changing managers if they failed to bring him what he wanted, the Champions League trophy.'[18]

As with the appointment to head Porto, this was very much a return journey for the man who became the Premier League's youngest ever manager. At both clubs before taking charge, he had spent a period of time working there under Mourinho. The unique environment at Stamford Bridge was therefore nothing new to him, and he was quick to distance himself from the sort of stance adopted by Mourinho, declaring himself far from being a 'Special One', although the club hardly helped matters in that particular pursuit.

On the day of his appointment, an official club statement hailed the new manager and his record of success, underscoring their confidence that he would lead them to 'greater success in major domestic and European competitions'.[19] As well as reportedly paying some £13.4m to buy out the remaining time of Villas-Boas's contract with Porto, it was said that he was being paid a £4.4m

17 Ross, Ian, interview with the author.

18 Addicott, Alan, interview with the author.

19 Chelsea FC statement, 22 June 2011.

salary. There were legitimate reasons for setting the bar so high.

The statement said, 'André was the outstanding candidate for the job. He is one of the most talented young managers in football today and has already achieved much in a relatively short space of time. His ambition, drive and determination matches that of Chelsea and we are confident André's leadership of the team will result in greater successes in major domestic and European competitions. André will bring his coaching experience back to a club he is already very familiar with, having previously worked here for three years. He has always been highly regarded at Chelsea and everyone here looks forward to welcoming him back and working with him.'[20]

Given that under their Russian owner, the club had won eight domestic trophies, reached a Champions League Final and made four semi-final appearances in the same competition, the aspirations were clearly high. An article in *The Telegraph* suggested that the new coach was anything but overawed by the task he faced. With a confidence born of a string of success, it suggested, 'Villas-Boas … is undaunted and is already understood to have taken soundings from senior Chelsea players.'[21]

As is so often the case in contemporary times with many major clubs, the first interview with the new coach was granted to the club's in-house television station. 'Don't expect something from one man. Expect us to create a dynamic group of everybody getting together, with the fans getting together, with people getting excited with the motivation that is in and around us. It is not about my arrival. It is about

20 Chelsea FC statement, 22 June 2011.

21 'New Chelsea manager André Villas-Boas – the fast track to Stamford Bridge', *The Telegraph*, 22 June 2011.

the continuous success of this club,' Villas-Boas asserted purposefully, adding later, 'Let's reflect on the success of the past six years at this club and what we have achieved and now what we can achieve in the next six years again. There is no doubt that the challenge for me is to keep winning. I am an individual who has that hunger for success and I want to keep it that way.'[22]

It was a mature and measured statement of intent, confident and proactive, but also inclusive and sharply in contrast to that of Mourinho. At his first press conference though, he was far more effusive, 'I wouldn't be satisfied if we don't win the Premiership. The domestic title is always the priority.'[23] It may have been just the sort of positive approach that fans wanted to hear, but also made the young manager a hostage to future fortunes, and one that would come back to haunt him.

With so many experienced players at the club having well-earned reputations for overly large egos, there was a danger that the young manager would be seen as being promoted above his worth by some in the squad. Ashley Cole was wheeled out to try and allay such fears. 'Age is just a number, he has experience of being at Porto, a big club,' Cole said in an interview with Sky Sports News. 'Hopefully he can bring that glory to Chelsea, but I don't think the age thing is anything to worry about, I don't think the players think about that. He is our manager now and we have to go out and fight for him. Whatever manager comes in we respect him, we are not kids, everyone thinks there are egos at Chelsea, but there aren't and we have to make Chelsea the

---

22 Interview with André Villas-Boas, Chelsea TV, 22 June 2011.

23 https://www.bbc.com/sport/football/17131298.

squad of a few years ago and win trophies.'[24] Not long into 2012, those words would seem to have a hollow ring.

Somewhat under the radar at the time, but hugely significant as later events played out, Chelsea also appointed Roberto Di Matteo to be assistant to the new man. The Swiss-born Italy international had pursued a coaching career following his premature retirement from playing through serious injury. Joining from Lazio in 1996 under Ruud Gullit, a debut goal against Middlesbrough rapidly endeared him to the Stamford Bridge faithful and he would enjoy a trophy-laden five seasons, winning two FA Cups, a League Cup, a UEFA Cup Winners' Cup and UEFA Super Cup, always seeming to save his goals for big occasions. In the 1996/97 FA Cup Final his long-range effort, again against Middlesbrough, after just 42 seconds of play, became the quickest goal in Wembley cup final history. He also picked on what seemed to be his favourite adversaries to score a goal in a 2-0 victory in the 1997/98 League Cup Final, before scoring the last FA Cup Final goal at the old Wembley to beat Aston Villa in the 1999/2000 final. As the fates transpired, it would be his last moment of glory as a player.

Playing in an away second leg UEFA Cup game against Switzerland's St Gallen, Di Matteo suffered a career-ending injury. Just past the half-hour, with Chelsea struggling, Di Matteo went into what seemed to be a regular sort of challenge against the home team's Daniel Imhof. It may have been the angle of the challenge or the way the legs collided but, with no blame attached to the St Gallen player, Di Matteo suffered a triple fracture of the leg. With numerous operations, recuperations and attempted recoveries, he

24 'Ashley Cole says Chelsea players will respect André Villas-Boas', *The Guardian*, 4 July 2011.

wouldn't play for 18 months and, in February 2002, was forced to concede that his career was over aged just 31.

A move into coaching followed and in July 2008 he took up his first managerial post at MK Dons, succeeding Paul Ince. In his only season there, he guided the club to a third-place finish in the league and into the play-offs, where they would lose out to Scunthorpe United in a semi-final penalty shoot-out. The following summer, after experiencing relegation from the Premier League, West Bromwich Albion sacked Tony Mowbray. Di Matteo was appointed to try and revive the ailing Midlands club and immediately achieved promotion back to the top division. Despite producing an attractive style of football and securing their status in the Premier League, a dip in results – they lost 13 of their previous 18 games – saw him moved out in February 2011. It meant that, when the call came from Chelsea, he was available and willing to take up the offer.

The appointment could perhaps have been seen as a step down for a man who had occupied the top job in his previous to posts, but Di Matteo was clearly happy to take up the role and return to Stamford Bridge, as was reported in *The Guardian* at the time. 'Di Matteo, however, insists he will have no difficulties making the transition back to an assistant's role. "It is obviously a challenge for me but I don't anticipate any problems," he confirmed. "I have got experience of being a manager, I know what it is like, and I know what it is to be a coach, so I have a bit of both and I am there to support André and any of the staff, to give what it takes for us to be successful. That's the ultimate challenge."'[25]

Di Matteo admitted it was an unexpected opportunity. '"[The] call came a bit out of the blue to be honest," said the

25 'Roberto Di Matteo happy to be No2 to André Villas-Boas at Chelsea', *The Guardian*, 4 July 2011.

41-year-old, who also had an impressive stint as MK Dons manager. "It is mostly based on the fact that he likes my football philosophy and that is why he wants me to be part of his team. I think he likes to play football and be positive and attacking and over the years if you have seen a game or two of the teams I coached I think we played the same way. I liked my teams to try and win games rather than not lose, to build, to pass. He is going to be in charge of it and we are going to be working the way he thinks is the right way to be successful.'"[26]

Bringing in a well-respected and popular figure was now a familiar move for Chelsea. It had played out reasonably well in the past, but on this occasion, it would bring the richest of rewards.

With Di Matteo now in place as his assistant, Villas-Boas took charge of his first official Chelsea training session on 7 July 2011. A week later, they would win their first game under the new management in a friendly against Wycombe Wanderers played at Chelsea's Cobham training complex. Purely designed to offer a gentle reintroduction to match action, and give the new man in charge an opportunity to see his players in what was, at least, a semi-serious game, Villas-Boas offered minutes to no fewer than 23 members of his squad and would have been broadly satisfied with a 3-0 result. The first goal came when Yossi Benayoun controlled a dropping ball in the opposing penalty areas, juggled it a couple of times, and then lobbed his shot over the goalkeeper with four minutes played.

Six minutes into the second period, a pass from Nicolas Anelka saw Torres sweep the ball home for the second goal. The last months of Ancelotti's reign had been dogged by the

---

26 'Roberto Di Matteo happy to be No2 to André Villas-Boas at Chelsea', *The Guardian*, 4 July 2011.

faltering play of the once ferociously deadly Torres, who took 903 minutes to notch his first goal for the Italian. Villas-Boas had needed to wait less than an hour. It was a promising omen. The final goal was added by Serbian centre-back Slobodan Rajković, who finished after a header on by Torres from a Yuri Zhirkov corner. The goalscorer, who had joined the club in 2007, would be a Chelsea player for four seasons but, other than friendly games such as this, would never make a first-team appearance, spending loan spells in the Netherlands with PSV Eindhoven, FC Twente and SBV Vitesse, before being sold to Bundesliga club Hamburger SV for a reported €2m six weeks or so after this game took place. It was a not unusual scenario for young players signed to Chelsea.

The fixture against Wycombe was the first in a series of six games in just 18 days, involving travels to Portsmouth, Kuala Lumpur in Malaysia, the Thai capital Bangkok, and then on to Hong Kong, before returning to the UK and a trip to Glasgow to round out the fundraising, meet and greet, promotional tour. For all the doubtlessly tiring experiences of travel, the results suggested things were going well. An own goal by former Blue Tal Ben Haim was enough for a victory in Portsmouth, before the party jetted off to Asia. Another single-goal win, thanks to a late Didier Drogba effort, accounted for a Malaysia XI in Kuala Lumpur on 21 July and, three days later, goals by Frank Lampard, José Bosingwa, Branislav Ivanović and Florent Malouda were more than enough for a comfortable win over a Thailand XI.

The party then flew to Hong Kong for the Barclays Asia Trophy. Local club Kitchee suffered similarly, being despatched in another four-goal romp thanks to Lampard, an own goal, plus strikes by Drogba and Daniel Sturridge, as Chelsea reached the final to play Aston Villa. A goal in the first minute by Josh McEachran gave Villas-Boas's team an ideal start and, when Torres added a second on the hour, the trophy was secured. It meant that the club had scored 15 goals across the half-dozen games without their defence conceding.

The final game before the real business began would take Chelsea to Ibrox and a meeting with Rangers on 6 August. On six minutes, a strike by Nikica Jelavić would puncture the Blues' defence for the first time under Villas-Boas, but a first-half brace from Sturridge and strike by Malouda ensured that the game was still won. Although inevitably half-paced at times, it would be difficult to paint these pre-season encounters as anything but encouraging. The razor-sharp competitiveness of Premier League or Champions League football may well have been absent, but seven games won out of seven can only breed confidence and the new man at the helm would lead his Chelsea team into the more meaningful competition with a sure-footed stride.

Just over a week later, the 2011/12 season would begin. Seven years previously, the club had plucked a relatively unknown manager from Portugal and begun an adventure that would lead to silverware, a brief domination of domestic football and the very cusp of European glory. José Mourinho had delivered trophies aplenty before the trauma and eventual breakdown in the relationship. Could Chelsea feasibly hope to repeat the feat with a manager widely regarded as Mourinho 2.0?

2

Dips, Dramas and the Group Stage

DESPITE THE early promise gained from an unbeaten run of pre-season games, the new regime guiding Chelsea ran into the buffers, as so many others had done, with an away fixture at Stoke City to open the season. A goalless draw in a physical battle was more than enough to drop a dollop of caution on top of the growing aspirations of Chelsea fans. If there was a more definitive way to welcome a newly appointed foreign coach to the realities of English football than a visit to Tony Pulis's Stoke, it's difficult to think of it. Not all Premier League teams played as the Potters did under the Welshman at the time, in fact few did, but unlike so many leagues around Europe there are very few easy games in the English top tier, and a visit to the Britannia Stadium has certainly never been one of them.

Being the first official match for the new coach, there was plenty of reason to reserve judgement. As well as fully deserving their obdurate reputation, Stoke's record made them more than reasonably successful. The previous season, they had reached the FA Cup Final, losing out by a single goal to Manchester City, and had already played their first round of Europa League qualifiers having defeated

Hajduk Split home and away. This was certainly no 'gimme' opening game.

The result may even have been an inadvertent boon to André Villas-Boas. Going to the Britannia Stadium was seen as a difficult task, and coming away with a goalless draw may even have been beneficial in that it served to rein in any overinflated ideas of what the new manager could reasonably have been expected to achieve so early in his time back in west London. Six days later, a home game against West Bromwich Albion offered a brighter prospect of victory and to build confidence in the new man at Chelsea's helm. Much later in the season, the return game in the West Midlands would produce the very opposite effect.

The game started poorly and Chelsea fell behind inside five minutes. A slip by Brazilian centre-back Alex allowed Shane Long to run clear and slip the ball past Hilário, who was substituting for the absent Petr Čech. If doubts had been born in the Potteries, they grew as the Chelsea defence looked anything but solid and Roy Hodgson's team – he had been chosen to replace Di Matteo, when the man now sitting on the home bench as assistant to Villas-Boas had been shown the door at The Hawthorns – could well have doubled their lead before home nerves calmed and Chelsea played their way back into the game.

José Mourinho had never hesitated to make changes when the flow of a game was going against Chelsea during his time in the Stamford Bridge hot seat, and Villas-Boas took a leaf out of his mentor's book when, ahead of the half-time break, he removed Salomon Kalou and brought on Florent Malouda. Eight minutes into the second period, with the new formation looking much more assured, Chelsea drew level when a Nicolas Anelka shot was deflected past Ben Foster by Jonas Olsson. While the visitors were still dangerous on the break, the momentum was now flowing mainly in one direction, although it took until eight minutes from time for Malouda to convert a cross from José Bosingwa and give Chelsea their first league win under Villas-Boas.

Although at this early stage the term 'project' was yet to gain the notoriety that would later be associated with it, the first couple of Villas-Boas team selections had begun to illustrate his desire to deliver on a controversial plan, apparently agreed with club owner Abramovich. Following his appointment, during one of his first press conferences on 22 June 2011, Villas-Boas had stated, 'When a manager comes, all radical changes are expected.'[27] It sounded nothing overly out of the ordinary, more the sort of noises that many incoming managers make when seeking to assert their independence and distancing themselves from any perceived failures of the previous regime. For Villas-Boas, however, there was substance in the statement and, as time went on, the project would be revealed as breaking the 'player power' that had come to be such a key factor in the way the club operated. Perhaps promoted by Mourinho, left undisturbed by Avram Grant as he surfed the success of leaving things well alone, and tolerated by Carlo Ancelotti's more permissive approach to management, the influence enjoyed by the likes of John Terry, Petr Čech, Frank Lampard and Didier Drogba, plus a few others, had grown. As well as delivering trophies, the new manager planned to change all that.

Any chance of achieving that aim would surely have been imperilled had Villas-Boas merely arrived and sought to rip up the existing order from day one. Taking on Terry and perhaps even Lampard would have immediately set him against the fans, especially with the result against Stoke and

27 '"Quitter" Roman Abramovich ruined our Chelsea project, says André Villas-Boas', *The Independent*, 12 July 2012.

the performance at home to West Bromwich Albion hardly sufficient to set the pulses racing. This would need to be an evolutionary process. Drogba had been left on the bench for the first two games, with Fernando Torres preferred to lead the line, although the Ivorian had joined the fray as a substitute in both, and Čech was unavailable for the Stamford Bridge fixture. Both appeared fairly uncontentious moves on the surface, but others would follow that would later bring the whole project into a confrontation that would make or break Villas-Boas and Chelsea's season, although fortune would have different fates in mind for the club and its manager.

Five days after the victory over West Brom, Chelsea's representatives were alongside contingents from another 31 clubs, seated in the plush surroundings of the Grimaldi Forum in Monaco for the draw for the group stages of the 2011/12 Champions League competition. Chelsea's previous success in the tournament had given them a coefficient rating of 129.157, comfortably establishing them among the top seeds in pot one, with only holders Barcelona and Manchester United, who lost to the Catalan club in the previous final, where Pep Guardiola's team delivered a masterclass display, rated above them.

At such times there's always a temptation to consider best and worst options for any particular club. The way the other pots were constructed, and bearing in mind that two clubs from the same association cannot be placed in the same group, for Chelsea, a grouping to avoid might contain Milan, Ajax and Borussia Dortmund. A more favourable route could be plotted from a section where the club would face Villarreal, Basel and APOEL. As is often the case though, when the draw was completed, Chelsea had avoided both of those scenarios and each of the clubs listed. Placed into

Group E, they would compete against Bayer Leverkusen, Valencia and the little-known Belgian club Genk, from whom they had signed goalkeeper Thibaut Courtois a few months earlier before immediately parcelling him out on loan to Atlético Madrid. It wasn't a 'group of death', but neither was it a draw that promised an easy qualification, and it certainly didn't turn out that way.

The summer transfer window didn't close until the end of August and, as well as Courtois, Chelsea would add several other players to their roster as the month drew on. Some would be significant in the coming months, others less so. Ironically, given the draw, Chelsea would take one of Valencia's prize assets from La Liga as Juan Mata moved to west London for a reported £23.5m. Joining him would be Oriol Romeu, who had played a single league game for Barcelona after graduating from the B team, and Romelu Lukaku, then a precocious teenage talent with Anderlecht. The combined fee for both would take another £20m out of the Chelsea coffers. Mata would appear in 54 games across the season – more than anyone except Čech, who featured in 56 – Romeu 24, and Lukaku a dozen. The other arrival would be Mexican Ulises Dávila, who joined from Guadalajara. As with Slobodan Rajković, the midfielder would be on Chelsea's books for five years, with loans spells in the Netherlands, Spain and Portugal, but never played an official first-team game before being sold to Mexican club Santos Laguna.

On deadline day, Raul Meireles also joined, moving from Liverpool, but was considered to be a second choice. Chelsea had fought long and hard to try and prise Tottenham Hotspur's Luka Modrić away from White Hart Lane and, as quoted in *The Guardian*, the Croat had been keen on the move, declaring, 'I would like to go to Chelsea. A lot of players would like to go there and play for Chelsea because it is one of the best clubs in the world, and so do I. I would like to play there. But we will see what will happen. Chelsea are a great club, they play in the Champions League every year, they have great players, they are ambitious and have an ambitious owner who wants to invest in the club and make it win the Champions League, the Premier League and other titles.'[28] Despite a series of increasing bids, however, Spurs chairman Daniel Levy would not to be persuaded to part with the player. Meireles was therefore taken almost as a consolation prize by the club, but the Portuguese would figure heavily, and significantly, in Chelsea's season with the £12m fee looking extremely good value. In among the issues of cup draws and transfer activity, there was also some football going on.

On the same day that Dávila crossed the Atlantic to join Chelsea, the club entertained Norwich City in their third Premier League game. Hilário retained his spot in goal, but Villas-Boas now paired Drogba and Torres as a front two. It was a move that Ancelotti had tried on any number of occasions during the previous season after the Spain striker had arrived, but without success. Much the same would result from Villas-Boas's selection. When Drogba had played alongside Anelka, the Frenchman had often dropped deeper to link the play and the pair worked well together. Despite Bosingwa scoring an early goal, the pairing up front hardly looked a good match and it was no real surprise when Norwich levelled in the second half.

With 20 minutes remaining, Drogba leapt to challenge Norwich goalkeeper John Ruddy for a high cross, but was inadvertently clattered by the goalkeeper, and out

---

28 'Luka Modrić reveals he wants to leave Tottenham for Chelsea', *The Guardian*, 18 June 2011.

cold before he hit the ground. Medical staff later told the striker that he was unconscious for six or seven minutes. He suffered concussion and sustained a perforated eardrum. Understandably, he would be unavailable for the next few games. A late Lampard penalty and an even later debut goal from Mata, coming off the bench, gave the home team victory. In truth, it had been a stumbling, unconvincing performance, but propelled Chelsea up into second place in the league.

Chelsea had one more league fixture to play before opening their Champions League campaign with a home game against Bayer Leverkusen. They visited the Stadium of Light on 10 September to face Sunderland. Čech had now returned in goal, and the back four took on a more recognisable look with Bosingwa, Terry, Branislav Ivanović and Ashley Cole. It was all change up front as well, with Daniel Sturridge and Anelka coming in as Drogba was unavailable and Torres dropped to the bench. A 2-1 victory kept thing ticking along. Now four games in, the league was taking shape. Chelsea had climbed from 11th to sixth, then fourth and, after this game, on up to third. Progress would stall from there though, and for the rest of the season they would hover between third and sixth. It was hardly a pedigree suggestive of the greatest season in the club's history.

For many players at the club, this Champions League campaign felt like a last chance of redemption after coming so close in Moscow, Drogba among them. 'Wow,' the Ivorian later recalled. 'I [was at the] end of contract [when the season ended] and for this generation, could be, could be the last one.'[29] Bayer Leverkusen had finished the previous season as

29 *Kings of Europe – The Chelsea Story*, Sky UK Limited, 16 September 2012.

runners-up to Borussia Dortmund in the Bundesliga, albeit seven points adrift of the champions. Their record suggested that they could score goals, having netted only three fewer than Dortmund, but the defence was less convincing. Conceding 44 in the 34-game season was twice as high as the champions, and was the same as that of Schalke 04, who finished in 14th position.

Having the advantage of the home game coming first, it seemed like a sound opportunity for Chelsea to register their intent and take a grip on the group if they could produce a good performance and a few goals against the German team. When Villas-Boas announced his selection, however, those not selected in the starting 11 made as much news as those who were. As expected, Drogba was still absent but, far less so, Terry was also missing – apparently purely at the manager's whim – and the team's main scoring weapon from midfield, Lampard, was left on the bench as Villas-Boas opted for a solid, rather than dynamic, central pairing in midfield with Mikel John Obi and Meireles. Sturridge, who had scored against Sunderland at the weekend, was paired with Torres, who had netted a single goal in 23 appearances for Chelsea. It seemed a perverse selection to leave Lampard out, especially with Terry not even in the matchday party, but perhaps the project was gaining momentum. If so, it's more than could be said for the game itself.

The first half was solid and stodgy with little in the way of Chelsea forward play suggesting a breakthrough as the Germans defended with growing assurance. At half-time the score remained goalless and the prospect of Chelsea dropping early points in the group grew alarmingly. After the hour, with the visitors enjoying a decent period of possession and offering more than a token threat on the home goal, it was time to accept that the team and formation was not working. A few minutes later, Sturridge and Meireles were withdrawn, with Lampard and Anelka replacing them. The cheers from the fans as Lampard entered the fray drew as much impetus from feelings of relief as they did of adulation. A few minutes later, perhaps a point had been proven to the manager as Chelsea went ahead.

David Luiz had arrived at Stamford Bridge in the same winter window as Torres, moving from Benfica. Always a controversial figure, he was popular with fans for his outgoing and ebullient personality, although often less so with coaches for his lack of defensive discipline and lapses of concentration. He hadn't featured since being substituted by Ancelotti back in May after a poor performance, and a thigh injury had delayed his return. Now he was slotted in to replace Terry and would offer some reward by scoring the opening goal on 67 minutes as he chased forward on to a lay-off from Torres to steer the ball round Bernd Leno and into the net. In typically flamboyant style, the Brazilian offered up his hands in thanks before falling to his knees and being swamped by relieved team-mates.

In stoppage time at the end of the game, neat interplay between Malouda and Torres saw the Spanish striker run clear of his marker and skip over a desperate lunging challenge by Ömer Toprak. Now at a tight angle and faced by a goalkeeper advancing to narrow any scoring opportunity, Torres slipped the ball across for Mata to tap into an empty net and make the game safe. It had hardly been a fluent performance, but a win and three points was the perfect start to Chelsea's Champions League campaign.

Interviewed after the game, Villas-Boas was intent on talking up the performance, suggesting that his team had displayed 'excellent work, excellent effort and tremendous possession'.[30] It was an analysis shared by very few observers. When reminded that the weekend would bring a visit to table-topping Manchester United, who had won all of their league games to date, including an 8-2 thrashing of Arsenal, Villas-Boas seemed to accept that Terry and Lampard may well be included from the start at Old Trafford. 'That will be a different kind of challenge altogether,' said the manager. 'We face United perhaps in their most tremendous moment of motivation, flair and style. But I think it provokes in us a good challenge. We will go there to try to win it.'[31] They were fine words, and very much what Chelsea fans expected to hear but, whereas the Blues had scored seven league goals and conceded three up to that point, Sir Alex Ferguson's team had scored 18 while only conceding the same amount. It hardly felt like a game that Chelsea were likely to win and, as the teams left the field at half-time at Old Trafford, that assessment was given a ringing endorsement.

It's often only with retrospect that matches can be identified as key turning points in a season. After only five games applying such a description to this encounter appeared to be rash but, looking back, so much that went wrong with Chelsea's season, as it progressed, could almost be compacted into this encounter as a microcosm. Three goals up at the break, United appeared to be coasting to success, with more goals for the home team being the most likely outcome in the second period. Lampard had been restored to the starting 11 but seemed to have been locked into a more defensive role; whether that was due to a tactical ploy, or merely the effects

30 'Juan Mata seals Chelsea Champions League win against Bayer Leverkusen', *The Guardian,* 13 September 2011.

31 'Juan Mata seals Chelsea Champions League win against Bayer Leverkusen', *The Guardian,* 13 September 2011.

of the flow of the game was unclear. At the back, Terry was reintroduced in place of Luiz, but with an early headed goal from Chris Smalling followed by strikes from Nani and Wayne Rooney, all seemed set for United to canter to victory. In a strange way, the first-half performance may even have been beneficial to Villas-Boas and his project. With only Drogba absent of the 'big four' perceived centres of player power at the club, the demoralising three-goal deficit may have provided grist to the coach's mill, confirming the need for change.

At least Villas-Boas didn't sit on his hands at the break. Removing Lampard for Anelka offered some forward momentum, and just a minute after the restart, an immaculate pass by the French forward saw Torres flick the ball nonchalantly past David de Gea in front of the Stretford End to offer a little hope to the visitors. For a brief second this was the Torres of bustling Liverpool vintage, as he dismissed the dark clouds of doubt that seemed to have been following him since he travelled down the M6 from Merseyside to west London.

Chelsea looked a different proposition after the goal and, although hardly dominant, at least they now had a foothold in the game. Ten minutes later, the potential fightback was nearly strangled at birth when a desperate challenge on Rooney by Bosingwa ended up with a spot kick for the home team. In an ironic twist of fate, Rooney echoed Terry's misfortune back in Moscow, slipping as he shot, and the ball flew wide. Did the miss offer Chelsea another chance? It seemed so with seven minutes remaining.

A pass from Ramires put Torres through with just de Gea to beat. A neat step-over by the striker deceived his compatriot, offering the opportunity to roll the ball home and set up a thrilling finish. Instead, however, he skewed the ball wide off his left foot, avoiding the gaping net when it truly looked easier to score. The Stretford End howled their derision as a former Liverpool player, now wearing Chelsea blue sank to his knees and bowed his head in disbelief. For the Manchester United fans, seeing a player who had performed so well against them for a bitter traditional rival, now playing for a new thrusting club trying to snatch their crown, the delight was unconfined, and they were quick to make the Spaniard aware of their joy as they wallowed in *Schadenfreude*.

If Torres's goal after the break had lifted his confidence, it had now sunk so deep into the ground to be almost subterranean. The game ended with a 3-1 defeat, Chelsea's brief four-match winning run was over and the gap between Villas-Boas's team and that of Ferguson was seen to be a gulf. The Reds were beaten finalists in the previous year's Champions League. Chelsea seemed light years away from the exalted heights of such games.

For Villas-Boas, however, the perspective was different. 'As I said before, nothing that happened here would mean anything in the Premier League table,' he said. 'It is an unexpected league. All of the five contenders are there. Anything can happen. The most regular is United at the moment but we showed we are up to the level of the champions.'[32] Was the statement intended to be encouragement for his players, mere bluster, or sincerely meant? Whatever the case, few would agree with the assessment.

It was the first time that Villas-Boas had experienced defeat in a league game for 17 months, but that felt like meagre compensation, and the golden image of this young

32 https://www.bbc.com/sport/football/17131298.

coach was beginning to lose a little of its glistening with some pundits. Alan Hansen accused the Chelsea defence as being 'wide open'[33] at Old Trafford. The Portuguese was quick to reply, declaring Hansen's assessment to be 'completely false,'[34] and explaining, 'It's just an unwillingness to make a correct comment on the game by having pleasure in criticising others.' He added, 'People like that go against their own principles. They don't know what to say and they basically just live by lowering others, which I find quite extraordinary. It doesn't annoy me because I respect to the fullness the opinion of people. It's just when it's football people, I find it really strange.'[35] Such a response raises the question as to whether it was driven by genuine indignation, or a perceived need to defend himself as the pressure began to build.

Three days after the defeat at Old Trafford, Villas-Boas sent out an under-strength team to face neighbours Fulham in the Carling Cup third round at Stamford Bridge. Using cup competitions, especially the Carling Cup, as an opportunity to offer fringe players some game time and also rest senior players had become very much the norm for any number of clubs, while retaining more senior options on the bench if required. This was the case with Villas-Boas's selection here. With Ross Turnbull, Terry, Bosingwa, Mikel, Lampard, Mata and Drogba on the bench there were plenty of upgrade options if the game wasn't going Chelsea's way – those options would be needed.

With half-time approaching after a fairly even game, Chelsea sustained a triple blow. Firstly, a goal from Sturridge

33 'Villas-Boas bites back at Hansen', Fox Sports, 24 September 2011.

34 'Villas-Boas bites back at Hansen', Fox Sports, 24 September 2011.

35 'Villas-Boas bites back at Hansen', Fox Sports, 24 September 2011.

was ruled out for offside before the same player was forced from the field with injury. Lampard was summoned to replace him. Then Čech was injured and was replaced by Turnbull at the break. The reserve goalkeeper was quickly called into action to face a penalty, with Alex being red-carded for the offence. Fortunately, Pajtim Kasami's attempt was saved and Chelsea survived, with the ten men seeing out the remainder of the 90 minutes, plus extra time, before winning a penalty shoot-out.

The games against Manchester United and then Fulham had hardly been suggestive of any kind of upturn in form, and yet the latter began a run of only one defeat in the following eight. Firstly, at the weekend, Swansea visited Stamford Bridge in the Premier League and were beaten 4-1. Lampard was again left on the bench, as was Drogba and, when Torres was dismissed on 39 minutes for an ill-judged lunge on Mark Gower, Chelsea were reduced to ten men again. Fortunately, by that stage they were already two goals ahead. Ten minutes earlier the Spaniard had collected a neat chip by Mata and efficiently converted the chance, before Ramires added the second after latching on to a ball by Cole.

After the break, Swansea pressed to get back into the game, exploiting their man advantage, but Chelsea held firm and, with 15 minutes to play, Ramires made the points safe with his second goal. Ashley Williams pulled one back with time running out, but Drogba celebrated his return to action from the bench for ten minutes with the last-minute strike to tie things up. Domestic matters were then put aside for a while as Chelsea travelled to Spain for their next Champions League encounter, against Valencia at the atmospheric Estadi de Mestalla on 28 September.

David Luiz returned to partner Terry, and Lampard was in from the first whistle. If the 33-year-old midfielder had a point to prove to his manager he did so with relish. The game was closely contested with neither team dominant, but with Lampard probing energetically, and former Valencia player Mata doing so with intelligence, Chelsea always seemed to carry the greater threat. Ten minutes after the break, it was Lampard firing home to put Chelsea ahead, as a cross from Malouda raiding in from the flank found him in space. From there it seemed the London club looked destined to add another three points to those accumulated in the win over Bayer Leverkusen and put themselves in a commanding position within the group. With the game seemingly petering out, Villas-Boas removed Lampard with half-a-dozen minutes to play, sending on Kalou to see out time.

The Ivorian forward has a chequered history with Chelsea; sometimes brilliant, but often exasperating, and it was the latter characteristic that defined his time on the field here. With three minutes to play, a Valencia corner swung in from the right was cleared away, but the referee spotted that it was Kalou's fist that had contacted the ball, and Roberto Soldado converted the penalty, sending the ball to Čech's left as the goalkeeper committed himself to a dive in the opposite direction. On the bench, Villas-Boas wore a look of bewilderment and disappointment. Two precious points had carelessly been cast aside, and later their loss would imperil Chelsea's progress to the knockout stages.

There were two more Premier League games before the next Champions League group match. First, Chelsea racked up an impressive 5-1 win away to Bolton. Lampard stamped his form with a hat-trick and Sturridge notched a brace. The following week, the improved performances continued with a 3-1 home victory over Everton before Belgian club Genk arrived at Stamford Bridge. Sturridge was again on the scoresheet, alongside Terry and Ramires.

Genk were struggling for form at this level and had yet to find the back of the net in their two group games so far. Things wouldn't improve on their visit to London and it took just eight minutes for the first goal to arrive. Collecting the ball in the middle of the Genk half, Meireles sauntered forward a couple of strides with the defence slow to close him down. Deciding to chance his arm he hit a speculative shot that bounced on its way to the target, but still deceived László Köteles in goal for the Belgian club. The Portugal international's celebration was probably as much to do with elated surprise as it was with the excitement of opening the scoring.

The second goal took another three minutes. A ball was played to Lampard advancing towards the Genk penalty area. A look up from the stand-in captain was sufficient to spark a run from Torres in behind the Genk back line. Lampard provided the slide-rule pass, and Torres the clinical finish. Fewer than a dozen minutes had been played but, to all intents and purposes, the result was now settled. There was little chance of the Belgians, in only their second adventure into the group stages of European football's elite tournament, finding a way back into the game, but the Blues were a long way from being finished with them, and on 27 minutes Torres added the third goal.

With Meireles in possession on the right flank, the striker anticipated the cross arriving and arced his run in front of marker Abel Masuero, leaving the defender floundering and unable to challenge. The ball met up with his run around the penalty spot and the flicked header was too accurate for Köteles, whose despairing dive was spectacular, but forlorn. There was still time for another strike before the break as a free kick from Malouda was powerfully headed home by Ivanović. Half-time must have been one of those rare occasions when the manager had little to say, and could merely enjoy his cup of coffee in quiet satisfaction. The only decision he made was to withdraw Cole, although the granted rest period on the bench was hardly much different to the easy time he had enjoyed on the pitch. Paulo Ferreira took his place.

The second half was played at an easy pace for the home team, with the visitors comfortably kept at arm's length and hardly any unnecessary energy expended. Lampard had controlled the midfield and on 68 minutes, it was time for him to take a rest as well, with Kalou sent on to replace him. The Ivorian would notch the final goal. Inside the last dozen minutes, Anelka fed a ball towards the goal line inviting Malouda to run on to it and cross. The Frenchman complied and found Torres a few metres from goal. His hat-trick strike was foiled by Köteles, but the ball fell out to Kalou, who volleyed home. The Belgians looked outclassed and like rabbits caught in a car's headlights, but they would exact a measure of revenge in the return game. For now, a side containing a young Kevin De Bruyne had been comprehensively outplayed.

Confidence may well have been growing at the club with the league successes and the bullying of Genk, but at such times, a fall often awaits, and so it was with the short visit across west London to Loftus Road and a Premier League game against Queens Park Rangers. Neil Warnock's team had experienced an up and down season so far, including a 6-0 defeat to Fulham and 3-0 victory away to Wolverhampton Wanderers. A confident, perhaps over-confident, Chelsea team may well have been ripe for the picking.

As early as the tenth minute a clumsy challenge inside the box by Luiz conceded a penalty, and the first goal, as Heidar Helguson converted to put the home side ahead.

Matt Barlow described the incident in the *Daily Mail*, 'The Brazilian defender may be prone to attacks of clumsiness and distraction – this was the third penalty he has conceded in 14 Premier League games – but it is always a shame to see strikers rewarded for their lack of strength. Contact was slight but Helguson crashed to the turf.'[36] From there things deteriorated badly. By half-time, Chelsea's on-field contingent was down to nine men as discipline fell apart and both Bosingwa and Drogba were dismissed. There were no more goals by the end of the game, but referee Chris Foy had plenty of things to keep him busy.

When the final whistle went, including the two dismissals, no fewer than nine Chelsea players had been carded by the official. Worse, much worse, was to follow, however. During the emotionally charged, frenetic game, Terry reportedly racially abused the QPR player Anton Ferdinand. Reports were filed with the police, who investigated the incident, including video footage and the Chelsea and England captain was formally charged.

On 3 February, with the court case pending, the FA decided to strip Terry of the England captaincy. Five days later, Fabio Capello resigned as the national team manager in protest. Although he was cleared by the court in July, Terry would be found guilty following an FA investigation in September 2012, and handed a four-match ban, plus a fine. At the time of the incident though, either due to expediency, a sense of loyalty or a genuine belief in his player's innocence, Villas-Boas supported his beleaguered captain, offering 'his backing to John Terry over allegations he racially abused Anton Ferdinand in the defeat by QPR'.[37]

---

36 'QPR 1 Chelsea 0: Blues are shaken up by their very OWN noisy neighbours', *Daily Mail*, 23 October 2011.

37 https://www.bbc.com/sport/football/17131298.

If the loss at Old Trafford had exposed fault lines in Chelsea's play under Villas-Boas, the events at Loftus Road on that late October afternoon suggested that the manager was also some way from having any kind of firm control over his players. The lack of discipline may well have been a symptom of growing ills at the club, rather than, as many painted it, a cause of them. After scrambling through a fifth-round Carling Cup tie at Everton in extra time, five of the next seven games would expose just how far short they were of being a team likely to achieve that 'greater success in major domestic and European competitions'[38] mentioned in the club's statement welcoming their new coach. With his project apparently stalling, the clouds were gathering for Villas-Boas.

Three days ahead of the return Champions League fixture with Genk, Chelsea faced a London derby against Arsenal. The Gunners had not started the season well and it had taken four games for them to register their first win, a 1-0 victory over Swansea, following the 8-2 humiliation endured at Old Trafford, but they arrived at Stamford Bridge on the back of successive victories.

At half-time, Chelsea led 2-1 thanks to goals by the 'Old Firm' of Lampard and Terry against a single strike by Robin van Persie. In the second half, however, especially the final ten minutes, things would change dramatically. With ten minutes remaining Mata scored to bring the game level after goals by André Santos and Theo Walcott had turned the game on its head, but on 85 and 90 minutes it was van Persie completing his hat-trick and exposing gaps in the home back line that fired the Gunners to victory.

---

38 Chelsea FC statement, 22 June 2011.

Momentum is such an important element in the fortunes of a football club and it seemed now to be swinging very much against Chelsea. Just as with Ancelotti, when things began to go wrong during the previous season and the Italian appeared unable to answer the questions that his team's performances and results were posing, Villas-Boas was confronted with a similar dilemma. A positive result in Genk, something that looked to be comfortably achievable following the five-goal romp against the same team at Stamford Bridge, was now assuming vital proportions.

On the first day of November, Chelsea visited Belgium's Limburg region to play the return rubber against Genk. Villas-Boas again appeared to opt for caution with an artisan rather than artistic midfield chosen and, once more, Lampard was on the bench. It seemed a perverse decision given his domination of midfield when the Belgian club visited Stamford Bridge, but such controversial decisions would increasingly feature among the Villas-Boas team selections as the season wore on.

Meireles, Romeu and Ramires were set alongside Malouda in the engine room of the team, with Anelka also dropping back to link the play and Torres as the lone striker. Given the tepid performance of the Belgians at Stamford Bridge, it was surely an over-cautious approach, when adding Mata or Lampard to the starting 11 rather than having them on the bench may well have eased Chelsea through what was now a critical fixture. Opting not to attack the home team, who would surely have been in an apprehensive state following the mauling in London, merely invited problems.

Perhaps the coach's caution, betrayed by his team selection permeated into the players and, far from the cavorting performance of October, this was a much closer contest. There was still a big enough gap in the retrospective talents on show though for Chelsea to go ahead midway through the first period, despite De Bruyne, whom Chelsea would later sign, being more prominent than in the earlier encounter.

The goal came from Ramires after neat interplay with Torres. Chasing on to a chipped ball from the striker, the Brazilian ran between defenders to fire home from an acute angle. Chelsea could then have gone on and put the game beyond redemption, but when the momentum is against you, things often fall agonisingly short. Meireles hit the crossbar, before a handball offence by Thomas Buffel gifted a penalty to the visitors. With normal spot kick expert Lampard sitting on the bench, the task was handed to Luiz, who saw his relatively tame shot comfortably saved by Köteles in the home goal.

After a home goalless draw against Valencia in their opening fixture, Genk had been beaten comfortably by Bayer Leverkusen and then Chelsea without finding the back of the net themselves. In the next game they would concede seven without reply in Valencia, before earning a 1-1 draw in the dead rubber of their closing game against the Bundesliga club. That goal against Bayer Leverkusen would not be their first in the competition though. That particular honour went to Jelle Vossen, as a left-wing cross from Fabien Camus found the striker who steered the ball past Čech from around ten metres to bring the scores level just past the hour.

The Cristal Arena celebrated as if they had won the tournament itself and, for the rest of the game, despite Chelsea pressing and Villas-Boas throwing on Lampard, Mata and Sturridge, it was all too late. The chance to kill the game off had slipped through Chelsea's fingers, and once the home team had their goal, their renewed determination to hang on to that hard-earned point was enough to see them over the line. Much later, when interviewed for a review of the campaign, Lampard was both political and restrained in his assessment, 'We'd made quite a few changes to the team, and put in a very lethargic kind of performance, and we'd left ourselves a little bit to do towards the end of the group.'[39]

They had indeed. Twice now, Chelsea had led in away Champions League games, only to see equalisers conceded. It was an irritating profligacy that bled into domestic fixtures. A game that should have brought a comfortable three points had turned into another disappointment and, after a scrappy 1-0 victory over Blackburn Rovers at Ewood Park in a Premier League fixture on 5 November, where there was very little in the way of entertaining fireworks, more disappointments would follow. The visit to Lancashire was significant, however, for Čech sustaining the nose injury that would mean him wearing a guard to protect it, as well as the now normal headguard. Batman had landed in goal for Chelsea. Appropriate superhero performances would follow in the denouement of the season.

There was one further game before what by now looked like a do-or-die encounter in Leverkusen, but this was also a big one. At home to Liverpool, Chelsea needed both a result and a statement performance to bring back some belief to their season. They would get neither. At this stage the Merseysiders were a top-eight club, but not much more, and would finish the league in that position. Their success in cup competitions, however, winning the Carling Cup and finishing as runners-up in the FA Cup, illustrated their ability to overcome most opponents in a one-off game – or even twice in rapid succession, as they would prove when

39 *Kings of Europe – The Chelsea Story*, Sky UK Limited, 16 September 2012.

returning to Stamford Bridge nine days later for a Carling Cup quarter-final.

With the visit to Leverkusen just three days away and progress in the Champions League hanging by a precarious thread, it was vital for Villas-Boas that his judgement in team selection for this game was spot on. Understandably reluctant to take any risks, other than Torres, who had long been perceived as the manager's first-choice forward, being left on the bench with Drogba starting, it was a pretty much full-strength side that faced Kenny Dalglish's team on 20 November.

Ahead of the game, rumours began to spread that Roman Abramovich was tiring of the Villas-Boas project. They were sufficient to provoke a rebuttal from the club as, 'Chelsea officials insisted before kick-off that reports of the first cracks surfacing in the relationship between Villas-Boas and owner Roman Abramovich were "total nonsense",' the BBC reported, before adding, 'but there is no question … form has deteriorated after a competent rather than spectacular start to the season.'[40] Matters were hardly helped when Maxi Rodriguez scored to give the visitors a lead at the break. Forced into a rethink, Villas-Boas used the half-time interval to rejig his formation, withdrawing the hard-working but hardly threatening Mikel for the forward-orientated Sturridge. Ten minutes later, the initiative was rewarded as the substitute profited from the skills of Malouda to equalise.

Chelsea now had the ascendancy, but chances came and went without any tangible reward. With time running out, Villas-Boas threw on two former Liverpool players, Torres and Meireles, in a vain hope that irony would win the day for

---

40 'Glen Johnson's late winner gave Liverpool victory as Chelsea's indifferent run of form continued', BBC, https://www.bbc.com/sport/football/15710566.

him. As it happened a player who had moved between the clubs would be the trump card, but he was not wearing blue. A draw would hardly have been sufficient to quash rumours of dissent in the Chelsea camp – and owner's mind – but even that small solace was denied when former Chelsea player Glen Johnson returned to his old stamping ground and struck the winning goal with just three minutes remaining.

It was a demoralising defeat for both club and coach. After completing a league double over the Blues in the previous season, Liverpool had now beaten Chelsea on three successive occasions, and would do twice more before the season was done. After losing that traumatic 5-3 game to Arsenal, this defeat meant it was the first time that Chelsea had lost consecutive Premier League matches at Stamford Bridge since Roman Abramovich bought the club in 2003. Despite those assurances of all being sweetness and light in the relationship between owner and coach, it was clear that the situation was deteriorating at an alarming rate, and should Chelsea fail to qualify from the group stages of the Champions League the end of the line for Villas-Boas, who had seemed so bright a prospect a few short months ago, looked imminent.

With a couple of games left to play in the group, Chelsea had two wins and two draws, placing them on eight points, with the visit to Germany and a home match against Valencia to come. Fortunately, both Leverkusen and Valencia had been falling over each other's feet. Each had won their home games against the other, and Valencia's opening draw away to Genk was looking like an expensive error. The Bundesliga club had six points and, after entertaining Chelsea, had to visit Genk. Valencia had five points. The Belgians' two points from their four games meant they stood adrift, and out of contention.

For all Chelsea's lack of consistent form in the group, they still sat top of the table, with a win in Germany guaranteeing progress to the first knockout round. A draw would put them on nine points, and vulnerable, with Leverkusen on seven and a highly winnable visit to Genk to come. Valencia had an appointment with the Belgians at home in their fifth game and, should they triumph, as they were surely overwhelming favourites to do, they would be on eight points with a visit to Stamford Bridge ahead. A defeat for Chelsea in Germany would guarantee Leverkusen's progress unless they lost in Genk, surely an unlikely scenario, with the west London club therefore highly likely to need a win against Valencia to progress.

Aside from the mathematical calculations, with performances and results dipping as the club endured the worst start to a Premier League season since Abramovich's arrival, anything but a victory in Germany would only add to the mounting pressure on Villas-Boas's young, but sagging, shoulders.

The portents were hardly encouraging on the day beforehand. Cole aggravated an ongoing problem during a training session and was ruled out of the game, as well as probably the weekend Premier League fixture at home to Wolverhampton Wanderers. It meant a reshuffle of resources with Bosingwa drafted in as left-back. The Portuguese had played there before, and was adaptable enough to be a more than adequate stand in, but it was just another sign that fate was not smiling on Villas-Boas. The situation was compounded when David Luiz reported that he was feeling nauseous and dizzy ahead of the game. He started, but lasted just over an hour before having to be withdrawn and replaced by Alex. By that time, however, things looked to have changed for the better.

The first half had been competitive but neither team could manufacture a breakthrough. Michael Ballack, who had left Chelsea in 2010 to return to Leverkusen, was the key midfielder for the home team, directing and organising. His ability on the ball and physical presence was a constant thorn in the side of the visitors. Wearing a nose guard not dissimilar to that of Čech, he came nearest to breaking the deadlock in the first period with a header from Gonzalo Castro's corner that crashed against the crossbar, before being cleared.

By now, Villas-Boas seemed to have switched the affections bestowed upon his two main strikers. While still offering public praise to Torres, it was Drogba who now seemed to be the 'go-to guy' in a big game, and the Ivorian repaid some of that faith three minutes into the second half. Receiving a pass from Sturridge, he rolled Manuel Friedrich with muscular ease, brushing aside the defender's challenge with disdain and, despite slipping as he shot, swept the ball past Leno to give Chelsea the lead.

In a season punctuated by bans, injuries and selection, it was only Drogba's second strike, but potentially of immense value. If Chelsea could keep the home team out it would not only mean that qualification was assured, but the result would also serve to lift some of the deepening gloom gathering over the club. Čech recalled the feelings of the team after the goal – and what happened later, 'We were winning the game. It looked like we had it under control and then, in the last 15 minutes, we totally lost control of the game.'[41]

Now facing the possibility of a home loss that would jeopardise their own European aspirations, Leverkusen swept

41 *Kings of Europe – The Chelsea Story*, Sky UK Limited, 16 September 2012.

forward with renewed vigour. Efforts came in from André Schürrle, Ballack again, and Stefan Kießling, but Čech stood firm, denying all that was thrown at him. On came Alex for the now struggling Luiz and, inside the final 20 minutes, Leverkusen coach Robin Dutt sent on Eren Derdiyok. Two minutes later his change brought the desired effect.

Ironically, it may have been an error by the substitute that created the goal. A crossfield pass seemed to arrow in on Derdiyok, but his attempt to control the ball, unless it was the most extravagant of dummies, only served to pull the Chelsea defence out of position. It allowed the ball to run into space on the right side of the Chelsea area, arriving with the unmarked Sidney Sam. Cutting in, Sam drew Čech towards him before lifting the ball over the goalkeeper for Derdiyok to head into the unguarded net as Terry raced back in vain desperation to block.

With enough time left for a winning goal, only one team looked likely to get it. The Bundesliga had assisted Leverkusen and moved their domestic fixture forward to Friday, giving them a few days' extra rest and preparation time more than Chelsea, who had been compelled to play that difficult league fixture against Liverpool just three days before travelling to Germany. A draw would have been serious enough, but fears that this game would go the way of so many others when Chelsea had taken the lead, only to gift away the advantage, proved to be well-founded in the very last minute of the 90.

A corner from the right was played into the box by Castro and, up from his defensive position to support the attack, centre-back Friedrich, redeeming his error of allowing Drogba's goal, looped a header over Čech and into the net. On television, the Sky commentator gave voice to Chelsea fans' anguish. 'Oh, it's in!' he described accurately but unnecessarily, adding, 'Čech is beaten by the header. It could be a killer blow for Chelsea.' The body language of the Chelsea players, as they trudged back to the centre circle, portrayed that they were having similar dark thoughts. There was precious little time, and apparently a similar amount of fight in the Chelsea team, to redeem the situation, and for the third time in away group games, Villas-Boas had seen his team lead and then concede crucial late goals. This time, however, the lapses had brought defeat, rather than a draw.

Elimination was now a clear possibility, if not probability. It was a feeling only compounded by the news that Valencia had overwhelmed Genk, scoring seven times without reply. The Germans were now on nine points, with the away game against Genk to complete their programme. Chelsea and Valencia both had eight, but that goal glut against the Belgian club had boosted the Spanish club's goal difference enormously. It stood at +8, while Chelsea's was +6, although in the crucial issue of goal difference between the two clubs, Chelsea's 1-1 away draw meant that a victory, or a goalless draw, in the final game at home to Valencia would see them progress at the expense of the Spanish club. It didn't sound an impossible task, but when you consider that Chelsea had only won twice in their previous nine games, and only kept a clean sheet twice in the last dozen, there was hardly a case for over-confidence either.

It may have been that the manager needed some reassurance as well, and sought a conversation with the owner to assess whether he still had Abramovich's backing. His comments afterwards suggested that it was the case, as the BBC reported, 'A bullish Villas-Boas says Roman Abramovich is fully behind him after revealing he has had talks with the Russian owner following Chelsea's slump in form. "Everybody wants to get out of a situation like this.

Self-confidence and self-belief is what we need now and everybody wants to get it," he said.'[42] If the manager was convinced, others were less so. As Matt Barlow commented in the *Daily Mail*, 'Villas-Boas may have Abramovich on his side at the moment but Chelsea's alarming slide must be halted before Valencia visit Stamford Bridge next month.'[43]

The first chance to do so would come three days later when Mick McCarthy took his Wolverhampton Wanderers team to Stamford Bridge. Had Villas-Boas been granted the opportunity to hand-pick his next opponents, he may well have opted for the struggling Midlands club. Sitting just a single place above the relegation zone before kick-off, they would end the season anchored to the foot of the table and relegated, winning just five times across the entire league programme and scoring only 40 goals in 38 games. Sometimes things don't go to form, but there was a measure of relief for the Chelsea manager when this particular game did just that.

Villas-Boas had again exhibited what seemed an undue amount of caution against a team whose own form made Chelsea appear world beaters by comparison. Romeu, Meireles and Ramires again formed the workmanlike midfield, leaving Sturridge and Mata to supply the ammunition for Drogba. Lampard was again on the bench. As the teams left the field for half-time though, the manager would have felt vindicated with his team three goals clear. Terry and Sturridge had both profited from Mata assists and the Spaniard had taken the third goal for himself. A goalless second period was efficiently delivered to lock up the points, but more stringent tests awaited.

42 https://www.bbc.com/sport/football/17131298.

43 'Germans pile pressure on Villas-Boas with late winner', *Daily Mail*, 24 November 2011.

Liverpool had proven to be the club's *bête noire* of late and when the draw for the quarter-finals of the Carling Cup paired the Anfield club with Chelsea, it would hardly have been a cause for raucous celebrations at Stamford Bridge. The win over Wolves had been expected, but at least it had been competently delivered and there would surely have been a strong temptation for Villas-Boas to send out a full-strength side in order to beat Liverpool and continue to rebuild confidence with the vital game against Valencia just ten days away. The dilemma was of course that, having already lost at home to them in the league, had a 'first 11' team been selected and still lost, the damage could have been terminal.

In the end, the manager opted for caution. Turnbull, Ryan Bertrand, Josh McEachran, Lukaku and Torres were all given a starting berth, alongside that semi-regular occupier of the bench, Lampard. Čech, Terry and Drogba didn't even make the 18-man squad. It was almost a parody of the fabled project succeeding. Perhaps things were dropping in Chelsea's favour though. The Liverpool hierarchy was less than impressed to be playing a quarter-final 48 hours after facing table-topping Manchester City in a Premier League game. When an early Malouda effort struck the bar and was then cleared though, Chelsea's hopes of overcoming a jaded visiting team were beginning to diminish, and would be subsequently vanquished when Liverpool scored.

Jordan Henderson neatly bisected Luiz and Bertrand with a perceptive pass that set Craig Bellamy in space, haring down the right flank. His low cross was far enough away from Turnbull to allow Maxi Rodríguez the relatively easy task of drilling home at the far post. Within five minutes the lead was doubled, and Chelsea's Carling Cup campaign over, when Martin Kelly inelegantly headed home at the far post to double the lead.

Too late, Villas-Boas sent on Mata and Anelka to seek to redeem matters but the visitors were home and hosed. It was Chelsea's third home defeat in four games, with Valencia the next team to visit. There was one more domestic fixture to be completed before that though, an encouraging victory was gained, but soon afterwards, more evidence of disquiet within the club bubbled to the surface.

A 3-0 victory away from home, almost regardless of the opposition, is a more than decent result and some reports of the game at Newcastle would have warmed the heart of the Chelsea manager. For example, Paul Wilson for *The Guardian* eulogised, 'Beating Newcastle is no mean feat these days and Chelsea returned to something like their fluent best in becoming the first visiting team to win on Tyneside this season. Their defence stood solid against some enterprising home attacks, with Oriol Romeu looking assured in front of the back four and Daniel Sturridge, Juan Mata and Ramires all showing speed of thought as well as movement. Newcastle were unhappy with a couple of refereeing decisions, and had every right to be, though there was no denying that, with slightly calmer finishing, Chelsea could have scored a hatful of goals.'[44] It was a theme that Villas-Boas was happy and eager to confirm. 'You could say 3-0 was excessive, but it was the fairest of results because of the number of times we were one on one with the goalkeeper,' the Chelsea manager insisted. Alan Pardew agreed with that. 'Tim Krul was outstanding,' he said. 'His penalty save alone was fantastic and he didn't deserve to be beaten three times.'[45]

---

44 'Daniel Sturridge goal seals controversial Chelsea win at Newcastle', *The Guardian*, 3 December 2011.

45 'Daniel Sturridge goal seals controversial Chelsea win at Newcastle', *The Guardian*, 3 December 2011.

Lampard had missed a penalty on 14 minutes, after Yohan Cabaye had illegally halted the run of Sturridge. Lampard, normally so efficient from 12 yards, was foiled as Krul threw himself left to stop the shot. It was a missed chance, but seven minutes earlier, Chelsea could have, and probably should have, been behind. Chasing a through ball, Demba Ba was hauled to the ground by Luiz, with the Senegal striker bearing down on goal. Although the offence occurred outside of the box, it was probably as close to the definition description of a professional foul as you can come. Mike Dean, ever the magnet for controversial moments, merely flourished a yellow card, and Chelsea escaped. Unsurprisingly Pardew was mystified and annoyed in equal measure. 'I can't understand why the referee didn't send him off,' he said. 'It could have been a very different afternoon.'[46]

Chelsea, and their young manager had certainly copped a break and when Drogba headed home Mata's cross on 38 minutes, it seemed the club's luck had taken a turn for the better. The second half was closer, but Chelsea still had the better chances and it was no great surprise that two further goals were added in the last couple of minutes, firstly by Kalou and then by Sturridge. A three-goal defeat may have reflected harshly on Newcastle's performance, but the Blues were happy to scamper away with the points and a boost of confidence ahead of the big game against Valencia. Drogba was becoming an increasingly important factor in Chelsea's season now that he had confirmed his number one status ahead of Torres. It was a trend that would continue, both into the next game, and then through to the end of the season.

---

46 'Daniel Sturridge goal seals controversial Chelsea win at Newcastle', *The Guardian*, 3 December 2011.

There was a sour note in the game though, when Lampard was substituted on the hour. Perhaps frustrated by his general restricted game time under Villas-Boas, the timing of the change in that game, the penalty miss, a general discord with the coach or a combination of many factors, the player was clearly less than happy. Perhaps, however, the manager was committing to some longer-term logic in the decision, with a desire to save the 33-year-old's legs with the Valencia game on the horizon? A few days later, that theory was proved to be well wide of the mark.

Lampard's display of discontent was perhaps an opportunity for the manager to emphasise his authority, but he took calmer counsel, perhaps appreciating that taking on one of the club's most popular players in the full glare of public scrutiny may not have been advisable. 'Frank is a top professional and every player wants to spend more time on the pitch. But the manager decides things for the team. The manager makes the decision,'[47] Villas-Boas declared. Of course that was true but the difference in the way the Lampard incident was dealt with, compared to the resolution of the scenario with Alex and Anelka may have suggested weakness, rather than wisdom.

Any mystery as to why defender Alex and forward Anelka had been absent from the party travelling to the north-east was explained by the manager during a post-match press conference. Rumours had spread that the duo had been told to train with the reserves and informed that they were no longer part of his plans. Villas-Boas confirmed that both players had submitted transfer requests, which had been accepted by the club, but then sought to defuse any sense of discord while still confirming his authority, 'They are top

47 'André Villas-Boas: Chelsea fans can have massive impact on Champions League crunch tie', *London Evening Standard*, 6 December 2011.

professionals and their professionalism and integrity is never in question but on recent results and form we have decided to try to get the group together and we have decided to assign different training times for them. The transfer requests were accepted but it doesn't mean it will happen and if it doesn't happen, they will return to full training.'[48] The Brazilian would join Paris Saint-Germain in January 2012 for £4.2m, reuniting with his former Chelsea manager Carlo Ancelotti. Anelka moved to Chinese club Shanghai Shenhua.

Ahead of the now dawning game against Valencia, there was much talk of accepting that the club was in some kind of tailspin. The necessity of getting the right result against the Spaniards was not lost on Čech. 'We were not doing well in the Premier League, you know, we were out of the Carling Cup, and the Champions League was really vital for us,'[49] he would later confess. The inevitable conclusion of a failure to progress would surely be the removal of Villas-Boas. The project had new become a millstone around the coach's neck, and threatened to be the thing that dragged the young Portuguese underwater as waves of criticism washed over him. Was elimination from the Champions League a price worth paying to be rid of Villas-Boas? Some fans thought so, and rumours of dissent among a group of the senior players, especially the targets of the project, seemed to have some sympathy with that assessment.

Perhaps aware of the tide of fans' opinions turning against him, Villas-Boas tried to rally the supporters and help drive the team to victory over Valencia. 'I have good memories of top European nights at this club,' he declared.

---

48 'Chelsea accept transfer requests from Nicolas Anelka and Alex', *Daily Express*, 3 December 2011.

49 *Kings of Europe – The Chelsea Story*, Sky UK Limited, 16 September 2012.

'And I know the atmosphere can be raised here, just like we did in the 4-2 against Barcelona. If they do that, we would have the right ambience to take on Valencia with that extra input.'[50] Perhaps the rationale for recalling that pulsating night when Chelsea defeated Barcelona under Mourinho, with Villas-Boas as part of his staff, was the manager's attempt to inculcate himself into the collective of the fans, convince them that he was part of them and had experienced the same triumphs. It read like a hollow call though, almost a 'please like me' earnest plea for sympathy and understanding. It was also unnecessary, if the desire was merely to rally the fans to support the team. Despite any random thoughts of paying the price of Champions League elimination to be rid of Villas-Boas and his project, at a game of this magnitude, there would be very few fans in Stamford Bridge not giving their all to help drive the team forward, regardless of any prompting from the manager.

For all the perceived failings of Villas-Boas, an inability to be consistent was not one of them. He clearly had some guns, he had some glue, and his default reaction was to apply the latter to the former whenever he was under pressure. At times, this characteristic can be appreciated as a steely determination and singular application to a cause. At others though, it looks obstinate, and predicated on a stubborn refusal to accept reality. When the announcement came out for the 11 selected to start against Valencia, where a win or at least a goalless draw was essential, Villas-Boas had left himself open to charges that the latter was the case. Lampard was once more on the bench.

That Lampard almost defined the modern game's role of the goalscoring midfield player is established in football

---

50 'André Villas-Boas: Chelsea fans can have massive impact on Champions League crunch tie', *London Evening Standard*, 6 December 2011.

folklore, but Villas-Boas was either unaware of this, disbelieving of it, or oblivious to its value. Also, the fate of games of this magnitude may be decided by a penalty and, back in Genk, had Lampard been on the pitch to take the spot kick that instead fell to Luiz, Chelsea may well have been through and able to play out this final fixture with a measure of comfort. There was, of course, an alternate view when considering the possibility of a penalty occurring in this game. After all, Lampard had failed to convert from 12 yards against Newcastle in the previous game, but such was his record of scoring penalties, the miss was probably much more likely to ensure that his next attempt from the spot would be converted, rather than squandered.

There may also have been a nagging, but persuasive, thought in the manager's mind, had there been some indecision about selecting Lampard, that the player's petulant reaction to being withdrawn at St James' Park was sufficient to sway the decision. If that had been the case, however, it would have been the ultimate act of self-harm, inflicted merely to illustrate a point. To coin the old military phrase, 'Only people who can't fight have to wear big hats.' Whatever the rationale for the decision, if the manager was looking for a hero to save his side, and probably his own hide, it wouldn't be Lampard. Fortunately, Drogba would assume the role. In poker parlance, Villas-Boas was going 'all in' and the Ivorian was the ace in his hand.

Even ahead of the game, during the warm-up and, perhaps significantly with the manager absent from the gathering, it was Drogba and Terry who called all of the players together to deliver their own pep talk. Talking later, Terry revealed that they were encouraging the players to believe, 'We've been there, we've seen the hard times. There's better times ahead. Make the most of these opportunities in life, you know, they don't come about often.'[51] Drogba's recollections were very similar, 'I think it's the best way to share the passion, and also, maybe it was also a way for me to get rid of the pressure.'[52] They're entirely reasonable things to say ahead of such a pivotal game, but there's perhaps also a question as to why senior players felt the need to try and motivate the remainder of the team. Was that not an essential part of the coach's remit?

As the game got under way, there were as many winsome glances from all corners of the ground towards the Chelsea number eight sitting on the bench as there were directed to the opening exchanges of the game. The manager needed an early goal before frustration had a chance to set in. Drogba delivered.

On the far post, Mata collected an over-hit cross and looked to play the ball back into the goalmouth. Aware of the massed ranks of white-shirted defenders crowded into the area, he paused. Drogba had stumbled over a fallen defender, as he followed the flight of the ball, and fell to the ground. Deciding that the striker was of no immediate danger, his marker then advanced to close down Mata. The movement afforded Drogba a brief second of space. Regaining his footing, he stepped back a few paces to fully exploit the opportunity. Astutely, Mata spotted the move and fed the ball to the striker. A dozen or so yards from goal, there was still plenty for Drogba to do as three defenders closed him down. Shifting the ball sharply from right to left foot opened up a lane of space and Drogba fired left-footed into the far corner as goalkeeper Diego Alves dived in a vain

---

51 *Kings of Europe – The Chelsea Story*, Sky UK Limited, 16 September 2012.

52 *Kings of Europe – The Chelsea Story*, Sky UK Limited, 16 September 2012.

attempt to save, the glancing touch of his left glove being insufficient to divert the ball wide of the post. Spinning away, Drogba celebrated, lighting the 'blue touch paper' of the game. On the bench, Villas-Boas allowed himself a quiet smile of satisfaction. There was plenty of time to go, and lots of things could still go awry, but it had been the perfect start to the game for Chelsea and their increasingly beleaguered young manager.

Strangely, cold logic suggested that the goal actually made no difference to the final equation of qualification. Whatever the result, Valencia could not progress unless they scored. Only a victory or a goalless draw would serve Chelsea's purposes; any other kind of draw would see the Spanish club progress. At the start of the game, with the score at 0-0, Valencia needed a single goal to put them into the qualifying slot. At 1-0 to Chelsea, that requirement remained the case. Cold logic, however, is ill-fitted to football, and the goal created a groundswell of momentum and positivity that had been lacking in so many recent games for the home team at Stamford Bridge.

The visitors were an accomplished team, however, and unlikely merely to be swept aside by a wave of optimism from the fans. They would finish the La Liga season in third place, topping the 'best of the rest' group behind the impenetrable duopoly of Real Madrid and Barcelona. Soldado had already proved his finishing ability by despatching that late penalty to earn a draw for his club when Chelsea visited the Mestalla in the earlier stages of the group and, in attacking midfielder Jonas, the Spanish club had their own version of Lampard. The Brazilian would score 19 goals across all competitions for the club that season. The goal stung Valencia into a rapid riposte.

Fleet-footed Jordi Alba, who would join Barcelona at the end of the season, nearly quelled the nascent positivity of the home fans. With Chelsea seeking to hold a line ahead of their penalty area, the left-back's run outside of Sturridge was spotted by Tino Costa, who lofted the perfect pass into the area. Alba controlled before firing powerfully past Čech, but the angle had grown acute and, despite beating the goalkeeper, the ball cannoned against the outside of the post and away. Alba held his head and grimaced at his team-mates in anguish, but more Valencia probes would follow.

Again, the Chelsea players were compelled to funnel back, opening up options from midfield. David Albelda was a stalwart at Valencia, coming through the club's youth ranks and making his senior debut way back in 1995, and had been a key player in the La Liga triumphs of 2002 and 2004. In more than 350 league games for the club, he would score only six times but, in matches like this, anything can happen and, when he drove forward from his defensive midfield role, a retreating back line encouraged him to try his luck. His thumping right-footed drive from 30 yards or so was headed for the top right-hand corner of Čech's goal, until the stretching hand, on the end of a diving goalkeeper's arm, pushed the ball around the post instead.

It looked increasingly likely that one goal was not going to be sufficient to settle the issue. With Chelsea now on the back foot, the Villas-Boas decision to pack his midfield with the resolute Ramires, Romeu and Meireles, rather than the more adventurous Lampard began to look a sound decision as the trio scurried around in front of the defence, harrying and tackling to subdue the visitors' attacks.

Fortunately for the home team, Drogba was minded to put on a *tour de force* performance, bullying the Spanish defence with his physical dominance, determined to drive his team on to qualification. Midway through the first period, with Valencia establishing some kind of ascendancy in the game, he collected possession in the Chelsea half. Muscular pace to the fore, he strode past one challenge and accelerated away from a second, driving forwards into the Valencia half, drawing defenders towards him, as a flame attracts moths, disrupting the Valencian defence that would shortly be burnt much as that insect is by the beguilingly fatal attraction of the flame.

With the elegant pace of a 200m sprinter, Ramires strode diagonally forward from the opposite side of midfield into the space vacated by the right-back's need to close on Drogba. Around 40 yards from goal, the striker released the pass into the Brazilian's path. Sensing the danger, Victor Ruiz had tracked the run, and seemed to have nullified the chance, but the pace of Ramires was too hot, with even a desperate late tug at the midfielder's shirt insufficient, and a jabbed finish past Alves doubled the lead.

The difference after the second goal was pronounced as Valencia now needed to score at least twice and Chelsea settled into a period of containment, while Sturridge still offered pacy options on the flank in any counter-attacks. Half-time passed and then, around the hour, perhaps with the game settled and his future assured – at least for the moment – maybe a hint of reconciliation was in the air as Lampard began to warm up. When the substitution was made though, with Ramires withdrawn, it was Mikel sent on, and Lampard remained on the bench. It wasn't reconciliation, it was restatement. The Villas-Boas gamble was paying off and he saw little reason to change things. It was a situation identified by Kevin McCarra in *The Guardian*, 'Lampard himself had seemed disgruntled when taken off against Newcastle United at the weekend but the manager saw cause to reassure only a single 33-year-old, Drogba.'[53]

As the game wore on belief drained away from the visitors. Attacks became both less frequent and less threatening. It was therefore of little surprise that the next goal came from the home team. Collecting an incisive pass from Mata, Drogba strode clear of a weary and almost disinterested Valencia back line, before flicking the ball past Alves for the third goal. There was no way back from there and, with ten minutes remaining on the clock, Villas-Boas withdrew Drogba, replacing him with Torres.

The Chelsea fans stood as one to acclaim the Ivorian's contribution to the cause, but perhaps the deepest gratitude was due from his manager. Villas-Boas had got his team over the line and into the knockout phase of the Champions League. The only question was whether the result would have an invigorating effect on the club or merely be a brief high point in a season with more downs than ups. Čech recalled how the performance raised previously depressed confidence. 'That game against Valencia, showed the team under huge pressure could cope and I think it was our best game. We played really well and we won 3-0,'[54] he said.

Certain sections of the press appeared to concur with the goalkeeper's assessment. In the *Daily Mail,* Matt Lawton opined, '[The game] felt like more than a result; more than Chelsea's progression to the next stage of the Champions League; more even than something that buys André Villas-Boas a bit more time. It felt like a pivotal moment. A glimpse into a future that might just involve a man who must have

---

53 'Chelsea see off Valencia to advance comfortably in Champions League', *The Guardian,* 6 December 2011.

54 *Kings of Europe – The Chelsea Story*, Sky UK Limited, 16 September 2012.

shock absorbers in his knees and the smallest waist in football management.'[55] Writing for *The Guardian*, Kevin McCarra hardly dissented from that view, 'This may be the night that constituted the true start of André Villas-Boas's reign as manager.'[56] Oliver Kay offered similar sentiments in *The Times*, 'It still feels too early in André Villas-Boas's tenure to be talking in terms of watershed moments, but this was an uplifting evening when the spectre of Champions League elimination was dismissed and a second emphatic victory in four days improved the mood at Stamford Bridge considerably.'[57] On top of the result and the following day's press acclaims, there was to be an unexpected bonus dropped into Chelsea's lap.

As fate would have it, in the other group game, Jelle Vossen – who would later play a season in the north-east of England with Middlesbrough – had doubled both his, and Genk's total of Champions League goals to put the Belgian club ahead against Leverkusen. As against Chelsea, it was Derdiyok who equalised late on for the Bundesliga club, but there were no further goals, and the game ended in a draw. It gave Genk their third point but also denied Leverkusen top spot in the group. That exalted position went to Chelsea who, despite the faltering performances and disappointing results had not only qualified, but had now done so as group winners, giving them the assumed advantage of playing a runner-up from another group in the first knockout round, rather than another group winner such as Benfica, Barcelona or Bayern Munich. Ironically,

---

55 'Top Drog fires Blues through and AVB can breathe a little easier', *Daily Mail*, 7 December 2011.

56 'Chelsea see off Valencia to advance comfortably in Champions League', *The Guardian*, 6 December 2011.

57 'Chelsea have little time for nerves after early strikes ease pressure', *The Times*, 7 December 2011.

however, fate would tie Chelsea to each of those other group winners as the tournament progressed.

There was also a substantial dollop of irony in one of the other groups. Back in September that 3-1 loss at Old Trafford had made Chelsea look a distance behind the Manchester United team that had lost out to the majestic Barcelona of Pep Guardiola in the Wembley Champions League Final of the previous season. The Old Trafford club were expected to drive on for another concerted run at the trophy in a group containing Benfica, the Swiss club Basel and unknown Romanians Oțelul Galați. On paper it looked like a comfortable group, but unexpected draws at home to both Basel and Benfica, plus an away defeat in Switzerland in the final round of games had seen them finish in third position, with Basel taking the second qualifying position behind Benfica.

Whereas Chelsea had won their final group game to qualify, United's fate had been the reverse. As Chelsea progressed in the major competition, United dropped into the Europa League, where they were joined by Valencia. It was a situation that most thought would play out in the opposite way. As things turned out though, that would be the least surprising aspect of Chelsea's European adventure.

3

Bleak Winter and the end of AVB

AT LEAST there were a few days for André Villas-Boas and the players to enjoy the satisfaction of a job well done and recover from the physical and emotional exertions of the Valencia game. The victory had come on a Tuesday, and Chelsea wouldn't be in action again until the following Monday, with television schedules requiring the upcoming home game against Manchester City to be moved.

Despite finishing third in their Champions League group, behind Bayern Munich and Napoli, causing them to drop into the Europa League alongside their neighbours from Old Trafford, domestically Manchester City were the dominant team, and on the way to their first league title since 1968. Funded by the wealth of the Abu Dhabi United Group, manager Roberto Mancini had brought together an exceptional and expensive squad in a bid to make the club the top dogs of English and European football. This league title would be the first step on a long journey.

The game at Stamford Bridge would be the 15th Premier League fixture of the season for both clubs, but while Chelsea appeared to be in an irritatingly consistent state of inconsistency, very much in the manner of Forrest

Gump's box of chocolates in that 'you never know what you're gonna get', City were a purring machine by comparison. As well as some notable victories – a 6-1 win at Old Trafford and a 5-1 triumph over Spurs at White Hart Lane being just a couple of examples – Mancini's team had yet to taste defeat, winning 12 of their 14 games by scoring 48 goals, and conceding just 13. The match would be a test for Chelsea. If, as had been suggested in some of the newspapers, the win over Valencia had been a turning point for both manager and club, here was the opportunity to prove it.

Understandably, Villas-Boas had wanted to send an unchanged team out against City, offering them a chance to prove that the victory over the Spanish club was something other than merely 'one of those nights'. His plan was foiled by David Luiz being unavailable though, so he reintroduced Bosingwa at right-back, and slid the versatile Branislav Ivanović into the centre of defence to partner Terry. It hardly looked to have overly weakened the defence, but when the first goal came, it was the Serb who was caught out.

For City, Mario Balotelli was a controversial figure, loved by the fans for his exuberance, but at times a coach's nightmare, exhibiting excellence and being exasperating in equal measure. Despite falling foul of his manager's code of conduct when breaking curfew on the night before the game, Mancini decided that the Italian's record of scoring in each of his last four league games was sufficient to return him to the starting 11 after being on the bench for their final game of the Champions League group. The decision would be quickly vindicated.

Out on the right, Sergio Agüero received the ball with his back to goal. Cutting inside, he played the ball on to Balotelli, who was closely marked by Ivanović. The quick feet of the Italian deceived the Chelsea defender, who slipped, allowing the striker a free run against Petr Čech. It was an uneven battle, a shimmy around the goalkeeper exposed an empty net and Balotelli coolly rolled the ball home. It looked as if, in that box of chocolates lottery, City had found Chelsea's soft centre.

The game was barely two minutes old and City were already smoothly moving through the gears, with an increasingly confident air boosted by the strike. The visitors continued to dominate, forcing Chelsea on to the back foot, desperate to avoid what, even at this early stage, would surely have been a killer second goal. It nearly came in the tenth minute. A mistake by Ashley Cole gifted possession to Agüero. The little Argentine skipped clear and left José Bosingwa on the floor as he closed in on Čech, but his effort flew wide and Chelsea escaped. The Portuguese defender was in peril of conceding a penalty soon afterwards, as a lazy dangling leg allowed David Silva to come into contact with it and plunge to the ground. Referee Mark Clattenburg was unimpressed by the extravagant tumble, however, and confidently waved City's semi-serious appeals away.

The first period was more than halfway through before Chelsea offered even a token threat on the visitors' goal as Joe Hart confidently saved from Didier Drogba. Whether their sustained domination had lulled City into a false sense of security, or their early frenetic start had emptied their fuel tanks as frustration at the second goal not arriving grew, as half-time approached Chelsea began to get a foothold in the game as the visitors' pace slowed. Ten minutes ahead of the break, out on the flank, Daniel Sturridge collected a pass, slipped past Gaël Clichy and crossed for Raul Meireles to volley home an equaliser.

The goal clearly upset the serene path that City's players assumed would be theirs for the taking, and the game became scrappy and ill-tempered. Meireles and Vincent Kompany were both yellow-carded by Clattenburg for being on less than friendly terms, and then another expansive bit of play from Sturridge saw Clichy trailing him again, before a pull on the shirt halted the forward's progress and Clattenburg added the French defender to his list of names.

The second period began in very much the same way, with play now more balanced, but Sturridge causing stress and strain on the left flank of City's defence. Clichy was coming under persistent pressure, and there would be a price to pay. As it was the young England forward causing most of the problems for the former Arsenal defender, it was somewhat ironic that it was a trip on Ramires, rather than Sturridge that brought Clichy's second yellow, and subsequent red, just ahead of the hour.

The man advantage encouraged Chelsea to push for a winner but, even being a man light, City were hardly in a backs-to-the wall situation. A game that had been ill-tempered at times now seemed to carry added malice. Oriol Romeu was carded for a foul on Balotelli just past the hour, and a minute later Mancini seemed to be looking to settle for a point when he withdrew star striker Agüero for the more muscular presence of Kolo Touré. If the game was going to develop into a physical battle the Italian coach wanted to ensure his team would not be bullied.

As City's change suggested caution, on 73 minutes, Villas-Boas seemed to indicate contrary intentions, removing the workmanlike Meireles for the increased goalscoring threat of Frank Lampard. Shortly afterwards, Ramires joined the list in Clattenburg's book after a less than graceful challenge on Balotelli. More changes and bookings followed. First, Mancini doubled down on his security-first approach, withdrawing Silva for Dutch midfield enforcer Nigel de Jong inside the final 15 minutes, then Drogba's clumsy tackle from behind on Pablo Zabaleta justly brought Chelsea's fourth yellow card of the game.

Inside the final ten minutes Mancini's ploy of locking things down and taking a point looked to be paying off but, with eight minutes to play, a handball by Joleon Lescott offered Lampard a chance to prove his penalty miss at Newcastle had been a blip. As Hart gambled with a dive, Chelsea's spot kick expert smashed the ball straight down the middle to bring the Stamford Bridge crowd to its feet.

Now the rationale for changes was switched. With time running down, Florent Malouda came on for Juan Mata, offering fresh legs to assist the defence and Mikel John Obi replaced Sturridge to add defensive nous to the midfield. Mancini threw caution to the wind replacing Lescott with Edin Džeko, but to no avail. Chelsea's back line saw out time. They had followed the victory over Valencia with a pulsating win against the previously unbeaten Premier League leaders.

Those newspaper pundits suggesting that Villas-Boas had turned a corner with the club, and his project, were giving themselves a pat on the back for their astute and timely judgement. It was a shade less than two weeks before Christmas, but as far as Stamford Bridge was concerned, the only person concentrating on issues regards a sack was Santa Claus. This was Chelsea though, and before the year was out, results and performances would diametrically change the attitude of the club and its fans.

Four days after the City game, immediate thoughts of upcoming fixtures were put to one side as the draw took place for the first knockout round of the Champions League. As a group winner, Chelsea would have the deemed advantage of playing the second leg – plus any accruing extra time – at home, but there was a large variation in the danger posed by possible clubs they could be pitted against. Options of a visit to Lyon, Marseille or Basel seemed less contentious than having to travel to Moscow to face CSKA or Saint Petersburg for a game against Zenit. With the matches scheduled for the third week of February, the Russian winter would hardly offer a warm welcome.

The remaining options, Milan or Napoli, may have presented less arduous journeys and more welcoming climates, but the two Serie A clubs were probably the ones to avoid in the draw. The *Rossoneri* had won the Scudetto the previous season, and had lost only one game when finishing as runners-up to Barcelona in their group. In their section, Napoli had forced Manchester City into third place, and the subsequent drop into the Europa League. They had beaten the Premier League leaders at the Stadio San Paolo, and only a late equaliser by Aleksandar Kolarov prevented the *Partenopei* completing a double for the Italians, as they finished in second place behind Bayern Munich.

When the whole ceremony was complete, Chelsea had avoided the worst-case scenario of an encounter with the champions of Italy, but any relief at that escape was quickly tempered. Instead, they had been handed the second-worst option of being paired with a resurgent Napoli team, comprising a forward line of Edinson Cavani, Marek Hamšík and Ezequiel Lavezzi, plus Gökhan Inler in midfield and Paolo Cannavaro at the back. Suddenly, those trips to Russia didn't look so bad after all. With their fate now set however, Chelsea had two months to concentrate on domestic matters, build on their recent impressive results and confirm those Mystic Meg predictions of the scribes correct as Villas-Boas forged forwards. The reality turned out to be quite different.

On the day following the Champions League draw, Chelsea needed to put thoughts of Neapolitan dreams away, and faced the more mundane bread-and-butter matter of a trip to Wigan Athletic. Understandably emboldened by the recent successes, Villas-Boas selected a more attacking line-up for the game, with both Mata and Lampard given midfield berths and Drogba, supported by Sturridge, further forwards. Wigan were struggling near the foot of the table at the time, and an energetic display from the visitors may well have kept the momentum flowing nicely. Roberto Martinez's team were not content to merely be bystanders for Chelsea's lofty ambitions though and, in a competitive first half, could well have been ahead early on had referee Martin Atkinson considered Ashley Cole's clumsy challenge on Jordi Gómez worthy of a spot kick, as most of the home players and bench did.

As the game wore on though, Chelsea slowly achieved parity and then a measure of ascendancy as the home team's ardour cooled, and they sank further back into studied and resolute defence. Often faced with the entire 11 home players between them and the goal when they had possession, Villas-Boas's team struggled to develop any penetrating play, and often resorted to long-range efforts that Ali Al-Habsi saved with varying degrees of difficulty. The nearest Chelsea came to a breakthrough was a 30-yard shot from John Terry that flew narrowly wide, and then another Al-Habsi save, plunging low to guide a volley from Romeu around the upright. Chelsea should have gone ahead on 40 minutes though when a clear headed chance for Drogba was nodded wide from a Meireles cross.

At this stage, it would have been against the run of play had the home team scored, but it should perhaps have happened when Atkinson again denied Wigan a penalty as a shot from Victor Moses struck Ivanović on the arm. Judging the impact to be accidental, however, Atkinson waved play on, although the replay suggested a distinct move of the Serb's arm towards the flight of the ball.

At the break, Villas-Boas's uncharacteristic determination to attack was lent extra weight as Romeu was withdrawn in favour of Salomon Kalou. An early combination with the substitute's compatriot nearly brought the first goal. Kalou got to the goal line before cutting the ball back to Drogba, but the striker's effort only found the side netting. Villas-Boas would have been cursing his luck then, but a goal was on the way. Just ahead of the hour, an incisive ball by Cole found Sturridge's run. The young forward was in a rich vein of form and, confidence flowing, he never looked like squandering the chance as he controlled before firing left-footed past Al-Habsi.

For a team that had reached the knockout stage of the Champions League and inflicted a first defeat of the season on the Premier League leaders, taking the lead against a team struggling at the foot of the table and having lost nine of their last dozen league fixtures, the points should have been secure, but they were not. With nothing to lose, Martinez gambled, sending on Hugo Rodallega and former Chelsea player Franco Di Santo for David Jones and Conor Sammon. Perhaps sensing a frailty in the visitors, Wigan suddenly applied pressure and the Chelsea defence creaked alarmingly. Čech was forced to push a shot from Maynor Figueroa wide and then a weak back pass by Ivanović offered Rodallega a chance on goal. Čech parried, and the ball ran free to Di Santo, who should have scored. But Ivanović redeemed his error by clearing from the goal line.

The worrying tendency for Chelsea to take the lead in games before surrendering it was about to be illustrated once more. It had been a recurring issue throughout the season and now they were under pressure again. Villas-Boas would have been increasingly on tenterhooks as time dragged into the final few minutes.

It was one of those sliding doors moments. See this one out, and the manager could laud the performance, define it as resilience under pressure, count the points and move forward with momentum uninterrupted. Concede though and the demons of doubt would be dancing around the manager once more.

On came Mikel for Mata, and later, Malouda for Sturridge as the Chelsea manager tried to lock out the victory. On occasions, when all around him seemed unsure and lurching from problem to crisis in defence, Čech had been the reassuringly solid, reliable figure, time and again rescuing his team. It was therefore more than a little symbolic that when the equaliser came, it was because of an error from the goalkeeper. On 87 minutes, Čech failed to securely collect a shot from Rodallega and Gómez gleefully fired home. On the visitors' bench, Villas-Boas slowly bowed his head. That sliding door was closing.

Interviewed after the game, the manager's attempts at being philosophical seemed almost an acceptance of an event that he saw as inevitable. 'We just let it slip in the end. It's disappointing, but we have to put it behind us and focus on a massive game against Tottenham on Thursday.'[58] Three days later, at White Hart Lane, the coach's selection suggested a reversion to the caution-first approach. Lampard was back on the bench, with Mata the sole creative spark in the workmanlike midfield of Mikel, Meireles and Ramires. Sturridge retained his place, as did Drogba. Despite

58 'Jordi Gómez grabs late Wigan Athletic equaliser to foil Chelsea', *The Guardian*, 17 December 2011.

conceding that late goal, Bosingwa, Terry, Ivanović and Cole also retained their starting berths.

Under the experienced Harry Redknapp, Spurs had become an entertaining and engaging team. The explosive pace of Gareth Bale was supplemented by the canny ability of Dutch playmaker Rafael van der Vaart, and the calm composure of Luka Modrić, the player Chelsea had tried so determinedly to sign in the summer. Up front there was the threatening presence of Emmanuel Adebayor who, on his day, was every bit as dangerous as Drogba at his muscular best. At White Hart Lane, there was a firm conviction that this season would see Tottenham's claim to be the top club in London given confirmation, and this was a chance to display their credentials.

Early on, they tore into Chelsea with vigour and Bale gave the right flank of the Chelsea back line a severe test. The opening goal came after eight minutes. Sturridge was dispossessed by Sandro, with Bale profiting from the tackle. A driven cross was finished by Adebayor and Chelsea were behind. Spurs dominated for a while but 15 minutes later, Chelsea equalised when Sturridge levelled the scores, tapping home Cole's cross on the volley. Protests from the Spurs players that the Chelsea man had profited from the ball striking his arm as he escaped a tackle from van der Vaart were waved aside.

Ten minutes later, Chelsea faced another setback when Ivanović suffered a hamstring injury and had to be replaced by Paulo Ferreira. Now into his 30s, the Portuguese defender had been one of the first purchases when José Mourinho joined the club as Roman Abramovich began his spending spree, and was a key factor in the club's early success. As time went on though, his appearances had dwindled to the point where he was now seen as more of a squad player, someone to draft in as required. Perhaps it was his long experience, a determination to prove his worth or a combination of factors, but Ferreira's ability to deal with the searing pace of Bale brought a new parity to the game and, while not completely extinguishing the Welshman's fire, at least kept its flames a little more under control. The change allowed Chelsea to ease into the game.

From there it was an end-to-end battle with both teams having chances, but being denied by the goalkeepers or last desperate defensive blocks. At the very end, it was Terry clearing off the line from Adebayor that maintained the point for Chelsea. If the draw at Wigan had been disappointing, this game only garnered the same sole point, but the performance, and especially the refusal to submit when the pressure was at its hottest, promised better things ahead. A few days ahead of Christmas, with entirely winnable home games to come against Fulham and Aston Villa after the festivities, there was a chance to draw breath and then move forwards again. Six points from those two games would be vital. Only one would be accrued though.

Unrest was still present and, on Chelsea TV, former Blues favourite Tommy Langley offered a relatively mild expression of the unease that some fans were feeling. Perhaps considering that his feathers had been unnecessarily and unhelpfully ruffled by Langley's comments, however, rumours abounded that the manager had insisted on the former player being sacked. If true, and some clearly thought it was, the situation hardly reflected favourably on the manager, as Malcolm Folley suggested in the *Daily Mail* following the Villa game, 'Villas-Boas is a man whose confidence borders on arrogance. Before Christmas he had former striker Tommy Langley fired from his role as a pundit on Chelsea TV for making the mildest criticism. Langley's loyalty to Chelsea is easily identified as he has four season tickets at the club. A friend of his said last night, "Villas-Boas appears to be a paranoid man."'[59] The old adage of 'just because you're feeling paranoid doesn't mean that people aren't out to get you' may have provoked the widely perceived overreaction from the manager.

Fulham were Chelsea's nearest rivals geographically if not, certainly in recent times, in terms of success. Games against the club perched on the side of the River Thames hardly felt like a local derby at all, and certainly not one where tension and pressure were particularly high. A home win was widely expected. More than 41,000 fans crowded into Stamford Bridge fully expecting to see a feast of attacking football from the home team, especially now that Lampard was back in the starting 11 alongside Mata, and there was even the bonus of seeing Fernando Torres assume the striking role as Drogba was either rested or dropped, depending on your perspective. Luiz returned to replace the hamstrung Ivanović. After beating Manchester City, Chelsea's hopes of challenging for the title had brightened considerably but, a mere two weeks later, as referee Kevin Friend brought the west London derby to a close, such thoughts were exposed as the wildest of fantasies with Chelsea trailing both Manchester clubs by an unbridgeable 11 points.

As would surely have been expected, Chelsea dominated much of the possession against Fulham, but failed to deliver any threat of real note. Reporting for the BBC, Owen Phillips suggested that the first half was an entirely tepid affair, describing 'a desperate first-half display which lacked

---

59 'Chelsea 1 Aston Villa 3: Night on the boos gives Villas-Boas a headache', *Daily Mail*, 31 December 2011.

urgency, quality and conviction'.[60] Two minutes after the restart there was promise of an improved performance as Mata put the home side ahead, striking a first-time shot past David Stockdale from the edge of the area. There was precious little time for the lead to be built on though as, within ten minutes, Clint Dempsey had equalised after comfortably evading Cole before finishing from close range. The final half-hour saw Chelsea press and have a number of chances but those that weren't put wide were dealt with by Stockdale and his defenders.

With the home team looking for inspiration from the returning Torres, they were merely repaid with the sort of shuffling and ineffective display that epitomised much of his time in Chelsea blue. Yet, when the substitutions came, it was Malouda for Lampard just past the hour and when Drogba came on inside the final 20 minutes, it was surprisingly to replace Sturridge, whose goals had been so important in recent games, rather than Torres, who had hardly scored at all in the league season up to then.

Any prospects of league title success had now been firmly vanquished and even Chelsea's absolute minimum requirement of a top-four finish was under threat. The Manchester clubs were long gone and over the horizon. Both Arsenal and Tottenham had designs on those Champions League slots assigned to third- and fourth-place finishes and Alan Pardew's Newcastle United were looking to elbow their way into the equation. The last day of 2011 saw the home game against Aston Villa. If the unthinkable happened, and Chelsea were defeated, it was entirely likely that they would slip out of the top four for the first time since the second game of the season. In the last decade, they had never

---

60 https://www.bbc.com/sport/football/16240767.

entered a new year outside of the top four. If Villas-Boas thought he had been under pressure previously, things were about to be ramped up to a whole new level.

The manager must have considered long and hard before making his selection for the game against the Birmingham club. Alex McLeish's team were sitting around mid-table and, although their season would deteriorate as they drifted down the table in the new year to finish a disappointing 16th, even at this stage they should have presented reasonably comfortable opponents for a team with aspirations of Champions League qualification. These were the dog days of the Villas-Boas tenure, however, when nothing can be assumed without a measure of hesitancy.

In what looked like a strange selection, Villas-Boas brought Ferreira into the starting 11 in place of Bosingwa. The veteran had undoubtedly excelled when subduing Bale in the game at White Hart Lane, but had hardly played throughout the season so far. In fact, he would only make three starts and three substitute appearances in the entire league programme. Lampard was relegated to a place on the bench again and Torres's brief return to first-team action was halted as Drogba returned.

The game began encouragingly with both Mata and Sturridge going close, but the visitors' tactical approach to strike on the counter-attack always looked threatening, exposing weaknesses in the home team's organisation and a worrying measure of tactical naivety. When Drogba netted a penalty after 23 minutes, there was a feeling that perhaps the goal would settle the home team, and discourage what had previously been eager Villa thrusts, using the pace of Gabby Agbonlahor. It wouldn't be the case. With Stephen Ireland bossing the midfield, the lead was short-lived. Within five minutes, Villa were level.

Given the flow of the game up to that point, it was entirely appropriate that Ireland should score the equaliser, converting at the second attempt after a run by Charles N'Zogbia. The goal clearly rattled the Chelsea players. They drove forward in a vain attempt to swamp the visitors, but the cool defensive organisation of Villa merely caused frustration and, as the Chelsea attempts became more and more desperate, the opportunity to counter-attack through the increasing number of gaps in the home defence grew. At the break, although the home team had controlled much of the possession, it was the visitors who looked the more likely to score. Little changed in the second period.

Villas-Boas, increasingly agitated on the sidelines as he moved from his characteristic crouch to standing tall and bellowing out feverish instructions, sent on Lampard for Romeu as the hour approached. Five minutes later, Torres replaced Sturridge, and then Bosingwa came on for Ferreira with a quarter of an hour to play. Chances came and went, but the scores remained unaltered and the home crowd, already frustrated by the insipid performance in the home draw with Fulham, vented their frustrations at the manager. All that was needed to compound issues now was a Villa goal. In typical fashion of underscoring the growing problems at the club though, Chelsea conceded not once, but twice. First Stiliyan Petrov coolly slotted past Čech, and then Darren Bent added the killer third goal after pouncing on a mistake by Lampard.

At the full-time whistle, the only home fans not booing were the ones who had left early, angered by the performance and impending defeat to a team that they, not unreasonably, expected their team to defeat with something to spare. The only packed part of the stadium was the area populated by Villa fans, saluting the performance of their favourites. It was the darkest day of the Villas-Boas reign so far, and the question on every Chelsea fans' lips was how much longer Abramovich would tolerate the tailspin that the club had now spiralled into.

Questioned about the fans' reaction afterwards, Villas-Boas offered a vague answer. 'Booing is the most valuable criticism we get,' he said.[61] Much as with the tactics, so easily torn asunder during the game, the implication was unclear, and it wasn't only Chelsea fans wondering how long before a change of manager was enacted. After the game, the *Daily Mail* reported, 'One of the largest bookmakers in the country had shortened the odds against Villas-Boas surviving 2012 to 7/2, placing him as third favourite to receive his P45.'[62] Villas-Boas reacted calmly, at least in public, to the enveloping crisis. 'You'll have to ask the owner if my job is safe,' he said. 'I have no information to the contrary.'[63]

Despite the stated absence of any knowledge of his position being under threat, the manager was clearly aware that things were dipping below what would be deemed barely acceptable by the club's owner, 'Now we are fifth, below the top four. But we have to wait and see. It can change within 48 hours, though. That's a good thing. We have a chance to produce something. Our reality is a fourth-placed finish, but that is not good enough.'[64] No one was likely to argue with that summary. All talk of the project, and cleaning out the group of older players while still maintaining the club's progress now looked like hubris and a plan riddled with

61 'Chelsea 1 Aston Villa 3: Night on the boos gives Villas-Boas a headache', *Daily Mail*, 31 December 2011.

62 'Chelsea 1 Aston Villa 3: Night on the boos gives Villas-Boas a headache', *Daily Mail*, 31 December 2011.

63 'Chelsea 1 Aston Villa 3: Night on the boos gives Villas-Boas a headache', *Daily Mail*, 31 December 2011.

64 https://www.bbc.com/sport/football/16324977

holes, through which the sands of Chelsea's season were draining away.

The league season was now halfway through. Two days after the depressing defeat to Aston Villa, Chelsea would travel to the Black Country to face a Wolverhampton Wanderers team struggling to fight their way clear from the clawing quagmire of the relegation zone, in a battle they would ultimately lose. Anything other than a win for Chelsea would surely see the curtain brought down and a merciful end to Villas-Boas's reign. Even a win may not have been sufficient to save his job. The individual who had arrived at Stamford Bridge as the brightest young coach in European football a few months ago now looked like a condemned man wondering which meal would be his last. Would it be served up to him at Molineux?

The portents ahead of the game were hardly encouraging. Drogba and Sturridge had both been deemed unavailable with injuries. In the case of the Ivorian, the problem was diagnosed as a minor foot injury. It should have only meant an absence of a single game but another issue would prolong that into almost two months.

The Africa Cup of Nations was played in the early months of 2012, with both Drogba and Kalou called up to represent Ivory Coast in the tournament. The hosting was shared between Gabon and Equatorial Guinea, with the continent's biggest international tournament beginning on 21 January. International protocol allowed national teams to require selected squad players' attendance 14 days ahead of the tournament's opening. It meant that the pair would be absent for the FA Cup tie against Portsmouth on 8 January and, should Ivory Coast progress to the final – as would turn out to be the case – neither Drogba nor Kalou would be available until the later weeks of February.

Villas-Boas would request a day's leniency from the Ivory Coast authorities, to allow Drogba to be available for the FA Cup tie, but the attempt would be rebuffed and, with the striker in the final year of his contract with the Stamford Bridge club, and probably facing the last real opportunity to take his country to continental glory, the player was unlikely to push the case for a moratorium either.

Rumours at the time suggested that both Manchester City and Arsenal had been more successful in their pleas to national coach Francois Zahoui to make the Touré brothers and Gervinho available for their games. Not unreasonably, had such uneven flexibility been shown, the Chelsea manager would have every right to feel aggrieved. The situation with Drogba, his relationship with Ivory Coast and its people, who were experiencing a traumatic period at the time, however, surpassed one of normal patriotic duty, as David Hytner explained. Writing for *The Guardian* he detailed, '... the sensitivity of the situation exacerbated by the civil war that Ivory Coast has endured and the way that this edition of the Africa Cup of Nations has been presented as the opportunity to raise the people's spirits. Ivory Coast are the hot favourites for the title, which they last won in 1992. Drogba's status in his homeland goes beyond that of a mere sporting icon and is quasi-presidential. Out of all Ivory Coast players, he is under the most pressure to meet the demand of the coach Francois Zahoui to report on time.'[65]

The loss of Kalou was perhaps a lesser issue for Villas-Boas, but with Torres struggling for any kind of goalscoring form, Drogba's absence would inevitably be keenly felt. Approaching his 34th birthday, the passing years and accumulated injuries had gnawed away at the forward's

---

65 'Didier Drogba to miss Chelsea's FA Cup tie at home to Portsmouth', *The Guardian*, 4 January 2012.

immense physical powers, but he remained a potent force at the top level of English football and, as with the likes of Lampard and Terry, was a talismanic presence in the team, as the game against Valencia amply illustrated. Villas-Boas probably needed very little further evidence that things were not flowing in his favour.

The depleted forward options meant a return for Torres and, with Lampard also invited back into the fold, the team selected suggested a cautious 4-5-1 line-up, with the Spaniard as the lone striker. Lampard and Mata were the creative pairing in a midfield also comprising Ramires, Meireles and Romeu, with the former nominally in the wide right attacking role, but often he drifted back into his more usual position, leaving Torres isolated.

With both teams enduring difficult times, albeit for different reasons, it was understandable that the first half was blighted by caution. The Blues were the stronger side and enjoyed more possession, but Wolves still retained a threat, and each time they pressed forwards, the experienced back line of Bosingwa, Terry, Luiz and Cole looked creakily inefficient and concerned, especially in the air. A free kick from Adam Hammill was met powerfully by Roger Johnson, but his header struck the upright. Then another set piece from the same player found the head of Stephen Ward but, with a wide expanse of goal to aim at, the Irishman nodded wastefully wide, with Terry berating his fellow defenders' lack of concentration.

Things could have been even worse for Chelsea. On 24 minutes Lampard lunged into a reckless tackle on Hammill, drawing howls of protest from the crowd and demands for a straight red card. It would have been difficult to claim that such a decision was overly harsh, but referee Peter Walton decided that a yellow was sufficient. At the break neither team had been able to break the deadlock. During half-time, Mick McCarthy replaced the young Anthony Forde with Matthew Jarvis, hoping that the winger's wide play would open up opportunities against what was a hesitant visiting defence. Ten minutes later, the first goal arrived, but it was at the other end, and the profligacy of those squandered chances in the first half came back to haunt the home team.

In keeping with the scrappy play of the game up to that point, it was a goal that owed much to luck and a few fortunate bounces before an emphatic finish. Playing a corner in from the left, Mata's cross dropped towards a posse challenging with Terry. The ball cleared the group and fell to Ramires with Ward in close attendance. After struggling briefly with the ball stuck between his feet as he turned, the Brazilian wriggled free and fired powerfully high into the net, offering Wayne Hennessey precious little time to react. The celebrations by the Chelsea players and bench betrayed as much relief at the goal as it did elation. Interestingly, and perhaps significantly, it was Roberto Di Matteo involved in the celebrations as Villas-Boas pushed his players back on to the pitch insisting on concentration, haunted by memories of how recent leads in games had melted away.

Even with more than 30 minutes remaining surely the lead should have been enough against a team struggling for goals and wins, but very much the same was true of the visit to Wigan where things had fallen away at the last. Chelsea continued to largely control the game, but as the minutes ticked away, nervous energy leaking from the coach to the players inevitably led to a deeper and deeper line. With seven minutes to play and the home side seeming to have run out of ideas, Mata was removed and replaced with the fresh legs, but inexperience of young midfielder Josh McEachran. Two minutes later the collapse at Wigan had an encore.

Chelsea players were dropping deeper and deeper, almost abandoning the midfield and allowing Wolves more possession. It gave fresh impetus to the home side and, with Jarvis on the field, there was always a chance that the winger would find an accurate cross to cause danger. Moving infield, the wide man crossed to the far post and Steven Fletcher, who had replaced Emmanuel Frimpong just past the hour, managed to flick the ball back towards the penalty spot. In the first half, Ward had missed a golden opportunity with his head. This time there would be no mistake. Closing in, he drove the ball home and Wolves looked to have rescued a point. On the Chelsea bench, Villas-Boas threw his arms in the air and then down by his sides in exasperated disbelief and frustration. The noose was tightening around the manager's neck.

Now it was Wolves who had something to protect, funnelling back deep to guard the precious point they had salvaged, but there was one more twist to come. Six, seven, and then eight home players stood defending on the edge of their penalty area as Chelsea desperately sought a winning goal. Understandably there were few gaps to exploit but, when Cole loomed up on the left flank, an intelligent pass by Torres saw the full-back in space. There were surely sufficient players back to cover the runs of Lampard and Ramires into the box but, transfixed, they hesitated as Cole drilled the ball across the box. The instincts that had served Lampard so well were to the fore and, reading the cross, he met it on the edge of the six-yard line and guided it unerringly past Hennessey. The home fans had barely had time to recover from the elation of the equaliser before they were cast into disappointment, and behind again. Lampard had rescued his team – and the manager. Or so it seemed.

Time was almost up when Ward shaped to hurl a long throw into the Chelsea area. There were no fewer than eight blue shirts, plus Čech, defending against the five players McCarthy had urged forwards, and yet two Wolves players got a touch on the ball before any defender. Firstly, Fletcher flicked it on towards goal and then Kevin Doyle got a touch at point-blank range. It was surely a goal, but Čech responded with instant reactions and managed to reach up to turn the ball over the bar. There was no time for the corner to be taken, and Chelsea had stolen away with the three points.

There had been times when Villas-Boas's team had fallen, or failed to hold on to a lead but, at others, it seemed that it was that group of experienced players, targets apparently of the project, that had come to Chelsea's rescue. Drogba's barnstorming performance against Valencia, Terry with the last-minute clearance to preserve a valuable point at White Hart Lane and now, Lampard and Čech had both been key elements in delivering the win at Molineux. At the big moments, the big players had stepped up and, as the season wound to its unpredictable climax, that would continue to be the case. Was the manager beginning to understand the value of what he had, and if so, had the dawning realisation arrived too late to save his job?

After four games without a win, and that dispiriting defeat at home to Aston Villa, the victory at Molineux, especially after it seemed certain that another advantage had been squandered late in a game, offered a small but much-needed boost. Early January saw the entry of clubs from the top two tiers into the FA Cup and Chelsea were offered what seemed a comfortable task with a home game against Portsmouth, but Chelsea's ongoing problems added an extra piquancy, as *The Guardian* reported: 'The Portsmouth tie has taken on increased significance in light of Chelsea's recent struggles and those of Villas-Boas to impose his will on some of the dressing-room's established names. The win at Wolves was the team's first in five Premier League matches. Home form has been edgy and confidence likewise. "It's true that we've had a little crisis of results," the midfielder Juan Mata said.'[66]

Chelsea's early progress in the FA Cup is described in detail in the next chapter, but suffice to say that although a 4-0 win looks comfortable enough, taking into account that it was a virtually full-strength starting 11 and, with five minutes left to play the Blues only held the slenderest of one-goal leads, the veneer of comfort quickly falls away to reveal the nerviest of progresses into the fourth round of the competition.

At least it was another victory though and their next domestic encounter was a home Premier League game against Sunderland. The Wearside club had experienced a fairly traumatic start to the season after a hugely encouraging 1-1 draw away to Liverpool on the opening day. By 30 November, following a 2-1 home defeat to Wigan, they had sacked manager Steve Bruce. The erstwhile manager's assistant Eric Black had been put in caretaker charge for a single game, a 2-1 defeat away to Wolves, before Martin O'Neill was invited to perform a rescue act.

Sunderland had certainly been in need of a lift. They had won just twice in 14 games, and had spiralled down the table, to second from bottom. By the time Sunderland arrived at Stamford Bridge though, the Northern Irishman had guided them to relative comfort in mid-table, having lost just once in six games, and that by a single goal away to Spurs. The team

66 'Didier Drogba to miss Chelsea's FA Cup tie at home to Portsmouth', *The Guardian*, 4 January 2012.

that Chelsea would face had been transformed from hapless strugglers into a resurgent and confident outfit, displaying a growing confidence and belief that had, in sharp contrast, been steadily draining away from the Chelsea players over the past weeks and months.

For all that, Chelsea had won the last two games, albeit thanks to goals in the closing minutes of both games, and another victory would at least keep that nascent run going. Understandably therefore, both Lampard and Mata were selected to add some creativity, alongside the more workmanlike Romeu, Meireles and Ramires. The ever-reliable Čech was in goal behind a back four of Bosingwa, Terry, Luiz and Cole that now seemed to be the coach's favoured defence. With Drogba absent, Torres led the line despite not having scored for more than 12 and a half hours of playing time on the pitch, and three months on the calendar. By the end of the game, the clock had clicked past 14 hours.

Perhaps just as significant, however, was two Chelsea players who did not play. Up in the stands, Gary Cahill waved to the crowd as the public address system introduced him as joining the club. A deal involving a fee of some £7m had been agreed with Bolton Wanderers, although it wouldn't be officially completed until a couple of days later. The 26-year-old centre-back may have merely looked like a usefully experienced addition to a squad where Terry, Luiz and occasionally Ivanović had first call in the heart of the defence, but Cahill would play a hugely significant part in the remainder of Chelsea's season.

The other non-starter was much closer to the action. Sitting on the bench and making his return to the first-team party was Michael Essien. The Ghana international had signed from Lyon in 2005 and had enjoyed success as his lung-bursting displays in midfield, coupled with some extraordinary goals, proved to be the perfect foil for Lampard. For example, his swerving, long-distance drive for a late dramatic equaliser against Arsenal was voted as Chelsea's Goal of the Season for 2006/07 and it was another dynamite effort from distance in the 2008/09 Champions League semi-final against Barcelona that so nearly took Chelsea past the Catalans, until Andrés Iniesta's late effort saw the Blues eliminated on away goals.

It was often said that, such was his fitness, after a game, he would sometimes need to go for a run, just to burn off his excess reserves of energy before beginning a warm-down regime. On top of his midfield performances, Essien also offered a versatility that proved invaluable to Chelsea managers. Under José Mourinho, in an away Champions League quarter-final second leg against Valencia, Essien was deployed to cover both right-back and wide right midfield slots at the same time. Chelsea had drawn 1-1 at home, and with the scores mirrored in Spain as time drifted away, it was Essien accelerating into an overlap position like a player who had been on the pitch for ten minutes, rather than one who had played a double role for the previous 90, who collected the pass and fired home the winning goal. It took Chelsea into the last four where the infamous 'ghost goal' at Anfield saw them eliminated.

In the final of 2008, Avram Grant trusted Essien to cover the right-back position in Moscow, knowing that he would be pitted against the potent force of Cristiano Ronaldo. It would be an onerous task for any experienced defender, but in typical fashion, Essien applied himself with dedication and commitment and, but for the salmon leap by the Portuguese star that any defender would have struggled to deal with, he acquitted himself well.

His time at Stamford Bridge would also bring much silverware. Premier League titles in 2005/06 and 2009/10 were complemented by FA Cup success in 2006/07, 2008/09 and 2009/10 and a League Cup in 2006/07. It should, however, have been so much more. The Ghanaian was plagued by recurring knee injuries, many of which had been attributed to his playing for the Black Stars in international matches on the bone-hard pitches of Africa. The first occasion came on 5 September when he sustained an anterior cruciate ligament injury while playing for Ghana. It was thought that the injury would mean the entire season was written off.

With typical single-minded fortitude though, he returned on 7 March to play in an FA Cup match, before starting against Juventus in his next game, and scoring in Turin. Another injury saw him miss the 2010 World Cup but he was fit to start the new season in Chelsea blue, before the next setback saw him out for two months. His value to Chelsea was clearly emphasised when, while he was absent, the team won just one of nine games.

The start of the 2011/12 season with a new manager promised a bright beginning, but injury struck again. A rupture to the anterior cruciate ligament and meniscus dampened expectations and surgery in July suggested that any return to fitness would, at best, be delayed for six months. Essien's single-minded determination and powers of recovery again defeated such forecast, and he began training again in November, building up strength and conditioning. A return to action in a reserve game in early January was enough to persuade the medical staff that he could now be considered for the first team. This led him to being on the bench for the game against Sunderland.

Ironically, had Essien not sustained that pre-season injury and been available to Villas-Boas through the season, he would have been unavailable now as Ghana had qualified for the Africa Cup of Nations. Being skipper of the national team, Essien would certainly have been away, along with Drogba and Kalou. His availability now therefore was both a quirk of fate and timing. His return to fitness had probably come a mere few weeks too late to merit selection for the tournament.

Arriving back in the first-team squad at Chelsea in mid-January should, therefore, have been a rare boon to Villas-Boas. By now though, the manager cut a beleaguered figure and was unwilling to put his faith in someone he knew little of. Essien was perhaps also one of those established players who was marked down to fall foul of the project. As with Cahill, however, despite never truly regaining the ebullient fitness he had enjoyed before the string of knee injuries gnawed away without mercy at his abilities and fitness, he too would contribute to the finale of Chelsea's season, before moving on loan to Real Madrid, where he was reunited with former manager Mourinho.

The Sunderland game itself was so in keeping with Chelsea performances of recent times. There was precious little fluidity to their play, with Torres seemingly fated not to score regardless of how hard he tried, and how much effort he expended. The forward's increasing burden of hours without a goal was clearly weighing heavily on his shoulders but, for the want of an inch or two, he could have thrown off that weight with the most spectacular of goals against the Wearsiders.

A deep cross from the right by Mata found the Spain forward beyond the far post. The ball was behind Torres but, throwing himself into the air to deliver a spectacular overhead scissor kick, he powered a spectacular shot on goal. The contact seemed perfect as the ball arrowed over a comprehensively beaten Simon Mignolet who had little time to react. It was a Goal of the Season strike but, being Torres and the way things were running for him, instead the ball crashed against the bar and, standing a few metres from the goal, it struck Lampard and rebounded into the net.

If ever there was a metaphor to illustrate how the fates had conspired that Torres couldn't buy a goal and why Lampard would feast on them, that was surely it. In fairness to the midfielder, after recovering composure from the initial shock of perhaps the most unintended goal of his long career, a beaming Lampard was quick to guide his celebrating team-mates across to where the Spaniard was climbing back to his feet, compelled to celebrate a goal for his team, but doubtless internally raging against the fates that had denied him a little personal glory and measure of redemption.

Somewhat perversely, the goal seemed to inspire Torres to have one of his better games for Chelsea. Malcolm Folley related for readers of the *Daily Mail*, 'The 27-year-old Spaniard was looking comfortable on the ball again and keeping it under control on the run, as we had been accustomed to witnessing through his years at Anfield.'[67] During the second half he could have had two penalties; the second one much more worthy than the first. A dozen minutes after the break, his tumble inside the area may have been a touch too theatrical to convince referee Phil Dowd, but ten minutes later, a challenge by Phil Bardsley inside the area looked likely to bring a spot kick. The official's decision, however, did little to disavow the forward that the world was against him. Dowd produced a yellow card, deciding that it had been simulation rather than Bardsley's challenge that

---

67 'Torres fails to score but he shines in victory', *Daily Mail*, 15 January 2012.

had caused the fall. It looked a terribly harsh decision – not least because it was.

Torres's frustration found an echo on the Chelsea bench as Villas-Boas fidgeted nervously. Was this going to be another game where a lead was not consolidated, and then squandered? If Chelsea fans had felt aggrieved by Dowd's refusal to award a penalty to Torres, visitors from Sunderland would share that anguish when Cole bundled Nicklas Bendtner off the ball in the time between the two Torres appeals. Frustration was also growing for Martin O'Neill. As time ticked on, Chelsea nerves became increasingly frayed. Essien was sent on to replace Lampard with 15 minutes remaining to cheers from the crowd, welcoming the player back into the fold. Then Malouda replaced Mata, but the chances were now falling to the visitors, both in increasing numbers and quality.

O'Neill jumped, spun, and berated his luck as his players seemed to form a queue to miss opportunities. James McClean, Craig Gardner and Bendtner all passed up chances that should have been taken as the sands of time drifted away. The joy and relief from the Chelsea bench at full time were not missed by the Sunderland manager. Villas-Boas and his entourage knew they had escaped with the win. 'When you consider how overwhelmed Chelsea's staff were to have won at the final whistle, you know we must have played all right. But it just gnaws away that we didn't get something out of that game,'[68] O'Neill lamented, frustration burning in his voice.

Villas-Boas looked at the half-full, half-empty glass of a game won, that could easily have been lost, and chose to emphasise the positives. 'We left the game on the edge,' he

---

68 'Torres fails to score but he shines in victory', *Daily Mail*, 15 January 2012

admitted. 'But it was a good performance, and an important weekend for us as it has shortened the distance to Tottenham.'[69] If the choice of emphasis was understandable, the assessment of the performance would have been disputed by more than a few observers, O'Neill included. More balanced judgement was noted by *The Guardian*'s Dominic Fifield, '"There's an obvious stigma around Stamford Bridge which is present for everybody to see," said Villas-Boas. "In the second half there was a tendency towards [nerves] because of recent happenings."'[70]

The words betrayed the growing sense of unease that was by now engulfing the club in ever deepening waves. Even at this stage, the possibility of Villas-Boas being able to dispel the clouds of doubt and disharmony felt remote. Three wins on the bounce had done little to help. None of the victories had spoken of belief and optimism, each having been chiselled out more by determination than ability. There should, however, have been a measure of empathy for the under-pressure manager, seeking to extract all the positives he could from the win. He wouldn't experience that feeling again until 25 February, and that would be his last before the inevitable happened, and he was dismissed.

A lunchtime game on Saturday, 21 January took Chelsea to Carrow Road to face Norwich City. Under manager Paul Lambert, the Canaries had established themselves in mid-table and would float around those positions until the end of the season. The turn of the year had seen them gain two successive away victories, winning 2-1 at both Queens Park Rangers and West Bromwich Albion. It hardly looked like an

---

69 'Torres fails to score but he shines in victory', *Daily Mail*, 15 January 2012.

70 'Chelsea cheered as Fernando Torres helps lift Stamford Bridge stigma', *The Guardian*, 15 January 2012.

easy game for Chelsea and, with his main striker not having scored for ten games, the team Villas-Boas selected seemed to accept the fact that goals would need to come from elsewhere. The midfield and front line looked equipped to help out.

Lampard was supported by Meireles and Ramires with Mata and Sturridge playing wider in support of Torres. Ironically, with Chelsea having scored at least one goal when more pragmatic selections had been deployed, this 11, at least on paper looking more adventurous, would draw a frustrating blank. With Chelsea comfortably enjoying the majority of possession, it quickly became clear that the home team would be more than satisfied with a point as the visitors sought to press. Their cause was hardly helped after 37 minutes when Lampard was forced to leave the field with a calf injury. Malouda replaced him from the bench. There was even a scare early on as Grant Holt latched on to a pass from Steve Morrison, evaded the challenge of Luiz, but fired his attempt wide of Čech's post. Had that shot passed the other side of the upright, it's questionable as to whether Chelsea's tepid and toothless display could have found a way back into the game.

The first half ended without any score and, despite plenty of huffing and puffing, there was little sign of a breakthrough for the visitors. Writing in *The Guardian*, Amy Lawrence described the Chelsea performance as being 'sluggish and short of sparks of invention from midfield. It took them until midway through the second half to exert their authority on a hard-working and enterprising Norwich team, and when they did a combination of careless finishing and the calm interventions of John Ruddy in goal ensured a shut-out.'[71]

As Lawrence suggests, like a fine wine, the second period improved with age, but an appealing bouquet failed to deliver

71 'Norwich and John Ruddy stand firm to deny Chelsea and frustrate Torres', *The Guardian*, 21 January 2012.

the satisfaction of the sweet taste of victory. Lawrence wrote, 'Chelsea began to turn the screw as the clock ticked on, seizing control and dominating possession. Juan Mata tested Ruddy on a couple of occasions, and the midfielders tried their luck. First Raul Meireles swept a shot just over the bar. Ramires then took aim with a piledriver that flew into Ruddy's midriff. Norwich's goalkeeper was equal to whatever Chelsea could summon, which in fairness was not that much.'[72]

Around the hour, it was merely the bitter taste of regret as another Torres chance came and went. A cross from Bosingwa was controlled well but the Spaniard's placed effort was inches wide. There are few groups of people more readily inclined to metaphorically kick an opponent when he's down than football fans. Savouring the opportunity to deliver a punishing barb, the home fans delighted in the miss, serenading Torres with chants of 'We'd rather have Grant Holt'. Given the striker's penchant for drawing such comments, it must have felt like one more strike on the back of a battered and fraying piñata. Not long afterwards, Villas-Boas removed Torres, sending on the young Belgian Romelu Lukaku, but it was too late to change things with Norwich well settled into their obdurate resistance and Chelsea running out of ideas. Essien also gained a bit more game time to push along his recovery, replacing Meireles with a dozen minutes to play but, at the final whistle the home bench celebrations were in sharp contrast to the disconsolate Villas-Boas demeanour.

Chelsea remained in fourth position but were losing ground on the clubs above and any realistic hopes of a late surge for the title had perished, as Duncan White confirmed in *The Times*: 'André Villas-Boas keeps playing possum. On Boxing Day, the prognosis for Chelsea's title challenge was

---

72 'Norwich and John Ruddy stand firm to deny Chelsea and frustrate Torres', *The Guardian*, 21 January 2012.

dire and after defeat at home to Aston Villa on New Year's Eve their prospects looked about as promising as those of a man paddling off into the North Sea in his canoe. … And Chelsea were still secretly in the hunt. In fact this game was Chelsea's final chance. Now it is definitely dead. Sort of....'[73]

For all the perceived faults of Villas-Boas, and he would later concede that he not only made several mistakes while at Chelsea but also that perhaps the chance at the top level came too soon for him, there's something admirable about his cussed refusal to bend the knee to an increasingly clear and inevitable truth. If White's implication was that the club should be looking at securing their fourth position against threats from below, it was a stance the Portuguese refused to accept, although conceding that, given more dropped points, the title was now a forlorn chase. '"It could have been a good last opportunity to threaten for the title," admitted Villas-Boas. The manager scoffed at the suggestion that he should keep an eye on what is behind him in the league table, insisting, "No, I am not worried about finishing lower than fourth."'[74] It sounded like hubris and, across the following weeks, it proved to be so.

On 28 January, a return to Loftus Road, scene of one of Chelsea's worst performances of the season, and Terry's legal problems, brought a tight single-goal victory in the FA Cup with Mata scoring from the penalty spot just past the hour. There are, of course, lies, damned lies and statistics, but if Villas-Boas wanted to accentuate the positives of Chelsea's fixtures since the turn of the year, he could point to an unbeaten record stretching to five

---

73 'Norwich City 0 Chelsea 0', *The Times,* 22 January 2012.

74 'Norwich and John Ruddy stand firm to deny Chelsea and frustrate Torres', *The Guardian*, 21 January 2012.

games. The run would next be tested by a visit to south Wales and Swansea City.

The Swansea manager at the time was Brendan Rodgers. The Northern Irishman had a linked back story with Villas-Boas, having also served as part of Mourinho's support staff in his first years at Chelsea. Rodgers had joined the Stamford Bridge club in 2004 to take over the reserve team after leaving Reading. He would stay there until 2008, when he was given his first managerial post at Watford. Rodgers' career was very much on the upswing, and his success at the Liberty Stadium, including the entertaining style that the Welsh club played, would lead to him taking control at Liverpool in the coming summer. For now, though, Swansea were, very much like Norwich, in a comfortable mid-table position in the Premier League when Villas-Boas and his Chelsea team came to visit.

Terry would miss the next few games as the knee injury compounded by a collision with the post in the FA Cup tie against Portsmouth grew worse. Villas-Boas would largely ignore – at least for a while – the claims of new signing Cahill, and draft in Ivanović to partner David Luiz at the heart of the Chelsea defence. With Lampard's injury also making him unavailable, the manager selected Malouda to add some width. Torres would maintain his place up front despite his lack of goals and deepening pit of low confidence. By the end of this game, wherein he only touched the ball nine times in the first period, the Spain striker would have completed 1,076 minutes of first-team action without scoring.

Facing a team with a growing reputation for slick play and intricate passing movements, Chelsea were second best throughout the first period. Returning his team to something resembling first-choice after resting several players for the FA Cup defeat against Bolton, Rodgers would have been delighted to see Swansea take a firm grip on the game. A free kick from Gylfi Sigurdsson led to a chance for Danny Graham, but Ivanović swiftly intervened. Not long after, a second chance fell to the hosts. A poor clearance by Čech fell to the feet of Sigurdsson, but again it was Ivanović saving Chelsea by clearing from the line and then Luiz blocked Graham's effort at a follow-up.

As is so often the way in football, when one team seems to be pressing, the best chance of the game falls the other way, and this would be no different. A cross from the left by Luiz was met by Sturridge, who controlled, swivelled and shot just wide of Michel Vorm's post. Had the effort gone in it would have been harsh punishment for the home team's profligacy, but just as the game was heading towards the break, Swansea scored.

Like so many others of the era, Scott Sinclair had been a promising youngster at Chelsea, after joining from Bristol Rovers as a 16-year-old in 2005. He would be on the club's books for five seasons, but during that period he only appeared in five league games, without troubling the scorers, and was loaned out to six clubs – Plymouth Argyle, Queens Park Rangers, Charlton Athletic, Crystal Palace, Birmingham City and Wigan Athletic – before being sold to Swansea for the princely sum of £500,000. There was, therefore, some measure of irony that, on the day Chelsea announced losses of £67.7m, they fell behind to a former player who had represented England at all levels from under-17 to under-21 and later played for Great Britain at the London Olympics, but had never really been given a chance to shine at Stamford Bridge; a Chelsea career washed away by a flood of expensive signings.

On 40 minutes, Sigurdsson's free kick into the Chelsea area was met by Bosingwa's fairly weak header. The ball dropped to Sinclair, whose left-foot shot screamed past Čech and into the top corner of the net. The player could have been forgiven for over-zealous celebrations had he considered that his goal had proven a point to his erstwhile employers, but his muted celebrations suggested an emotion of regret at the way things had panned out for him in London, rather than any triumphal exuberance. It sent the teams into the half-time break with contrasting emotions. The home side would have considered themselves well worth the goal lead that Sinclair had given them, and the Chelsea players would have known that they needed to improve massively if there was to be any chance of salvaging something from the game.

The break may have come at the wrong time for the home team. With time to reflect on their lead, there may have been a natural inclination towards caution, to protect the advantage. Whether that was the case or not, Chelsea were improved in the second period and, despite perhaps not being as dominant as the home team had been before the break, they began to build a forward momentum that had been sadly lacking earlier.

An equaliser remained elusive, however. Villas-Boas sent on Essien for Romeu just past the hour and the Ghanaian emphasised his increasing return to full sharpness with an energetic display, both driving his team forward and denying Swansea any kind of midfield dominance. He came close to delivering the equaliser with a 25-yard drive that just passed wide of the target. As time drifted away though, it became clear that the visitors were running out of ideas, especially with Torres still being the bluntest of blunt instruments as an attacking threat. Villas-Boas threw Lukaku on for Malouda inside the final ten minutes, but Swansea were holding out fairly comfortably. On 86 minutes, all hope seemed to have gone for Chelsea when a clumsy lunge by Cole on Nathan

Dyer brought a second yellow card from Andre Marriner and Chelsea were down to ten men. Cole would also miss the next league game, banned for the visit of Manchester United to Stamford Bridge. Villas-Boas looked down at the ground as Cole trudged from the pitch.

As things turned out though, it would be Chelsea's other full-back who lightened the coach's depression a little. Playing his 100th game for the club, Bosingwa gained possession on the right flank. Dipping first one way, then the other, he turned past substitute Kemy Agustien before delivering a cross towards the near post. The ball clipped defender Neil Taylor and eluded Vorm, slipping inside the near post for a more than fortunate equaliser. At the final whistle, it was difficult to avoid the conclusion that Chelsea had escaped with a draw despite the now regular attempt by the manager to accentuate the positive.

'I think it was [two] completely different halves,' protested Villas-Boas, who claimed Chelsea will 'continue to persist' with Torres despite the Spaniard's glaring lack of confidence. 'In the second half we were competent and managed to create a lot of problems by pressing them. In the first half we conceded the initiative and they found spaces to create problems. They were magnificent.'[75] The loss of Cole for the game against Manchester United was a blow, but there was also encouragement in the performance of Essien. The resurgence of a fully fit Essien could have the same effect as signing a new player, but as time went on, it appeared that Villas-Boas was less than fully convinced.

The draw at least kept the unbeaten run going but, aside from statisticians, very few others saw much value in it when the preponderance of results had only yielded a single point.

---

75 'Ashley Cole sees red as Chelsea leave it late to deny stylish Swansea', *The Guardian,* 31 January 2020.

The club were still in fourth, but the gap to Spurs in third was increasing, and the two Manchester clubs were uncatchable. The real, and growing, issue was that in fifth Liverpool were closing in and both Arsenal and Newcastle United also looked dangerous. That comment from Villas-Boas claiming that he was 'not worried about finishing lower than fourth' looked increasingly likely to come back and bite him.

On the previous evening, at the Nuevo Estadio de Malabo in Equatorial Guinea, Ivory Coast had defeated Angola to complete the perfect group stage in the Africa Cup of Nations, winning all three games, with both Drogba and Kalou scoring to drive the Elephants forward to the knockout phase. Had Villas-Boas been harbouring vague hopes that perhaps Drogba would be returning by the end of January, chastened by his nation's early elimination, and back in blue with a renewed hunger, they were gone. The comment that Chelsea will 'continue to persist' with Torres may well have been driven by the fact that, other than the vastly inexperience Lukaku, there were few options.

Ever since the arrival of Abramovich, and the club's first league title for precisely 50 years, games against Manchester United have carried that extra little piquancy for Chelsea fans and, although followers of the Old Trafford club would still count Liverpool as their most-hated rivals, for a few years, Chelsea were an irritating itch that Manchester United needed to scratch. With the club's fortunes on a decidedly downward trend, Chelsea's home league game against Sir Alex Ferguson's team could have been a boon or a bane for Villas-Boas. Victory and a decent performance would do much to expunge recent bad memories, reinvigorate the club and suggest that perhaps things were coming together at long last. Lose, however, or turn in another disappointing performance and the clamour for the manager's head would surely intensify. In a game described as 'insane'[76] by Matt Lawton in the *Daily Mail*, each one of those scenarios was at times in play before being vanquished and, in the end, the waters had just been muddied even further.

There was a significance in the side that Villas-Boas sent out against United on that early February Sunday. For the first time in four years none of the quartet of Terry, Cole, Lampard and Drogba would start a Premier League game for Chelsea. Although this was perhaps a potential intended consequence of the project, the absences were not down to any kind of Villas-Boas determination. Lampard was still recovering from his calf injury and Terry's ongoing knee problem also prevented him from being considered. Cole's red card in Wales ruled him out, and Drogba's ongoing international duty had him scoring twice the previous evening to eliminate the hosts in a 3-0 victory over Equatorial Guinea that took Ivory Coast into the semi-finals of the Africa Cup of Nations.

With both Cole and Terry absent from what would have been a first-choice back four, Villas-Boas shuffled his pack and brought Cahill in for his first taste of first-team football since 4 January. Only Luiz kept his regular position as it was 'musical shirts' all around him. Ivanović returned to right-back following his stint as a central defender. Bosingwa switched flanks to play on the left, and Cahill joined Luiz in the centre.

Further forward, Essien was given a starting berth alongside Meireles, in a pair expected to offer space to Mata as the prime creative force, with Malouda and Sturridge operating wide and the seemingly impotent Torres at the not very sharp end of the attack. Mata would very much star in

76 'Chelsea 3 Manchester United 3: Head boy Hernández completes stunning fightback', *Daily Mail*, 5 February 2012.

his role, having a hand in all of the home team's successes and so nearly bringing the game to a glorious conclusion for Chelsea.

In a game that saw contrary emotions as the fates twisted one way and then the other with an apparent malevolent ecstasy, the home crowd's vitriolic anger targeted at Rio Ferdinand was a bleak reminder of an unacceptable behaviour still staining the game. The defender was apparently identified, in a totally unjustifiable way, as a surrogate target for the problems assailing Terry amid the alleged racial abuse of the Manchester United player's younger brother at Loftus Road back in October. In some misguided way, perhaps it was driven by a desire to offer support to the captain, but manifested itself as merely boorish and shameful. It helped no one.

With the game of high importance to both clubs – United battling their 'noisy neighbours' at the top of the table, and Chelsea searching for something to grip on to as a man swept away in a surging torrent of problems – full commitment to the cause was the minimum requirement for those on the pitch, and the early minutes of the game reflected that prerequisite. Later, focusing on different events, both managers would offer criticism of referee Howard Webb and his assistants, with varying degrees of validity. With the eager, often overly eager, start to the game though, a level of leniency from the referee was probably sensible and seemed to favour both sides rather than have a partiality for which he would later be accused.

The first 15 minutes saw Rafael da Silva fortunate to escape any kind of personal sanction for a crunching challenge on Torres, and Cahill, perhaps a little rusty following his weeks of inaction, was treated similarly after abruptly halting Danny Welbeck's run. Cards in either case would have been justifiable, but Webb allowed the frantic early emotions to cool. Leniency was probably not the reason that Bosingwa's tug on Ashley Young's shirt wasn't punished with a spot kick though, the action escaping Webb's attention, which was fortunate for the Portuguese, and the home team.

As things settled down, it was the visitors who had the advantage and appeared the more likely to score. Such being the case, the goal they conceded on 35 minutes would have particularly frustrated Ferguson, not only for it being against the run of play, but also for its scrappy and unfortunate nature.

Sturridge picked up the ball on the left of the visitors' box as it squirmed to him from Mata's initial probe that clipped Ivanović in transit. Hitting the byline to elude Patrice Evra, the young forward drove the ball across the goalmouth. Standing by his near post, David de Gea jabbed out a foot to divert the cross away, but the ball cannoned on to the thigh of a hapless Jonny Evans and rebounded into the net. If Villas-Boas and Chelsea were in need of a slice of luck to send them on their way, here it was. Ten minutes later, Webb's whistle brought the first period to an end with only smart goalkeeping from both Čech and de Gea preventing further goals. A mere 20 seconds after the restart, however, Chelsea scored again.

Out on the right flank, Torres hit a cross into the box. Perhaps it was over-hit or, if offering a little generosity, it may have been that the Spaniard saw his compatriot in space on the far side of the area. Whatever the intent, the ball passed above the players gathered in the middle of the goal and found its way on to Mata's left foot, from where it exploded in a ferocious volley into the top of the net. It was a strike of rare beauty, and suddenly the Blues were coasting. Five minutes later the points were surely sewn up when

Mata's free kick was met by Luiz exploiting an unforgivable amount of space in the Manchester United penalty area. The defender's header glanced off Ferdinand and left de Gea flat-footed and beaten. On the bench Villas-Boas punched the air in celebration. Three goals ahead, each with a slice of good fortune attached. The crossroads of a game was now revealing itself as a turning point for Chelsea's young manager. Or so it seemed.

After going three goals clear, Chelsea needed a solid ten minutes or so of defensive security. Attacking intent could be put on the back burner for a while. Defending now was the key requirement. The problem, of course, was that with 40 minutes remaining on the clock and Manchester United driven on by both an angry frustration and the glowering countenance of their manager, such a ploy was bound to bring with it a period of sustained pressure from the visitors, and so it did.

Released from defensive duties, both visiting full-backs provided ammunition for the forwards as they launched raids down the flanks. It was from such an attack that United found their way back into the game. Young had already been withdrawn for the impish Mexican forward Javier Hernández, when Patrice Evra received a pass from Ryan Giggs and drove into the Chelsea penalty area, pursued by Sturridge. It was an almost mirror image of the opening goal scenario when the roles had been reversed. With the young forward chasing back, the experienced France international was canny enough to cut across the recovering run of Sturridge and the contact brought the inevitable penalty decision from Webb. Čech gambled low left as Wayne Rooney swept the ball high and to the goalkeeper's right. From a position of apparent comfort, Chelsea's fragile confidence would now endure a thorough examination in the remaining half-hour or so.

Ten minutes later, another penalty tugged at the jangling nerves of Chelsea players and manager, but if the foul on Evra had been clear enough then this incident was much less so. Breaking, Hernández played a pass to Welbeck, but with Chelsea players recovering position, the danger looked manageable. Closed down by Ivanović, Welbeck played the ball wide of the Serb who looked to challenge for the ball, then withdrew his leg. With the ball drifting away and Cahill poised to clear, Welbeck took his chance. Jabbing his left foot out, he contacted the defender's foot and fell to the ground.

Blinded from the action by a gaggle of players, Webb's sight was less than clear but, significantly, the assistant on the far side with a clear view offered no indication of an offence, and no signal of a penalty. Nevertheless, the referee made up his mind. A second spot kick was awarded and this time Rooney went to Čech's left as the goalkeeper committed himself in the other direction. Fate had coquettishly offered a teasing smile towards Villas-Boas before dashing it away. It's often said that the darkness of the night is only amplified by a glance at the brightness of day. The evening was rapidly closing in above the Chelsea coach with the momentum now strongly in favour of the visitors.

In an apparent admission that it had become a game that Chelsea saw as a rearguard mission, Sturridge was replaced by the more defensive inclinations of Romeu. The game was now an emotional roller coaster and very much in the balance. Even from here, there was much to be gained for Villas-Boas if Chelsea held out. A victory in such circumstances could be portrayed as both defiant and signifying a togetherness at the club that many considered patently absent. Sadly for the coach, he would not have the opportunity to paint that picture.

With five minutes remaining, and United in full flow, Rooney pivoted and shot from the edge of the area, but Čech threw himself to his right and parried the ball away. It ran out towards Giggs, who controlled before crossing. Standing in the space between Cahill and Luiz, the ball arrowed towards the head of the diminutive Hernández and the Mexican's header from five yards gave Čech little chance to react. Despite the goalkeeper getting a flailing hand to the ball, it was insufficient to prevent the equaliser. The lead had disappeared and the manner in which Welbeck quickly recovered the ball from the net suggested that Ferguson's players now had the clear scent of victory in their nostrils. In contrast, for Chelsea, blue was the colour of the players' mood as well as their shirts.

There was one final twist to come. A minute into added time, a typically clumsy tackle by Scholes brought Chelsea a free kick some 25 yards or so from goal. Regardless, Mata chanced his arm and fired the ball towards the top-right corner of the net. A goal then would have crowned a remarkable game and still given Villas-Boas the solace of victory, but de Gea flung himself acrobatically to turn the ball away with his right hand.

In the final analysis, despite being three goals ahead, the denouement of the game only served to demonstrate Chelsea's continuing decline. Never in the history of the Premier League had the club been three goals clear and failed to win the game. Another damning statistic. Another sad episode in a dispiriting season. Another nail in the Villas-Boas coffin? The following weekend would see the situation deteriorate further.

Following the dramatic collapse, reports emerged that Abramovich had visited the Chelsea training centre at Cobham, but what happened while he was there is less than clear. Given the Russian's intolerance of failure, it's unlikely to have been to proffer a personal vote of confidence to Villas-Boas. More likely, as some rumours suggested, it was to speak with some of the senior players and gauge their thoughts on the manager and where the club was headed. If that proved to be the case, it would only serve to undermine the manager and confirm to the players that he was drinking in the Last Chance Saloon, as was suggested in *The Guardian*, 'Villas-Boas has endured unrest within the ranks which, with the owner [...] making a point of observing training at Cobham recently, has suggested that his ideas are not backed by all of his players.'[77]

Everton had experienced a strange season. By the midpoint of the fixtures, they had been defeated in ten of their 19 games. Yet, from there, David Moyes would rally his team and suffer only a further three reverses in the remainder of the league programme, eventually finishing in seventh position. Chelsea's second visit of the season to Goodison Park – their first had seen a 2-1 victory after extra time in the League Cup – would be to face a confident team on a run of four games undefeated, including a victory over Manchester City.

With his one-game ban now served, Cole returned at left-back, requiring another shuffle in the Chelsea defence. Bosingwa moved back to his more regular position on the right and Ivanović moved back into the centre, with Cahill returning to the bench. Lampard had now recovered from his calf injury and returned in midfield alongside Essien and Meireles. Sturridge and Mata flanked Torres. After the disappointment of watching a three-goal lead slip through his fingers against Manchester United, a strong and resolute

77 'Roman Abramovich is backing my Chelsea project, says André Villas-Boas', *The Guardian*, 20 February 2012.

start was the order of the day for Villas-Boas. It failed to materialise.

A mere five minutes into the contest, Bosingwa's throw-in aimed towards Lampard was careless, compelling the midfielder to contest possession with Tim Cahill. The ball looped up towards the Chelsea penalty area where Steven Pienaar, making his return to the club on loan from Spurs, brushed past a weak challenge by Ivanović, controlled with his chest and hammered the ball home to put Everton ahead.

Understandably, the goal served to increase the Everton confidence and their midfield buzzed around the pitch every time Chelsea tried to play with any control. The home team's harrying and hustling ploy prevented any cohesion developing from the visitors and Everton energetically dominated the early phases. As the minutes ticked by and the early zeal eased a little, Chelsea did manage a couple of forward flurries. Sturridge saw a shot deflected by Phil Neville and Lampard dragged a left-footed effort wide, both chances created by Mata. At the break, Tim Howard had hardly been troubled, and nothing much changed as the second period got under way.

With 20 minutes to play, Villas-Boas tried to change things, in the hope of some improvement. He removed Essien and sent on Malouda, but the decision was greeted with derision from the travelling Chelsea fans with chants of 'You don't know what you're doing'. They may have been right. Just two minutes later the game was settled by Everton's second goal. Neville dispossessed Cole with a sliding tackle and Landon Donovan eluded a challenge from Luiz to put Denis Stracqualursi through on Čech. The Argentine coolly converted and, as Chelsea had struggled to muster anything of note as an attacking force for the first 70 minutes of the game, the likelihood of them striking back twice in the remaining 20 was slight indeed.

Not long afterwards, the after-effects of Neville's challenge forced Cole to hobble off with Ryan Bertrand joining from the bench. A minute later, Lukaku came on for Mata, but to no avail. As Chelsea looked impotent and Everton stroked the ball around with the confident conviction that the win was secure, it was the turn of Everton fans to serenade Villas-Boas. 'You're getting sacked in the morning' was hardly original, but there was a ring of the inevitable about it. At the final whistle the cheering of Everton fans was almost drowned out by the booing of the Chelsea contingent – at least by those who hadn't left the stadium in frustration already.

To emphasise how poor Chelsea had been, despite Everton's improving performances they had failed to score more than once in their last 13 games, but had achieved that with plenty of comfort against a Chelsea team now without a Premier League victory in four. In the post-match interviews, Villas-Boas could hardly deny that the result increased pressure on his position, 'It was one of our worst displays of the season – if not the worst. Today we couldn't be ourselves and express our football and we ended up heavily defeated. If there is one defeat that the manager should take the blame, it is this one so I will go back to my pre-planning and decision-making because maybe it wasn't right to help the players.'[78] In the *Daily Mail*, Nick Harris detailed the manager's reaction to the abuse from the club's fans, 'Asked how it felt to be derided vocally by his own fans, as he was in the second half, he said, "It's part of the job. At the moment we're sitting fifth in the league and it's not good enough. "'[79]

---

78 https://www.bbc.com/sport/football/16884797.

79 'Everton 2 Chelsea 0: Villas-Boas jeered by own fans as Blues fall again', *Daily Mail*, 12 February 2012.

It wasn't. Since Abramovich took control of the club in 2003, they had never finished lower than third in the Premier League. They were now fifth and Chelsea's total of 43 points from 25 games was their lowest at the same stage since 2001, when they ended in sixth position. They had only accumulated 12 points from their last ten league games, and just three from the last four outings. It was relegation points accumulation, produced by relegation performances. There was now just a single game before the Champions League campaign swung back into gear and Chelsea visited Napoli for the first leg of their round of 16 tie.

On 18 February, an FA Cup fifth round game at home to second tier Birmingham City brought a struggling 1-1 draw with a virtually full-strength team, other than Ryan Bertrand standing in for Cole, who hadn't fully recovered from the knock he sustained in the Everton game. After conceding an early goal from David Murphy, it took until the hour before Sturridge equalised and earned Chelsea a replay. Lampard had been dropped to the bench once more, and Essien omitted from the party altogether. There was at least some comfort for the fans in seeing Drogba and Kalou back in the squad.

The previous week, Ivory Coast had lost out in a hugely disappointing Africa Cup of Nations Final. The game had ended goalless after extra time, before Zambia triumphed 8-7 on penalties.

Three days after the Birmingham game, Chelsea would face Napoli in the intimidating atmosphere of the Stadio San Paolo. The stadium would be a cauldron of passion and if the team were to return to England with a decent chance of progression, the case-hardened experience of Chelsea's international players would surely be key. And yet, when Villas-Boas's team was announced, so much of that experience was sitting alongside him on the bench.

Defiance in the face of conventional wisdom was nothing new for Villas-Boas and he was quick to assert that neither success nor failure in the tie against the Serie A side would define his future at Stamford Bridge. After he had spoken to the press ahead of the game, *The Guardian* reported, 'The Portuguese [was] already "excited" and "confident" about the team's prospects for next season.[80]'

The coach had also let it be known that there were some injury concerns for him to ponder ahead of selecting his team. He expressed concern about whether Cole would be able to return to action, even after missing the Birmingham game, which had seemed merely precautionary. He appeared likely to play, with his big-game experience of enormous value for such an encounter, along with the likes of Lampard and Essien, especially as the captain would surely be absent.

Terry was a major doubt. He took part in the Monday evening training session, but his participation was peripheral at best with the rain-soaked surface of the Stadio San Paolo hardly conducive to anything more, for a player struggling with a knee condition further damaged in the FA Cup tie against Portsmouth on 8 January. Villas-Boas announced that the captain's fitness would be assessed following the training session, before any decision was made, but it seemed a forlorn hope that he would be available.

As things turned out, the situation was worse than just missing one more game. Later, Villas-Boas would reveal that the problem was not responding to periods of rest and surgery would be required, with a further absence of a month the likely prognosis, 'Four weeks would be excellent, but

80 'Roman Abramovich is backing my Chelsea project, says André Villas-Boas', *The Guardian*, 20 February 2012.

normally it's six weeks. We'll have to wait and see how the operation goes. Four weeks? Hopefully the player can return in that time frame.'[81] In fact, Terry would return comfortably inside that period, regaining his place in the starting 11 for the league game against Stoke City on 10 February. Even that wouldn't be early enough for Villas-Boas though. By that time, he'd been sacked. Of course, that still lay in the future and, at least in public, the manager seemed blissfully unaware of the ground breaking apart beneath his feet.

His team selection emphasised the point, as Matt Lawton reflected in the *Daily Mail*, 'When this breathless European encounter ended, the Napoli supporters might have been addressing André Villas-Boas with the anthem they sing to mark victory at the Stadio San Paolo. *Il Soldato Innamorato* tells the tragic story of a soldier writing his last letter home and there was a sense here that Chelsea's manager may have done something rather similar within the context of his career. The team sheet he submitted read to some like a professional suicide note and while that might sound a touch melodramatic the first 11 names that appeared below "Chelsea FC" could yet amount to a Portuguese P45.'[82] Lawton may have been overstating the point for dramatic effect, but the assessment was not wholly without merit. On Sky's presentation of the game, Jeff Stelling described news of the starting 11 as 'startling'.[83]

It was, however, more the players who were not selected, than those who were in the 11, which caused most discussion. Cole was omitted although the player considered himself

81 https://www.bbc.com/sport/football/17131298.

82 'Napoli 3 Chelsea 1: Villas-Boas gets it wrong and Cavani doubles his misery', *Daily Mail*, 4 February 2012.

83 *Kings of Europe – The Chelsea Story*, Sky UK Limited, 16 September 2012.

fully fit and willing to play. Rumours later arose that perhaps the manager's stated concerns about him being an injury doubt were merely camouflage to justify a decision already made. Talk was that Cole's omission had arisen as a result of a 'clear-the-air' meeting at Cobham, where Villas-Boas had invited any member of the squad who had doubts about his methods to voice them directly to him. Cole had apparently availed himself of the opportunity. Despite the meeting being declared an open forum for debate by the coach, Villas-Boas had reportedly taken umbrage at the defender's remarks and considered him as not being fully committed to the cause. If the rumours were true, it was a poor managerial decision and merely emphasised the gulf between manager and players.

Essien was also left out and sat alongside a frustrated Lampard, who Lawton suggested 'responded to the news by communicating his disappointment directly to his manager'.[84] One can imagine that it was not a cordial discourse. Mikel completed the trio of disaffected and experienced midfield players looking on from the sidelines, along with Torres, Kalou and back-up goalkeeper Ross Turnbull.

Apart from Čech, who regardless of any other considerations was surely as certain a starter when fit as any, the team was a combination of shuffled positions and those players that the manager considered worthy of his trust. Ivanović was back defending the right flank of the defence, with Bosingwa again switched to cover for Cole. The absented defender spoke in restrained terms when later interviewed about the decision to leave him, and others, out of the team. 'There's a lot of players was [sic] not happy, but that happens in football, every player wanted to play in that

84 'Napoli 3 Chelsea 1: Villas-Boas gets it wrong and Cavani doubles his misery', *Daily Mail*, 4 February 2012.

game because it was such a big occasion for the team and,' he paused a little as if selecting the right words, 'it happens in football. You can't play every game, so I had to take it on the chin.'[85] It's significant that Cole made no reference to any injury concerns being the reason for his absence. In his mind, it was clearly the manager's decision.

Cahill was brought in to partner Luiz. It was a largely untested combination, and one that would be ruthlessly exposed in the game. Bosingwa was a fellow Portuguese and both Luiz and Cahill were relatively new to the club, with the latter being a Villas-Boas signing. In midfield, Malouda was selected alongside Meireles, who joined the club at the same time as the manager and Ramires. The forward line was Mata, whose situation was as with Meireles, accompanied by the two players who it seemed had spoken up earlier for the manager, Drogba and Sturridge, while Cole, Lampard, Mikel and Essien sat on the bench, deemed to be unneeded, and perhaps untrusted, by Villas-Boas.

In sharp contrast, home manager Walter Mazzarri had deployed all of his star players in the starting 11. The South American pair of Edinson Cavani and Ezequiel Lavezzi was a potent force and supported by Marek Hamšík and Gökhan Inler from midfield, their progress to this stage at the expense of Manchester City had been well deserved. Even with a fully united team and the best 11 starting, which by most calculations, this was palpably short of being, escaping the Stadio San Paolo with a decent result would have been a stern test for Chelsea. With so much talent and experience sitting on the bench, it appeared that Villas-Boas had chosen to take on the task with one arm, metaphorically, tied behind his back.

---

85 *Kings of Europe – The Chelsea Story*, Sky UK Limited, 16 September 2012.

Inevitably, as the game got under way, both teams opened cautiously, but Napoli quickly achieved a measure of ascendancy and Čech was called into action to make saves first from Cavani and then Christian Maggio. The Chelsea coach's plans were also compromised when his decision to bench Cole was reversed following an injury to Bosingwa just 12 minutes in. The fact that the defender then came on and played the remainder of the game illustrated the folly of the coach's assertion that he was not fit to play. The appearance of Cole apparently intentionally standing with his back to Villas-Boas as the manager sought to impart last-minute instructions before the substitute entered the pitch may well have been an illustration of the state of the relationship between the two men.

The home club had somewhat of a cavalier style of play that marked them out as exceptional in the more traditionally pragmatic Serie A environment. It brought goals but, on occasions, they were vulnerable to counter-attacks and, approaching the half-hour, that ethos cost them the first goal. Drogba broke up a Napoli move developing in their own half, sweeping the ball out to the right for Sturridge. Attempting to play a volleyed pass into the path of Mata, the forward slightly mishit the ball, and it ran ahead of the Spaniard towards Paolo Cannavaro, younger brother of the *Azzurri* World Cup-winning captain Fabio. Slightly off balance, and under pressure as Mata closed him down, Cannavaro sliced his clearance, spooning the ball into the air behind him. Seizing the opportunity, Mata ran forward to meet the dropping ball just past the penalty spot and coolly placed a left-footed shot beyond an advancing Morgan De Sanctis in the home goal.

The playing area of the Stadio San Paolo is surrounded by a running pitch and the almost constant rain over the previous few days had caused a number of puddles to settle on the red-surfaced track, and the Chelsea players splashed through them celebrating the goal. On the bench, Villas-Boas stood and applauded, hoping that it meant fate wouldn't rain on his parade. Could Chelsea exploit the advantage though?

As with the game in Leverkusen, Čech recalled thinking that things were heading in the right direction, 'Once we got 1-0 up, I thought that was the moment where it will be okay. We will get the result, good result from the first leg.'[86] Unfortunately for Chelsea, the goalkeeper's assessment had been awry in Germany, and would prove to be so in Italy as well.

Taking the lead in an away leg, especially in such a febrile atmosphere, is best exploited by a period of controlled possession, drawing the sting out of the game and making the home team appreciate the depths of their problems as frustration grows among the fans. It's a well-worn tactic but one that the Chelsea team on the pitch were unable to deploy, as Daniel Taylor later reported in *The Guardian*, 'Instead Chelsea capitulated. Mata's cool finish was the one moment of the night when this chaotic, throbbing stadium was thrust into silence. Yet Chelsea did not have the wit to keep the ball. These were moments, undoubtedly, when they badly missed John Terry's experience. What Chelsea really needed was some leadership but Frank Lampard started on the bench and Cole was also a substitute, despite declaring himself fit. Between them these three players have made more than 1,300 appearances for the club.'[87] Add in that Essien and Mikel were also sitting alongside the coach and

---

86 *Kings of Europe – The Chelsea Story*, Sky UK Limited, 16 September 2012.

87 'Swashbuckling Napoli expose Chelsea's lack of maturity', *The Guardian*, 22 February 2012.

the self-inflicted wounds were there for all to see. Whereas the goal should have encouraged the Chelsea players to grow into the game, the reverse was the case, and Napoli's attacks increased in both quantity and vigour.

It was an intensely difficult period for the visitors, with Čech called upon on three occasions. And yet, very much against the run of play, the lead could have been doubled when Luiz headed over from a Mata corner, but it was just a brief respite. Ten minutes after Mata's strike, the value of the away goal was already being eaten into when Lavezzi equalised. Despite having half a dozen players back behind the ball, a simple pass and a diversionary run tore gaping holes in the Chelsea defence. Illustrating the lack of cohesion in the partnership, Luiz and Cahill challenged each other for a ball on the edge of the area, neither getting sufficient contact for a convincing clearance. Napoli recycled possession and Cavani received the ball around 20 yards out from goal. Seeing Lavezzi in support, the Uruguayan played the ball inside before pivoting and running forward for a return pass. The run attracted a trio of Chelsea players like a magnet, including Meireles who had previously been covering Lavezzi. Exploiting the space, the Argentine advanced a step before hitting a shot from the edge of the penalty arc as Cahill threw himself forward in a vain attempt to block. Unencumbered by any challenge, the shot was deadly accurate, eluding any effective contact from Čech's outstretched left hand, the barest of glancing touches being insufficient, and finding the corner of the net.

The stadium erupted into a frenzy and Villas-Boas stood, punching the air in frustration. Looking downcast, he raised his arms trying to enthuse his players with a confidence that seemed to be lacking in himself. There were seven minutes left to play ahead of the break. The manager needed his team to hold out for that period, get them into the dressing room and settle things down. Those seven minutes were too long.

The entire 11 black-shirted visiting players were compressed into an area surrounding the Chelsea area as the energised home team pressed for another goal. Out on the right flank, the Napoli players exchanged passes, working the Chelsea back line and trying to create an opening. Eventually, the ball was funnelled back to Inler with space and time to look up and pick his cross. Standing on the edge of the penalty area, the glance up from Inler was the signal for Cavani to make his run. Driving past Cahill, he reached the six-yard box by the far post as the Switzerland international's cross arrived slightly behind him. Instead of reaching back though, the forward used his shoulder to divert the ball home with Cahill hopelessly out of position and Ivanović unable to intervene. The Serb lay on the ground as the Uruguayan sprinted towards the fenced area of the Napoli *tifosi*, bellowing his elation.

In the Chelsea dugout, Villas-Boas rubbed his hands over his face in exasperation, as if to ask, 'How can this have possibly happened?' before sitting down again. It may well have been the moment that sealed the manager's fate. As the teams left the field at the break, the elation of the Mata goal felt like a long time ago, and it was difficult to see the second period being anything other than a long rearguard action to try and retain a finger-hold in the tournament or, even worse, avoid humiliation.

Perhaps the break would have afforded Villas-Boas a period of reflection. There were plenty of options on the bench who may have been able to influence the game, but Chelsea began the second period unchanged – as was the flow of the game. Cavani squandered a decent opportunity. Then Lavezzi did the same with an even better one, but another goal was inevitable, and it came after 65 minutes, in almost 'comic cuts' fashion. Čech later conceded, 'We were all over the place.'[88]

A long ball forward found Cavani cutting in from the right. It should have been a standard challenge for Luiz, but the Uruguayan simply brushed past him with ease. Feeling exposed, Čech advanced to narrow the angle but, instead of shooting, Cavani played the ball wide to Lavezzi as Luiz raced back to cover the goal line. All composure destroyed, Čech ran across his area to try and confront the Argentine, while Cahill first slipped then regained his footing as Lavezzi's shot whistled past him. Luiz's half-skip, half-jump on the line was pointless. As the Napoli players celebrated, Cahill shouted in frustration, 'So bad!' He wasn't wrong. 'It was my first Champions League appearance,' the defender later recalled. 'So, it's not one that's really [sic] got fond memories of. I don't think I played particularly well. I know, the team, we struggled that night.'[89]

Five minutes later, with the damage now done, Villas-Boas sent on both Lampard and Essien. It felt like a gesture of condemnation – 'Could you have done any better, then?' – more than one of remorse or regret. The game did settle a little, but that may have had as much to do with the home team being sated by their three goals and confidence in completing the job at Stamford Bridge rather than any improvement in Chelsea's performance. The damage could

88 *Kings of Europe – The Chelsea Story*, Sky UK Limited, 16 September 2012.

89 *Kings of Europe – The Chelsea Story*, Sky UK Limited, 16 September 2012.

have been even worse. Maggio had a late effort cleared from the line by an off-balance Cole.

A fourth goal would surely have been a killer strike, as the defender recalled, 'You look back at it and I think 4-1 would have been a disaster for us.'[90] Months later, Roberto Di Matteo was to describe the clearance as 'probably the most important moment in our Champions League campaign'.[91]

It didn't feel like it at the time and at the final whistle Drogba could see the exit door opening in front of Chelsea, and beckoning them forward, 'I was, I was really down. I was like, again, you know, it's going to be the same, the same old song. You know, quarter-final, or Chelsea is out, or semi-final Chelsea is out.'[92] The Chelsea fans leaving the stadium in Naples that night were of a similar mind, as author and long-time supporter Mark Worrall remembered, 'Walking out of the Stadio San Paolo in the rain after that 3-1 first-leg defeat against Napoli the ire of Chelsea supporters was directed at André Villas-Boas. The Blues' inability to defend was shocking.'[93]

Chelsea had now gone five games without a win and Villas-Boas cut a sad and lonely figure walking back towards the tunnel. Writing in *The Guardian*, Daniel Taylor peered into the manager's thoughts, 'These are the moments when André Villas-Boas, for all his outward confidence, could be forgiven for wondering how much longer a man with Roman Abramovich's lack of tolerance is prepared to stand

---

90 *Kings of Europe – The Chelsea Story*, Sky UK Limited, 16 September 2012.

91 *Kings of Europe – The Chelsea Story*, Sky UK Limited, 16 September 2012.

92 *Kings of Europe – The Chelsea Story*, Sky UK Limited, 16 September 2012.

93 Worrall, Mark, interview with the author.

by him when the evidence of Chelsea's deterioration is so overwhelming.'[94]

Two days later, Villas-Boas revealed that following the defeat, Chelsea's technical director had been deputed by Abramovich to seek an explanation from the manager for his team selection in Naples.[95] Even for someone who had publicly expressed the owner's support for him and brazenly spoke of plans for the new season with a confident air just a few days earlier, the writing on the wall surely clear enough to see.

If it wasn't, the owner was there in person to reinforce matters the following weekend, as Bolton Wanderers arrived at Stamford Bridge for a Premier League game. In public, Villas-Boas was quick to defend his selection against Napoli, but the 11 who began against Bolton suggested that the conversation – albeit through a third party – with the owner had at least been in some way influential. Back into the starting line-up came Cole, Essien and Lampard.

Although not firing on all cylinders, when the game began, it was clearly a Chelsea team more at peace with itself. Inside the first five minutes a run from the halfway line by Sturridge drew a save from Ádám Bogdán in the visitors' goal. Drogba also looked threatening but, as the early phase of the game passed without a goal, Chelsea began to look more like a side woefully short on confidence, who had forgotten how to win matches. Owen Coyle's team had struggled throughout the season and barely been out of the relegation places for any length of time. They were, however, precisely the sort of team that had caused Chelsea problems of late and the Scot had his players well-drilled and

94 'Swashbuckling Napoli expose Chelsea's lack of maturity', *The Guardian*, 22 February 2012.

95 https://www.bbc.com/sport/football/17131298.

organised at the back, even if they were somewhat limited going forwards.

Chelsea's attacks became sporadic and increasingly unconvincing as Abramovich looked down with irritation and frustration etched on his face. Occasionally Chelsea tested the Bolton defence. On the half-hour, Bogdán plunged to palm away a Drogba effort and then David Wheater thwarted a long Luiz pass that seemed bound to release Sturridge. On other occasions though, the attacks were more slapstick than slick. A clever pass by Lampard opened up an opportunity, but it was squandered as Ivanović and Drogba collided with each other as they sought to prosper from the opening. Early in the season, Chelsea had visited Bolton and won 5-1. There seemed little prospect of that score being repeated as the half-time whistle was sounded.

Chelsea needed a spark and it came inside three minutes of the restart. Bolton's attacking had been sporadic at best, ineffectual at worst, in the first period and Luiz had taken the opportunity to sally forward when the chance presented itself without exposing the Chelsea defence to much danger. The opening goal came when he seized possession high up the pitch, charged forward and curled a shot past Bogdán. The celebrations were as much of relief as joy. Villas-Boas had only seen his team keep two clean sheets at home all season. One goal was hardly likely to be enough.

The goal did instil some belief, however, and twice Chelsea came close to adding a second. First a Luiz header from a corner clipped a post before going behind, then Drogba's curled shot struck the top of the bar. Despite his advancing years, on occasions, Drogba's physical muscularity was overwhelming and, on the hour, he brushed away a challenge from Fabrice Muamba to head home a Lampard corner. With Bolton now unlikely to change the course of the game, play became easier and Essien nearly added a third. Worryingly though, Drogba was forced out of the action, limping as he left the pitch to be replaced by Torres. The Ivorian had been a match-winner already in the season, and would be again. His loss would be a blow, but the injury was slight and he would recover in time for the following game.

Fortunately, the change did little to affect the flow of the action and, a few minutes after Drogba left the field Lampard confirmed the win with the third goal, converting at the far post from a Mata cross. It was the midfielder's 150th strike for the club, taking him past Jimmy Greaves on the all-time league scoring list. He also became the first Chelsea player to hit double figures in nine successive seasons. The chants of 'Super Frankie Lampard' must have burnt Villas-Boas's ears as they were as much directed at him as they were to the goalscorer. Afterwards, Lampard would admit that his relationship with the manager had 'not been ideal'.[96] It was hardly a surprise to anyone, and it showed in Villas-Boas's post-match interviews.

The game was the club's first win in seven games, but afterwards it seemed to give the manager little solace. Asked about Lampard's scoring milestone, the response seemed unnecessarily guarded. 'It is great personal satisfaction and I congratulate him for that,' he said. 'Frank's satisfaction comes from scoring one more time, overtaking another legend at the club. Frank goes on and on breaking the club's records and that is important for him.'[97] It sounded begrudging and unnecessarily dismissive. Had the win offered Villas-Boas some kind of lifeline, ironically handed to him by Lampard?

---

96 https://www.bbc.com/sport/football/17131298.

97 'Chelsea 3 Bolton 0: Frank Lampard's right royal answer…', *The Express*, 22 February 2012.

The next game would test that theory out as Chelsea visited West Bromwich Albion.

Ahead of the game reports emerged that only emphasised the deepening chasm between coach and players. With Villas-Boas displaying a less than gentle touch by delivering his latest lesson in man-management, he informed his squad that they were, in case they thought otherwise, inferior to Manchester City's group. While the statement was in no way inaccurate – Chelsea stood in fifth position and sliding, and City were challenging for the title – it's not unreasonable to consider that any number of the players were thinking that responsibility for much of that lay with Villas-Boas himself, and perhaps a similar charge could be laid at his door when compared to the coach leading the Manchester club. Perhaps it was a symptom, as much as a cause, of the breakdown in relationship between coach and players, but it was hardly chapter and verse from the book *How to Win Friends and Influence People*.

Having won their last game, changing the team would have been obtuse, so it was an unchanged 11 that took the field at The Hawthorns. Roy Hodgson had been appointed to replace Di Matteo at the Black Country club, and the experienced coach had led a sustained revival, with Albion now comfortable in mid-table and with a resolute defence. They were also facing Chelsea on the back of two encouraging victories. A 4-0 home win over Sunderland had followed a 5-1 victory over Wolverhampton Wanderers in the Black Country derby, which offered bragging rights to all Baggies fans who worked, lived or socialised in the vicinity of any fans of the Molineux club.

Hodgson had developed his team into an effective unit, drilled to defend in depth and strike on counter-attacks. Strangely in this game, the tactic was almost rendered redundant as, for the most part, it was the home team enjoying the bulk of possession and delivering the more potent attacks. The attacking unit of Peter Odemwingie, James Morrison, Jerome Thomas and Marc-Antoine Fortune was hardly a celebrated quartet but all were more than capable of unsettling Chelsea's defence, and were unlucky not to score on several occasions. It was fortunate for the visitors that Cole was in good form and Luiz had deigned to have one of his less exuberant days and defended solidly, with unusual consistency. They were also blessed in having the dependable Čech as the last line of defence. A diving save from Morrison was typical of his contribution.

Chelsea's own attack was tepid but even on such occasions there are periods when a team can build a little momentum. So rare was the occasion though that it was vital for Chelsea to score in those precious few minutes of ascendency, but they failed to do so. Even when shots were not wide, or blocked by Hodgson's back line, Ben Foster looked in commanding form and dealt with anything that penetrated the defence in front of him.

Half-time came and went, but the flow of the game was unaltered. The home team were disciplined and organised, if not particularly threatening on any consistent basis; the Blues were laboured and ragged, offering even less threat. Sturridge was removed for Malouda, then Essien for Torres as Villas-Boas sought some kind of breakthrough, but without any tangible reward. In fact, if anything, the changes galvanised the home team into more concerted efforts on Čech's goal. Luiz's solidity couldn't last all game, and an error offered a chance for Fortune to run in on Čech, but the goalkeeper rescued the situation, turning the ball for a corner. Moments afterwards, following another error in defence it was Fortune again threatening, this time firing from distance and forcing Čech to parry the shot away.

With defensive errors providing openings for the home side, it was no great surprise when, on 82 minutes, another one led to the opening goal. A cross from Keith Andrews on the Albion left flank was only half-cleared and, as the ball fell to Gareth McAuley, he crashed it past Čech. In the remaining time, Chelsea huffed and puffed, but the Albion defensive house was made of bricks, not straw, and hardly looked like being blown down. The final whistle sounded like a death knell for the manager.

The victory over Bolton was now exposed as a mere brief respite in the continuing downward spiral. The light at the end of the tunnel was nothing other than an express train coming to mow down the career of Villas-Boas at Stamford Bridge. Chelsea had not lost a league fixture against West Bromwich Albion in 33 years and won the previous 11 games against them. They were 20 points behind table-topping Manchester City, and four adrift of Arsenal in fourth, occupying that last Champions League qualification slot. Chelsea not qualifying for Champions League football in 2012/13 had moved from possibility through probability to be an almost certainty.

Throughout the game, especially after the goal, the home fans had delighted in serenading Villas-Boas with, 'You're getting sacked in the morning.' So often these chants are just hollow taunts. This time, however, they were accurate. In Shakespeare's *Julius Caesar* the Bard has a soothsayer warning the eponymous emperor to 'Beware the Ides of March.'[98] It's doubtful whether many, if any, of those West Bromwich Albion fans would consider themselves to be soothsayers but,

---

98 Shakespeare, William, *Julius Caesar*, 1599.

on this occasion their prediction was accurate, and Villas-Boas wouldn't even survive until 15 March, as Caesar had done. Stamford Bridge wasn't Rome, but it was certainly part of Roman's Empire. Less a case of 'Et tu, Brute?'[99] and more one of 'Et tu, Bruce (Buck)' perhaps?

The following day, a statement on the official Chelsea website confirmed the dawning of a day that had seemed increasingly inevitable over recent weeks and months, 'André Villas-Boas has parted company with Chelsea Football Club today. The board would like to record our gratitude for his work and express our disappointment that the relationship has ended so early. Unfortunately, the results and performances of the team have not been good enough and were showing no signs of improving at a key time in the season. The club is still competing in the latter stages of the UEFA Champions League and the FA Cup, as well as challenging for a top-four spot in the Premier League, and we aim to remain as competitive as possible on all fronts. With that in mind, we felt our only option was to make a change at this time. With immediate effect, Roberto Di Matteo has been appointed first-team coach on an interim basis until the end of the season.'[100]

Some may argue that appointing the former Chelsea player was just a case of Di Matteo being in the right place at the right time, and far enough distanced from Villas-Boas not to have been perceived as part of the failed regime. Alan Addicott would suggest there was far more to the appointment than that though, 'As far as I was concerned it was a stroke of genius. Di Matteo was a big favourite with the fans, was well-respected as a player at Chelsea by his

99 Shakespeare, William, *Julius Caesar*, 1599.

100 Chelsea FC statement, 5 March 2012.

fellow pros and helped them win numerous trophies and most importantly of all, was one of "them". Di Matteo had already won the players over, he didn't have to prove himself to them or the fans. Another key to Di Matteo's success was appointing Eddie Newton as his assistant. Newton came through the ranks at Chelsea so was another familiar face for the players. You could argue that Di Matteo was in the right place at the right time but he quickly proved his worth. I don't think appointing yet another new manager from the "outside" would have been as successful. It would have taken the new man in charge quite a time to get Chelsea's house in order, and time was a thing the Stamford Bridge outfit didn't have.'[101]

In the end, the dismissal felt merciful. Both parties, club and coach, had seemed locked together in a doomed embrace that each was finding more and more difficult to sustain, as hopes and dreams faded into despair and disappointment. For Chelsea, sacking a manager, even in mid-season was nothing particularly new, but for Villas-Boas, failure had been a novel, and chastening, experience. He later tried to rationalise why things went wrong, 'The Chelsea experience was too much too soon. I wasn't flexible as a manager at that time. I was communicative, but I wasn't flexible in my approach.'[102]

Perhaps that was the reason, but there may have been many others as well. Ian Ross certainly thought so. 'It always seemed to be a case of "I'll show you" with Villas-Boas. That attitude was clearly evident in his desire to move on Chelsea's older, senior players with almost indecent haste – that was a big mistake. I believe it was too much far too soon. The

---

101 Addicott, Alan, interview with the author.

102 'André Villas-Boas was "blinded by love" of José Mourinho', skysports.com, 4 October 2016.

staggering thing was that he moved on to Spurs only to suffer an almost identical fate.'[103]

Addicott considered the demise inevitable as performances and results continued to deteriorate, 'Morale was low at Chelsea at the time and I think from the off he never really gained the respect of the players, a key element to any success for a man in charge at the Blues. Dropping out of the sacred top four in the league finally put paid to him, I think.[104]' Perhaps the change was not as obvious and desirable as some recalled though, as Ryan Baldi suggested, 'Maybe he was the wrong appointment from the start. But given Chelsea fought hard to get him, paying a record compensation fee to Porto, you'd perhaps expect a little more faith.'[105]

It's difficult to summarise the feeling of Chelsea fans at this stage, but Mark Worrall may well have been speaking for many when he recalled that, 'The Chelsea board clearly thought they were hiring Mourinho 2.0 and were dazzled by AVB's "project management" PowerPoint slides. With hindsight it was a naive appointment given his lack of experience as a manager and the fact he'd never played the game. Trying to gain the respect of a dressing room full of world-class stars and strong personalities was a non-starter especially when it became transparent that he'd been hired to move the older players on. Factor in hopeless in-game management and that curious crouching stance in the technical area and he soon became an object of ridicule among supporters and once that happens the end is usually nigh.'[106]

---

103 Ross, Ian, interview with the author.

104 Addicott, Alan, interview with the author.

105 Baldi, Ryan, interview with the author.

106 Worrall, Mark, interview with the author.

Lifelong fan Danny Ridgeway, who saw his first Chelsea game in 1962, had drawn a similar conclusion, 'Despite having just done a great job at Porto, winning the treble and going undefeated in the league, I think Villas-Boas lost the respect of the dressing room and with so many big-name players having a huge influence within the club it was always going to be an uphill battle. Too big a job too early is probably spot on!'[107]

Ironically, it was the defeat to West Bromwich Albion, the club that had sacked Di Matteo in the summer, that had hammered the last nail into the Villas-Boas coffin, and led to the former Chelsea and Italy player taking charge at Stamford Bridge. The decline had stopped, precisely because the club had decided there was simply nowhere else to fall. It was the lowest point for Chelsea in a season that so far had featured very few positives.

From this point though, things would change and, far from being one of the club's most harrowing of recent seasons, it would lead to an event that, commentating for Sky Sports, Martin Tyler would describe as 'the greatest night in the history of Chelsea Football Club'. There were plenty of hurdles, many of them set very high, to clear before that day though, and on the way another trophy would be secured. Two months after Di Matteo took charge, he would guide Chelsea to FA Cup victory.

---

107 Ridgeway, Danny, interview with the author.

4

Stumbling Steps along the Wembley Way

ACROSS THE years leading up to the 2011/12 season, Chelsea had enjoyed a rich history of success in the FA Cup. Victory over Manchester United in 2006/07 when the final returned to Wembley from its sabbatical in Cardiff was the first of three wins in four years, with Didier Drogba scoring what would almost become his regular goal in the showpiece event to secure the trophy.

The following term looked likely to offer the club another success when Portsmouth defeated Manchester United in the first of the quarter-finals. With Chelsea facing a game against second-tier Barnsley, and the other ties to be contested by Middlesbrough, Cardiff City, Bristol Rovers and West Bromwich Albion, all seemed set fair for the Blues to retain the trophy. A shock defeat at Oakwell scuppered the plans, and Avram Grant's side instead had to focus on a Champions League campaign that would fall at the final hurdle in that rain-lashed Luzhniki Stadium, where hopes were washed away.

The following year, Chelsea returned to Wembley to defeat Everton 2-1 and regain the trophy. Guus Hiddink was now at the helm after replacing Luis Felipe Scolari mid-season and, after Louis Saha scored the fastest ever FA Cup Final goal – usurping Roberto Di Matteo's strike against Middlesbrough – to give the Toffees an early lead, inevitably it was Drogba equalising midway through the first period, before Frank Lampard scored the winner in the second half. In 2009/10 Drogba again notched the sole goal of the game to retain the trophy, defeating Portsmouth and setting up the Double for Carlo Ancelotti.

In February 2011, Everton exacted a little revenge for that final defeat in 2009, defeating Chelsea on penalties in a Stamford Bridge fourth-round replay. In extra time, Lampard had given Chelsea the lead and with no further score, entering the last minute, the Blues seemed destined to progress, before Leighton Baines netted from a free kick to necessitate the lottery of penalties. Misses by Nicolas Anelka and Ashley Cole left it open for Phil Neville to put the winning spot kick away and eliminate Chelsea. It was the first time that the club hadn't reached at least the quarter-finals since 2004/05. Despite enduring an increasingly harrowing season, by the time Chelsea entered the 2011/12 competition on 8 January, the club were hopeful of welcoming back an old friend to their trophy cabinet.

Chelsea's pursuit of the FA Cup began with a home game against Portsmouth. As related in the previous chapter, the call of the Africa Cup of Nations had reduced André Villas-Boas's selection options with both Drogba and Salomon Kalou on international duty. There had been a small lift in the squad's morale after the victory at Molineux, the first in four games; another win could help build a little momentum.

With the resumption of the Champions League more than a month away, an early exit from the League Cup and any aspirations of a run at the title merely a pipe dream, there was little reason for the manager to select anything other than the strongest side he had available. Matt Hughes noted in *The Times*, 'André Villas-Boas's team selection was an admission of Chelsea's status as Barclays Premier League also-rans, but the bigger worry was that, for long periods, his strongest side were only just good enough to beat a team then languishing 17th in the Npower Championship.'[108]

In more recent times, such ties against nominally weaker opposition would be an opportunity to allow some minutes of first-team action for that most neglected of squad members, the back-up goalkeeper. Understandably though, Villas-Boas was in no mood to take unnecessary risks and Petr Čech was denied any rest. The defence consisted of José Bosingwa, John Terry, David Luiz and Ashley Cole.

The left-back was in pursuit of his seventh FA Cup winners' medal. Amazingly, aside from penalty shoot-outs, he had lost only one of the last 38 FA Cup ties he had played in, going all the way back to Arsenal's 2001 final defeat by Liverpool. The second-tier visitors were hardly fancied to blot that record, with Portsmouth in a decline far worse than Chelsea's. Crumbling under periods of financial mismanagement, they were in the process of falling through the divisions. They had lost their Premier League status two seasons ago and would end this one in 21st place in the Championship, and be relegated to League One.

In midfield, Ramires partnered Lampard and Raul Meireles and, in the absence of having the option of selecting Drogba, Fernando Torres led the line, flanked by Florent

108 'Chelsea 4 Portsmouth 0: Limp Chelsea are flattered by scoreline', *The Times*, 9 January 2012.

Malouda and Juan Mata. Daniel Sturridge was sidelined with a hip problem, so there were few other options for the forward line.

If the win against Wolverhampton Wanderers had given a lift to the Chelsea players, it hardly manifested itself in the first period. Their play was ponderous and Torres, who was barracked by the Portsmouth fans chanting, 'We'll take you on loan,' played precisely like a player who hadn't found the back of the net since October, and had no idea where his next goal was coming from.

The visitors even had the better opportunities to open the scoring. Inside the first minute, a move by Dave Kitson and Márkó Futács had Terry and Luiz dragged out of position. Fortunately, Kitson failed to hit the target, then Aaron Mokoena committed the same sin when he should have done better with a free header from a corner. At the other end, with Torres comfortably controlled by Ricardo Rocha and Jason Pearce there was little to concern Pompey manager Michael Appleton. When the half-time break came, Villas-Boas would have been increasingly concerned; Appleton increasingly confident. The opening goal, three minutes after the restart, would change the complexion of the game.

Up supporting the forwards, Cole blocked an attempted clearance by Kitson and the ball bounced free towards Malouda. Instead of chasing back, Kitson stood pleading with the referee that Cole had blocked the ball with his hands. It was a costly loss of concentration. Anthony Taylor was unmoved, and the replays proved the official correct as the ball struck the back of Cole's arm while folded into his body at point-blank range. Seizing the advantage as the defenders hesitated, Malouda scampered towards the penalty area from the left flank, jinking past Mokoena and hitting the byline before pulling the ball back for Mata to tap home for his sixth strike of the season.

The goal should have been the spark to ignite Chelsea's play and add further confidence, but it hardly seemed to do so. Despite having more of the play, they still looked vulnerable, especially with problems of their own making. A free kick conceded allowed Liam Lawrence a chance to curl in a cross, but Terry cleared efficiently under pressure. The next chance was even closer.

Bosingwa played the ball back to Luiz out by the right-hand touchline as the Brazilian was closed down by Kitson. Never shy of over-indulgence in inappropriate areas of the pitch, Luiz attempted an extravagant drag-back to beat the forward. Embarrassingly for the defender, Kitson was unimpressed and stole possession, quickly whipping the ball inside to Futács. The Hungarian dragged the ball inside of Terry and shaped to shoot left-footed. Čech read the danger though, and by the time the shot came in he had closed the gap between him and the forward to just a few yards. The ball struck his hip and flew high towards the edge of the box where Greg Halford rose to head towards the empty net with Čech trying to recover his ground. It seemed a certain goal until Terry, who had made an instinctive run on to the line to cover for his goalkeeper, appeared and slid across to clear the ball. The clearance fell to David Norris, who hit in Portsmouth's third attempt on target in the space of a few seconds, but by now Čech was back in position and he fell on the ball, gripping it tightly in relief, as if clutching a Ming vase thrown down to him from a fifth-storey window.

There was a price to pay, however. Terry had been struggling with a knee problem for a few games, but with cussed belligerence and Alex on the brink of departure, he had continued to play. After clearing Halford's header, his momentum had carried him into the post and a collision with the same knee. Whatever his sins, a charge of feigning injury could never be levelled at the Chelsea captain, and when he raised a hand towards the bench in obvious pain it was clear that something was wrong. In typical fashion, after treatment he continued and played out the remainder of the game. The initial prognosis, at least for public consumption, was encouraging. 'He'll be fine,' shrugged assistant manager Roberto Di Matteo, when asked about Terry.[109] He wouldn't be. The effects of the collision with the post on the pre-existing problem would later mean a prolonged absence from the action.

Fortunately for the home team, by now the Portsmouth efforts were beginning to wilt as fatigue set in and Chelsea achieved some measure of control, but more goals wouldn't arrive until the final five minutes. Ramires always seemed to have a full fuel tank and his industrious energy and pace was becoming an increasingly potent weapon for the home team. A cross by Cole found Torres on the far post. His header back across invited a diving header by the Brazilian midfielder, but the challenge by Rocha was just enough to disrupt Ramires's dive and Stephen Henderson comfortably collected the ball.

Next time they wouldn't be as fortunate. With five minutes to play, Ramires collected possession around the halfway line and drove through the tiring Portsmouth midfield, checking one way, and then the other, before slipping a pass to Lampard, who fed it on wide towards Mata. His cross found Torres, who headed down for Ramires to slip the ball home with Henderson stranded. When the Brazilian arrived at Stamford Bridge, he had been handed the number

109 'Chelsea 4 Portsmouth 0: Brazilliant! Ramires double sparks late FA Cup goal rush', *Daily Mail*, 9 January 2012.

seven shirt previously worn by Andriy Shevchenko, and the way he snaffled the opportunity was a decent imitation of the Ukrainian in his pomp.

A few minutes later he notched his second of the game, and this one would have impressed Shevchenko even more. Breaking from defence, Torres carried the ball to the halfway line before releasing a perfect pass that allowed Ramires to exploit his pace and run clear from 40 yards before adroitly flicking the ball past Henderson. Although he hadn't scored, Torres had created both of the Ramires goals and the Stamford Bridge crowd, ever eager to find something – other than goals – to celebrate in the striker's games acclaimed his achievement.

The final goal came when Lampard received the ball in the area, pivoted and shot home. By then though, the game was over. 'It was possibly a bit harsh,' said Pompey boss Appleton afterwards. 'But I've learned it can be very hard to come to a top-six Premier League team, especially if you don't get an early goal to hang on to. Conceding two minutes into the second half after a good first-half display doesn't help but we got ourselves back into the game. You could sense some nervousness before they got their second but we are a Championship club and fatigue and concentration come in and they have players who can be clinical.'[110]

Portsmouth wouldn't be a Championship club much longer, and it's unclear who Appleton was referring to as Chelsea's 'clinical' players. The four-goal margin of victory certainly flattered the home team, but at that time of the season no one from Stamford Bridge was going to complain. Their fifth-round assignment would have a much tighter scoreline.

---

110 'Chelsea 4 Portsmouth 0: Brazilliant! Ramires double sparks late FA Cup goal rush', *Daily Mail,* 9 January 2012.

With the draw being held later that same day, Chelsea shouldn't have had long to wait to find out who their next opponents would be. As it turned out, when ball number 28 was pulled out of the bag, it meant that they would face an away game at either MK Dons or Queens Park Rangers. The clubs had played out a 1-1 draw the day before with a goal from Heidar Helguson earning the Hoops a replay as the game entered the final minute. Dean Bowditch had given the home team a lead midway through the second period, but the League One side just failed to see out the game against their Premier League opponents.

The replay was played on 17 January and, as logic would have suggested, the MK Dons' best chance had gone. In a tight game, defender Danny Gabbidon scored the only goal, securing progress for Chelsea's neighbours. It meant that on 28 January, the Blues would revisit Loftus Road, scene of that catastrophic game back in October, when both Bosingwa and Drogba were dismissed before half-time and Terry's alleged remarks to Anton Ferdinand led to legal proceedings, inquiries, a ban and retirement from international football. Chelsea had also lost the game to another Helguson goal. It had been just their second defeat in the league, but also a milestone as their season began to unravel.

With Ferdinand certain to be in the home line-up, there were rumours that Terry may well be rested for the game in order to allow his knee time to recover more fully. Whether any such thoughts even crossed the mind of Villas-Boas or not is a moot point. When the team selections were announced Terry was included as captain. The court case would not be heard until July and, understandably adopting the 'innocent until proven guilty' maxim, there was no reason not to select the captain. Ironically, however, with the knee problem becoming more difficult to cope with, even after resorting to painkilling injections, this was Terry's last game for some six weeks or so. On his return, a different man was in charge at Stamford Bridge.

The FA had taken precautions to try and avoid any potential explosive points, decreeing that there would be no customary pre-game handshakes. Again, some had speculated that it would have been an opportunity for a measure of reconciliation between the players that perhaps could have defused the situation. On balance though, it's easy to understand the FA's caution, especially with emotions bound to be running high off the pitch, almost regardless of the behaviour of the players on it.

Following the holiday debacle of the home defeat to Aston Villa, Chelsea had at least gone into 2012 on a run of four games without defeat, winning three of them. None, however, had been gained without prolonged periods where they had struggled for any kind of cohesion. In fact, since the victory over Portsmouth, in successive games against Sunderland and Norwich they had scored only one goal, and that only occurred when Torres's shot against the crossbar struck an unknowing Lampard and cannoned into the net against the Wearside club. There could be no repeat of that in this game as, although Torres was again leading the line, Lampard wasn't even given a place on the bench.

The first half was poor from both sides, with the best chance falling to Mata following a swift counter-attack by Chelsea. It began after a home free kick by Joey Barton was headed clear by Luiz. It was the sort of defensive header beloved by coaches, having both the height and distance to allow the defence to scamper out of the penalty area before the ball dropped to the ground. This one achieved that aim, falling to Luke Young by the halfway line. The full-back attempted to hoist the ball back towards the Chelsea area but it fell woefully short, dropping to Torres as he charged out of the back line.

Suddenly there was a break on. The home defenders chased back as Ramires loomed up alongside Torres, with Mata to the left out wide. Looking to pass the ball on, Torres fed it left towards his compatriot. As with Young's attempt a few seconds earlier, however, the pass was short, and should have been easily collected by the recovering full-back, but a slip by Young turned a poor pass into an inviting one. Mata collected, skipped past the fallen Young, and ran on towards goal. Driving into the area he got a clean shot off, but Paddy Kenny dived low to block, and the ball was scrambled away for a corner.

The Blues were the better side in the first period, but without offering much genuine threat. A strike from distance by Meireles flew harmlessly wide and Ramires, chasing on to a neat back-heel pass from Mata, the outstanding creative influence in the game, crossed dangerously, but no Chelsea player could exploit the opportunity. The best that the home side could offer was a 20-yard effort from Barton that was well wide of Čech's post. For a game that had been regarded as a potential boiling point given the Terry–Ferdinand situation, the encounter had hardly reached a gentle simmer by the break.

The second period began brightly for Chelsea. Torres and Sturridge combined to give the latter an opening but his powerful shot was wide. Searching for a little more penetration, former Chelsea favourite Mark Hughes, now in charge at Loftus Road, had thrown Federico Macheda into the fray at the break, replacing Helguson, but to little avail. There was earnest effort but little cutting edge to the home attacks, and they could have conceded a penalty when Clint Hill's less than graceful challenge sent Sturridge tumbling, but Mike Dean ignored the claims. Moments later however, a spot kick would be awarded.

Another former Chelsea player, Shaun Wright-Phillips, drove into the box and cut a low cross back from the byline. It looked a dangerous move and, indeed, it led to a goal, but at the other end of the pitch. Čech parried the ball and it fell to Ramires, who engaged the after-burners, sprinting 70 yards or so with opponents trailing in his wake before spreading a pass to Mata on the left. Looking up, he crossed towards the far post, where Sturridge was making a run. With the ball heading towards the forward, Hill ran into the back of Sturridge, who fell to the floor. Dean pointed to the spot. Initially, it looked like a generous decision, perhaps influenced by Hill standing over the fallen Sturridge suggesting that the forward had made far more of the contact than was warranted.

Hill was furious at the decision, but perhaps with the earlier incident still resonating in his mind, Dean was unmoved. More timely review using the replay from behind the goal shows that Hill certainly came into contact with the back of Sturridge as he was preparing to jump for the ball, which may have put him off balance, and made the tumble appear more theatrical, but it was clearly a debatable decision. There was also an echo of that tempestuous game at the same ground back in October when Luiz conceded a penalty in a similar fashion. Mata sent Kenny sprawling in the opposite direction and Chelsea hit the front on the hour. Given the paucity of threat offered by the home team, whichever way the goal came about, it was probably a fair reflection of the flow of the game.

The goal did provoke some response from the QPR players, but it was handled with unusual composure by a Chelsea defence that had seemed anything but assured in so many previous games when defending a lead late on. With a dozen or so minutes to play, Ramires injured himself blocking a shot from Hill, and had to be taken off with what was feared to be damage to his knee ligaments. Romeu replaced him.

Chelsea dropped deeper to contain the more determined efforts of the home team, but coped without too much distress, even allowing for the almost eight minutes of injury time added to compensate for when Ramires was being attended to. At the end of the game, the FA hierarchy would have breathed a heavy sigh of relief that what could have been a hugely controversial encounter had turned into a damp squib. In *The Times*, Rob Shepherd disdainfully described it as, 'The grudge match that never was … settled by a penalty that never was.'[111] Even allowing for a little poetic license about the second part of the sentence, no one would argue with the initial assertion. Villas-Boas and Chelsea were just relieved to be in the hat for the next round.

The draw for the fifth round took place on 29 January and Chelsea were again favoured with what looked like a more than appetising fixture, at home to Championship club Birmingham City. The previous term, the St Andrew's outfit had overcome the odds to lift the League Cup, defeating Arsenal in the final, before going on to be relegated from the Premier League. Even without the team firing on anything remotely resembling all cylinders, few Chelsea fans would have complained about the draw, and confidence of getting into the last eight would have been high.

Much of that confidence may well have evaporated though by the time the game took place on Saturday, 18 February as their 12.30pm kick-off opened the weekend's

111 'QPR 0 Chelsea 1: Rangers go quietly after Mata's penalty', *The Times*, 29 January 2012.

FA Cup fixtures. Since that victory at Loftus Road, Chelsea had played three Premier League games without recording a win. A 1-1 draw at Swansea was followed by the 3-3 roller-coaster ride with Manchester United at Stamford Bridge where a three-goal advantage was squandered, then a defeat at Everton completed a miserable fortnight. The game against the other Blues, from England's second city, would offer small comfort.

Given the last few results, there was little chance that Villas-Boas would risk putting out an under-strength team against the second-tier opponents, despite the natural inclination to rest some players. Cole hadn't fully recovered from the injury sustained at Goodison Park, so Ryan Bertrand was drafted in at left-back. Cahill came in for Terry, whose knee problem was now beginning to cause real concern, and Ramires returned to the starting line-up after recovering from the injury sustained in the previous round. There was also a measure of comfort for the home fans in seeing both Drogba and Kalou available after their return from the Africa Cup of Nations. In a strong group of substitutes, the Ivory Coast pair sat alongside Lampard, Essien, Bosingwa, Malouda and third-choice goalkeeper Hilário.

Despite the trials and tribulations endured at St Andrew's, Chris Hughton had performed a minor miracle with the club and, when visiting Stamford Bridge, Birmingham had an impressive unbeaten run of 13 games behind them. Comparing that to Chelsea's recent performances and results, it should have been of little surprise that it was the Championship side that had the better of the early stages of the game.

An early warning came when a corner from Jordon Mutch reached the head of Luiz. His attempted clearance was miscued, and the ball struck David Murphy before bouncing to safety behind the Chelsea goal. It was a danger signal that should have been heeded. That it wasn't led to the opening goal. Approaching the 20th minute, another Mutch corner caused problems for Luiz as the ball eluded both the Brazilian and Meireles at the near post, allowing it to bounce in the area. It's the sort of defensive indiscipline that an under-12 team coach would pull his hair out at. Somewhere in the Stamford Bridge stands, the injured Chelsea skipper may have been doing precisely the same thing.

Curtis Davies attempted an overhead kick but missed the ball as he fell back, claiming a tug by Cahill. On the ball went bouncing a second time in the six-yard area before running on towards Murphy, who crashed it past Čech from a couple of yards. As the visiting fans celebrated a sudden hush fell over the Chelsea faithful. It wasn't one caused by shock, but that a gnawing dread of inevitable disaster had now been made real in front of their eyes. On the sidelines, Villas-Boas stood motionless, hypnotised by the events, paralysed by the continuing malaise of his team.

Shortly afterwards, there was a chance for redemption. Ramires had possession in the box and played the ball past Wade Elliott. A fraction slow in responding, the defender jabbed out a leg and brought the Brazilian down. The expression on Elliott's face confirmed both the offence and his disappointment. Having converted from 12 yards at Loftus Road in the previous round, Mata stepped up with confidence. He drove the ball low and to Colin Doyle's right-hand post, but the goalkeeper had guessed correctly and palmed the ball away.

He would later also deny a Luiz free kick from distance, pushing the ball safely over the crossbar, and then he dived to collect a Mata header. Sturridge had also volleyed narrowly wide as the chances continued. The Irishman was back-up to Maik Taylor for the place between the posts and, in his dozen years as a Birmingham player would only play 31 league games for the club, plus another 17 during various loan spells. This was his moment of glory, however. Chelsea seemed keen to make it somebody's day, just not their own. At the break, the lead was intact and deservedly so. Writing for the BBC, Owen Phillips summed up the scene at the break, a goal down, 'The Chelsea manager cut a forlorn figure on the touchline as his lacklustre side left the Stamford Bridge pitch to a chorus of boos and chants of support for former manager José Mourinho.'[112] Phillips described the Chelsea performance as 'woeful'[113] and 'far too typical of Chelsea in the past two months – slow to start, ponderous in midfield, sloppy in defence.'[114] It wasn't an exaggeration and the boos from the home fans at the half-time whistle confirmed the fact.

During the break, Torres was removed and Drogba sent on in his place. Villas-Boas later rationalised the change. 'It was a decision that we had to make,' Villas-Boas said. 'We were going much more direct, based on the running of the game we wanted to up the tempo [so] Didier could act as a target man.'[115] Following the game, a television channel reported that after leaving the dressing room and out of earshot of the manager, Drogba corralled the Chelsea players and delivered a pep talk of his own, before the team returned to the pitch.

Understandably, when Villas-Boas was informed of the report during a post-game interview, he was clearly angry.

---

112 https://www.bbc.com/sport/football/16994719.

113 https://www.bbc.com/sport/football/16994719.

114 https://www.bbc.com/sport/football/16994719.

115 'Sturridge saves Chelsea and André Villas-Boas against Birmingham', *The Guardian*, 18 February 2012.

'The response of the Portuguese, who had removed the now perennially disappointing Fernando Torres at the break, came laced in sarcasm. "Yeah, right, fantastic, of course," he said. "Because he has to do team talks, it's up to him. It's ridiculous. Which channel is it?" When informed it was ESPN, he said, "It makes no sense. It's a pity because I just gave an interview to ESPN and I'm sure I wouldn't have done it if I knew that was the case."'[116]

Whether the angst was driven by a feeling of being undermined, ignored or mere frustration is not clear, but the change, and at least one of the half-time talks produced a marginal improvement in Chelsea's play as the second period got under way. Mata had been the prime, perhaps only, real threat to Birmingham's back line and, with his team now on the front foot, more chances fell to the little Spaniard. A long ball from Luiz found him in the area. He controlled with accomplished ease but his shot flew wide of the near post. At least Chelsea had begun to offer some threat, as the visitors slipped further back into defence to protect their lead. With the team now at least having a measure of control against their Championship opponents, the coach further increased the forward momentum a dozen minutes after the break, replacing Mikel John Obi with Kalou. A few minutes later, a tangible reward arrived. A Branislav Ivanović cross from the right was headed home by Sturridge and Chelsea drew level.

The goal brought as much relief as joy to the home fans, but the London Blues were now pressing for a winner. A scramble from a Mata corner saw the ball fly out towards Meireles, but his low drive was deflected over the bar with Doyle struggling to make any significant movement. Had the ball been a foot or so lower, he would surely have struggled to

---

116 'Sturridge saves Chelsea and André Villas-Boas against Birmingham', *The Guardian*, 18 February 2012.

prevent it entering the goal. With seven minutes left, Villas-Boas sent on Lampard. If it was a move to placate the angry fans, however, it was rendered ineffectual when the number ten was shown, indicating that it was Mata being replaced. Boos, accompanied by angry chants of 'You don't know what you're doing', spoke of both frustration and incomprehension.

With time draining away, Chelsea came so close to suffering their first home FA Cup defeat to a lower-league club since losing to Oxford United in 1991 when a defensive calamity saw Nathan Redmond go clear, but his effort was tired and ineffective. At the final whistle, the boos echoing around Stamford Bridge told Villas-Boas all he needed to know about how the fans felt, with the big game against Napoli looming in a few days.

Without anywhere to hide, Villas-Boas was honest in his appraisal of the performance. 'No, it was not good enough, for sure it wasn't,' the Chelsea manager said. 'But we take the game to St Andrew's – a difficult game and Birmingham are undefeated in the league there – and I am sure that there we'll put on a more decent challenge. [In] the first half there were a lot of opportunities for us, and [it was] better in the second half, but not enough to win the game. So it is never satisfying when you draw at home to a Championship team.'[117] Few, if any, Chelsea fans would have disputed that.

Writing in *The Times*, David Walsh drew a comparison between the two managers, their past and recent performances, 'Oh, for the life of the manager. You're Chris Hughton, you've done a good job at Newcastle and then, unfairly, you get sacked. You fear your life is over. Not like André Villas-Boas who, still in his managerial nappies, does well at Porto and is tempted by the jingle of Roman

117 'Sturridge saves Chelsea and André Villas-Boas against Birmingham', *The Guardian*, 18 February 2012.

Abramovich's silver. He thinks his life has just begun. But football turns nightmares to dreams, riches to rags. Sunk by Mike Ashley, Chris Hughton resurfaced at Birmingham and his team are now unbeaten in 14 games and threatening to return to the Premier League. Their run wasn't seriously jeopardised by Chelsea in this FA Cup tie as they worked hard and were well organised, like a team that is being well managed.'[118] The implication carried by those final half-dozen words was clear and, when Chelsea visited St Andrew's for the replay on 6 March, they would be led by a different man.

With Villas-Boas finally surpassing the patience of Abramovich following the unedifying Premier League defeat to West Bromwich Albion, he was sacked on 4 March and replaced by erstwhile assistant Roberto Di Matteo as interim head coach, with Eddie Newton brought in to help him. The appointment was announced as being effective until the end of 2011/12, but would go beyond that as Chelsea's season, and their fortunes, would undergo a radical change of direction.

In the FA Cup, under Villas-Boas Chelsea had played through three rounds. Each had been a struggle against teams that their status suggested should have been dispensed with by a comfortable margin. Only the 4-0 victory over Portsmouth looked anything like the sort of result produced by a side with aspirations to challenge for the Premier League title, but that scoreline was massively distorted by three goals in the dying minutes of the game, camouflaging another poor performance. After Di Matteo's appointment though, the following games in the competition would produce much improved performances, that led to a final

---

118 'Chelsea 1 Birmingham City 1: Villas-Boas in crisis', *The Times*, 19 February 2012.

triumph over a fancied team playing in red. The remaining ties would serve as a microcosm for what was left of Chelsea's extraordinary season.

5

See Naples and Live!

ON 14 August 2010, Roberto Di Matteo arrived at Stamford Bridge for his first game in charge of West Bromwich Albion. The man who had won two FA Cups, a League Cup, a Cup Winners' Cup and a UEFA Super Cup while wearing Chelsea blue received a rapturous welcome as the home fans sang his name ahead of the game. Ninety minutes later, following a chastening 6-0 defeat, the first glow of being in charge of a Premier League club playing at Stamford Bridge had been badly tarnished for the Swiss-born former Italy international.

Just over 18 months later, the dismissal of André Villas-Boas had presented Di Matteo with the opportunity for a second chance, at a second coming. With the Chelsea squad in turmoil, lacking in confidence, and with a £50m striker unable to find the back of the net, perhaps taking that West Bromwich Albion team to Stamford Bridge and trying to get a decent result may have been a less difficult task in comparison. A former Chelsea manager certainly saw things that way. 'Villas-Boas won everything and will continue to be a champion,' Luiz Felipe Scolari asserted. 'The club needed to change seven or eight players. He knew that from the moment he got there, but he wasn't able to. Now it's going to be hell for his successor.'[119]

Was there a hint of residual resentment from the Brazilian following his sacking in 2009? Di Matteo had certainly been handed a difficult task but, aside from being a former Chelsea player and the kudos that his history would carry around the club and among its fans, he had one great advantage over his predecessor. Simply put, he wasn't André Villas-Boas.

If a former manager of Chelsea had severe reservations about whether Di Matteo could succeed, one of his old team-mates, Gianfranco Zola, took a different view. Quoted in the *Evening Standard*, he explained: 'Roberto has got a big opportunity and I personally believe he's got the qualities to do a good job. I really hope that he's going to do well. He's a Chelsea boy as well, he's a Chelsea hero, and so he's well represented.'[120]

The same article also asserted that Chelsea's owner did not consider that all of the blame for the club's problems was the sole responsibility of the dismissed manager, 'Abramovich reportedly read the riot act to Chelsea's players after sacking Villas-Boas, telling them they were as much to blame for the club's plight as the Portuguese. Speculation is rife Abramovich will jettison some of the older squad members this summer'.[121]

Zola, who left the club as the Russian oligarch arrived responded when the situation was posed to him, 'All I can say is that they are players who are 33, 34, and I believe

---

119 https://www.thenational.ae/andre-villas-boas-was-the-man-with-the-plan-but-found-no-support-1.595066.

120 'Di Matteo can succeed at Chelsea – Zola', *Evening Standard*, 7 March 2012.

121 'Di Matteo can succeed at Chelsea – Zola', *Evening Standard*, 7 March 2012.

that they have still got something to give. Whether they're going to be giving it for Chelsea or for another club, I don't know.' There were constant rumours of dressing-room unrest under Villas-Boas and Zola said, 'When you want to achieve something, one of the main things is to stick together. Only by doing that can you go through the difficulties. I think it is the moment where Chelsea players, managers, club, and supporters have to do that.'[122] The former player's words would prove to be prophetic.

The first task for Di Matteo was to safely negotiate the FA Cup replay against Birmingham City. It was the only time in the cup run that Chelsea had needed to venture outside of London. Home draws and a visit to Queens Park Rangers would be followed by a semi-final and final at Wembley, but before those sorts of things could be contemplated, there was the visit to St Andrew's to deal with first as, just two days into the job, Di Matteo led his team into the West Midlands for his first game in charge.

If anyone had been expecting a revolutionary change to the starting line-up, they were to be disappointed. Other than bringing in Salomon Kalou to replace Daniel Sturridge, who was dropped to the bench, Di Matteo left well alone. It meant that alongside the dropped forward, the list of available substitutes comprised Frank Lampard, Michael Essien, Didier Drogba, Romelu Lukaku and Hilário, plus the encouraging sight of an apparently now fit John Terry.

Since the first game, Birmingham had extended their unbeaten run to 17 games, but Chris Hughton had problems of his own. As well as three players who had featured strongly being cup-tied, a further five were injured. It was, therefore, a make-do-and-mend team that took to the field to face

122 'Di Matteo can succeed at Chelsea – Zola', *Evening Standard*, 7 March 2012.

Di Matteo's first Chelsea 11. Despite their deficiencies though, the home side were still playing with confidence and belief, and the first half offered only a slight improvement in Chelsea's performance, if discernible at all, and yet they nearly had the perfect start.

From a throw-in on the right, the ball was hooked forward to release Juan Mata closing in on Colin Doyle. Had he squared the ball across the box, Kalou was unmarked and would have had a simple tap-in. Instead, the Spaniard elected to shoot, and Doyle plunged down to his near post to deflect the ball wide. On the sidelines, Di Matteo put his hands to his head. An early goal would have been the ideal way to settle any nerves.

Responding at the other end, a cross from Jordon Mutch found the towering Nikola Žigić ducking to contact the ball, but he still directed his header towards goal, forcing Čech to tip the ball over the crossbar. The final minutes saw a move by Fernando Torres that epitomised his time with Chelsea. Standing on the edge of the area as a ball was fed into him, he instinctively turned his defender to open up a clear chance but then, with time to think, he dragged his shot horrendously wide as the home fans jeered mercilessly, and that was pretty well it in an uninspiring first period.

Very much in the manner of that woefully wasted missed chance, once again, Torres resembled a busted flush in Chelsea blue; a pale shadow of the menacing striker who excelled at Anfield. Ryan Baldi suggested, however, that a decline in the effectiveness of Torres, once the most feared striker in European football, had begun before the transfer to Stamford Bridge, 'The move to Chelsea is always cited as the point at which Torres went off the boil, but I think the origin of his downturn can be traced back a little further. His form had already begun to slide somewhat in his final half-season with Liverpool. Injuries certainly played a part. After his first, electric season in England, he made only 22 and 24 league appearances in the next two campaigns, missing 11 of Liverpool's last 18 Premier League games in his final full season at Anfield through a knee injury. Although he recovered fitness the next season – before joining Chelsea in the January – he never got his momentum back, scoring a pretty average (by his standards) nine goals in 26 games.

'The £50m fee was huge at the time, a British record. But had he been sold a year earlier, I think the fee would have been even higher, such was the level he was performing at. Of course, following the move to Chelsea, his form deteriorated further, which always seemed, from the outside looking in, a matter of spiralling confidence; the run of goals he so desperately needed just never came for him. One goal in his first 18 league games for Chelsea, and only three from his first 38, and he looked less a malfunctioning striker than a broken man.'[123]

After the break, Chelsea picked up the pace. Ten minutes in Ramires hustled possession away in midfield and drove down the flank before crossing. The ball dropped between two Chelsea players in the box, as Mata and Kalou seemed to compete to see who could fall over it first. Then, perhaps enjoying a slice of fortune seemingly perpetually denied to Villas-Boas, Di Matteo watched as Mata stabbed out a foot and sent the ball past Doyle. It was hardly a goal of great grace, but its importance outweighed any deficiencies in artistic impression.

It's tempting to say that the goal broke the dam, and to some extent it did. Chelsea suddenly seemed quicker to the ball and Birmingham's infrequent forays forward

123 Baldi, Ryan, interview with the author.

became increasingly rare. Not long after the goal, Branislav Ivanović stole possession around the halfway line. An exchange of passes with Ramires saw the Serb out on the right in an ideal crossing position. The ball went in and Mata's header on the far post was narrowly wide, but Chelsea had begun to threaten. Six minutes after the first goal, the visitors doubled their lead. Again, it was an Ivanović cross creating problems. This time, a low ball into the area was controlled and quickly transferred to Raul Meireles on the edge of the box who powerfully struck home, offering Doyle little chance of any meaningful intervention.

There should have been a third goal, when Torres turned quickly to deceive his marker and receive a return pass before being bundled over in the area by Guirane N'Daw's clumsy challenge. Mata took the ball in determined fashion, keen to remedy the miss from the spot at Stamford Bridge but, once more, Doyle confounded him and saved. It mattered little. At the end of the game, Chelsea had prevailed by being little more than competent, but even that was an improvement on the recent dark days, and Di Matteo was keen to promote a feeling of positivity after the game, 'We had a difficult task given the last few days but the attitude was right.' Di Matteo added the priority had been to progress to the next round and show the supporters 'that we care.'[124] It had been largely achieved.

The new man in charge was also keen to promote a united front when asked about his team selection that had left some of the big hitters on the bench. Had it been a brave decision? 'Was it a brave selection choice? It was nothing to do with bravery. They were all on board. They know the

124 'Di Matteo: Chelsea dressing room united', *The Express*, 7 March 2012.

targets we have to achieve. They are big players for this club. We have a squad and we have to utilise the squad. We have to try to get the best out of these players. It was a question of freshening up the team a bit, giving it some energy and fresh legs for a game like this. We had to fight today. It has been a difficult time. It's been difficult for the whole club but you have to deal with it. Tonight we had to focus on this game and move on as a club, put it to one side and move forward. We faced a difficult task given the events of the last couple of days, and it was important for us to get through to the next round. We had to do a job.'[125]

When asked about Terry being on the bench, just two weeks after undergoing surgery to solve his knee problem, Di Matteo suggested that he hadn't been fit enough to start, but being the player he was, just having him in the matchday squad had given the entire group a lift, and that he would be available for the league game at home to Stoke City four days later. The win, plus the prospect of having a fully fit Terry back in action, was a tonic for the Chelsea fans, as well as the coach and his squad. Just four days after the game against Stoke, Chelsea would play their second leg against Napoli, needing to overturn the 3-1 defeat suffered in Italy. What had looked like a mountainous task just a few short days ago was now feeling much more possible. If a week is a long time in politics, two days since the departure of Villas-Boas seemed even longer at Stamford Bridge.

Given that the previous Premier League game had seen the end of Villas-Boas, and that the Champions League encounter with Napoli was following in a few days' time, Chelsea fans would have been comforted to see a more regular looking 11 line up for the game against the team

---

125 'Di Matteo: Chelsea dressing room united', *The Express*, 7 March 2012.

from the Potteries. The ever-impressive and reliable Čech was in goal, but Terry returned to a back four comprising Ivanović and Ashley Cole on the flanks, with Gary Cahill partnering the skipper and David Luiz on the bench. In midfield, Lampard was back with Meireles and Mikel. Ramires offered width and pace on one flank, Kalou was on the other, with Drogba leading the line. The average age of the starting line-up was 28.5 years, but this was a game when precious little other than the result mattered, and in such games, experience is key.

If the match at Birmingham had been a hesitant first step on a road to some rediscovered confidence, the result attained there had clearly helped things along. Stoke hadn't won a league game at Stamford Bridge in almost 38 years, and the opening minutes suggested that their drought was unlikely to end anytime soon. During an encouragingly bright start, an Ivanović header from a Lampard corner whistled narrowly over the bar. Then Cahill ventured forward from his defensive position to fire in a shot from the edge of the area, but Asmir Begović dived to save. A Stamford Bridge crowd, denied entertainment and optimism for so long, fell upon the encouraging signs like a starving man at a banquet, roaring on their approval. In a period where Chelsea dominated, the visitors were limited to one brief sight of the home goal, when a slip by Terry allowed Jonathan Walters a clear run at Čech, but the increasingly reliable Cahill recovered to block the effort.

Despite needing little help to control the game, Stoke gifted Chelsea a further advantage on 25 minutes. A petulant stamp by Ricardo Fuller on a fallen Ivanović brought an inevitable red card for the Jamaica international, and the visitors were compelled to play with ten men for more than an hour. It was a key factor in deciding the fate of the game, as Rob Beasley described in *The Sun*, 'Fuller cost his team dear with a shameful moment of madness. An act of pure thuggery over-shadowed the game – and it decided the match just as much as Drogba's goal. The Stoke striker's vicious stamp on right-back Branislav Ivanović in the 25th minute was a disgrace and deserved a straight red card.'[126]

Seizing the moment, Di Matteo decided that, with the visitors now restricted to even less frequent forays forward, he could do without so much midfield defensive cover, and he removed Meireles to add the attacking flair of Mata. Without any criticism of the Portuguese player being withdrawn, the crowd roared their approval of the positive instincts of the new man taking charge in the dugout. Despite Terry and Ivanović both striking the woodwork, the change brought no tangible rewards ahead of the break, but Chelsea headed to the dressing-room with applause rather than boos echoing around the stadium. Optimism had replaced pessimism.

At the restart, the consequences of Fuller's action seemed to have caught up with Ivanović and Luiz emerged to begin the second period, with the Serb still in the dressing-room receiving treatment. The change made little difference to the flow of the game, with the majority of the action at the other end of the pitch. In sharp contrast to the actions of their dismissed striker, the visitors were disciplined and organised, but with Chelsea attacking almost without break, they were tested to the full, and Begović was called into action on several occasions. The Bosnian did particularly well to deny Drogba from a free kick that looked bound for the net.

---

126 Chelsea 1 Stoke 0, *The Sun*, 10 March 2012.

Just past the hour, a shot from Terry scraped by Begović's post as Chelsea frustration began to grow. A goal was on the way though. On 68 minutes, Mata slipped a delicate through pass to Drogba, who collected the ball a dozen or so yards from goal and guided it past the goalkeeper. It made him the first African player to notch a century of goals in the Premier League but, just as importantly, it virtually settled the game as well.

With manager Tony Pulis driving them forwards from the sidelines, Stoke pushed for a quick reply, but Chelsea jealously guarded the hard-earned lead. Andy Wilkinson nearly caught Čech off his guard with an audacious effort from around halfway, but most of Stoke's attacks were blunted by the commanding presence of Terry and Cahill at the heart of the home defence who, despite playing their first game together, gave the impression of a well-established pairing. Late on, Mata nearly doubled the lead as his free kick struck Begović's post; the third time that the woodwork had denied Chelsea. Sturridge, who had come on for Mikel a minute before Drogba's goal, then drove in from the right flank but fired wide.

At the final whistle, one goal was enough to secure the points. It had been a tight game, despite the one-man advantage Chelsea had enjoyed for more than an hour. There was, however, perhaps extra merit in that. The win took Chelsea back up to level on 49 points with fourth-placed Arsenal. The Gunners had a game in hand, but after a dark period for the club, there were some green shoots of recovery beginning to show, as *The Guardian* suggested, 'This was not a performance to have the Napoli scouts trembling, ahead of the Champions League last 16 showdown here on Wednesday night, but for Roberto Di Matteo and everyone connected with Chelsea, the result was everything. After the angst of recent weeks, on and off the field, which culminated in the sacking of André Villas-Boas last Sunday, there was comfort to be located in a narrow victory.'[127]

Napoli would provide an entirely different kind of test. Just over a week before the Serie A side visited Stamford Bridge, another Italian club had arrived in London with a seemingly comfortable lead from the first leg, confident that progress to the quarter-finals was assured. AC Milan had enjoyed a 4-0 victory over Arsenal at the San Siro and very few, if anyone at all, expected anything other than elimination for the Gunners. It turned out that way, but not before the Italians were on the ropes at half-time having conceded three goals. It meant that, with both Manchester City and United being eliminated from the Europa League the day after Chelsea's game, if the Blues could spring a surprise and overturn the deficit conceded in Naples then they would be English football's sole remaining representatives in continental competition. Despite undeniable improvements in performance, and Arsenal's brave, but ultimately forlorn effort to climb a not too dissimilar mountain offering a sliver of encouragement, achieving that status still looked an improbable task for Chelsea.

Napoli had won their previous six games, scoring 17 goals, while despite the recent hesitant tentative steps hinting at recovery, Chelsea's form had been inconsistent at best with two wins, two draws and two losses from their last half-dozen games. The visitors also had Marek Hamšík, Edinson Cavani and Ezequiel Lavezzi all fit and available after minor knocks. Di Matteo did have the opportunity to bring talismanic skipper Terry back into the starting 11, but was denied the services of Meireles, who was suspended for

127 'Didier Drogba's neat finish gives Chelsea victory against Stoke City', *The Guardian*, 10 March 2012.

the game. It had also been three years since Chelsea had won a home leg of a Champions League knockout tie and, even if they could break that run, it may not have been sufficient to see them through to qualification.

Walter Mazzarri, Napoli's coach, who appeared likely to be given UEFA dispensation to appear on the touchline despite serving a suspension, had a dozen years' experience in Italian football. It was a massive contrast to an interim head coach who had never once taken charge of a club in European competition previously. Lampard recalled, however, a slight feeling among the team of not having much to lose at that stage, 'Because we had been so bad in Napoli and been on a downer as a team, there was this kind of defiance as a group to try and show character and show spirit. We knew it was a tough battle, but at the same time, where we had been so bad, we could only get better in that game.'[128] The defiance and spirit that had been largely absent in Napoli, would return on an emotional night at Stamford Bridge, and as the official Chelsea website relates, see Di Matteo deliver 'the most famous European coaching debut in our history'.[129]

Ahead of that though, there was the press conference on the day before the game, where Di Matteo would be accompanied by Terry. Later the Chelsea skipper would recall an event as he headed towards the press conference with the coach, 'As we were walking up to the lift, he stopped me [and reminded me that] ten years ago, I was an apprentice here, he was playing in the first team, we would never have pictured being in this position. He said, "Just take a moment before we go into this press conference and

---

128 *Kings of Europe – The Chelsea Story*, Sky UK Limited, 16 September 2012.

129 https://www.chelseafc.com/en/international/usa/usa-news/2020/05/top-matches-napoli-2012.

tell them how it is." You know, and we went in there, and we said, you know, from the heart, how we felt and what we felt we could achieve, and we went and done [sic] that. Everyone was a bit like "well, they will say that, they don't really believe that they can do it, and that kind of thing". But we really believed and we were getting that message across from the other lads in the belief we'd seen.'[130]

That growing feeling of belief was also recalled by Cole, 'Not many people had confidence in us but, as a team, as a squad, and the management staff, we had confidence that we could overturn the deficit.'[131] There's always a temptation to look back at events with 20/20 hindsight, and paint a picture of the time with the wisdom of knowing how it turned out. Would Terry and Cole have had the same recollections if the game had turned out badly? No one can say of course, but the perhaps unconsciously inclusive narrative identifying Di Matteo as an intimate part of the group, rather than an adjunct to it, is possibly the most telling element in both discourses.

In previous key games, Chelsea fans had often considered the team to be hamstrung by unexpected, and often unfathomable, selections by Villas-Boas. For the fixture on 14 March, that was certainly not the case. With Čech in goal, the defence looked solid with Terry back from injury and Cole back from the bench. The former slotted in alongside Luiz and Ivanović guarded the right flank. The midfield also had two players who had been placed on the bench for the first leg. Both Lampard and Essien were brought back into the fold, alongside Ramires. Mata, Drogba and Sturridge were in attack.

---

130 *Kings of Europe – The Chelsea Story*, Sky UK Limited, 16 September 2012.

131 Kings of Europe – *The Chelsea Story*, Sky UK Limited, 16 September 2012.

The team had a feeling of the 'Old Contemptibles'; battle-scarred, sometimes defeated, but hardly ever bested for belligerence or bloody-minded refusal to bend the knee. It wasn't a case of the Spartan-like ritual of returning with your shield or carried on it, but the fans knew that there would be no lack of fight in the unlikely pursuit of the required victory margin, and they responded by building a pulsating backdrop to the game. Mazzarri, who had indeed won his appeal allowing him to take his place on the sidelines, was clearly acutely aware of the raucous atmosphere. Walking over to shake hands with Di Matteo he looked around at the crowd with noticeable concern, perhaps appreciating, had he not done so already, that this tie was anything but over.

Mark Worrall recalled the pulsating atmosphere at the stadium, 'AVB's sacking … and his replacement with assistant and club legend Roberto Di Matteo was a masterstroke on the part of the board. Immediately the fans were back onside and while team selection played a part in the second-leg victory it was perhaps as much to do with the way the crowd got behind the new manager and players. Rival fans will joke about plastic flags at Stamford Bridge, but the atmosphere in the stadium that night was as raucous as any I'd previously experienced including when The Shed was a terrace.'[132]

The spine of Čech, Terry, Lampard and Drogba gave the team a backbone often denied it during the last dog days of the previous regime. Early on in the game though, that spine would be tested to the full. Inside the first five minutes, Sturridge had a snap-shot turned aside by Morgan De Sanctis but, with Chelsea needing a minimum of two goals, it was concerning that most of the flow of the game was going in the other direction. Full of confidence,

---

132 Worrall, Mark, interview with the author.

Napoli swept forward in waves of attacks. A single away goal would probably quieten the crowd and put the tie beyond the reach of Chelsea, and Mazzarri had clearly sent his team out to achieve that target. Cavani blazed wildly over after a poor headed clearance by Terry from a corner landed at the Uruguayan forward's feet. Čech blocked with his feet from Hamšík despite apparently falling the wrong way. Then an effort by Cavani, a dozen minutes in, found the side netting after a dangerous cross from Christian Maggio, on the counter-attack, found the forward in space at the far post.

Lavezzi was on a run of scoring five goals in his previous five games and on the lookout to make it six in six. The next minute saw him make a diagonal run to the right, springing a disorganised Chelsea offside line. Closing in from a tight angle, it was difficult to find a way past the perfectly positioned Čech, and the goalkeeper beat the powerfully struck shot away. Seconds later, Čech was forced to plunge low to his right to parry away a shot from distance by Hamšík. On 17 minutes, Juan Zúñiga hit in a shot from distance that flew high and wide. On the touchline, Mazzarri danced around in frustration. His team were almost shooting at will but, despite all of their opportunities, they had nothing to show for their domination. At such times, football's perverse nature often delivers a punishment for such profligacy.

Just ahead of the half-hour, that sanction was delivered. Out on the left flank, Ramires hit a hopeful ball long towards the Napoli penalty spot. Drogba later recalled that ahead of kick-off he was aware that 'this may be [his] last Champions League game.'[133] Such realisations can often inspire. So far, with Napoli in the ascendency, he had been

---

133 *Kings of Europe – The Chelsea Story*, Sky UK Limited, 16 September 2012.

mainly a peripheral character in the play, but that was about to change.

The diving header that he met the cross with, to power the ball into the net, suggested that the Ivorian was not prepared to give up on his Champions League aspirations just yet. Running back to the halfway line, he whirled his arms round in upsweeping movements, encouraging the crowd along. There was hardly any need as with slightly more than an hour to play, Chelsea now just needed one more goal, accompanied by a clean sheet, and they would be through to the quarter-finals. The fans were acutely aware of the basic mathematics and the noise in the stadium was ratcheted up.

It's said that with London buses, after a long wait for one, often two arrive together, and that old maxim nearly played out with regard to Chelsea goals. A couple of minutes after Drogba's strike, a run and low driven cross from the right flank by Sturridge arrowed towards a waiting Drogba on the far post, but he was denied a tap-in by the outstretched foot of Hugo Campagnaro diverting the ball for a corner. Chelsea had the wind in their sails. With emotions high though, there was a danger of getting washed along by a tidal wave of fervour, in frantic pursuit of that second goal. Drogba had ignited Chelsea's hopes, but from that corner, they were nearly extinguished. A clearance and rapid counter-attack developed into a three on two overload for the visitors and a chance for Cavani on the edge of the penalty area, but he dragged his shot wide.

The game was now open, probably more open than either of the coaches would have preferred, but there was little they could do to prevent the urgent surge of emotion rolling down from the stands drowning out any calls for caution. Sturridge glanced a header wide, Lavezzi had a shot diverted narrowly wide by a blocking defender, and then, following a poorly defended corner, Luiz was found in space, to the right, inside the Napoli area. His shot was dragged across goal but, with two Chelsea players ready to convert, Cannavaro slid in to block and the ball rolled into the welcoming arms of De Sanctis.

Despite all of that feverish activity, there were no further goals at the break. As they had done in every Champions League fixture up to that point, Chelsea had struck the first goal of the game. One, however, wouldn't be enough and, if the first half had been dramatic enough, there was plenty more of the same to come after the players had drawn breath and returned for the second period. If the individual dressing rooms had been full of urgings of restraint and composure, all of that went up in the air inside two minutes of the restart.

Chelsea earned a corner on the right and Lampard floated the ball towards the near post. Drogba ran towards the ball, but it passed over his head, and that of the marker he had attracted to him. As the ball travelled on, Terry advanced into the space left by the striker and glanced a header towards goal that described a perfect parabola, arcing over De Sanctis and dropping into the far corner of the net. 'Bedlam at the Bridge!' bellowed Martin Tyler commentating for Sky. He was right. After slightly less than 47 minutes of the second leg, Chelsea had wiped out the deficit conceded in Naples and were now ahead thanks to the away goal scored by Mata.

Kieran Allen was among the Chelsea supporters that evening at Stamford Bridge and recalled the pulsating feeling around the ground, 'Napoli's fans were so loud that night at the Bridge and Chelsea's situation so desperate but we rose to the occasion and the atmosphere was electric which seemed to inspire both teams to engage in end-to-end combat. Napoli were probably the better team but somehow

Chelsea were 2-0 up soon after half-time.'[134] Calling full time on the game now would have been ideal, but there were still more than 40 minutes to play, and Chelsea's advantage would only last for eight of those.

It would be wrong to say that the goal spurred Napoli into action. They had done most of the attacking up to that point regardless, but now there was an increased urgency in their thrusts. Pressure mounted and Chelsea began to be forced back, with a couple of scrambles being hastily cleared. Given the Serie A club's attacking power it was always likely that they would find a breakthrough, and it came with 35 minutes to play. A cross from the left was met by an uncharacteristically weak header from Terry that dropped towards Gökhan Inler, some 20 yards or so from goal. Quick to bring the ball under his spell with chest control before any defender could close him down, the Switzerland international advanced and, with outstanding technique, struck a low half-volley past Čech, finding the bottom corner of the net.

Now it was the turn of the Napoli fans crammed into one corner of the ground to celebrate, as the remainder of the crowd greeted the goal with stunned silence, before raising voices again to drive the home team on. In contrast to Di Matteo's exuberant joy at the Chelsea goals, Mazzarri was calmness personified in response to Inler's strike, as if he knew the goal was going to happen all along. Waving his hand in a calming motion, he told his players that things were back on track and to concentrate on not conceding again. Chelsea now needed to score at least once in the remaining 35 minutes. The problem, though, was that as they committed to attack, gaps at the back were increasingly

134 Allen, Kieran, interview with the author.

likely to appear, and one more goal from a Napoli break would inevitably be a *coup de grâce*.

For the next few minutes, Chelsea pressed, but the disciplined Napoli back line looked composed, keeping De Sanctis well protected. Just past the hour, Di Matteo sent on Torres for Sturridge. A couple of minutes later, Ivanović hit in a powerful shot from an acute angle that the Napoli goalkeeper was happy to merely parry up and away. A shot on the turn by Drogba was also turned away, but the pressure was building and, driven on by the crowd, Chelsea began to find gaps in the tiring Napoli back line.

There was always that lurking menace of a Napoli goal however, and with time ticking on, the likelihood of any goal for the visitors killing off the game increased with each passing second. On 70 minutes, Zúñiga had a chance but Čech blocked the shot and the ball was cleared. Chelsea's desperation increased and a series of corners from the right brought hope, but nothing tangible.

On 75 minutes, however, one from the other side was far more profitable. From the cross, Ivanović powered in a header that seemed to be deflected away. Amid Chelsea appeals, German referee Dr Felix Brych had spotted that it was the hand of substitute Andrea Dossena blocking the effort and pointed determinedly to the penalty spot. Napoli complaints were more formulaic than convincing and quickly dismissed by the official.

There was little doubt who would take the spot kick. With a calmness belying the situation, Lampard hammered the ball down the middle of the goal as De Sanctis threw himself left, gambling on making a save. The scores were now mirrored across both legs and, unless either team could break the deadlock in the remaining 15 or so minutes, extra time would be required to settle the issue. Perhaps it was emotional exhaustion piled on top of the physical variety, but both teams now seemed spent and, although there was plenty of effort, the 90 minutes was reached without any further goals. It was now extra time with, perhaps, penalties to follow. The 12-yard lottery wouldn't be required, however.

In the first period of 15 minutes, the visitors looked the more threatening in possession, but the first sight of goal came from an Ivanović header meeting a corner from the right and flicking the ball just wide of the far post. The full-back had now offered up several warnings of his attacking prowess; Napoli's failure to take heed of them would prove expensive. The visitors' best effort of the first period was a tired-looking volley from Hamšík that initially looked to be threatening Čech's goal, but drifted away. With only seconds of the first period remaining, Ivanović finally made Napoli pay.

Out on the right, despite being closed down by two defenders, Ramires managed to smuggle the ball past them to Drogba on the flank of the penalty area. Flicking the ball with his heel to deceive the defender, Drogba pivoted and played it into the box. Ivanović had stayed froward from a previous attack and was unmarked as the ball reached him by the penalty spot. Eschewing any thoughts of controlling the cross, he swung his right foot at the ball and it arrowed into the roof of the net.

With a shout that would be echoed a few months later with a sky blue-shirted Argentine's name on his lips, Tyler adroitly defined the moment with a single word. 'Ivanović!' he yelled as the Serb defender's shot hit home. Alongside him, all Gary Neville could offer was a gently soothing 'Ahhh' that would find full-throated orgasmic fulfilment in Catalonia the following month. Lost in his own ecstasy of the moment, Ivanović ran towards the touchline, throwing himself into a celebratory double-knee slide, channelling a nine-year-old on a wedding reception dance floor, before jumping to his feet, thumping the club crest on his shirt in front of the celebrating fans. The Blues were back in the box seat. A few seconds later the break arrived and everyone paused to take stock.

Seb Hutchinson is a freelance sports commentator and has worked on the biggest tournaments and events in the world, including the World Cup, Champions League, the Olympic and Paralympic Games, Rugby World Cup and more. These roles meant that he was often in attendance at some of the biggest games. This was one of them. He recalled, 'This was a roller coaster of a game that could easily have gone either way. But considering the deficit that Chelsea carried going into the contest, it had to be approached in that matter. When you are behind in a knockout cup match, why play with the handbrake on?'[135]

By the break, Di Matteo had replaced Mata with Malouda, and the tiring Terry, playing his first game since the injury lay-off was substituted for Bosingwa, with the resultant shuffle in the back line seeing Ivanović partner Luiz in the centre of defence. Mazzarri responded to the goal with changes of his own. Goran Pandev came on for Hamšík, and Eduardo Vargas replaced the defender Salvatore Aronica. As the players took on much needed liquid, the interval gave both coaches a chance to restate the situation to their players. Napoli still only needed one goal. It had taken them a mere eight minutes to quell Chelsea's ecstasy after Terry's header. The home team now needed to keep the visitors at bay for probably twice as long as that, if Ivanović's goal was to send them forward. The tie was far from settled.

---

135 Hutchinson, Seb, interview with the author.

Seeing a brighter future? When Villas-Boas was dismissed, Di Matteo was appointed to replace him. The change reinvigorated the club's fortunes

Cavani celebrates the goal that puts Napoli 2-1 ahead. Later, a third goal for the Italian club would push Chelsea to the brink of Champions League elimination.

Branislav Ivanović celebrates after putting Chelsea 4-1 ahead in extra time against Napoli.

Di Matteo and Drogba celebrate after eliminating Napoli. The victory resurrected Chelsea's Champions League campaign.

After enduring constant abuse from Benfica fans, Meireles celebrates his winning goal.

Drogba's goal against Barcelona was mishit, but meant so much.

Chelsea in trouble at the Camp Nou, as Terry is rightly dismissed.

Chelsea in deeper trouble at the Camp Nou. Iniesta puts Barcelona 2-0 up against ten-man Chelsea.

Ramires executes a delicate chip over Valdes to throw Chelsea a lifeline in the Camp Nou.

Messi's penalty strikes the crossbar and Chelsea breathe again.

Torres rounds Valdes and scores to send Chelsea to the Champions League Final.

Torres celebrates the goal that gave him instant iconic status among Chelsea fans.

Chelsea are on the brink of defeat, as Müller's header gives Bayern a late lead in Munich.

Drogba's header defeats Neuer to equalise and prove that 'They never die!' (Gary Neville).

Čech saves Robben's extra-time penalty.

Čech's save from Schweinsteiger's shootout penalty set up Drogba's finale.

Drogba's penalty makes it 'The greatest night in the history of Chelsea Football Club – Champions of Europe!' [Martin Tyler]

Roman Abramovich with the Champions League trophy.

Di Matteo celebrates with the Champions League trophy at Chelsea's victory parade.

For the home fans, the second 15 minutes dragged like a man hauling an anvil up a mountain. For the Italian fans, fretting in their corner of Stamford Bridge, they flew with the speed of that same anvil plummeting from the mountain top. A couple of half-chances fell to the visitors with two free kicks causing mild palpitations around the stadium. Now it was Chelsea pulling all their players back to defend, with hardly a thought to attacking. On a rare sally forward Drogba hit a cross-shot wide, but defence was all that mattered. Perhaps the Serie A side had shot their bolt, their attacks gradually diminished and, when a free kick for offside against Cavani was awarded, and Čech cleared upfield, Dr Brych prescribed the medicine that all Chelsea fans had required to quieten fevered heart palpitations, blowing for full time.

Di Matteo ran on to the pitch celebrating with his players, at one stage jumping into the arms of Drogba like some excited schoolboy welcoming home his long-lost father. The elation was matched around the stands of Stamford Bridge, except in the corner where the Napoli fans had watched their team being eliminated. The months of disappointment at below-par performances had been washed away in a single evening. The importance of the night was not lost on Di Matteo, 'It was one of those nights in Chelsea Football Club history that will probably go down as one of the greatest European nights.'[136] Some of the players who had been shunned by André Villas-Boas were the most significant factors in getting the club over the line. It was hardly a low-key event.

There was perhaps even more to it than that though. It was a statement of intent by some of the players who had apparently been the target of the now defunct, unlamented

136 *Kings of Europe – The Chelsea Story*, Sky UK Limited, 16 September 2012.

project, as Danny Ridgeway remembered, 'Drogba was immense, scoring one and assisting Ivanović's winner in extra time as well as forcing a couple of great saves from the Napoli keeper. Without the Drog, Chelsea never would have made it to the final let alone won it!'[137]

It appeared that there was certainly life in the 'old Drog' yet. Abramovich's words that the departing coach had not been the only one at fault had produced the required reaction from a team that looked to be in almost terminal decline. Some would say that if a team can put in such different performances across a gap of a few weeks against the same opponents, does it say as much about the players as it does about the manager? That argument fails to acknowledge, however, that four of the 11 that started the second leg were absent from the team that kicked off in Naples. Terry was injured and unavailable for selection in the first leg, but any similar claim for the absence of Cole hardly stands up to scrutiny, given he played virtually all of the game after being called on to replace Bosingwa. Lampard and Essien had merely been deemed surplus to requirements in Italy.

Terry illustrated the point. 'Everyone was against us. Everyone writ [sic] us off. And everyone came together … And then you look at that Napoli at home, things are meant to be, when myself, Didier and Lamps score, you couldn't have writ [sic] it any better.'[138] Perhaps with the hint of a reference to the now departed former manager, Lampard echoed the sentiment, 'Sometimes, when circumstances change a little bit, you're even more determined.'[139]

---

137 Ridgeway, Danny, interview with the author.

138 *Kings of Europe – The Chelsea Story,* Sky UK Limited, 16 September 2012.

139 *Kings of Europe – The Chelsea Story,* Sky UK Limited, 16 September 2012.

Many of the reports in newspapers recognised the difference between the two performances. This was the new 'old' Chelsea. In the *Daily Mail*, Matt Lawton acknowledged, 'John Terry said this could be one of their greatest nights and so it was, this ageing Chelsea team simply refusing to die, to give up on a dream, on a quest for the ultimate prize.'[140] Writing for *The Guardian*, Daniel Taylor took a similar tack, 'Ultimately this was the night when Chelsea remembered what it is to be a team of serious ambition and from here they should approach the rest of the season with a new zest. At the very least they have restored some pride and dignity to what has been a difficult and sometimes turbulent season.'[141]

Ian Ross's memories echo that sentiment, declaring that the victory was, 'Vital for the club – a magnificent performance. It was typical of a team's reaction to the sacking of a manager they had clearly lost faith in. It was the chance for the "old hands" to show Villas-Boas that his selection and tactics had been wrong – particularly in the 3-1 first-leg defeat. While supporters will always back new arrivals, it is the established – if ageing – stars they love. The 4-1 second-leg win was a form of reuniting of fan and player.'[142]

Perhaps Shaun Custis summed it up best for readers of *The Sun*, 'That Didier Drogba – what a donkey, eh? John Terry? His legs have gone. And, as for Frank Lampard, there has been a space marked "Reserved" for him for months down at the knacker's yard. Well, that was the theory anyway – and it is one the sacked André Villas-Boas had signed up to. But the gang of three were not ready to stand aside this

---

140 'Chelsea 4 Napoli 1 AET (agg 5-4): Old guard march on as veterans seal last-eight spot,' *Daily Mail*, 14 March 2012.

141 'Branislav Ivanović seals dramatic Chelsea win over Napoli', *The Guardian*, 14 March 2012.

142 Ross, Ian, interview with the author.

season. There was still far too much fight left in these proud men who refused to be pensioned off. They proved it as each netted last night on the way to a stunning aggregate success, which was completed when defender Branislav Ivanović slammed home the clincher in extra time. Villas-Boas went about it the wrong way when he tried unceremoniously shunting some of the oldies aside, only to discover that, without them, there was no team. Interim boss Roberto Di Matteo recognised it. Of the side which started last night, only Juan Mata was signed by AVB.'[143]

At home, the game was deemed to be not only as a tonic for Chelsea, but also a boost for the flagging reputation of the Premier League in overcoming a two-goal deficit to a successful Serie A club. In Italy, however, a different slant was taken on the outcome. Alex Frosio, a journalist with *La Gazzetta dello Sport*, explained, 'At the time Napoli was considered – and it was, actually – an inexperienced team at the highest level, never going past the last 16 in the Champions League. So, the match at Stamford Bridge was considered a big chance to "make history" but *La Gazzetta* never considered Napoli favourite to go through, despite winning 3-1 at San Paolo. In fact, after the defeat, the perception was, "Okay Napoli, you tried, thanks anyway!"'[144] The perception was that the club's three front men, their stars – Cavani, Hamšík and Lavezzi, who were known as the 'Three Tenors' – performed poorly. Luigi Garlando, the newspaper's lead writer, reported at the time, 'Drogba, Lampard or Terry are not as good as they used to be, but they still have the voice for a glory night.'[145] It seems that

143 'So the old guard are finished are they?', *The Sun*, 14 March 2012.

144 Frosio, Alex, interview with the author.

145 *Gazzetta dello Sport,* 15 March 2012.

perception is everything, and if disappointment at Napoli's elimination was muted in Italy, English football, and particularly Chelsea, were more than happy to give it full-throated celebration.

Two days later, the draw for both the quarter-finals and semi-finals was made. In the last eight Chelsea would face Benfica, playing the first leg in Lisbon and the return at Stamford Bridge. Should they prevail, they would either face AC Milan or Barcelona, the previous season's champions of Serie A and La Liga respectively. Any pathway to a final in Munich looked bedevilled by huge hurdles. Before the visit to the Portuguese capital on 27 March though, there were domestic issues pending.

On 18 March, Leicester City visited Stamford Bridge for an FA Cup quarter-final. Di Matteo had apparently worked wonders on rejuvenating a team struggling to recover its identity. Following the Leicester game, it looked very much like he had performed a similar trick for a striker who had forgotten where the back of the net was.

After the physical and emotional rigours of the Napoli game, tweaks to the team selection were inevitable for the visit of the Foxes, and Di Matteo rang the changes. Čech was retained but in a re-organised back four, Bosingwa came in on the right with Ivanović – the only survivor from the starting 11 on Wednesday – moving into the centre to partner Cahill and young Ryan Bertrand played on the left. The theme was continued in the midfield. Mata, Mikel and Meireles provided an entirely new unit and, up front, only Sturridge survived with Torres taking up the central striker role and Kalou attacking from the left.

Of course, it was a gamble to change so many players but it may have been a bigger one not to do so. The club now had a solid sense of positive momentum about it, something that had been absent for so long. Perhaps this wasn't Chelsea's first 11, but with the glass now seen as half full rather than half empty, confidence around Stamford Bridge was not in short supply.

It was a similar situation on the pitch as well as Chelsea got off to a positive start against Leicester, dominating the first exchanges and looking threatening whenever going forwards. The opening goal came on 12 minutes. A Mata corner from the right was met by Cahill, who headed down and past Kasper Schmeichel. It was his first goal for the club and a more than decent imitation of the sort of strike the rested Terry would specialise in. In the Leicester goal, Schmeichel's exasperation at his defenders' insipid challenge on the goalscorer was wholly justified as Cahill jogged towards the corner flag, lifting his shirt to reveal a vest adorned with the words 'Pray 4 Muamba'.

A team-mate of the goalscorer when Cahill was with Bolton Wanderers, midfielder Fabrice Muamba had collapsed during an FA Cup game at White Hart Lane the previous evening after suffering a cardiac arrest. Despite his heart stopping for a reported 78 minutes, he did recover, although his footballing career was, understandably, over.

There seemed little problem with the heart shown by the Chelsea players as they scored again just six minutes later. Whatever the words Di Matteo had used to rouse Torres from his apparent goalscoring torpor, they seemed to work. The striker, who had not found the net in 24 appearances spanning 24 hours of playing action since his last goal in the victory over Genk on 19 October, now looked like a player inspired, and it was his searing run down the right flank that created the goal.

So often in the past Torres had failed to deliver at the last moment. A mishit pass or a sliced shot heading towards the corner flag had brought hoots of derision from opposition fans. This day was different though. Outstripping Richie Wellens for pace, Torres tore the visitors' back line asunder, and the Spain forward selected the perfect moment, and the perfect pass, to set Kalou free to slide the ball past Schmeichel to double the lead. If there had been a wave of optimism before kick-off, the team were surfing it on the way to the FA Cup semi-finals, and washing away any Leicester aspirations at the same time.

Torres was clearly enjoying himself, and he nearly added a third when drifting across the edge of the box before firing in a right-footed shot that the overworked Schmeichel was happy to turn away with a diving save. It wasn't all one-way traffic though, as a stumble by Cahill allowed Neil Danns a sight of goal, but Čech's fingertips were enough to guide the ball inches outside of the post. Two goals clear at the break, the game seemed safe with the home team looking far more likely to secure the next goal. Despite plenty of pressure, it didn't arrive until the 68th minute, and although hardly a thing of beauty, for Torres it meant the world.

Meireles ran on to an incisive pass by Sturridge before squaring to Torres standing around the penalty spot. The ball bobbled unkindly as he sought to control with his left foot, but the following shot with his right still had enough pace and direction to find the corner of the net. Sometimes it's said that strikers need a goal, no matter how ugly it is. That couldn't have applied more to the Spaniard, whose smile betrayed as much relief as it did joy. Now apparently free of self-doubt, Torres nearly added another goal, sweeping a shot just over the bar after a run and pass from Sturridge, with Schmeichel flailing forlornly at the ball as it passed him.

Leicester did get a goal when Jermaine Beckford followed up after a shot from Danns cannoned back from the post with a dozen minutes to play, but it looked like a consolation rather than the start of a comeback, and so it was. Eight minutes later, Torres rose at the near post to head home from an acute angle following a Meireles corner. The game was done but not the scoring. A minute later Ben Marshall curled home from 25 yards to make it 4-2. Fittingly, however, it was Torres who had the last word. Cutting in from the left, he drove into the area, drawing defenders towards him before slipping a pass to Meireles – repaying the favour as the Portuguese had offered assists for both of the Spain forward's goals – to net the final strike. In the Napoli game, Chelsea had shown that they had rediscovered their form and identity. Was this game the turning point for Torres? Could he get back to his Liverpool form?

The dramatic fall from being one of the top strikers in Europe to someone who looked bereft of confidence had shocked many. Ian Ross, who had also worked for the *Liverpool Daily Post* and *Liverpool Echo*, recalled, 'The swift decline of Torres absolutely astonished those of us who had regularly watched him deliver world-class performances in the red of Liverpool. Having said that, Liverpool only rarely make mistakes in the transfer market – very few players who leave Liverpool move on to become better players. The only two I can think of are Jimmy Case and Peter Beardsley. Even so, his fall from grace was inexplicable – brilliant one minute, decidedly average the next. Only he will know the reasons behind that.'[146]

146 Ross, Ian , interview with the author.

Writing for *The Guardian* after the game, David Hytner was initially a little less than charitable, quipping, 'The T-shirts are on their way to the printers. "I was there when Fernando Torres scored."'[147] It was understandable though, and with a brace secured and a man of the match award pocketed, perhaps even Torres himself could laugh at the remark. Suitably, a little more elegant in *The Telegraph*, Henry Winter restricted his references to music rather than merchandise, '"Fernando Torres, he scores when he wants," sang the Chelsea fans after 67 minutes, borrowing Arsenal's paean to the prolific Robin van Persie. It had been 25 hours and 40 minutes since Torres last scored, a barren stretch of Kalahari proportions.'[148]

More importantly, Hytner also recognised the importance of the forward's vastly improved form, 'Torres looked transformed and, when he galloped through and skated across the edge of the area, the crowd implored him to shoot. Instead he squared to Meireles, his provider, for the Portuguese to give the scoreline a more accurate reflection of Chelsea's control. Torres had also set up Kalou's goal and if the cynics might point to the Championship opposition – and Championship opposition who had defended particularly badly, at that – he could simply savour a man-of-the-match performance which was gilded by positive numbers. As Chelsea look ahead to defining tests, at home and in Europe, it will feel good to have Torres's confidence bolstered. The club's run goes on. It is four wins in four matches under the caretaker charge of Roberto Di Matteo and John Terry, the captain, who did not play here, banged

---

147 'Fernando Torres ends goal drought as Chelsea ease past Leicester', *The Guardian*, 18 March 2018.

148 'Chelsea's Fernando Torres finally breaks goal drought in FA Cup win over Leicester', *The Telegraph*, 18 March 2018.

the drum for optimism when, with opportunities in the FA Cup and Champions League, he suggested, "It could turn out to be one of our finest seasons ever."'[149]

A quick dose of Di Matteo had seemingly cured all of Chelsea's ills in a couple of weeks, and some were left to wonder if promotion to the top job had always been the real target for the former Chelsea player and, indeed, whether he had done much to engineer the outcome. It was something that he was quick to dismiss. 'Blues legend Di Matteo has overseen a dramatic upturn in the club's form since assuming control after unpopular Villas-Boas was axed by owner Roman Abramovich three weeks ago. But Di Matteo, who was AVB's right-hand man, said, "I did not conspire against him and all the decisions we took, we took together. I have always behaved with the utmost professionalism and loyalty towards the club, the staff, the team and fans."'[150] It seemed to put the matter to bed, at least for a while. Chelsea's turnaround man had other issues to worry about.

With two resounding cup successes in a few days, it was back to the bread and butter of the Premier League now, and the vital, but increasingly difficult, matter of ensuring that the club qualified for the Champions League by finishing in the top four. Chelsea had been down in fifth place since the 2-0 loss to Everton on 11 February, and Premier League points were now vital currency if that key top-four place was to be anything like a realistic hope. The upcoming games away at Manchester City and at home to Tottenham Hotspur would cast that aspiration into serious doubt though, and put a stumble into Chelsea's nascent recovery march.

---

149 'Fernando Torres ends goal drought as Chelsea ease past Leicester', *The Guardian*, 18 March 2018.

150 'Di Matteo: I didn't go behind AVB's back', *Daily Mirror,* 19 March 2012.

Roberto Mancini's team had surprisingly lost at Swansea City in their previous Premier League fixture, and with it the top spot in the league that they had held since beating Aston Villa 4-1 back in October. The defeat in South Wales halted a run of five successive wins and, for Mancini, a win over his fellow former *Azzurri* international team-mate's club was essential. Equally, Di Matteo needed to keep the momentum building and he selected a strong side for the visit to the Etihad Stadium where City had won their previous 19 games in succession.

Ivanović, Cahill, Luiz and Cole provided the back line in front of Čech, with Meireles, Mikel and Lampard in the middle. Mata and Ramires nominally supported the supposedly in-form Torres from the flanks, although for periods of the game, were compelled to drop back into midfield as City pressed.

There were plenty of solidly logical reasons for Di Matteo keeping Torres in the starting 11, not least the possibility of destroying any new-found confidence should he be dropped in favour of Drogba. Psychology to one side though, selecting the physically dominant Ivorian may well have been the better ploy. Both of City's first-choice centre-backs were missing and, filling in for the absentees, Micah Richards and Kolo Touré would have been much more comfortable confronting Torres than Drogba.

Strangely, City were in a run of form that would see them win only one game in five, before then recording six successive wins that would eventually land the title. Unfortunately for Chelsea, that single win was on this day. Things started poorly for the visitors with Ivanović suffering a thigh strain and being replaced by Bosingwa inside the first 20 minutes. For much of the first period the play was disjointed with neither team fashioning many openings, despite City having the majority of possession and hitting the bar.

At the break, Mancini removed Mario Balotelli, who was having one of his less impressive nights, and sent on Gareth Barry. Very little changed in the pattern of play. When Di Matteo made his first change approaching the hour though, as Essien arrived for Meireles, a goal followed quickly, but in a totally unrelated way.

City had already struck the woodwork again, before a Chelsea corner from the right saw the ball fall to Cahill inside the box. His shot took a slight deflection that wrong-footed Joe Hart and Chelsea were in front. Both teams now faced a test – for different reasons. After losing to Swansea, another defeat would seriously dent City's title aspirations. For Chelsea, if they could add another win, any claims that their recovery was a false dawn could be vanquished. Both managers sought to aid their teams. Mancini sent on Carlos Tevez and Edin Džeko for Nigel de Jong and David Silva to spruce up the attack and Di Matteo sent on Drogba for Torres. The Spaniard hadn't played badly and, in flashes, had offered impressive passages of play. When under pressure however, and looking for an 'out ball' to someone who could retain possession and get the team up the field there were few, if any, forwards in the Premier League more suited to the role than Drogba.

Inside the last 15 minutes it looked like Chelsea would hold on for a vital win, but fate would take a cruel twist. With 12 minutes to go, a headed clearance from the Chelsea penalty area fell towards Pablo Zabaleta running into the box from the right. Essien moved to close the full-back down, turning his back as the Argentine shot. The ball struck the Ghanaian's hand and, with the linesman frantically flagging, referee Mike Dean pointed to the spot. The offence was clearly unintentional and the trajectory of Zabaleta's shot would surely have taken it high and wide, but that mattered little and Sergio Agüero coolly slotted home the equaliser from 12 yards.

There would only be one winner now and, eight minutes later, Tevez controlled the ball on the edge of the box before slipping an intricate pass through for Samir Nasri to clip over Čech and secure the win. City's title hunt was back on track. Chelsea's recovery was derailed and their hopes of a top four place were being shunted into the sidings. The next game, at home to Spurs three days later, was now assuming 'must win' proportions if the club was to maintain any kind of grip on a high enough league position to ensure Champions League qualification. The visitors were five points ahead of Chelsea with matches beginning to run out, but there was also an added edge to the game.

The draw for the last four of the FA Cup had been made a week or so earlier, pairing the two London clubs in one semi-final and matching up the Merseyside duo of Liverpool and Everton in the other one. It's questionable whether Chelsea fans considered the league or FA Cup encounters to be the more important. The club would surely have preferred the points rather than a visit to Wembley for a final. Champions League qualification was key to their finances. As things turned out though, months later, despite failing to overcome Spurs in the league game Chelsea would achieve FA Cup glory, and Champions League qualification for the following season, albeit in a way that very few would have predicted, and Tottenham would miss out on playing in the Champions League despite finishing fourth.

The game was scheduled for the Saturday lunchtime kick-off slot, and mixed blessings were on the menu for the Chelsea defence. Terry was back, but Ivanović hadn't recovered from the injury sustained a few days earlier in Manchester and Bosingwa continued to deputise. Essien, Ramires and Lampard looked a combative midfield and Drogba was back in the centre of attack, flanked by Mata and Sturridge. Despite being five points ahead of Chelsea, Spurs hadn't won a league game since 11 February, and with Chelsea's loss to City upsetting their flow, it was hardly surprising that the first period was pretty much guileless – and goalless. Writing for the BBC, Tom Rostance described the first 45 minutes as 'turgid'[151] and few would argue. The best chance came right at the end of the period when Rafael van der Vaart was denied first by Čech, and then Cole after Luka Modrić had created an opening.

The second half did improve a little, at least in terms of chances, with Mata hitting a post and Gareth Bale putting a late header against the bar. In the end, the goalless draw probably suited the visitors more than it did Chelsea. 'It's a step back for finishing in the top four but we have eight games left and we will try to win them all,'[152] Di Matteo later conceded reluctantly.

Three days later, his team would visit Lisbon for the Champions League quarter-final first leg. The growing feeling of renaissance engendered by the cup wins over Napoli and Leicester City had now begun to lose their shine a little after struggling against first Manchester City and then Tottenham with the growing realisation that a fourth-place finish was a distant prospect at best. If anything like an encouraging result was to be gained in Portugal, an upswing in form would be required.

---

151 https://www.bbc.com/sport/football/17412539.

152 https://www.bbc.com/sport/football/17412539.

6

Eagles, Cockerels and Flights of Fancy

BENFICA HAD finished as runners-up to André Villas-Boas's Porto in the 2011/12 Liga ZON Sagres, and would do so again at the end of this season as the man Porto selected to step in when their manager resigned to take charge of Chelsea, Vítor Pereira, retained the title for *Os Dragões*. Despite this domestic success, Porto had faltered in the Champions League, finishing third in a group from which the Cypriot club APOEL and Zenit Saint Petersburg had qualified. With the champions vanquished to the Europa League, it was left for Benfica to carry the flag for Portuguese football.

They had reached the quarter-final stage by topping Group C ahead of Basel with Manchester United in third place. Two victories over Romanian club Oțelul Galați and a commendable win at Basel, coupled with draws in the other games gave them an unbeaten record and a tie with Saint Petersburg in the round of 16, ironically facing the club who had edged out Porto. Playing the first leg in Russia, a goal by Óscar Cardozo with three minutes remaining on the clock looked to have given Benfica a valuable 2-2 draw with the home leg to come. Their hopes were slightly dented though when Roman Shirokov scored an even later goal to edge the Russians ahead.

A couple of weeks later, nearly 50,000 watched at the Estádio da Luz in Lisbon as goals in injury time at the end of the first half, and then the end of the game, by Maxi Pereira and Nélson Oliveira respectively were just in time to ease the Portuguese club into the last eight, where they were to play Chelsea. The first leg was scheduled for 27 March, warm enough on the Iberian peninsula for some Chelsea fans to take advantage of the game's location and add in a few extra days of sunshine away from the grey English skies at the time.

In October of 2020, the author spoke with Luís Mateus, the respected Portuguese journalist, football writer, analyst and pundit, about the two ties, and he offered comments from a Portuguese point of view. As it transpired, it was an opportune moment. Mateus explained, 'The Benfica–Chelsea matches of 2012 came again into discussion just a few weeks ago when Jorge Jesus was again put in charge of the Portuguese giants. In his first period at Benfica, he led the team back to an era of national success with three championships out of six, and he has also achieved two Europa League finals [lost against Chelsea and Sevilla] in consecutive years [2013, 2014]. Jesus has come close to getting Benfica a continental trophy, and the club and coach have now guaranteed that his comeback has international success as his primary objective, mostly in the Champions League. Again, he has failed in his first attempt, ironically in his first match, in the third qualifying round against PAOK. Nevertheless, some pundits defend that, even more than in the EL finals, Jesus came close to winning the Champions League in 2012, in his third season there.'[153]

Despite the recent disappointing league results, whatever happened in Lisbon, Chelsea would still have the prospect of an FA Cup semi-final against Spurs to look forward to in around three weeks' time, and while any thoughts of an unlikely success in the Champions League was still very much the stuff of capricious daydreams, the domestic cup competition offered a realistic hope of silverware after the dismal first part of the season. Mark Worrall was one of those who opted for the extended stay in the Portuguese capital, 'The game in Lisbon was treated as a holiday by an intrepid band of Blues supporters who made a week of it, basking in the sunshine. Expectations and chatter were more related to winning the FA Cup given the semi-final pairing with Tottenham Hotspur. The Champions League was viewed as a wild card. With Robbie at the helm, the fans had "their" Chelsea back and a defeat to Benfica wouldn't have deflated that sense of unity they felt for the Italian to the point of not questioning team selection or tactics.'[154]

It was a reasonable point of view. Arsène Wenger had famously – or infamously, depending on your perspective – declared that finishing in the top four of the Premier League and qualifying for the Champions League was worthy of a trophy. 'The first trophy is to finish in the top four,'[155] he said after his team had lost an FA Cup tie at Sunderland during the previous month. For all the Frenchman's persuasive tones, however, it was perhaps a sentiment that found more empathy in the boardroom than in the stands.

---

153 Mateus, Luís , interview with the author.

154 Worrall, Mark, interview with the author.

155 'Arsène Wenger says Champions League place is a "trophy"', *The Guardian*, 19 February 2012.

Of course, fans want to see their club qualify for European competition but, in the final analysis, that can only be a means to an end, rather than an end in itself. Directors may care more about brass, but for fans, silver is the currency that pays for elation. It was also interesting to note Mark Worrall's comments regarding team selection. After months of Villas-Boas selecting starting 11s that defied the logic of so many fans, Roberto Di Matteo had returned to the tried and trusted, and been duly rewarded, that is until the setbacks against Manchester City and Spurs in the last two league games. When the interim head coach announced the team that would face up to Benfica at the iconic Estádio da Luz however, it looked like Di Matteo had taken a leaf out of the Villas-Boas playbook.

Whether he had been persuaded by a perceived need to send out a team more used to the weather conditions in a southern European spring or merely to refresh the squad, the team selected had a strikingly Iberian identity. In front of Petr Čech, Portuguese full-back Paulo Ferreira was drafted in to guard the right flank. It was his first game since the 3-1 defeat to Aston Villa. The experienced defender had hardly featured on the bench in recent games, let alone started, but now he was thrust into a last-eight game of the Champions League, with Ashley Cole on the opposite flank. In the centre, John Terry was paired with David Luiz, who had played for Benfica for four seasons before signing for the London club.

The midfield comprised Mikel John Obi and two players with experience of the game in Portugal. Along with Luiz, Ramires had also played for Benfica before joining Chelsea, and Portuguese midfielder Raul Meireles had spent six years with Benfica's bitter rivals Porto before joining up with Liverpool. Those years would make him a target for abuse from the Benfica fans across both games, leading to a memorable finale in the second leg. Up front, Salomon Kalou would play alongside the Spanish pairing of Fernando Torres and Juan Mata.

It meant that only Terry of the scorers from the Napoli game would start in Lisbon. Branislav Ivanović was still unavailable while Frank Lampard and Didier Drogba sat on the bench, alongside Ross Turnbull, Gary Cahill, Daniel Sturridge, Michael Essien and José Bosingwa. Despite Iberian inclinations apparently influencing his selection, following the Villas-Boas tactic of leaving out Cole for Bosingwa for such a difficult away leg probably never entered Di Matteo's mind. How difficult? 'Benfica hadn't lost a home game in Europe for two years, I think,'[156] Di Matteo explained. It was also true that they'd only suffered one domestic defeat at the Estádio da Luz all season. Add in the fact that Chelsea hadn't won away in European competition for more than a year, and the enormity of the task was clear.

Benfica fans were confident of success and progress to the semi-finals and beyond. Luís Mateus recalled, 'Chelsea was facing a lot of problems, had changed from an unconfirmed "next Mourinho", André Villas-Boas, to a more pragmatic Roberto Di Matteo, and the team was not that scary, with Lampard, and Drogba already 32/33 years old. Chelsea has also been struggling in the Premier League. So, leaving Manchester United behind in the group phase and getting by Zenit with ease led fans to believe that the team could really get to the final – even if there would be a probable semi-final with Barcelona, Real Madrid or Benfica's nemesis Bayern Munich.'[157]

---

156 *Kings of Europe – The Chelsea Story*, Sky UK Limited, 16 September 2012.

157 Mateus, Luís, interview with the author.

If, however, the radical team changes wrought by Villas-Boas in Naples had produced an incoherent and hugely disjointed display, in Lisbon, the reverse was very much the case, as Daniel Taylor explained, writing in *The Guardian*: 'Here, like then, we had the story of a manager leaving out key names, not afraid to prick a few egos if it meant following his convictions. The difference this time was that there was structure, resilience and not a hint of panic. Napoli had overwhelmed André Villas-Boas sides but Chelsea have already come a long way since Roberto Di Matteo became the latest man to answer to Abramovich.'[158]

As with the Napoli side that tore into Chelsea at the Stadio San Paolo, Benfica was sprinkled with South American attacking talent. Paraguayan striker Óscar Cardozo would feature strongly in both games, as would the Argentine Nicolás Gaitán and the wily skills of his compatriot, Pablo Aimar. Whereas Edinson Cavani and Ezequiel Lavezzi were the spearhead of an attacking Napoli display, the tactics of Benfica seemed much more restrained, but still carried menace.

After a quiet period of play as the teams settled into the game, Benfica began to press. On 18 minutes, the first threat on the visitors' goal appeared when another South American, Brazilian midfielder Bruno César, created an opening for Cardozo. Chasing a through pass, he controlled the ball with his chest inside the box, but the challenge from a recovering Terry was sufficient to ensure the resultant shot failed to trouble Čech. As would be expected from a team with such an outstanding home record, the Portuguese side dominated much of the first half, but this Chelsea team maintained a calm resolution in defence, rarely looking rattled and limited

158 'Salomon Kalou's goal gives Chelsea Champions League win at Benfica', *The Guardian*, 27 March 2012.

many of the Benfica thrusts to long-range efforts that Čech handled with comfort.

Just past the half-hour, it was the Brazilian midfielder César who again offered up a threat. Cutting inside from the right, pursued by Cole, he hit in an effort from 30 yards or so. At such a distance it would take a shot of extreme power and direction to defeat the Chelsea goalkeeper. This shot had neither of those required elements and Čech calmly clutched the ball to his midriff. While many of their efforts were concentrated on studied defence, Chelsea did venture forward briefly when the opportunity presented itself. On occasions, Torres had lurched between effective and inept across the season. This game saw much of him as the former. Collecting the ball as the 40th minute approached, he cut inside the area, but fired narrowly over. His confidence to attack the Benfica back line would pay dividends after the break.

Before half-time however, Meireles, who had been relentlessly taunted by the home fans for his time with Porto, nearly offered the most appropriate of ripostes. Torres played a ball down the left to Kalou, who collected and then fed back to the onrushing Portuguese midfielder. Meireles's shot was struck low and hard, but Artur dived to his left to turn the ball away for a corner. It was the last significant action of the first period, and there was every reason for Di Matteo to be satisfied with his team's performance. They had contained the home team's attacks with a calm assurance that was hardly reflective of their early season performances. A goalless draw would be a valuable result with the home leg to come.

Having what had surely amounted to a vocal injection of urgency from manager Jorge Jesus during the break, Benfica opened the second period with what amounted to their biggest threat of the game inside the first couple of minutes. A long throw from the right caused temporary problems in the Chelsea box and the ball fell invitingly to Cardozo, who fired off a first-time shot. The effort eluded Čech but, having one of those rare games of self-assured calmness, Luiz blocked on the line. The red-shirted players appealed forlornly for handball, but the ball had clearly struck the defender squarely in the chest.

A few minutes later a chance at the other end showed that Chelsea still carried some attacking threat, even if it had been restrained for much of the game. A Torres cross was fractionally too high for Kalou, and the Ivorian could only head tamely over. On the hour the best chance of the game fell to Mata. A long goal kick by Čech was allowed to skip through the Benfica back line, who assumed that Artur would collect unchallenged.

Reading their intent, Mata raced forward from the right and nudged the ball past the advancing goalkeeper on the edge of the area. The movement took him wide to the left though and with the net unguarded, his shot hit the outside of the post and bounced away. By now, fatigue was setting in for both teams and, inevitably, chances resulted. A cross from the left by Gaitán found two Benfica players beyond the far post, but the resulting header was turned away by Čech. It looked like a goal was coming though and with 15 minutes remaining it arrived from what many Chelsea fans would have considered to be an unlikely source.

Energetic as ever, Ramires drove down the right and evaded a challenge before playing the ball on to Torres. Brushing Jardel aside far too easily, he ran into the box, but the angle was tight and Artur advanced to narrow it even more. Dismissing the option of a surely blocked shot, the Spaniard played the ball across the goalmouth instead. The pass evaded the attentions of Luisão and Nemanja Matić, who had arrived from the substitutes' bench a few minutes earlier, to meet up with the run of Kalou, who steered the ball under Artur to give Chelsea the lead. 'Often maligned by fans, Torres and Kalou combining to score the only goal of the game underlined the growing belief that Di Matteo was both an inspired and inspiring coach,'[159] Mark Worrall recalled.

Torres stood from where he had crossed the ball and punched the air in celebration. Despite apparently tweaking a hamstring as he stretched to convert the cross, Kalou smiled through the wince of pain as he limped over to join the Spaniard. Mata unknowingly leaping on Kalou's back could hardly have helped, but at times waves of elation can, at least temporarily, wash away pain. Kalou would soldier on for a further five minutes or so, before being replaced by Sturridge as the game entered its final ten minutes. By this time, the quietly efficient Ferreira had also been replaced by Bosingwa in a move that maintained Chelsea's on-field Portuguese quota. Five minutes before the end, there was a brief glimpse of a potential second Chelsea goal when Mata attempted to chip over Artur after a run and pass by Sturridge, but the ball drifted over the bar, and with it went the last minutes of the game. Against the odds, Chelsea had come away with a 1-0 victory and, on balance, few would say it was undeserved as Di Matteo's team selection and tactics had played out perfectly.

Quoted in the *Daily Telegraph*, the Italian explained his reasoning, 'We've been playing all these games, and they're all high intensity, against City, Spurs and tonight was another. It's just a question of trying to energise the

---

159 Worrall, Mark, interview with the author.

team, freshen up the team. We knew Benfica play at a high tempo so we needed fresh players who could run. That was the reasoning behind it.'[160]

Writing for the *Daily Mail*, Matt Lawton not only hailed the success, but also the bravery of Di Matteo's decisions, 'Roberto Di Matteo's reputation has certainly been enhanced, the decision to omit certain senior players paying off when much the same approach had proved so costly for André Villas-Boas in Naples in the previous round. What happened against Napoli actually made the team selection of the interim manager all the more courageous. Torres ahead of Didier Drogba, Raul Meireles ahead of Lampard, David Luiz ahead of Gary Cahill; even John Mikel Obi ahead of Essien. All big calls, all of which enabled Chelsea to record their first away win in Europe in 13 months.'[161]

Sometimes the word 'bravery' is overused in such circumstances, but it's not beyond the realms of possibility that Di Matteo was risking his newfound promotion with his selection. Ian Ross certainly thought it may have been the case, recalling that, 'It was a latish goal but a wonderful result. I don't believe for one second that Di Matteo expected to get the job on a permanent basis – so, yes, had they fallen at the quarter-final stage I suspect he would have been out of the door. Abramovich is hardly an owner renowned for either his patience or his loyalty. Perhaps [Di Matteo] saw something in Torres which many or most others believed had long gone. Chelsea defended exceptionally well. Any win away from home in Europe is absolutely huge.'[162]

---

160 'Chelsea manager Roberto Di Matteo's risk taking pays off in "terrific" Champions League win against Benfica', *Daily Telegraph*, 27 March 2012.

161 'Benfica 0 Chelsea 1: Advantage Chelsea as Kalou strikes on perfect night for Di Matteo', *Daily Mail*, 27 March 2012.

162 Ross, Ian, interview with the author.

It's an obvious point, but one whose significance is magnified by Chelsea's lack of ability in achieving such victories over the previous year or so. Di Matteo was also aware, however, that the task in hand was far from being completed, as he explained: 'You'll see other players who have played a little less in the past playing more of a role in the future. It's impossible for us to play every three days and reach the fitness levels needed to win games. It's terrific, we couldn't have hoped for a better result. Nothing is over. There is still another 90 minutes to play. But we have home advantage and we are pleased that we're in a different position going into the second leg. We had a mountain to climb against Napoli [following a 3-1 first-leg defeat]. We still have a mountain to climb.'[163]

Those last words would have been grasped with relish in Portugal, where there was belief that the tie was far from done and dusted. Luís Mateus attended the game, and recalled the notes he made for his report, 'Of course, the defeat in Lisbon, in the first match, cooled down the euphoria. I was there in the end at the stadium writing my ideas about the first match, and my conclusions were something like this, "Benfica is not good enough at this level; Chelsea has a lot more solutions in the squad than the Portuguese team." In my article, I also wrote that Emerson had a game to forget, "a nervous night" and he shouldn't have finished it, even if there was not an obvious substitute, because Capdevila was in the stands. He was one of the players to blame in Kalou's goal as he didn't manage to stop Ramires – afterwards Jardel also let Torres escape. But it was just 1-0, and there was a consensus Jesus could pull it off tactically in London.'[164]

---

163 'Benfica 0 Chelsea 1: Advantage Chelsea as Kalou strikes on perfect night for Di Matteo', *Daily Mail*, 27 March 2012.

164 Mateus, Luís, interview with the author.

There was a gap of eight days before Benfica visited Stamford Bridge for the return leg and, before that, Chelsea had a Premier League fixture away to Aston Villa to face. The Birmingham club had inflicted that shattering 3-1 home defeat on the last day of 2011, in a game that may well have served to underscore the futility of any title ambitions Chelsea may have harboured. The game was played on the last day of March, and against the backdrop of Villa captain Stilian Petrov's announcement 24 hours earlier that he had been diagnosed as having leukaemia. The popular Bulgarian would watch the game from the stands as both teams demonstrated their support to him. Chelsea wore T-shirts bearing the words 'Our Thoughts Are With You' during their pre-match warm-ups and Villa's said 'Support Stan'.

After the unexpected selections in Lisbon, the starting 11 at Villa Park seemed very much back to the normal state of affairs. Ivanović was now recovered and assumed his regular place at right-back. Ferreira disappeared back into the shadows, not even making the bench. The other three members of the back line, who had coped so well in Lisbon, were retained. In midfield, Mikel and Lampard were added to Mata, and up front, Kalou and Torres were joined by Sturridge. After losing their last three away league games, and in order to maintain the momentum of the win over Benfica, a good start would be required and it was delivered as Chelsea went ahead after just eight minutes.

Chelsea had already squandered a chance to take the lead after just six minutes, when a through ball from Luiz put Torres in the clear, but he contrived to shoot directly at the goalkeeper and Shay Given saved. Two minutes later, Kalou's cross from the left was short and arrived in the box at around knee height. Marking Torres around the penalty spot, Nathan Baker dived to try and head clear as the forward jabbed out a foot to divert the ball towards Mata closing in from the left edge of the area. Torres got to the ball first though and Baker looked to have collided with the Spaniard's leg and lay on the floor as Mata closed in on goal. Given advanced to block any shot but Mata instead played the ball back across the goalmouth towards Torres. As the forward shot though, Stephen Warnock hurled himself in front of the effort and the ball spilled out to the right where Sturridge was waiting to lash it into the net. The Villa fans hollered their displeasure, claiming that Torres should have been penalised for the collision with Baker. Referee Lee Mason was unmoved though, and replays of the incident suggested that he was correct in being so minded. It was an ideal start, and on the touchline, the broad smile on Di Matteo's face told its own story.

Villa battled hard to get into the game, but with emotions of the day running high, football may not, understandably, have been at the forefront of their minds. Midway through the first period Chelsea nearly doubled the lead but Mata's effort struck a post. The home team's best effort came just ahead of the break. Barry Bannan slid a perceptive pass to Gabby Agbonlahor inside the Chelsea area. Quick control won a yard of space, but his shot was turned on to the crossbar and away by a diving Čech. The single goal remained the only strike of the game as the half-time whistle sounded, but five minutes into the second period, Chelsea struck again.

Cahill had replaced a struggling Luiz at the break and was called into early action. Villa had started the second half strongly, forcing Chelsea on to the back foot but, when they conceded a disputed corner on the Chelsea left, defensive insecurity let them down. The ball was flighted in towards the near post and, as Baker hesitated, the returning Ivanović stabbed the ball home. Di Matteo punched out with both fists. Six minutes later, it looked like he was seeking to lock down the game. Kalou was removed and Ramires sent on to strengthen the midfield. Then, 15 minutes later, Mata was replaced by Malouda. If the Chelsea boss thought that, with only the final quarter-hour to play, the game was done, two goals in a shade over two minutes would harshly disavow him of such hopes.

Villa were pressing, but more with hope than any apparent intent, then, a long throw-in from Eric Lichaj reached the head of James Collins and the rugged defender nodded simply past Čech. It was the sort of set-piece goal that any team can concede, but also the sort of goal that infuriates coaches. The marking in the Chelsea box was poor and duly punished. From the relative comfort of a two-goal lead, the Blues were now under pressure to stay ahead. Their defensive resolve lasted less than three minutes. Marc Albrighton had been sent from the substitutes to replace Chris Herd half a dozen minutes before Collins struck and, with ten minutes to play, he would create the equaliser.

Running down the left flank, he crossed a ball that flew between Čech and the Chelsea back four. The cross was too far out for the goalkeeper to intervene, but too near to the goal for a defender to risk trying to intercept, lest he divert it into his own net. As the ball reached Cole on the far post, he tried to help it on its way, but only delivered an air shot as, outside of him, Lichaj capitalised and smashed home the equaliser. Standing by the Chelsea bench, Di Matteo stood, hands on hips, slowly shaking his head. Those few minutes had almost seemed like a return to the bad old days when, under Villas-Boas, time and again, Chelsea had proved incapable of closing out a game when leading into the late minutes. With ten minutes to play, it would now be a test for his team. Would they wilt under the pressure as Villa now surged forward in search of an unlikely winner, or could they rediscover the composure that had taken them into the lead in the first place?

Within four minutes of the equaliser, he had his answer. Another left-wing corner found Torres's blond locks on the near post and as he flicked the ball on, it collided with the side of Ivanović's head and flew into the net. It may be generous to say that the Serb's reactions were lightning fast, he saw the deflected cross heading towards him and redirected it home, although he clearly seemed to duck into the ball as it arrived. Whatever the case however, Chelsea had the lead again. Now Villa were pressing for an equaliser, rather than a winner, but they would get neither. Two minutes past the regulation 90, the points were secured.

A Villa free kick on the halfway line was hoisted towards the Chelsea box with many of the home players committed to what was surely a last throw of the dice. The ball was headed clear and, suddenly with defenders thrown forward, Chelsea had a three-on-two break. Sturridge sprinted on over the halfway line before playing a perfect pass to Torres, who drove the ball across Given and into the far corner of the net with his first touch. The points were now safe, and Torres had his first league goal since September.

At the end of the game, despite losing those two goals and being pegged back, Di Matteo probably had more to be satisfied with than if his side had successfully closed out the game at 2-0, although he would hardly confess to that. After seeing their lead snatched away, his players had displayed the resilience to go and win the game again, as the *Daily Mail* related, 'Men who had declined to rouse themselves for the previous manager were now toiling urgently for Roberto Di

Matteo, and the manner of their success occasionally evoked faint echoes of the Chelsea of old.'[165]

Chelsea were now just two points behind fourth-placed Spurs, who had a game in hand, and the momentum of the win over Benfica had been reinforced. Writing for *The Observer*, Russell Kempson suggested that, if not maybe completed as yet, the Chelsea revival was under way, 'If they are not yet wholly convincing under the stewardship of Roberto Di Matteo, the interim replacement for André Villas-Boas, they are now resilient instead of fractured. It was Di Matteo's sixth win from eight matches in all competitions since he stepped into the breach. As job interviews go, he is stating his case quite emphatically.'[166] Di Matteo was keeping his feet firmly on the ground. 'I will enjoy this for about an hour,' he said. 'Then we prepare for the next game.'[167] On Wednesday, 4 April, that game would be the second leg of the Champions League quarter-final against Benfica. It would mark the completion of Di Matteo's first month at the helm.

The strong Iberian flavour of the team that had faced Benfica in Lisbon was watered down somewhat for Chelsea's home leg. The same back four that had performed well at Villa Park, save for that panicky three-minute period, remained intact. In midfield, Lampard replaced Meireles to partner Mikel and Ramires, although the Portuguese would enter the fray late in the game and offer an iconic denouement. Mata and Kalou formed the front line along with Torres. There was also the comforting sight of a returning Drogba back on

---

165 'Aston Villa 2 Chelsea 4: Torres ends Premier League drought as Petrov watches on', *Daily Mail*, 31 March 2012.

166 'Stilian Petrov watches as Chelsea beat Aston Villa in six-goal thriller', *The Observer*, 31 March 2012.

167 'Stilian Petrov watches as Chelsea beat Aston Villa in six-goal thriller', *The Observer*, 31 March 2012.

the bench if needed, plus the extended number of substitutes allowed in the competition saw Ferreira materialise again, although his services wouldn't be called upon as Chelsea sought to qualify for the semi-finals of the competition for the sixth time in the last nine seasons.

Ahead of the game, Benfica had a selection issue to resolve. They were missing no fewer than four centre-halves with injuries, including both of the Brazilians, Luisão and Jardel, who had been on duty in the first leg. The former Real Madrid midfielder Javi García, who would leave Benfica for Manchester City at the end of the season, and Emerson were drafted in to cover. Luís Mateus recalled Jesus's dilemma, 'Already without the injured Ezequiel Garay, the plan seemed somehow compromised with the loss of the two centre-backs Luisão and Jardel, which has forced Jesus to change defence and midfield at Stamford Bridge: left-back Emerson – who had an awful first match, as said before – and defensive midfielder Javi García were dragged to the centre of defence, and World Cup winner Joan Capdevila, who never convinced the coach during his loan, had his chance as left-back; Matić, by then an attacking midfielder, was pulled back to the defensive midfield position.'[168] There would be a price to pay for this unavoidable patched-up solution though, as García's understandable lack of experience in his new position would cost the Portuguese club dearly.

After securing an early goal at Villa Park over the weekend, Chelsea started the game as if acutely aware of the dangers of allowing Benfica the luxury of a similar start. Defending deeply, they inadvertently gifted the ascendancy to the visitors, as Benfica began as if determined to wash

168 Mateus, Luís, Interview with the author

away the stain of the home defeat a week earlier. In midfield, as Chelsea sat back, Aimar was granted the sort of time and space on the ball that should always be denied to players of his ability. The statistics would later indicate that across the game, the visitors enjoyed 60 per cent of the possession, and it certainly felt that way in the early stages. There was little cohesive play from either side but, in such games, tension tends to paper over any cracks in the quality of play. Terry, at one point, was even drawn into berating his team-mates to push further forward and, as Benfica continued to be the better side, it was such a forward run by Cole that brought the first goal.

Sprinting to get on to the end of a lofted pass, Cole quickly got on to the wrong side of the stand-in centre-half as García belatedly recognised the danger posed. Racing to recover, he barged into Cole, sending the full-back sprawling to the turf. 'So many changes had of course some costs, with Javi García fouling Ashley Cole in the penalty area to give Chelsea the lead,'[169] as Luís Mateus acknowledged. Slovenian referee Damir Skomina had no doubts, and pointed to the penalty spot.

The regulation protests required at such times drew a yellow card for skipper Maxi Pereira. Although somewhat peripheral to the events of the moment, the full consequences of the sanction would be revealed five minutes before the end of the half. Lampard stepped up to take the spot kick and fired low to Artur's right-hand corner. The goalkeeper was unlucky to be beaten and got a solid hand on the ball as it went below his dive and into the net. It was all smiles on the Chelsea bench as Di Matteo clenched both fists in front of him. At 2-0 with that away goal already banked, if

---

169 Mateus, Luís, interview with the author

not clear and comfortable, Chelsea looked to at least be in a commanding position in the tie.

Benfica sought to fire straight back, and a sublime rehearsed move nearly brought an instant equaliser. From a free kick midway inside the Chelsea half, Aimar lofted a cross towards the far post. Instead of heading for goal, the ball was nodded back across the box and then headed down towards Cardozo in space by the penalty spot. With defenders drawn towards the brief period of head tennis around the goalmouth, the Paraguayan had lost his marker and met the ball with a crisp volley that had Čech beaten, but Terry cleared from the line. With half-time approaching the game swung further in Chelsea's favour.

Pursuing a poorly controlled ball as he tried to drive his team forward, Pereira slid, studs up, into Mikel bringing the midfielder crashing to the ground in pain. The grimace on the Benfica captain's face matched that of Mikel as he realised the consequences that would inevitably follow. The challenge had hardly carried much malice but the contact on the Nigerian's shin was both clear and condemning. Pereira stood in grim silence as the referee first produced a second yellow, followed by a red. Reluctantly he accepted his fate and trudged from the pitch as the Chelsea fans cheered the decision. Luís Mateus recalled how the Portuguese coach was forced into another adjustment, 'Jesus needed to improvise again, giving centre midfielder Witsel the right-back role.'[170] Two goals up and now facing a depleted ten-man Benfica, the semi-finals were beckoning. Around the stadium, the half-time conversations centred on who Chelsea would be playing in the final four.

---

170 Mateus, Luís, interview with the author.

That issue had been settled the previous evening, when a brace of first-half penalties by Leo Messi and a goal from Andrés Iniesta early in the second period overwhelmed a Milan side who only had a single goal from Antonio Nocerino to offer in reply. The first leg in the San Siro had finished goalless meaning that, should Chelsea see out the game against Benfica without any mishaps, they would face the onerous task of playing Pep Guardiola's all-conquering *Blaugrana* team.

Over the previous few years, the Catalans had been collecting silverware with the zeal of a magpie on heat. Three successive La Liga titles were matched by their success in the Supercopa de España to underline a domestic dominance. If anything, their record in continental and global encounters was even better. Two Champions League wins – both against Manchester United, 2-0 in Rome in 2008/09 and 3-1 at Wembley in 2010/11 – added to a brace of UEFA Super Cups and the same number of FIFA Club World Cup triumphs suggested that, at that time, Barcelona were probably the best club side on the planet. For Chelsea, getting to the Champions League semi-final, especially given their early-season form, would surely represent success by any reasonable measure, but aspirations of progressing past Barcelona looked fanciful at best, outrageously optimistic at worst.

On the same evening that Barcelona had booked their place in the last four, Bayern Munich were matching the achievement, beating Marseille 2-0 in the Allianz Arena to complete a comfortable 4-0 aggregate scoreline. The Bavarian club looked highly likely to be facing Real Madrid. At the same time as Chelsea faced Benfica, *Los Blancos* were easing their way through what was little more than a leisurely stroll against the Cypriot club APOEL in the Estadio Santiago Bernabéu. A 3-0 victory in the away leg had rendered the return in Madrid of interest to statisticians alone. While Chelsea fans, at half-time in London, were contemplating the prospect of facing Barcelona, Real Madrid had added a further two goals to their lead and would coast to a 5-2 win, completing an 8-2 aggregate victory.

It all meant that the two semi-finals looked like being Chelsea playing Barcelona, and Bayern Munich facing Real Madrid. Three of the four represented the aristocracy of European club football. Barcelona were reigning European champions and widely regarded as the best club side in the world. Mourinho's Madrid would later take the La Liga title back to the Spanish capital, and had won the continent's top club title no fewer than nine times. Bayern had established themselves as the dominant force in Germany and had been champions of Europe on four previous occasions. Likely to join them were Di Matteo's Chelsea, who had reached the semi-finals of the FA Cup, but stood in fifth place in the Premier League and struggling to rise above that. The club's only European successes had been two Cup Winners' Cup triumphs back in 1970/71 and 1997/98. For any Chelsea fans, it was probably best not to think too much about the possibilities of the future. The game against Benfica remained to be completed and, before the end, the ten men of the Portuguese club would put any and all thoughts of glamorous games against Barcelona in peril.

The first significant act of the second period should have been a warning that the tie was far from settled. Although leading 2-0 on aggregate, a goal for Benfica would have meant that they would then be just a single strike from eliminating Chelsea, and the first step along that road so nearly came just two minutes after the restart. Clever interplay on the edge of the Chelsea box ended with Cardozo clipping a shot towards the top corner of the goal, but Čech went full length to claw it behind. Chelsea only half-cleared the resultant corner and Aimar underscored the visitors' threat by rattling a powerful shot into the side netting.

Two minutes later, with the Portuguese voices still raised in song after their early encouragement, Chelsea should have secured the win. An overhit cross from the right found Kalou beyond the far post. Jinking first right, then left, he closed in on Artur before playing the ball low across the gaping goalmouth. Running in from the right, Ramires had a simple tap-in from less than a yard out. It should have been game over, but the Brazilian somehow contrived to get his foot ahead of the ball, and it struck his ankle and bounced away. 'Oh, how did he miss?' questioned Clive Tyldesley commentating for ITV. 'Literally, all he has to do is make any sort of contact and it goes in,' replied Andy Townsend sitting alongside Tyldesley. The replays suggested the former Chelsea player's assessment was awry, however. Ramires did contact the ball, but the effect was to divert it away from the net, rather than in. Ramires ended up in the back of the net, but the ball was hacked clear into the crowd. A goal then would have negated what would become a fraught final five minutes.

After those two near misses, the game settled into a pattern; Chelsea pressed but still with caution. Conscious of the potential peril should they concede on a break, composure was key, and vigilance to the fore. For the visitors it was a case of having fewer attacks but seeking to make them as effective as possible. From one of Chelsea's forward thrusts, Torres had possession on the edge of the box. A neat turn opened up space but Emerson got the slightest of deflections on the shot, barely enough to turn it inches wide of the post with Artur beaten. Benfica were walking a tightrope between trying to score and knowing that a further goal conceded would be terminal.

Approaching the hour, another chance fell to Chelsea. Mata skipped away from Axel Witsel, now moved from his normal midfield berth into a full-back role to cover for the dismissed Pereira. After exchanging short passes with Torres, the diminutive Spaniard had wriggled clear of the Benfica back line and stuck his shot powerfully. Artur had seen the danger though and advanced to cut down the angle, forcing the shot to go high. He dived to parry away and Torres just failed with an acrobatic attempt to turn the ball home.

Even before play restarted, Jorge Jesus made the surprising decision to remove Cardozo and send on the young forward Nélson Oliveira. Across both legs, the Paraguayan had been the main danger for the Portuguese and unless the striker had a less than obvious injury, it seemed a perverse decision, especially as the replacement had a mere ten minutes of Champions League experience. That Cardozo walked slowly to the back of the rows of Benfica coaches and slumped down without receiving any medical attention suggested the move had been tactical.

A couple of minutes later, injury or fatigue was clearly the issue when Terry was replaced by Cahill, before the Benfica coach doubled down on mystifying changes by removing the dangerous Argentine Gaitán for another young player in Yannick Djaló. It marked a change in formation as well, as Jesus gambled by going with three at the back in search of a goal that would give his team a foothold in the game.

By now, Chelsea had resorted to almost playing in second gear and, on the break following another Benfica attack that broke down on the blue wall of the home defence, Mata fed Kalou in space inside the visitors' area, but his effort was tame and Artur parried it away. With 20 minutes to play it was Mata firing across goal and wide of the far post from a similar position. Scoring didn't seem to be of massive importance to Chelsea. As things lay, Benfica still needed two goals and their attacks were beginning to lose purpose and belief as fatigue inevitably set in. César was the next player removed by Jesus for former Bolton Wanderers player Rodrigo.

Approaching the last ten minutes, Di Matteo signalled his intentions. The creative Mata was removed for the more solid and hard-working Meireles, and the change provoked the inevitable chorus of whistles and boos from the Benfica fans. Each time he touched the ball, the catcalls would rise again, perhaps fed as much by frustration at their team's failure to score as anything else. At least it gave them something, or more accurately someone, to vent their ire at. Then, with a mere five minutes to play and with dreams draining away like sand through fingers, suddenly their hopes were given a fresh and unexpected renaissance. A header from Djaló had Čech stretching towards his far post to tip the ball away for a corner. The goalkeeper climbed to his feet, bellowing at his defenders to maintain concentration, insisting that the job wasn't done yet.

It certainly wasn't. From the resultant corner and with barely a Chelsea player moving, García was allowed to stroll towards the near post, leap and flick the ball home. The goal, that by this time looked like it was never going to happen, had now arrived, dropped like a rock into a shallow pool. The ripples of concern were suddenly washing all over Stamford Bridge. With six minutes to play, Chelsea stood on the edge of elimination. Another goal conceded, with precious little time left, would be a killer blow. Chelsea fans sank into subdued concern as Portuguese voices were raised in expectation.

The pressure was on now. Oliveira had a chance but his inexperience probably let him down as Di Matteo sent on Drogba, now recovered from the toe injury received in training, to replace Torres. With balls likely to be loaded into the Chelsea box, the physicality of Drogba could be key in defence, and perhaps to hold the ball further upfield when clearances could be played towards him. Minutes passed slowly, and the team that had ten tired men a mere minute ago now looked to have a dozen, all full of running, as Chelsea sank further and further back to protect what was now the slimmest of threads from which their Champions League aspirations were hanging.

Finally, the Chelsea fans found their voices in support of their team as the seconds ticked away. Past the regulation time, an extra four minutes were added on. The first of those was drifting away when Drogba tangled with García competing for a high ball, but was penalised by Skomina. A free kick partway into the Chelsea half meant a chance to load the area for Benfica. It was a 'Last Chance Saloon' moment, and Benfica were thirsty for glory. Aimar stood over the ball before flighting it towards a crowded Chelsea penalty area.

Unforgivably, the ball was short, and Mikel stooped to head away, but the ball was running back towards the taker as Meireles pursued it. As the Argentine slightly ducked to head the ball away from Meireles, the Portuguese jabbed out a foot and flicked it past Aimar into what seemed to be acres of clear grass. In such situations, many referees may well have punished Meireles for a high foot, but the Slovenian official merely swept both of his arms forward, indicating that play should continue.

Meireles needed no second bidding. On he went for 40, 50, 60 yards. Emerson was the only player between him and

Artur as Ramires loomed up alongside with his searing pace and distracted the defender. A pass may well have been the better option, but Meireles only looked ahead. Reaching the edge of the area, he crashed the ball high into the roof of the net to decide the game, before peeling off to offer a wave to the Benfica fans who had taunted him mercilessly across both legs. It was the sweetest of ripostes.

Seb Hutchinson recalled the emotion of the moment, 'I was at this game, and when Meireles scored his goal, the pressure balloon popped for the first time in the knockout stages of the competition. Chelsea felt relatively comfortable.'[171] The joy of celebration for the Chelsea fans was certainly mixed with relief at the drama of the denouement. Mark Worrall was also at the game and the combination of the importance of the goal, the way it was scored and that it was Meireles delivering the *coup de grâce* was iconic. If the fans needed some kind of line drawn in the sand to show that page had been turned, this was it. Worrall said, 'There was something filmic about substitute Meireles's goal. The fact that, with his Mohican haircut he looked like the Travis Bickle character in *Taxi Driver*, added menace to the midfielder's persona and, when he swung his boot high to bring down Mikel's headed clearance and made a swashbuckling run from inside the Chelsea half before unleashing a ferocious volley at the Benfica goal, there was only going to be one outcome. It was an absolute belter of a strike and embodied how fearless the Blues had become since AVB's sacking and the change of management and philosophy.'[172]

---

171 Hutchinson, Seb, interview with the author.

172 Worrall, Mark, interview with the author.

Worrall's delight had its counterpoint in the disappointment and sad acceptance of Luís Mateus and Benfica fans, as the journalist recalled, 'Ironically again, it was former FC Porto player Raul Meireles who confirmed Chelsea's qualification. It has been seen by Benfica's fans as a kind of karma. The first leg's defeat, the forced changes made for the second match and its consequences – Javi García's error in the penalty – and Maxi Pereira's individual mistake with the red card have cut the Eagles' wings in the quarter-finals. Murphy's law says it can always get worse, and that was what has happened with Meireles's goal. FC Porto is Benfica's biggest rival. The Italian approach by Di Matteo has paid off in the end, but Benfica made a good second half, getting the equaliser near the end (with Javi García redeeming himself), and forcing Petr Čech into some nice saves, including one that denied Oscar Cardozo's shot aiming [at] the top corner – Kalou had some chances for the Blues too, exposing Witsel's speed and lack of positional awareness. There was also a late, almost miraculous, chance which could give Benfica the second goal, but the youngster Nélson Oliveira unfortunately tried a curve ball when he had Yannick unmarked just beside him to score.'[173]

The fans burst into song and the remaining time ebbed away. Chelsea had reached the last four of the Champions League again. Di Matteo had delivered so much progress in his first 31 days in charge at Stamford Bridge. The club may have been facing a near impossible mission to get past the reigning European and world champions, if they were to deliver on the dream of a return to the Champions League Final, but that was for another day. It had been a nervous ending but progress to the semi-finals was all that mattered.

---

173 Mateus, Luís, interview with the author.

'In knockout football,' Ian Ross underscored, 'winning is all that matters. This game was nervy and it was close. Indeed, Benfica showed their true self at Stamford Bridge and did actually look capable of overturning the first-leg deficit. It was some way from being Chelsea's best performance of the campaign but they did enough – just.'[174]

Three days later, Chelsea would have a Premier League fixture at home to Wigan Athletic, followed by an away game at Fulham. The Easter fixture list is always a busy time in English football. After that, they would face Tottenham Hotspur in the FA Cup semi-final at Wembley on 15 April before entertaining Barcelona three days after that. It was a hectic schedule, but that was only because Chelsea had stayed in contention for trophies and, given the situation the club was in precisely 31 days earlier, that was no mean feat.

Unsurprisingly, when Wigan arrived at Stamford Bridge, Di Matteo selected a team that reflected both the exertions of the Benfica game and the crowded schedule across the next ten days or so. Such decisions always require the delicate poise and balance of a tightrope walker. Plough on with tired minds and legs and the cost can be both immediate, losing the game, and carry longer-term consequences, with player fatigue and the increased potential for injuries. Make too many changes though, and the momentum of victory can easily be squandered by a below-par performance and poor result.

Ivanović, Luiz, Cahill and Ryan Bertrand formed the line in front of Čech. It's questionable whether he would have been selected anyway, but Terry was unavailable through injury. What had been seen initially as a means to inject fresh

---

174 Ross, Ian, interview with the author.

legs into a tiring defence when he was substituted against Benfica on Wednesday turned out to be caused by the skipper having difficulty in breathing due to cracked ribs. Bertrand's selection was also compelling with Cole unfit.

In the middle of the field, Essien was promoted from the bench to play alongside Mata and Meireles – the hero of Wednesday night receiving a particularly raucous cheer from the home fans when his name was read out over the public address system ahead of the game. Lampard was absent with a thigh injury. Malouda and Sturridge had the flanks and a fully fit Drogba led the line.

Despite the changes, the course of the game would emphasise the difference in character – if not the characters – between the Chelsea team under Di Matteo, and the one that had laboured and struggled, often in vain under Villas-Boas.

The visitors were in the early days of an impressive run of form. A disappointing home defeat to Swansea on the day before Villas-Boas had been dismissed sparked a run that would include just two defeats across 11 games to the end of the season, and see them climb from the foot of the table to the relative comfort of 15th position. Successive victories, away to Liverpool and then home to Stoke City, made manager Roberto Martinez's selection of an unchanged starting 11 an entirely logical decision.

The game began with Chelsea pressing eagerly, but without any tangible reward. The nearest they came to opening the scoring in the early part of the first half came after Cahill fired in a shot from 30 yards or so that forced Ali Al-Habsi into a flying save to pluck the ball from the top corner of the goal. Wigan were anything but compliant victims, however, and Victor Moses offered threats cutting in from the flank to shoot, or play crosses into dangerous situations. His direct attacking style gave the young Bertrand an uncomfortable time.

Ten minutes ahead of the break, Chelsea should have been in front. A pass by Drogba put Mata into a good position. The Spaniard cut inside his defender before shooting but was denied by Al-Habsi's parry. The ball dropped to Drogba who headed for goal, but Maynor Figueroa cleared from the line. At the break the game was still goalless. Chelsea had seen plenty of possession but their performance had been stodgy and far from incisive. There may have been emotional fatigue at play, and certainly a revitalised Wigan team were well worth being on level terms, but for a team supposedly fighting for every point in pursuit of a top-four finish, the first 45 minutes had been disappointing.

The first threat of the second period came from the visitors. On the opposite flank to Moses, Jean Beausejour had also been threatening, and his cross was met by a charging run by Emmerson Boyce, but the header flew comfortably wide of goal. Ten minutes in, Chelsea began to apply a little more concerted pressure. A Mata chip to Drogba and a left-footed shot from the striker brought another save from Al-Habsi and then a slip from Sturridge on the edge of the box meant that his shot from a dangerous position flew high and wide.

With the home team pressing but looking like the very definition of a blunt instrument, there were repeated calls from the crowd for Torres to be introduced, a situation that Brian Glanville, writing for the *Sunday Times*, found worthy of mention, 'If for nothing else – and indeed there was little else – the game was memorable for the reception given to the once derided Fernando Torres. Believe it or not, and you would never have done just a few weeks ago, the crowd was roaring in chorus for the Spaniard before he arrived as a substitute after 59 minutes.'[175] Rather than replace Drogba though, as would have been the expected call, it was Malouda who was hauled off, allowing the Ivorian and Spaniard to form a partnership that should, by all reckoning of form over the previous few seasons, have been the most potent of pairings but, in reality, had been the flattest of disappointments. A few seconds later, Chelsea scored. Suffice to say that neither striker was involved.

Chelsea had been awarded a free kick for a challenge on Ivanović. Mata floated the ball into the area, but the cross was headed clear. Collecting the clearance, Meireles chose to deliver the ball back into the area. It found an isolated Ivanović, who scored. Immediately, if only for the space that the Serb found himself in, it looked offside, and replays confirmed that to be the case. Guided by the advice of his linesman Dave Bryan however, referee Mike Jones awarded the goal despite the frantic protestations of the enraged Wigan players.

Fired with apparent righteous indignation, Wigan sought an immediate riposte and Moses again threatened. Driving into the box, his attempt to go round Čech failed as the goalkeeper blocked. On hand though was former Chelsea player Franco Di Santo, who fired the rebounding ball on target, but Ivanović frustrated the visitors once more as he cleared from the line. Entering the last 20 minutes, with Chelsea apparently flagging and under pressure, Martinez gambled, sending on Mohamed Diame, who had returned to the bench after missing two games with a groin injury, and Ben Watson.

Pressing forwards was always going to increase the danger of conceding a second goal and Chelsea twice came

175 'Chelsea 2 Wigan 1: Mata lifts the Blues', *Sunday Times*, 8 April 2012.

near to sewing the game up. Drogba rose to head on a long ball from Čech and found Mata on the edge of the visitors' box, but his hurried effort was high and wide. Next, it was Sturridge who benefited from a Drogba assist but, from a tight angle, his effort was also wide of Al-Habsi's goal. Di Matteo looked to strengthen his midfield by sending on some fresh legs with 15 minutes to go. On came Mikel for Essien, with just seven minutes to play, then Chelsea conceded the equaliser. Twenty yards from goal, Diame collected a pass, turned and hit a ferocious shot that Čech watched fly past him and into the net.

Back in December, Chelsea had endured a similar setback when playing the reverse fixture at the DW Stadium. Leading from a Sturridge goal on the hour, they had conceded a late equaliser and squandered two valuable points with the sort of performance and result that had inexorably gnawed away at the diminishing belief in Villas-Boas. Now, faced with a comparable position, had anything really changed between the Chelsea of then and now?

Now it was Di Matteo's turn to gamble. A draw would be of little use in that increasingly forlorn pursuit of fourth place, and a loss would hardly make the position any worse. Kalou was sent on to replace Sturridge and the change almost brought immediate dividends. Torres crossed but, in space, Kalou failed the composure test and shanked his shot horribly wide.

It looked like the last throw of the dice with the points surely likely to be shared as the game entered injury time, and yet, the Blues were now looking as threatening as they had throughout the entire game, with the visitors forced on to the back foot. Was there still a chance of redemption? Three minutes into injury time, Drogba hit a cross towards the far post and, when Torres's shot struck the woodwork with Al-Habsi struggling, Mata was on hand to bundle the ball over the line with his knee. There was some doubt as to whether the Spaniard was offside when Torres had hit his shot. It certainly wasn't as clear-cut a case as when Ivanović had scored, but there was sufficient doubt about it to add to Wigan's frustration. Soon afterwards, Torres squandered a chance to give the scoreline a most unrealistic look, but Chelsea happily settled for a 2-1 win and the three points.

While Martinez and Wigan returned home feeling ill-served by the officials, Chelsea fans could console themselves not only with the three points but also the fact that the team, even when hardly playing well, and after being dragged back to parity in the dying minutes of the game, still got the job done. Few were aware at the time, but that dogged refusal to accept what seemed to be an inevitable fate. would be the club's most valuable asset as their season, and particularly their Champions League campaign, was played out.

There was one more league fixture to be played before Chelsea faced three semi-final games – first in the FA Cup against Tottenham Hotspur and then the two Champions League legs against Barcelona – in four games across nine days, with a visit to Arsenal in the Premier League thrown in for good measure. On 9 April they would make the short journey to Craven Cottage and an away game against Fulham.

Earlier that same day, Chelsea received an unexpected boost to their Premier League aspirations when Norwich City visited White Hart Lane and left with a 2-1 victory. The loss for Spurs meant they had only won once in their last eight league games. It was the sort of form that Chelsea had been experiencing earlier in the season. Perhaps the door was opening for the Stamford Bridge club to claim that all-important fourth place, but there was also competition for that coveted spot from Newcastle United, who were now only trailing Spurs on goal difference. A win at Craven Cottage would not only increase the pressure on Harry Redknapp's team in the league, but also put down a marker for the upcoming FA Cup semi-final the following weekend. In a frustrating game, however, Chelsea would not only fail to exploit the opportunity opened up by Norwich's victory but also demonstrate that, despite the battling win over Wigan, they looked a distance from being capable of offering much resistance to a Barcelona team set on a return to the Champions League Final.

Di Matteo had made six changes from the team that had scrambled over the line against Wigan a few days earlier. Terry was back, despite carrying heavy strapping around his damaged rib area, and Lampard also returned to the starting line-up after recovering from his thigh injury. Mata was dropped to the bench, but that was probably more to do with the games coming up than any comment on his recent performances. Torres led the line.

In a worrying echo of the Wigan game, Chelsea held a lead inside the final ten minutes but then conceded a poor goal. A Lampard penalty on the stroke of half-time was controversial enough to suggest the fates were smiling on the visitors. For much of the first period, it had been Fulham dictating the pace of the game and looking far and away the more likely to score. Going in at the break with the lead was, therefore, just the sort of boost to convince Di Matteo's team that the three points were within their grasp, if they could raise their game. As Andrew Dillon wrote for *The Sun*, however, 'Chelsea were eventually lucky to get out of their neighbours' house with a point, such was the pummelling they took in the final stages of a match which slowly got into gear after Lampard tucked away his spot kick.'[176] With eight minutes to play, Clint Dempsey headed the equaliser from a set piece. There was no late goal for Chelsea and three points were reduced to one.

The result, and more particularly the performance, cast the victory against Wigan in an entirely different light to that in which many Chelsea fans had chosen to see it. Instead of demonstrating that important ability to win games when not playing well, it suggested something far less positive. When taken together, the two games now simply looked like a couple of poor performances, with a fortunate last-minute goal against Wigan merely the sort of momentary distraction that can temporarily paper over the cracks that were running deep throughout the club's recent performances. It was a point highlighted by Henry Winter in *The Times*, 'Once again, Chelsea had conceded a goal in the final ten minutes of a game, the fifth time in the last four outings and their 20th this season. Fitness? Concentration? "It's been a pattern this season, conceding late goals," said their interim head coach Roberto Di Matteo.'[177] It certainly had, and Chelsea were heading into the most significant ten days of their season so far with that cloud of anxiety and doubt, once thought to have been banished for good by Di Matteo, now gathering strength again above them.

Being involved in the semi-finals of two competitions in the space of three days is a demanding enough scenario. To do so when the outcome of those few days is likely to shape the destiny of the entire season only adds to the pressure. Chelsea were still two points adrift of Tottenham Hotspur, despite Spurs' slump in form, with games running out and

---

176 'Fulham 1 Chelsea 1', *The Sun*, 9 April 2012.

177 'Chelsea's hopes are dented by Clint Dempsey leveller as Fulham claim 1-1 draw at Craven Cottage', *The Times*, 10 April 2012.

facing a more challenging run-in than the White Hart Lane club had to negotiate. Add in the unwelcome ingredient of a resurgent Newcastle elbowing their way into the fight for fourth spot, and qualification for European football's premier club tournament through the Premier League placing was becoming more and more of a distant dream with each game played – and each point surrendered.

The cup competitions offered an alternative pathway to European football. Win the FA Cup and a place in the Europa League – taking over from the UEFA Cup in 2009/10 and including a merger of the Intertoto Cup – could be gained. With an owner as ambitious as Abramovich, however, that would inevitably be deemed a poor consolation.

The alternative was to win the Champions League and qualify as holders for the following season, but with form fluctuating between lucky and poor, that seemed akin to discovering perpetual motion, finding the secret of the Alchemist's Stone or perhaps even solving that most perplexing of issues, the age-old quandary of why no England manager could ever truly unite the talents of Gerrard and Lampard.

Given Di Matteo had been handed the poisoned chalice of taking over from Villas-Boas with the club apparently locked into a downward spiral, perhaps delivering the FA Cup and reaching the last four of the Champions League, despite finishing outside of the top four in the Premier League, was a reasonable enough achievement. The problem was, of course, that 'reasonable' was hardly a word often heard around the chambers of Chelsea's inner sanctum.

For all that, the first task was to play the semi-final of the FA Cup at Wembley on Sunday, 15 April against Tottenham Hotspur. The teams appeared to be fairly evenly matched. Spurs were slightly ahead in the league, but across history, when the clubs had met in FA Cup ties, victories had been split precisely 50/50. One way or the other though, the balance of that record would have shifted by the end of the game. With extra time and penalties to be used if required, no replay would be possible.

At the time, Harry Redknapp was widely reported as being courted by the FA for the post of England manager. Such press musings turned out to be well wide of the mark afterwards but, had there been merit in them, the White Hart Lane boss, may well have been inclined to offer a curt reply after referee Martin Atkinson was widely criticised for making a controversial decision in the game. Despite the outcome, Chelsea would also come away with major concerns.

Di Matteo had selected a team that looked solid, rather than bursting with expansive potential. With Ivanović suspended, Bosingwa was slotted into the back four, alongside Terry, Luiz and Cole. With Gareth Bale and Aaron Lennon offering plenty of width for Spurs, the full-backs looked destined for a busy time. Mikel and Ramires provided the solidity in midfield with Lampard alongside them. Further forwards, Mata and Kalou had the flanks with Drogba leading the line. So often a big-game player, the Wembley turf seemed to have an irresistible appeal for Drogba. He had already scored seven times there, more than at any other stadium – excluding Stamford Bridge. The striker's star would shine bright again on that early evening in April. In the opposite goal, hoping to foil his old team-mate, was former Chelsea hero Carlo Cudicini.

After the inevitable tentative early period of the game, as both sides settled into a type of shadow boxing, offering little real threat and concentrating on not conceding, the initiative seemed to be with Spurs. Before that though, a long high ball saw Drogba chase into the area, but his attempt at a spectacular left-footed volley only brought a mis-hit effort that bobbled gently towards Cudicini. Then, following a Spurs corner, a mis-hit back-pass by Kyle Walker set Kalou sprinting forward on a break, but it came to naught as Mata failed to collect the final pass. As the half drew on though, a couple of opportunities may have brought tangible reward.

Spurs began to press with Adebayor's pace threatening and, from a cross, Terry blocked Rafael van der Vaart's header on the line, when the Dutchman should surely have scored from just a few yards out. Then, the same player arrowed a through ball towards Emmanuel Adebayor in full stride, as the Spurs forward entered the area. Compelled to try and react to any contact, Čech was motionless as the ball evaded Adebayor's foot but bounced clear off the post. On another day Spurs could have been two goals clear but, with nothing to show on the scoreboard, they would pay the price.

Lampard hit a long ball towards Drogba, who was closely policed by William Gallas. The French former Chelsea defender was muscled aside as Drogba controlled and turned with typically physical insistence, before rifling high into the net beyond a despairing Cudicini. As trademark goals go, this one could have been patented by Drogba. At the break, despite probably having the better of things, Spurs went in a goal down. Four minutes after the restart, the lead would be doubled in the most controversial of circumstances.

A quick start from Chelsea saw Mata's shot turned aside for a corner by Cudicini but, when Lampard crossed in, mayhem ensued. A Luiz header was acrobatically saved by Cudicini, but the ball flew straight up into the air before dropping down again inside the six-yard box. Shots and blocks followed with bodies obscuring much of the action and, often, the location of the ball. As a Spurs foot hacked clear, Chelsea players were claiming a goal. Atkinson agreed and the Spurs players erupted in fury.

There seemed little evidence in the replays to support claims that the ball had crossed the line, and Atkinson would later admit his error. Redknapp later said, 'I spoke to [the referee] and he said he feels worse than I do about it – I said, "I don't think so."'[178] The manager's frustration was understandable. Of course, nothing said afterwards would change anything on the pitch, and Spurs were now two goals down and needed a quick riposte.

It came just six minutes later, and to compound Chelsea's disappointment, it brought with it a hamstring injury to Luiz. Adebayor chased a through ball with Luiz in pursuit, before the tell-tale hop and skip of the Brazilian betrayed the injury. The Spurs striker ran on, but was felled by Čech in the area. As the ball broke free, it rolled to Bale, galloping up in support and the Welshman calmly passed it into the empty net. Fortunately for Di Matteo, Cahill was on the bench and he slotted in alongside Terry in the centre of defence as Luiz hobbled away. The longer-term consequence was that the Brazilian would surely miss both legs of the semi-final against Barcelona and, in the unlikely event of Chelsea progressing past Guardiola's European champions, any hopes of a return for the final would be slim to the point of emaciated.

Chelsea still had the lead but, fuelled by a righteous indignation at Mata's goal, Spurs had the momentum and for the next 20 minutes they pressed Di Matteo's team back, searching for the equaliser. As Chelsea defended with resolution, however, and Spurs' forays became increasingly urgent, the threat of a punishing counter-attack was ever

---

178 https://www.bbc.com/sport/football/17649443.

present. Inside the last 15 minutes, Chelsea confidence grew as they continued to frustrate their opponents and, following a period of studied possession, a clever clipped pass from Mata found Ramires running clear of Benoit Assou-Ekotto, and the Brazilian midfielder eased the ball past Cudicini to restore Chelsea's two-goal margin. To all intents and purposes, the game was now done.

With the Spurs resistance broken, Chelsea plundered two further goals to give the result a varnish that the balance of the game had hardly justified. Inside the final ten minutes, Lampard hit a speculative free kick from around 30 yards that deceived Cudicini in flight and found the far corner of the net and, in the last minute, with Redknapp's players looking for the final whistle to end their miserable evening, Malouda, on as a late substitute for Ramires, ran into the area to slip home the fifth goal. At the end, Spurs looked a well beaten team, and Chelsea would return to Wembley on 5 May to face Liverpool, who had eased past Merseyside neighbours Everton with a late Andy Carroll winner after Nikica Jelavić had put the Toffees ahead. It would be Chelsea's third FA Cup Final in the last four seasons.

Before that, however, there would be the little matter of the Champions League semi-final against Barcelona. The first leg at Stamford Bridge was now just three days away and, while the Wembley success would build confidence, facing Pep Guardiola's all-star team remained a daunting prospect. History offered a little encouragement, though. Until his time of exiting the Camp Nou, Guardiola only failed to have a winning record against one club – Chelsea.

7

Un-be-lievable

REACHING THE final four of any major competition should surely be a cause for hope, if not expectation. For Chelsea though, given their torturous Champions League campaign so far, their place alongside Barcelona, Real Madrid and Bayern Munich must have felt like a triumph in itself, and many doubted their chances of progressing further.

The BBC related that former Chelsea manager José Mourinho, now leading *Los Blancos* in pursuit of their tenth continental triumph and the coach's own third success, was summarily dismissive of his former charges' prospects, reporting, 'José Mourinho has written off his former club Chelsea's hopes of reaching the Champions League final, branding their semi-final opponents Barcelona as "super-favourites" to progress … Asked why he had told Telemadrid that Barcelona would advance, he said, "Because they are very good. Barcelona aren't the favourites. They are super-favourites." He added, "Let me be honest, I don't think the final will be a Real Madrid/Chelsea final. It could be Bayern or Barcelona, I just don't think it will be Real Madrid v Chelsea and we know why.'"[179] As was often his wont, Mourinho didn't go on to expand on 'why', leaving it for others to merely concur with his assessment. Many – fans of the club foremost among them – did.

Alan Addicott was, and remains, a Chelsea supporter but at the time there had been sufficient hard-headed realisation to appreciate that the odds were heavily stacked against his club, 'No chance. Here we go again. Barcelona – again. Messi and co. are just too good. We've done well to get this far. Just some of the thoughts that went through my mind having drawn the Spanish giants in the semis of the Champions League! Having played – and lost – against Barcelona in this competition on numerous occasions, my hopes were not very high on reaching the final to be honest. Chelsea had been put out by Barça, sometimes in controversial circumstances, a few times in the past. Surely, they would be too good again? It wasn't a case of simply giving up before a ball had been kicked, it was just what happened against Barcelona wasn't it? They were the better team, weren't they? Messi, Iniesta, Busquets, Piqué, Fabregas, the list goes on. Chelsea had performed miracles to reach this stage. Oh well, there's always next season!'[180]

Feelings were very much the same in Catalonia, as fans of Barcelona savoured the prospect of meeting arch-rivals Real Madrid in a Champions League final to decide the best club on the continent, and – more importantly – the top club in Spain. Jason Pettigrove was content editor at FC Barcelona, and was aware of how the tie was perceived in Spain, and particularly Catalonia. 'The talk of the *El Clásico* final was incessant in the lead-up to Barça's game. The Spanish press,

---

179 'José Mourinho writes off Chelsea's Champions League Final hopes', *The Guardian,* 5 April 2012.

180 Addicott, Alan, interview with the author.

perhaps not unfairly, were convinced that both would make the final, and it wasn't even contemplated that the Catalans wouldn't be able to finish the job at home.'[181]

Without the first leg even being played, the outcome of the tie was deemed a foregone conclusion – both in England and Spain. Barcelona's towering triumph over Manchester United – a team widely acknowledged as being comfortably superior to Chelsea – in the previous year's Champions League Final was evidence enough of the dominance of Spanish football over the best that England had to offer. Andy West is Spanish football correspondent for BBC Sport and commentator for La Liga TV. He was keenly aware of the accepted wisdom ahead of the tie, 'Barcelona were very much expected to advance. This was less than a year after the brilliant Champions League Final victory over Manchester United which many people regarded as the best club performance ever, and the prospect of Barça facing Real Madrid in the 2012 final was never out of the newspapers. Chelsea were certainly respected and not taken lightly, but they were not feared.'[182]

According to the old adage, familiarity is deemed to breed contempt. Despite meeting on several occasions in the same tournament over the years, however, there was a grudging respect between the two teams, but perhaps an unresolved irritation, rather than contempt. Having lost out to the Catalans 'sometimes in controversial circumstances a few times in the past' as Alan Addicott claimed, at least in west London, there was a feeling of having a few scores still to settle.

---

181 Pettigrove, Jason, interview with the author.

182 West, Andy, interview with the author.

The most recent issue was from three years previously, when Tom Henning Øvrebø's controversial officiating granted Barça a passage to the Champions League Final that many felt should have been Chelsea's by right. That feeling was compounded by the *Blaugrana* going on to win the trophy. After that tempestuous evening, Barcelona had flourished and improved to become widely regarded as the best team on the planet, while Chelsea's fortunes had waned as their key players aged. Now into the last four for the first time since 2009, the club had to show that it still had the capacity to compete with the very best.

The FA Cup victory over Spurs at the weekend had given the club a lift and offered a welcome boost in confidence. Plus, with the 'feel good' factor of Roberto Di Matteo still broadly holding sway – nine victories from 12 games with the Italian at the helm – perhaps it wasn't a bad time to face such a stern test. At least outwardly, players were expressing confidence, despite their undoubted underdog status in the tie. Sky reported Frank Lampard as insisting that Chelsea were not scared of the reigning European champions[183] and later John Terry said that he felt Barcelona 'feared us a little bit.'[184] Perhaps it was akin to whistling in the dark, but at least the players seemed to be in tune with each other.

There was plenty of other talk, however, suggesting that 'the dark' contained plenty of perils, with such talk inevitably finding its way through to the players, but perhaps even that aided Chelsea's cause. Petr Čech recalled the consensus among pundits and the media, 'Chelsea are out. Barcelona are the best team at the moment, and Chelsea are at the

---

183 https://www.skysports.com/football/chelsea-vs-barcelona/preview/258579.

184 *Kings of Europe – The Chelsea Story*, Sky UK Limited, 16 September 2012.

worst moment in their last, how many, years.'[185] Conversely however, even that seemed to solidify team spirit. Čech continued, 'Okay, we thought. We have nothing to lose, so we will just prove everybody wrong.'

After his trials and troubles under André Villas-Boas, Lampard had been given a fresh lease of life when Di Matteo arrived and was widely expected to feature in the upcoming home tie against Barcelona, probably aided by a solid supporting cast in midfield, and Didier Drogba broadly ploughing a lone furrow up front. With David Luiz absent thanks to that hamstring injury, Di Matteo would have been relieved to have the option of supplementing his defensive forces with Branislav Ivanović being available. The Serb's domestic three-game ban was not applicable in the Champions League.

There was little doubt that the Barcelona team Chelsea would face at Stamford Bridge was superior to the one that benefitted from those controversial refereeing decisions back in 2009. Lionel Messi was in prime form, and had netted no fewer than 14 goals in the season's Champions League campaign. In the group stage, Barcelona had scored 20 times in their six games, ending up undefeated and topping the group by a clear seven points. In the round of 16 they had added a further ten goals against Bayer Leverkusen and three more in disposing of AC Milan in the quarter-finals. If Chelsea's progress had been a stumbling struggle, Barça had been easing confidently through games at a canter. When Villas-Boas had been dismissed, there had been renewed newspaper speculation that Roman Abramovich had settled on another determined chase to acquire the services of Pep Guardiola. With the contrasting fortunes of the clubs

185 *Kings of Europe – The Chelsea Story*, Sky UK Limited, 16 September 2012

however, there was little surprise that the Barcelona manager dismissed such talk as mere 'fantasy'.[186]

Despite his team's almost serene passage to this stage of the competition, Guardiola still had issues to resolve ahead of the game and – at least publicly – acknowledged the threat that Chelsea posed to Barcelona's pursuit of a third European title in four seasons. Andreu Fontàs was out for the season with a knee injury, but was unlikely to have been in the starting 11 anyway. More significantly, David Villa was a long-term absentee with a broken leg and utility forward Seydou Keita was unavailable for the first leg with a thigh problem. He didn't even make the journey to London.

On a more positive note, Ibrahim Afellay had recovered from damage to his knee ligaments and was available for selection along with Gerard Piqué, whose thigh problem was unlikely to prevent him taking his assumed place alongside Carles Puyol and Javier Mascherano in defence. When the team was announced though, Piqué missed out and had to settle for a place on the bench. Also in contention for a starting berth, after recovering from a thigh injury, was right-back Dani Alves. In contrast to Piqué, the Brazilian would play. His rampaging forward runs had been a key feature of Barcelona's success across the season, both domestically and in continental competition. In this game, however, that perceived asset was exposed as a vulnerability that would cost the reigning European champions dearly.

When the teams were announced, there were few surprises. Chelsea's 11 were set up to defend and deny where possible. Barcelona's 11 looked full of goals. In front of Čech and the back four of Ivanović, Terry, Gary Cahill and Ashley Cole, alongside Lampard, Juan Mata was the only other

186 https://www.skysports.com/football/chelsea-vs-barcelona/preview/258579.

creative force in the middle of the field with the combative trio of Raul Meireles, Mikel Jon Obi and Ramires more inclined to defend. Drogba wouldn't see much of the ball. The one interesting choice was the stationing of Ramires on the left of midfield, nominally as the wide player it seemed. That selection and positioning would become significant as the first half drew to a close. In contrast, Barcelona's front five would enjoy an almost rampant monopoly of possession, and with the talents of Xavi and Andrés Iniesta prompting the attacking triumvirate of Alexis Sánchez, Cesc Fabregas and Messi, any result that kept Chelsea in the tie when the return leg was played could be looked upon as a victory of sorts.

When the game got under way, Di Matteo's pragmatic tactics quickly became clear, as Lampard later explained, 'We didn't care about possession. We didn't want to fight them on possession basically … We allowed them possession around the halfway line, and probably in towards our half and what we were more concerned about was staying tight.'[187] It was a system destined not to entertain but rather to frustrate. Di Matteo's reluctance to get into a basketball-type slug-fest with football's equivalent of the Harlem Globetrotters was, however, both understandable and sensible. And yet, as Jonathan Northcroft, the *Sunday Times* football correspondent who was at the game remembered, the contrasting styles and sheer drama of the occasion made for 'a fantastic night at Stamford Bridge'.[188]

The game was bookended by the visitors striking the woodwork. Sanchez hit the bar early on and substitute Pedro struck a post with time ebbing away and the most

187 *Kings of Europe – The Chelsea Story*, Sky UK Limited, 16 September 2012.

188 Northcroft, Jonathan, interview with the author.

unexpected scoreline on the cards. In between, the home team took a possession battering of fearful proportions.

Barcelona certainly started as if they meant to settle the tie as quickly as possible. Terry later conceded, 'Those first 20 minutes, you know, they battered us. I don't think we had a touch. I think possession was about 82 per cent or something.'[189] Although that estimation of possession looks exaggerated, to anyone watching the early period of the game, it may even have felt like an understatement.

The first big chance fell to Sanchez, as Cole recalled with a wry smile, 'It was hard, not just physically, but mentally. It takes it out of you, I think. You're constantly looking over your shoulder to see where the players are. They're constantly running in behind you … But you have to stay with it 100 per cent in that game because it takes just one second for them to score.'[190] Just eight minutes in, that demand for unremitting concentration caught Cole out. A lofted pass by Iniesta found Sanchez clear on the edge of the area with just Čech to confront. Beaten by the astute run, Cole appealed forlornly for offside as the Chilean clipped the bouncing ball over the advancing Čech towards the gaping net.

Convinced he had opened the scoring, Sanchez wheeled away in celebration but, not for the first or last time in their Champions League campaign, fortune favoured those in blue. The ball struck the bar and Terry hacked clear with relief. Chelsea had escaped the first real danger, but the pattern of the game had been set. In training sessions, coaches often set up an 'attack v defence' drill to work on defensive solidarity, marking and countering runs. Each

---

189 *Kings of Europe – The Chelsea Story*, Sky UK Limited, 16 September 2012.

190 *Kings of Europe – The Chelsea Story*, Sky UK Limited, 16 September 2012.

time the defence clears the ball, inevitably it is returned and another attack ensues; pressing, probing, pushing for openings. That was the format of this game.

The next chance fell to Fabregas. Messi was already testing and teasing the Chelsea back line and this time he created an opening for Iniesta to fire in on goal. The shot was on target but Čech plunged to parry. The ball dropped out to the former Arsenal captain a mere eight yards from goal, but he horribly skewed his shot and the ball went wide.

Messi tried his luck with a header from the edge of the box, running on to a cross, but the distance precluded any real danger and Čech comfortably collected. For all the artistic ebullience in their approach work, Barcelona's final-third performance was of an entirely different order. Time ticked on and, as more chances slipped by, Chelsea's belligerent midfield and back line, marshalled and inspired by Terry's insistent demands, held firm under the unrelenting pressure – always bolstered by the hope of a break at the other end, as Terry later recalled, 'You're soaking up the pressure, but you still believe. And you're getting battered by the best team in the world, on your home pitch, in front of your own fans, but knowing that we will get a chance and, if that falls to Didier or if that falls to Frank, Rami or one of the big players, it'll get taken.'[191]

As the end of the first period approached an incisive pass from Messi created an opening for Fabregas. His shot got the better of Čech, but Cole had scrambled back to cover his goalkeeper and cleared from the line. Into injury time, Chelsea had very nearly reached the sanctuary of the break without conceding. It would have been a worthy reward for their pugnacious determination and the organisation drilled into his players by Di Matteo and translated on to the pitch

191 *Kings of Europe – The Chelsea Story*, Sky UK Limited, 16 September 2012.

by Terry. The final seconds of the half would bring a much greater prize though.

Reports later suggested that Di Matteo had placed the speedy Ramires on the left of Chelsea's midfield with a specific plan in mind, should the opportunity to deploy it present itself. It took little imagination to realise that Barcelona would dominate possession, as had turned out to be the case, and that the regular forward forays of Alves from his nominal right-back position would become increasingly prevalent should Chelsea deny the visitors an early breakthrough. As Alves ventured forwards, the gap left by the Brazilian's attacking could be a vulnerability, but with the visitors so dominant in possession and territory it seemed to carry little threat, and it was largely discarded, but not by Di Matteo.

Another run forward by Messi into Chelsea's right flank was halted when the Argentine maestro tried to nutmeg Lampard, but the ruse went awry and possession was snaffled away. Looking up, Lampard saw Drogba set off on a run down the Chelsea right, but the forward was heavily marked and, perhaps with his manager's words reverberating in his ears, the midfielder eschewed the obvious ball down the line and looked across to the left.

As had been his wont with increasing regularity, Alves had committed forward to support the attack, leaving swathes of empty grass behind him. He was out of position, stranded upfield. As Lampard looked up, the blue blur of Ramires appeared on the left wing sprinting into the space, and Di Matteo's plan took flight.

Lampard angled his pass to exploit the midfielder's run and Chelsea sprang forward in a rare flurry of activity. The Barcelona defence had been drawn to Drogba as the perceived danger and were now compelled to recover position as Ramires ran on towards the area. Entering the penalty box, the Brazilian twice looked up to see where Drogba was. A recovering Xavi, Puyol and Mascherano hurtled back to cover, but astutely, Drogba hung slightly back, allowing the black-shirted Barcelona defenders to run past him.

It meant that when Ramires played his pass across the goalmouth, the ball passed behind the three defenders, throwing each off balance as they tried, in vain, to turn. Adriano had tracked Drogba's run, but wasn't close enough to make any sort of challenge when the ball reached the Chelsea forward. If the move so far had been executed with the exquisite precision of a well-practised routine, the denouement was hardly perfect, although no less effective for that.

Compelled to hit the ball with his left foot as it came across his body, Drogba's strike was mis-hit and the ball almost immediately cannoned into his right foot on the way towards goal. Víctor Valdés had been drawn to cover his near post as Ramires closed in on goal, but now scampered back across to recover his position as the ball headed on goal. The double contact on the ball meant that the strike was tame and seemed certain to be blocked by the goalkeeper but, instead of diving to reach the ball with his hand, Valdés instead opted to stretch out a foot, with his arm behind it. A glancing touch from his left boot was insufficient to deny Drogba, and merely diverted the ball away from the goalkeeper's glove that may have otherwise saved it.

Somewhat unbelievably, Chelsea had the lead. Drogba later confirmed that the goal had been conceived on the training ground, 'I was really happy, because this is exactly what we were working on the last few days in training.'[192]

---

192 *Kings of Europe – The Chelsea Story*, Sky UK Limited, 16 September 2012.

Drogba turned and slid on his knees towards the corner flag offering salutes as he did so. It was a moment of joy tinged with an understandable disbelief that only added to the lustre of the moment.

Jonathan Northcroft recalled not only the goal, but how it almost exemplified the contribution that Drogba had made to Chelsea's Champions League campaign, and to the club as a whole, 'Generally, I'd say that the triumph of 2012, I kind of see as being 60 per cent Chelsea's and 40 per cent Didier Drogba's alone, because his role in the latter stages particularly of the Champions League was just unbelievable. If ever a man's willpower helped give a team that extra bit of power, energy, drive, belief and quality, then Drogba was just on a mission. Drogba was the example. He was probably even more important in the final of course, but that goal [against Barcelona] was an incredible contribution, because the way Di Matteo played was so focused around his Italian principles of keeping things very compact and tight and trying to hit on the few breakaway opportunities that a defensively minded team were ever going to get, and Drogba was the ideal attacking weapon to provide that "one-man forward line" that he was. I don't think I've ever seen anyone [play] the "one-man forward line" as well as him, and that was an example.

'I think it was Chelsea's only real chance of the game, if I remember right. A classic breakaway goal just before half-time. A quite difficult finish, a deceptively difficult finish, where the ball's slightly behind him and he has to adjust slightly, check his run and get enough contact to get it over the line. I think that one brutal moment of decisiveness from Drogba gave – I wouldn't say it made you think that Chelsea were then going to go and do what they did in the Camp Nou – but it did put a question mark against the tie.

I think it did put a bit of doubt in Barcelona's mind, and it did demonstrate the weapon that Drogba was. It was a memorable goal and, of course, the sight of Abramovich celebrating in the directors' box. I remember it well.'[193]

It's questionable how many Chelsea fans crammed into Stamford Bridge, or watching on television, could believe what they had seen, as German referee Dr Felix Brych – the same official who had awarded the penalty to Chelsea in the epic round of 16 tie against Napoli – ended the first half. Perhaps the man with the whistle was a lucky charm for Chelsea. They had overcome the odds against the Serie A team to progress in the previous month and, although this task was undeniably a much sterner challenge, they had hit the front.

It had been an unbelievable first 45 minutes, borderline surreal, the stuff of tall tales and outlandishly heroic *Boys' Own* comic stories. Chelsea had been on the back foot for almost all of the first period and yet held the lead. If the good doctor was indeed a lucky charm for the home team, they would need whatever good fortune his presence had to offer in the second period. Should anyone watching have considered that the goal would change the pattern of the game, or dent Barcelona's insistent will to place a more realistic scoreline on it, they were to be proved as wide of the target as some of the Catalan club's finishing had been.

Barcelona had an iron-clad belief in their pattern of play. As victors in the continent's premier tournament twice in the previous three seasons, and three times in the last six, why wouldn't they? In each final they had defeated the best that the Premier League had to offer. First they overcame Arsenal and then twice beat Sir Alex Ferguson's Manchester

193 Northcroft, Jonathan, interview with the author.

United, and they had blitzed Chelsea's defence in the first half. Surely they would enjoy better fortune after the restart if they continued in the same vein.

Aside from the teams changing ends at the break, the new period was very much akin to the first half. As was their style, Barcelona continued to play in the same manner, seeming to disregard the fact that they had fallen behind. It was a minor irrelevance soon to be consigned to the footnotes of the game, washed away by a flood of vengeful goals. All the visitors needed to do was to convert their superiority and dominance into the tangible currency of goals. The problem was that their profligate finishing from the first half also remained unchanged and, when they did hit the target, Čech was proving an impenetrable barrier.

Chances came and went. Adriano forced Čech into a save and then Sanchez just failed to connect with a scooped pass from Fabregas. Time was ebbing away and still the visitors had yet to find an equaliser. Chelsea sank deeper and deeper into defence, but each passing minute added to their resolve and confidence as belief slowly began to drain away from Barcelona. Jonathan Northcroft recalled, 'Even though Barcelona dominated, they didn't threaten enough, or as much as their possession suggested they should.'[194]

In an effort to add more vigour to his attack, Guardiola removed Sanchez and sent on the energetic Pedro, but to little effect. Into the final 20 minutes, Di Matteo began to feed fresh legs into his team as well. Salomon Kalou came on for Mata. It had hardly been a game suited to the skills of the little Spaniard but, as with all of the players in blue he had fulfilled his obligations to the team and looked a spent force as he trudged slowly from the field.

---

194 Northcroft, Jonathan, interview with the author.

Guardiola rolled the dice again in the hope of plucking a goalscoring rabbit from his hat. Thiago Alcántara replaced Fabregas and later the young wide player Isaac Cuenca came on for a frustrated Xavi. Di Matteo removed Ramires for the extra defensive nous of José Bosingwa inside the final few minutes. The home team had precious little intention of attacking. All that mattered now was the beckoning glory of victory, and a clean sheet to take to Spain six days later.

Puyol was now playing as an auxiliary central striker, having little to do in his day job, as waves of late attacks repeatedly broke on Chelsea's defensive wall. The lion-maned captain so nearly delivered for his club when a flicked header following a Messi free kick looked destined for goal, until Čech plunged to his right and reached out a hand to divert the ball wide of the post.

In a final crescendo of action, a Barcelona goal seemed inevitable. A sliding challenge by Terry broke up another attack, but the ball broke towards the left flank of the Chelsea penalty area, with Pedro closing in. By now the blue-shirted players were running on pure adrenalin with energy fuel tanks at zero. The Spaniard hit a low right-foot shot as Ivanović and Cahill threw themselves forwards in a desperate attempt to block, and Cole dropped back behind Čech. The ball arced behind the two defenders as each jabbed out a heel and appeared to clip the back of the Serb's boot, altering its direction perhaps only by millimetres, but vitally so. Čech's dive to his left was a mere gesture as the ball closed in on goal. On the line, Cole stuck a left boot out, but missed the ball as it thudded into the upright.

Messi stood, ominously waiting, on the edge of the goal area. Had the ball bounced out towards him, it would have been a simple tap-in, but Ivanović's slight glance on the ball had affected its trajectory, not only denying a goal but also sufficiently so that the rebound bounced in the opposite direction, away for goal, and away from Messi. The danger was not over though. Sergio Busquets charged in to meet the ball around ten metres from goal. Čech was still struggling to regain his feet after plunging in pursuit of Pedro's shot. Almost any effort on target would surely have found the back of the net, but in that moment, Busquets's technique, or perhaps his nerve, failed him. Leaning slightly back, his shot flew high over the bar and Chelsea escaped. 'Against the post and over! Unbelievable finish here,' exclaimed Alan Parry commentating for Sky. It was one of those rare occasions when such descriptions cannot be dismissed as mere hyperbole.

The penalty area was a seething mass of emotion. Relief for the high-fiving Chelsea players and exasperation for those who had travelled from the Catalan capital. Busquets lay on the floor with his hands on his head in dismay. Seconds later, the referee brought proceedings to a close. Jonathan Northcroft's description of the game as 'a fantastic night at Stamford Bridge' hardly seemed to do the events justice.

Had the game been a boxing match, any referee would surely have stopped the fight to prevent Chelsea from taking more punishment as Barcelona piled on the punches, one after the other, but without landing that knockout blow. This was football however, and, as the old adage goes, 'every dog has its day' – something true even of underdogs – and this had been Chelsea's day. The match statistics were both revealing and conversely, to any Chelsea fan at least, irrelevant. The visitors had enjoyed more than 70 per cent of the possession across the game and had 25 attempts on goal, compared to Chelsea's four. Fifteen of Barcelona's efforts had been on target. Chelsea's total was a paltry two, but one of those had beaten Valdés and decided the game. It was difficult to recall the other one, but that hardly mattered.

Suddenly, the impossible dream was now merely improbable; the mountain could now be perceived as merely a steep hill. For a watching Seb Hutchinson, the game had perfectly laid out a blueprint for Chelsea's tactics in the return leg, 'This result meant you knew exactly how they would approach the game at the Camp Nou; sit deep, "park the bus" and frustrate the home faithful.'[195] A belligerent confidence had certainly taken root among Chelsea fans, as Mark Worrall confirmed, 'With the Barcelona game coming three days after Chelsea had walloped Tottenham Hotspur 5-1 at Wembley in the FA Cup semi-finals, the belief now was that Robbie Di Matteo was a football god and Barcelona, irrespective of Messi, any repeat of the dubious refereeing that had stalked fixtures with the Catalan club in the past, or indeed suspicions of UEFA bias, were there for the taking. There wasn't a "True Blue" soul inside Stamford Bridge that night that didn't believe Robbie had worked Pep's tactics out. It was brilliant. "One Di Matteo, there's only one Di Matteo" never sounded sweeter and there was a growing sense that maybe, just maybe, this was going to be Chelsea's year especially given the fact Barça should have scored enough goals to secure the tie but left SW6 with nothing.'[196] Perhaps it was a new-found confidence built on the fragile foundations of euphoria, but no less understandable for that.

Others were less convinced. The game had been a thrilling encounter, high on emotional energy fuelled by a passionate home support. Cold, hard logic would suggest that a single-goal lead to take to the Camp Nou was akin to

---

195 Hutchinson, Seb, interview with the author.

196 Worrall, Mark, interview with the author.

trying to mask naked embarrassment with a pine needle – offering wildly insufficient cover. Ian Ross was of that mind, 'I didn't think 1-0 would be enough. Barça had around 70 per cent of the possession but missed a couple of inviting chances. Chelsea defended well – particularly Cahill and Cole who succeeded in keeping Messi relatively quiet. It was a good, solid performance but I suspect both teams headed to the second leg in Spain suspecting Barça were on track for another final appearance.'[197]

The point about Messi was entirely valid, and it may have been that the Argentine was beginning to develop a complex about playing the Stamford Bridge club. He had scored 243 goals in his Barcelona career by that stage but had also failed to find the back of the net against Chelsea in seven matches. That statistic may have come into play in the second leg.

A check of Barcelona's home form at the time would have been sufficient to calm any excited expectancy taking root among Chelsea fans. In 30 games at the Camp Nou that term, the *Blaugrana* had won 27 and drawn the remaining three. They had scored 104 goals in those 30 games, and conceded just 16. Averaging almost 3.5 goals per game, if Barcelona performed to anything like that level, Chelsea would probably need to score at least twice to have any hope of progress.

The defeat in west London was the first game, either domestically or in European competition, where Barcelona had tasted defeat since a 3-2 loss to Osasuna in Pamplona on 11 February. Since that time they had played 11 La Liga matches and won every one, scoring 33 goals and conceding just eight. They had also played four times in the Champions League, beating Bayer Leverkusen across both legs for an

---

197 Ross, Ian, interview with the author.

aggregate 10-2 margin before drawing 0-0 in Milan and then winning the home leg 3-1. Merely a steep hill? Perhaps it was still a mountain after all.

In Catalonia, the Stamford Bridge defeat was seen as an irritating setback but hardly a catastrophe. With the home leg to come and an opportunity to put things right progress was still expected, as Jason Pettigrove explained, 'Opinions remained as they had beforehand. Nothing had convinced supporters, players or media otherwise, particularly given the first-leg performance. It was put down as one of those games that come along occasionally where, no matter what you do, it's not your night.'[198] Besides, there were other matters to concentrate on before the second leg.

In December, Barcelona had visited the Estadio Santiago Bernabéu and, despite falling behind to a Benzema goal in the first minute, had triumphed 3-1. Sanchez had equalised on the half-hour and second-half goals from Xavi and Fabregas gave Guardiola's team victory in the first *Clásico* of the season. Three days before Chelsea were to visit the Camp Nou for the return leg on 24 April, *Los Blancos* would travel to Catalonia for the reverse fixture. With the clubs locked in battle for supremacy, it was almost a title-deciding encounter.

In front of more than 99,000 fans, José Mourinho's Madrid team claimed a pulsating encounter 2-1, with the winner almost inevitably coming from Cristiano Ronaldo. In the space of a few days, Barcelona had lost twice after going more than two months without defeat. If there was some question as to which defeat was the more significant, Andy West had little doubt, 'A significant backdrop to the [Chelsea] tie was that it was punctuated by a *Clásico* league

198 Pettigrove, Jason, interview with the author.

game at the Camp Nou which was essentially a title decider. Real Madrid won that game 2-1, more or less sealing the title for the hated José Mourinho's team. So, in a strange way, the Chelsea tie was almost an afterthought to the *Clásico* that came between the two legs,' he suggested. 'The first leg was more or less forgotten as soon as it had been played due to the *Clásico* which took place a few days later, and there's no doubt that Barça's morale was knocked by their loss in that game to Real, which effectively ended their title challenge. That, more than the first leg, cast a shadow over Barça as they prepared for the second leg.'[199]

Chelsea also had domestic business to take care of before their thoughts could return to the enticingly romantic notion of eliminating Barcelona from the Champions League. There were six fixtures remaining to complete their Premier League programme. Their next appointment would be the short journey to the north of the capital, and a visit to the Emirates Stadium to play Arsenal. Holding sixth in the table with so few games to go suggested that any faint hopes of top-four qualification were even more extreme than the prospect of winning the Champions League. It meant that Di Matteo was forced to, once more, walk the tightrope of team selection. He needed to choose a team worthy enough to do the club justice in a traditionally difficult game, while still protecting as many of his players as possible for the midweek visit to Catalonia. The result was a starting 11 largely bereft of the responsibility for turning hope into reality in the Camp Nou a few days later.

Resting goalkeepers is hardly ever considered a worthwhile gamble, and Čech kept his place, as did Terry and Cahill in the centre of defence. With Ivanović still

199 West, Andy, interview with the author.

serving his ban, Bosingwa deputised at right-back. Cole was rested, and Bertrand took over, covering the left flank of Chelsea's defence. In midfield, Essien and Oriol Romeu were the solid pairing with Florent Malouda offering some measure of creativity. Kalou and Daniel Sturridge flanked Fernando Torres in attack. The Spaniard's return to the starting 11 was probably inevitable anyway, given the gravity of the next match, but reports out of Chelsea suggested that Drogba had been left out due to concern over a niggling knee problem. Arsenal were also in the hunt for a European spot, but far better placed than their opponents and, with no distractions from other competitions, could field a full-strength team.

The 60,000-odd crowd may have been hoping that the lunchtime fixture would offer up a feast of attacking football, in line with the eight goals shared back in October when the Gunners ran out 5-3 winners at Stamford Bridge. It wouldn't be the case. In a game of fairly stodgy fare, Chelsea largely contained the home team with a resilient display built on the back of that deployed against Barcelona a few days earlier. Arsenal had the better of the game, and struck the woodwork twice in the opening period. At the full-time whistle though, the scoreline had remained goalless.

The result certainly did nothing to breathe new life into a Chelsea Premier League campaign that was on its last legs both with regard to fixtures and ambition. They were now four points adrift of Newcastle United, who had climbed into fourth place, and one behind a Spurs team that had seen their season deteriorate badly. Di Matteo at least had the consolation of leaving north London without any injuries to his key players. The journey to Barcelona was next on the agenda.

On the day of the game, the English press were reporting on upbeat comments from Di Matteo at the previous day's press conference. In *The Times*, Matt Hughes related the Chelsea coach as declaring that 'he would not be sending [his team] out to grind out a goalless draw'.[200] Perhaps that was true, perhaps not. The comment may have been informed by the acceptance that another clean sheet for his team against Barcelona was highly unlikely, and therefore, in all probability, Chelsea would need to score at least once if they were to progress. In fact, Barcelona hadn't failed to score at least once in a home Champions League game for more than three years. The last club to deny them a goal on their own ground in the competition, however, was Chelsea.

Had someone, there and then, offered the Italian a dull goalless draw achieved through a grinding performance though, he would surely have snatched their hand off and Chelsea had been given a practical lesson in how to achieve that very thing by a former manager. Two seasons ago, José Mourinho had taken his Inter Milan team to the Camp Nou at the same stage in the competition and delivered a tactical masterclass in smothering the attacking flair of Guardiola's team, before going on to win the final against Bayern Munich at the Bernabéu in the perfect audition for the Real Madrid job. And, just a few days before Chelsea landed in Spain, he had repeated the trick with *Los Blancos*, winning the game on this occasion.

Di Matteo also confirmed Drogba was fit to play and that he planned to begin the game with the same starting 11 that had earned the all-important victory at Stamford Bridge. The Italian had the comfort of knowing that Barcelona had failed to beat Chelsea in any of their last six

---

200 'We can win Champions League says Di Matteo', *The Times*, 24 April 2012.

meetings, and had only scored one goal across their most recent three encounters. That statistic was suggested by a couple of questions fired at the coach during the press conference, but the Italian was wise enough not to take the bait and allow himself to be portrayed as over-confident.

In what initially seemed like a strange turn of events, according to an article by Rory Smith in *The Times*, Harry Redknapp was reported as publicly wishing Chelsea well in the game, but his statements had little to do with the fact that nephew Lampard would be involved. The Spurs manager's hopes had a more pragmatic driver. The more games Chelsea had to play, the more tired, and potentially increasingly distracted their players would be in the Premier League encounters remaining, offering up Spurs a better opportunity to clinch that vital fourth place. 'I'll be rooting for Chelsea,' Redknapp said. 'From our point of view, if we keep Chelsea in it and they have got a final to prepare for, they have got a lot on their plate then, haven't they?'[201] The 65-year-old should perhaps have been experienced enough to know you should be careful what you wish for. Despite experiencing a rugged period where his club only accumulated six points from a possible 27, Spurs would recover to secure that fourth place. Chelsea would still deny them that coveted Champions League place, however.

Maybe it was his team's poor record against Chelsea, or perhaps the nagging doubts put into his mind by succumbing to successive defeats but, in the Barcelona coach's meeting with the press, Guardiola was unusually combative and reacted angrily to criticism of one of his younger players for his performance against Real Madrid. Not holding anything back, he defended 20-year-old Cristian Tello with a bristling

201 'Blue is the colour for Redknapp as Tottenham seek lifeline', *The Times*, 24 April 2012.

aggression, lapsing into profanity, 'You can criticise the veterans, but not the young players. You attack Cristian. Analyse, don't criticise. He played a f****** good game and most of the dangerous chances created, were created by Tello.'[202] Barcelona had not lost three consecutive games for nine years. Was Guardiola feeling the pressure? There was some positive news from the coach though concerning Messi. The Argentine had missed training on Sunday due to a gastric illness, but had recovered and would play.

When the teams were announced, Di Matteo had made good on his desire to begin the game with the same starting 11 from the previous week. He wasn't to know it at that stage, of course, but, before a dozen minutes had been played, his planning was in need of adaptation. Twenty-five minutes after that, the game plan was in tatters and Chelsea were heading for the Champions League exit door.

With Piqué now available, Guardiola had switched to a back three, abandoning the line of four he had deployed at Stamford Bridge. Alves was consigned to the bench with Mascherano and Puyol alongside the reinstated Piqué. Busquets was in his normal *regista* role ahead of the defence with Xavi and Iniesta primed to prompt and probe. Fabregas, Sanchez and Cuenca formed the forward line, with Messi allowed the freedom to link the attacks and pick his moments to strike. As with Di Matteo however, Guardiola would also be forced into a rethink early on, although he wouldn't have to deal with the crisis the Chelsea coach faced eight minutes ahead of half-time.

There was one other selection that some would later deem significant while, for others, it would be the very epitome of ephemera. At Stamford Bridge, Barcelona had

---

202 'We can win Champions League says Di Matteo', *The Times*, 24 April 2012.

worn an all-black strip, rather than the traditional *Blaugrana* colours, to avoid the potential colour clash with Chelsea's all blue. When the teams emerged from the Camp Nou tunnel to the regular strains of the Barcelona anthem 'Cant del Barça', it quickly became clear that the visitors hadn't adopted a similar approach, although an all-black strip was labelled as the club's first change colours. Instead, their third kit, a virtually all-white ensemble, had been chosen, and the Blues temporarily became the Whites.

Walking into the cauldron of Catalan commotion, Chelsea were wearing a kit redolent of the one worn by the 'real' *Los Blancos* a few short days earlier, when Mourinho's team from the capital had all but secured the La Liga title in the same stadium. Chelsea's shirts were not quite all-white, but had two bands, one blue, the other yellow, stretching down from shoulder to chest. It hardly distracted from the overall effect, and the chorus of boos when the visiting team was read out carried a little extra venom.

Whether the decision to wear that kit, rather than the black one, was influenced by innocent concerns over a lack of contrast to Barcelona's *Blaugrana,* or merely as a tool to increase any siege mentality the club was trying to foster is open to discussion. The real reason may never be truly revealed. Regardless though, not only did it reinforce the painful recent memories of the loss to Real Madrid, pouring salt into open wounds, it also conjured up memories from previous Chelsea visits to the Camp Nou when, under the charge of Mourinho, spicing the animosity of the home fans was seen as an indispensable aid to victory. Any incantations, intentional or otherwise, conjuring up the ghost of Mourinho, the eternal *bête noire* of the *cules* (as Barcelona fans are known), would only intensify the atmosphere. Whether that would aid Chelsea, or hinder them, was less clear.

Had the decision to wear white been influenced by the recent and more distant past? Ian Ross was sceptical about any such ploy, 'The wearing of white shirts a la Real Madrid possibly annoyed the Catalan hordes – but I don't believe it would have unduly bothered the Barça players.'[203] It's a reasonable assessment but the decision just added a little more grist to the mill for anyone seeking to inject a little devilment into the growing rivalry between the clubs.

Chelsea's 'lucky charm' official Dr Felix Brych, who had taken charge of the first leg, had been replaced by Turkish referee Cüneyt Çakır for the second leg. Although FIFA-listed since 2006, Cakir had only been a member of the UEFA Elite group since 2010. To some, it appeared a strange decision to award a game full of explosive potential to a relatively inexperienced official, and many Chelsea fans would argue that, in the second period, that inexperience may well have contributed to a decision going against them.

The visitors also had six players carrying yellow cards into the game, with the potential of any further indiscretions costing a place in the final should Chelsea prevail. Just over 38,000 had packed Stamford Bridge six days earlier for the first leg. In the steeply layered tiers of the Camp Nou, that number was nearly 97,000. This was a stage set for theatre. If the first leg had been tense and enthralling, this game would have a drama all of its own and a denouement that few novelists would even dare to contemplate writing.

When the game started, Chelsea even had the temerity to mount the first attack. Inside the first 30 seconds, Cole and Ramires exploited the gap on the right flank of Barcelona's back line, with the three-man defence bereft of full-backs. Cole's hopefully hit pass for the Brazilian's run

---

203 Ross, Ian, interview with the author.

was intercepted by Valdés though, and Barcelona assumed their expected dominance.

A couple of minutes later, Barcelona's first threat came at the other end. A neat wall-pass between Sanchez and Messi had the little Argentine galloping into the area but, as Čech advanced to close down the angle, he fired narrowly wide, rippling the side netting as the ball passed and offering a brief, but ultimately forlorn, hope of a goal for the home fans. The pattern of the game had been set, and Chelsea sank back further into defence. Seb Hutchinson was watching the game from a position near to Čech's goal and recalled, 'Chelsea's players were camped in their own half as Barça probed away. The unity and defensive cohesion of the Chelsea players was notable; every member of the team was prepared to sacrifice any individual footballing freedom to keep Barça out.'[204]

Less than five minutes had been played when Di Matteo's planning began to unravel. A through ball had Sanchez running to collect inside the area, pursued by Cahill. As the forward turned with the ball, Cahill slipped. Performing an intelligent 'splits' movement, for a moment the defender resembled Bambi on ice as his legs splayed forward and aft and the tell-tale sign of a hand reaching to the back of his left thigh told that the tumble had caused a hamstring injury. Čech caught the resulting cross, but the urgings of his team-mates to put the ball out of play only confirmed that Cahill had a serious problem. It was a similar injury to that suffered by Luiz in the FA Cup semi-final against Spurs. Initially Cahill tried to walk it off, but it was pointless. A few minutes later, with his lack of mobility threatening to unhinge the Chelsea defence, Cahill limped away to the sidelines.

---

204 Hutchinson, Seb, interview with the author.

Chelsea only had one defender on the bench. Fortunately, it was Bosingwa and it only required a minor adjustment for the Portugal international to take up his usual right-back position and Ivanović to move into the centre to partner Terry. Derided by some pundits and Chelsea fans during his time at Stamford Bridge, Bosingwa was hardly a weak link and had already picked up a Champions League winner's medal during his time with Porto, under a certain José Mourinho. In this game, he would also prove his adaptability and perhaps offer his most effective, and certainly most valuable, performance in Chelsea blue. It was just as well because Barcelona were now upping the pressure and beginning to lay siege to the visitors' goal. With Drogba falling back to help the midfield, the home team had cause to leave just a single defender to guard Valdés while the remainder of the team swarmed forward. Chief among the threats, inevitably, was Messi. Receiving possession, playing short neat passes and gracefully avoiding tackles, he was as darting as a wasp, evading clumsy attempts to swat him. Plus he carried a sting.

On 15 minutes Guardiola faced his first problem of the game. A long kick from Čech carried into the Barcelona penalty area. Drogba chased unconvincingly, tracked by Piqué, but Valdés hurtled from his goal to punch clear, flattening both players as he did so. As the ball ran out of play, the penalty area resembled a war zone with all three players flat out on the ground.

The replays revealed a sickening contact between the leaping goalkeeper's hip and the side of the unsuspecting Piqué's head. After treatment, he returned to the game but, as with Cahill, it was brave but ultimately pointless. Before he left the action though, Barcelona had their best chance so far as an advancing Messi was only foiled by the outstretched leg of Čech. Terry blocked Iniesta's shot from the rebound. On the sidelines, Guardiola threw his hands up in the air before holding his head. It was a sign of frustration, and perhaps an increasing worry that the memories of the misfortunes and missed chances of the previous week were haunting him.

Just past the halfway mark of the first period, Drogba received a forward pass and shrugged off a tepid challenge by Piqué, exposing the fact that he still had not recovered from the collision with his goalkeeper. The chance came to naught, but the struggles of Piqué were sufficient evidence for Guardiola, who called his defender off the field. Walking to the sidelines like someone a little the worse for wear, Piqué was replaced by Alves. With the muscular, menacing figure of Drogba offering a physical challenge when the ball was occasionally delivered forwards, the height of Piqué had been important. It meant that the back three of Barcelona were now all relatively small, and it would need all of Puyol's combative intensity to make up for the missing inches when challenging the Chelsea forward.

Just past the half-hour, Xavi fired in a shot from 25 metres or so, but it was pulled well wide of the target and Čech watched it run away to safety. The pattern of the game was settling into the same format as the first leg a week previously. Barcelona monopolised possession but Chelsea's rearguard had, for the most part, kept the attacks at a safe distance from their goal and, even on the odd occasion when the home team penetrated the white wall, Čech looked at his commanding best.

If Di Matteo's team could maintain this concentration and discipline for a further 15 minutes and get into the dressing room at half-time without incurring any damage, confidence would soar. It wouldn't be the case, however.

That period would see the semi-final swing dramatically in favour of the home team.

When the breakthrough came on 35 minutes, strangely, it was almost a surprise. The packed crowd were growing impatient and increasingly frustrated. For the previous ten minutes Chelsea had seemed as comfortable as at any time in the entire tie, not totally untroubled by the home team's attacks, but dealing with them effectively and with a growing assurance. At such times, however, perhaps the guard was dropped slightly. It was all the invitation Barcelona needed.

A corner from the right was headed clear to Alves midway inside the Chelsea half. With the massed ranks of white shirts deep inside the box, the Brazilian galloped forward into the inviting space before playing the ball off to his left, finding Cuenca. The young winger, who would be celebrating his 21st birthday three days later, got the party going a little earlier than that. Driving into the box, he drew Čech towards him before looking up, then delivered a low cross along the six-yard line towards the far post, where a lurking Busquets swept the ball home. For all the star forwards Barcelona had on the field, there was an irony in Busquets being the man who delivered where others had failed. It was only the midfielder's second goal in two years.

Tension released, players and fans exploded with joy. The dam had been breached, the wall had fallen, and Chelsea's back line suddenly looked vulnerable. The English club's lead had vanished and, with an hour left to play, the omens were looking bad for the visitors. Ten minutes to play until the break. It was a time for cool heads and steely concentration. A little over 100 seconds later though, things would look much darker.

Just two minutes after the goal, as another Barcelona attack broke down, a chorus of whistles erupted from the crowd. The referee stopped play and walked to the edge of the Chelsea penalty area where Sanchez was lying on the floor apparently writhing in pain. Terry stood over the fallen forward trying very hard to look innocent and confused as to what had happened. The referee pointed towards the Chelsea goal to indicate a Barcelona free kick, then immediately reached into his breast pocket and flourished a red card at the Chelsea captain. Terry initially looked aghast. It was the affected and overworked innocent look of a perpetrator caught out.

The incident had been missed by so many watching, and the Sky television commentary team of Alan Parry and Gary Neville covering the game. Replays of the incident also confirm that the referee had not seen what had happened either. Had a linesman or the fourth official alerted him to the offence? Minutes later, Parry reported that information from the linesman was indeed the source.

Once replays were shown, however, there was little cause for Terry's apparent anguish. Unprovoked, he had walked up behind the Chilean forward and driven a knee into the back of his upper leg. It was blatant, it was stupid and surely it was going to be catastrophic. Any number of watching Chelsea fans feared the worst.

Watching the game on Sky at home, Danny Ridgeway spoke for many of them as he recalled the incident, 'Terry lost his head in the moment on the big stage and we were all sure at the time [that] his sending-off would lead to another failure in the CL.'[205] Seb Hutchinson had a ringside seat, and found it difficult to argue, 'On another day Terry may have got away with it, it happened off the ball. I wasn't that far away from the incident – it transpired so quickly, and

205 Ridgeway, Danny, interview with the author.

Sanchez certainly made the most of it. But Terry's face gave the impression that he knew he'd made a mistake and that he may have cost Chelsea any hope of progression.'[206]

Despite continued and increasingly desperate attempts at looking the injured and unjustly punished party, Terry was eventually ushered from the field by Čech. The grim reality of the situation sank in as he crossed the white line and past Di Matteo. He appeared to say something to the Italian, but there was little response. Chelsea's coach had more pressing matters to concentrate on.

With Cahill already off injured and now the captain dismissed and a man down, a reshuffle was required. Had there been another defensive option on the bench, he may have looked to make a change, but that wasn't a possibility. Looking to at least cobble together some kind of recognisable back line until the break, when he could reconsider his options, Bosingwa was moved into the centre alongside Ivanović and Ramires slotted in as an emergency right-back. Thirty-five minutes earlier, Di Matteo had sent out a team with an experienced and largely settled back four. Of that defensive unit, only Cole was still in his starting position and the first choice pairing at the centre of the defence were both now back in the dressing room.

There were eight minutes until Chelsea could get to the sanctuary of half-time. With Barcelona now full of confidence and Chelsea struggling to retain an orderly back line, Mark Worrall feared the worst, 'John Terry's sending-off was a bit of a choker as I immediately thought back to Paul Gascoigne getting booked playing for England against Germany in the Italia 90 World Cup semi-final. Gazza would have missed the final through suspension had the

---

206 Hutchinson, Seb, interview with the author.

Three Lions won through and JT was going to miss the Champions League Final if Chelsea got past Barcelona. With the Barça game level at 1-1 on aggregate, I immediately thought the tie would be settled by penalties and then thought back to the shoot-out loss to Manchester United at Moscow. All these thoughts went through my mind as Terry left the pitch. Psychologically I was all over the place and wondered if Chelsea's reorganised defence would be as well.'[207] Only six of those eight minutes had passed when Worrall's concerns were validated. The inevitable happened, and Chelsea's roof fell in all around them.

Messi's shot as the free kick was tapped to him by Fabregas came to nothing. Rather than an escape however, the squandered chance was merely a brief reprieve. After a few minutes of fairly ineffective probing, the defensive naivety on the right flank of Chelsea's defence was ruthlessly exposed. Sanchez fed Messi who waited until the perfect moment before slotting the ball on to Iniesta with Ramires cruelly isolated by the speed and precision of the play. A touch to control and a side-foot finish past Čech delivered the goal. 'Chelsea's hopes are crumbling here,' declared Parry to the watching millions. As statements of the obvious go, it was right up there. The *cules* celebrated as if the match had now been won, and Chelsea fans resigned themselves to elimination and the end of a dream for another season at least.

Alan Addicott had accepted that it was all done and dusted, 'Barcelona dominated much of this game. So, despite taking a goal advantage into the second leg, I still believed a place in the final just wasn't going to happen. It was no surprise to me when Barcelona took a two-goal lead at their

---

207 Worrall, Mark, interview with the author.

place. They did what they do best, dominated possession and created chance after chance. Then John Terry got sent off and that was it, end of the road.'[208] The feeling was echoed on the field, throughout the team.

'I thought we were going out,' Lampard later confessed, 'and I thought it was about trying to save our embarrassment and not giving away too many goals.'[209]

Cole's thoughts were travelling in the same direction. 'If I'm honest, I thought, "This is it." You always have that little bit of belief but they scored straight away and, you're like, it's too hard to come back from this.'[210]

'We were 2-0 down,' Drogba said later, grimacing at the memory, before adding with a laugh and a shake of his head, 'It don't look good.'[211]

Čech agreed, 'Down to ten men, over here, with Barcelona in full confidence, with no defenders, or completely different defence than we would have played all season, you think that it's going to be very difficult.'[212]

In the commentary box, sitting alongside Parry, Gary Neville echoed the emotions of the players in white below him, 'This is going to be painful for Chelsea.'

Across the entire semi-final, it was Chelsea's lowest point. As if to pour further woe on to the visitors, Ramires was booked as well. It meant the Brazilian would potentially miss the final, although any thoughts along those lines were

---

208 Addicott, Alan, interview with the author.

209 *Kings of Europe – The Chelsea Story*, Sky UK Limited, 16 September 2012.

210 *Kings of Europe – The Chelsea Story*, Sky UK Limited, 16 September 2012.

211 *Kings of Europe – The Chelsea Story*, Sky UK Limited, 16 September 2012.

212 *Kings of Europe – The Chelsea Story*, Sky UK Limited, 16 September 2012.

surely of a mere academic nature now. All hope seemed to have drained away in those few short minutes, defeat accepted, almost two hours of stoic application to defence wiped away, with only the pride of avoiding a heavy defeat to keep the players going. 'I don't think any Chelsea fans thought it was possible and were just hoping that we could keep it to a respectable scoreline and hold our heads high against one of the best, if not the best team in Europe at the time,'[213] recalled Danny Ridgeway. And yet, after an even shorter period of time than when the tie had seemingly been lost, hope would be renewed.

Barcelona were now in their pomp and, as Čech suggested, looked full of confidence. They quickly sprang forward again, crisp passing picking at holes in a now threadbare Chelsea defence and only a late challenge on Sanchez prevented another strike on Čech's goal. Then Messi nearly profited from a deflected pass, but Čech collected. In the first leg, the 45 minutes of the first half had drifted into injury time when Drogba struck. As Čech rolled the ball out, added time had just begun in this match.

Possession was quickly spirited away but an attempted through pass was cut out by Mikel, deflecting the ball to Meireles and, a couple of short passes later, it was with Ramires on the right flank, striding forward enthusiastically. The ball was played forwards to Lampard around the halfway line, who was quickly closed down by Mascherano. Brushing the Argentine aside, Lampard glanced inside to see Ramires continuing his run into the Barcelona half. On the half turn, the newly promoted Chelsea captain fed a superb pass into the path of the speedy Brazilian, its accuracy cutting out three Barcelona players. Onside by a comfortable

---

213 Ridgeway, Danny, interview with the author.

margin, the speed of Ramires had now taken him clear of the *Blaugrana* back line as Puyol and Busquets chased in vain pursuit. Compared to the lithe stride of the Chelsea player, they were running through treacle.

As Ramires entered the penalty area, Valdés committed himself forwards to confront the danger. With a calm assurance, the Brazilian deftly clipped the ball over the goalkeeper's head and turned away as it landed in the unguarded net. 'It's a goal,' exclaimed Parry, as Neville let out a long sigh, rehearsing for a more prolonged version that would follow an hour or so later. It had been a remarkable passage of play.

Lampard's vision and execution of the pass was sublime, only matched by Ramires's lofty ambition and composed finish. The impudent skill of his team-mate was lauded by the creator, 'Running at that speed, and to produce such a deft touch, I think, you couldn't expect that of Messi or Ronaldo … You know, it's one of those moments where he produced something that completely outstanding and, again, he picked his moment perfectly.'[214]

If the goal had a distinctly Brazilian touch to it, the celebratory dance of Ramires was very much less the case as, on the field, in the stadium and beyond, emotions flipped in that moment. 'The goal of Ramires was a complete turning point,' Lampard added. 'Because without that goal, before half-time, then I think we could have ended up on a fair beating with ten men.'[215] Now it was the Chelsea bench celebrating as Guardiola rubbed his forehead as if trying to wipe away the strange reality that had now engulfed him.

---

214 *Kings of Europe – The Chelsea Story*, Sky UK Limited, 16 September 2012.

215 *Kings of Europe – The Chelsea Story*, Sky UK Limited, 16 September 2012.

The *cules* were stunned into silence. Sitting near to where the Boixos Nois, the loudest of the Barcelona fans, were located, Seb Hutchinson remembered the impact that the goal had on their ranks, 'The Ramires goal was the match's turning point – I remember 30 seconds before the goal the Barça fans were emitting an air of arrogance – 2-0 up and facing ten men, they were cruising. The truth of the matter was that Chelsea just needed one goal. Scoring that goal gave them something to defend again and boy, did they defend!'[216]

At least there was a measure of hope again now and, with the precious away goal pocketed, amazingly Chelsea led in the tie. Progress was far from secured, but that dread resignation of another Champions League elimination had been put aside, replaced with hope, as Danny Ridgeway recalled, 'The Ramires goal was massively important and definitely gave a glimmer of hope.'[217] Keen to keep a lid on any outlandish expectations trying to force their way to the front of his mind, Alan Addicott was containing his emotions, 'Slim chance now? Hmm. Maybe not.'[218] A minute or so later, with the Barcelona fans now recovered from the shock of the goal and trying to rouse their players, the referee ended the first half.

The goal had come at the perfect time for Chelsea. Had play gone on another five minutes or so, perhaps a quick riposte and another Barcelona goal would have deflated all thoughts of an unlikely recovery. Now, not only was there an opportunity for Di Matteo to reset his tactics and offer new inspiration to his players, but in the home dressing room, the

---

216 Hutchinson, Seb, interview with the author.

217 Ridgeway, Danny, interview with the author.

218 Addicott, Alan, interview with the author.

Barcelona players were forced to contemplate how they had let the visitors back into the game, and the tie overall. They had it all to do again.

It was a situation not lost on the Chelsea players, as Čech explained, 'We were ahead. We just need survive another 45 minutes and everything is possible. So, we just say we will make it as hard as possible for them, and if we can hold on another 20, 25, 30 minutes, it will become difficult for them.'[219]

The rationale was sound and, being a man short, there was little inclination to go forward and leave gaps to be exploited. Di Matteo had his revamped back four in place with Mikel, Lampard and Meireles forming a narrow line in front of them. The flanks were guided by Mata and Drogba. In formation terms it read a little like 4-5-0. It was a theme that Seb Hutchinson quickly picked up on, 'At the time all that mattered was surviving the Barça onslaught and if they picked up cards it didn't matter – the final itself would not have crossed their mind until the final whistle.'[220]

As Čech alluded to, the early minutes of the second period would be key. Chelsea needed to deny their opponents an early goal. They need time to drift away without offering Barcelona the oxygen of a breakthrough. Deny them for a while and frustration would grow in the same proportion that confidence would drift away. It was a ploy that depended on having luck on your side. Fortune had smiled on Chelsea many times in their Champions League campaign, but such things are always liable to turn. There's only so many times a blindfolded man can dip his hand into a barrel of water and come up with an apple. Three minutes into the second

---

219 *Kings of Europe – The Chelsea Story*, Sky UK Limited, 16 September 2012.

220 Hutchinson, Seb, interview with the author.

half, that empty hand appeared as Fabregas hurled himself to the ground inside the Chelsea penalty area as Drogba challenged for the ball. Bowing to the baying screams of the crowd, and perhaps convinced by the Spaniard's dive, Cuneyt Çakır pointed to the spot.

Replays suggested that there had been no contact between the players, but it would be ungracious for Chelsea to bemoan ill fortune after so much had fallen for them in this tie, not to mention the earlier games as well. 'I didn't touch him,' Drogba later confirmed, before adding for good measure, 'After [the game], he told me "no, but I had to play the penalty tactic". And he did it well. But, you know, I was worried.'[221] There was plenty of cause for concern. Concede from the spot kick and all Di Matteo's carefully laid plans would be torn asunder. Trail by two goals, and Chelsea would need to score at least once more, and that looked unlikely in the extreme. The fate of Chelsea's Champions League ambitions lay in the gloved hands of Čech, but also in his mind.

After any penalty decision there is a minute or so of protests, delays and discussions. It both allows a goalkeeper time to collect his thoughts and decide on his tactics and for the taker to feel the pressure build up on him. Čech was convinced that, as Messi stood waiting to take the penalty, he had been repeatedly made aware of his record in games against Chelsea, 'He had never scored against us. Everybody kept reminding me and him that Messi never scored, so I think [he was feeling] a little bit of extra pressure from that.' That belief fed into Čech's tactics. If Messi was going to score, he was not going to make it easy for him, 'My target was not to move. If you move slightly, he can see that you're

221 *Kings of Europe – The Chelsea Story*, Sky UK Limited, 16 September 2012.

preparing to go left and he will shoot, he will just pass it on the other side.'[222]

Whether Čech's thoughts had merit, or were merely akin to drawing the comfort blanket of a plan around him in order to bolster his own confidence, is unclear. There's no doubt however that, as Messi moves forward to strike the ball, he looks up at Čech – was he seeking any hint of a move from the goalkeeper? – before looking back down at the ball as he strikes it. Čech picks up the action, 'In the end, because I was not moving, I think, he decided to go with the strong shot on top, and he hit the bar.'[223] Barcelona's early chance to get back into the lead had gone. The ball cannoned clear and, as the camera closed in on Čech, he gave a barely perceptible nod of satisfaction to himself.

Whatever the merits of his approach and the belief that drove it, all that mattered was that the ball had stayed out of the net, and Chelsea had stayed in the game. The goalkeeper also recalled sensing a change in the atmosphere of the crowd, 'The pressure started rising and the mood in the stadium changed … You could feel the anxiety of the whole place. Suddenly, things were not going the right way.'[224]

One thing certainly not going Chelsea's way was the yellow card shown to Ivanović among the protests against the penalty decision. With Luiz and Cahill both hamstrung and severe doubts if Chelsea got to the final, Terry suspended for his red card and now Ivanović's third yellow meaning he too would be unavailable, the centre of Chelsea's defence

---

222 *Kings of Europe – The Chelsea Story*, Sky UK Limited, 16 September 2012.

223 *Kings of Europe – The Chelsea Story*, Sky UK Limited, 16 September 2012.

224 *Kings of Europe – The Chelsea Story*, Sky UK Limited, 16 September 2012.

for any potential final was looking less threadbare and more non-existent.

It seems a little contrary to say it but, as events transpired, conceding the penalty actually served Chelsea's purposes quite well. Not only did it eat up a precious couple of minutes in the melee of protests and posturing but, as the ball bounced from the crossbar, it also inevitably pushed those nagging Barcelona doubts further to the front of their minds. Was this just one of those games where they were fated not to prevail? Some observers regarded the missed penalty as a pivotal moment, not only in this leg but the tie as a whole.

Andy West saw it that way, 'Lionel Messi's penalty miss was the moment when Barça fans – and the players on the pitch too, you sensed – started to fear that things were getting away from them. They had lost the first leg despite playing well, lost the league to Real Madrid a few days earlier, and now the best player in the world missed a spot kick. At that moment, their confidence or even absolute belief that they would progress was significantly eroded.'[225]

Jonathan Northcroft had similar feelings, 'The Messi penalty miss just fades into the general weirdness and madness of that match, but it was a very important moment in the game clearly, because having taken control of the tie, and then surrendered it to the Ramires goal, I think Barcelona could have killed Chelsea off, really, had Messi converted. With so much of the second half to go, they would probably have gone on and scored again but, by hitting the bar, it kept that door open and, looking back, it just shows the fine margins that these ties are made of. I suppose you might liken it to [Dennis] Bergkamp's penalty miss in 1999 in the semi-final of the FA Cup, which [Manchester] United

225 West, Andy, interview with the author.

then went on to win, and win the treble. It had that kind of impact.'[226]

Jason Pettigrove agreed, 'I'd suggest [the key moment of the game] was the penalty miss from Messi. Ramires's goal clearly made life difficult, but had Leo scored from the spot, Chelsea would really have had to open up. Given how long there was left in the game, I'm almost certain Barça would therefore have scored at least one more goal, probably more.'[227]

If the miss caused doubt in the Barcelona ranks, it had the opposite effect on the Chelsea players, as Mikel recalled, 'It was just amazing for us and, from there, we kind of had the belief, okay, that this is the time for us to actually beat Barcelona and go through.'[228] If the whole penalty incident had served Chelsea well, there was still in excess of 40 minutes to play, and just a single goal for the home team would be sufficient to tilt the tie back in their favour. If Chelsea fell behind, it was difficult to see a way back for them. They would be walking a precarious tightrope, and Barcelona began to pour forward with renewed vigour in search of that goal.

For the few minutes following the missed spot kick, the attacks on Čech's goal appeared urgent, almost frantic, where previously they had been steady and calm, built on a confidence of success. In need of a rapid response to the setback they seemed set on scoring quickly to redeem things. If Chelsea could remain resolute for the next ten minutes or so, and stem the rising tide of attacks that were now threatening to break over them, growing doubt and

---

226 Northcroft, Jonathan, interview with the author.

227 Pettigrove, Jason, interview with the author.

228 *Kings of Europe – The Chelsea Story*, Sky UK Limited, 16 September 2012.

frustration in Catalan minds could be the English club's greatest ally.

The nine white-shirted outfield players were compressed into a narrow ribbon running across the edge of the Chelsea penalty area as Barcelona pressed incessantly, and their massed ranks, time and again, served to cut out the attempted 'eye of a needle' passes designed to create an opening. There was space on the flanks but, even with Ivanović as the lone genuine centre-back in Chelsea's defence, there was a marked reluctance for Barcelona to send crosses into the box. None of Sanchez, Fabregas or Messi were particularly tall of course, but the main reason may well have been that such manoeuvres were simply not how this team played. It meant that, so long as Chelsea kept their barrier of players between the ball and Čech's goal, it would take a move of rare majesty to prise open a gap.

On the occasions when Barcelona did chance their arm with a high cross in the box, conversely results were encouraging. With 53 minutes played, Ramires lost possession among a maze of Barcelona players around the halfway line. The ball was whisked out to the right flank where Alves, now hardly required to undertake any kid of defensive responsibility as one of three nominal centre-backs, crossed for Sanchez to head narrowly wide, with Čech struggling to cover.

Perhaps it shouldn't have registered as a legitimate attempt at goal, but a break out of defence by Drogba a couple of minutes later saw him drive clear of Cuenca and then evade a challenge by Puyol before attempting the most outrageous of shots from around the halfway line. The dramatic dive to collect the ball by Valdés gave the effort a gleam it hardly deserved, but also illustrated how forlorn any Chelsea raids would be as the game progressed.

A dozen minutes into the second period, Di Matteo made his second change. Mata had worked hard but playing as a defensive wide man was not the Spaniard's forte. He had neither the physical presence nor speed on the break to secure possession or participate in any rare chance of a counterattack. Instead, Di Matteo deployed the energetic Kalou, and his fresh legs, to assist the cause. Over the past months, the Ivorian had at times been inconsistent and lacking in concentration – the late penalty conceded in Valencia being a case in point. Such misdemeanours could not be tolerated here.

Approaching the hour, Čech walked behind his goal to retrieve a ball back-headed wide by Puyol as another Barcelona attack came to naught. It would be mendacious to suggest that the goalkeeper did not see such situations as an opportunity to eke out a few extra seconds before getting the ball back into play but, increasingly every time he was called upon to restart the game, he was roundly booed and whistled by the home crowd. Eventually, the referee bowed to the pressure of the baying fans and yellow-carded the goalkeeper. Gary Neville commented sagely, 'There's nothing in the rule book that says you have to sprint for it. He walked to the ball, picked it up, brought it back to his six-yard box, and the referee books him. A ridiculous decision.'

In fairness, Neville may have failed to notice, or declined to mention, that Čech had been handed a ball by a ball boy, but passed it straight back, instead walking a couple of steps further to retrieve the original one. The difference was minimal and, given the situation, the card was probably harsh. The more worrying element for Chelsea though was that the official had now shown how he could be influenced by the seething atmosphere and vitriol rolling down from Barcelona fans. The caution to the goalkeeper was fairly insignificant, but what other decisions would be influenced by the mounting pressure? Whether he'd been told to do so, or merely acted on his own initiative was unclear but, the next time the ball ran beyond Chelsea's goal for a goal kick, rather than passing or throwing the ball to Čech, the ball boy threw it on to the pitch before chasing after the original ball to make the goalkeeper's mind up for him.

Reaching the hour, Ivanović thumped a low cross from Cuenca clear, and Chelsea had survived the first 15 minutes of the second period. The angry passion of Barcelona's play immediately following the penalty miss had now abated somewhat, and they were back to their more meticulous lock-picking exercise. For Chelsea though, they were now five-sixths of the way through a tie that hardly anyone gave them much chance of winning and, albeit by the narrow margin of an away goal, they were in the lead.

Passes went sideways, back, out to the flanks and back inside, then a few metres forwards, before repeating the process. Chelsea's back line of nine watched the intricate movements each time the ball came near to them and, unless there was a direct threat, they resisted the temptation to be drawn out of position. Once again, passes went sideways, back, out to the flanks and back inside, then a few metres forwards, before repeating the process. Concentration was key for the defenders. The wall would remain solid unless a single brick was removed. Once more, passes moved sideways, back, out to the flanks and back inside, then a few metres forwards, before repeating the process. It was an adherence to their established pattern of play, albeit one that seemed incapable of opening up the visitors' defence, that would be criticised by at least one media outlet afterwards. The wall remained in place, and Barcelona's players and fans became increasingly frustrated as time ticked on.

Finally there was an opening. Cuenca was in on Čech, but from a tight angle. The goalkeeper rushed out to block. The game was now in its final half-hour and, since the break, it was the first real save Čech had been called on to make. On the sidelines, the frantic tactical handwaving of Guardiola may have carried little real purpose to his players, but it betrayed that the growing tension on the field was spreading to the usually calm coach as well.

Tension was also mounting for Chelsea fans as the impossibility of denying Barcelona with just ten men, unbelievably, began to look possible. Kieran Allen endured the roller coaster of emotions as the drama of the game unfolded. 'We watched at home with a bunch of Chelsea fans,' he recalled. 'And 2-0 down [approaching] half-time with Terry off the main hope was that we would not get embarrassed. Ramires's great goal just before half-time lifted the spirits but none of us were thinking about the final at that stage. But after Messi missed the penalty early in the second half, we felt hopeful, but not confident.'[229]

That confidence may have flared briefly after 63 minutes when, with typically muscular insistence, Drogba won a corner following a long punt downfield from Čech. It was a rare, if limited triumph, and only the second time Chelsea had earned a corner across both legs of the tie. From Lampard's cross, scandalously, Ivanović was allowed to leap unhindered around six metres from goal with Valdés stranded in no man's land, but the ball ricocheted off the Serb's shoulder and bounced harmlessly wide. As things had gone for Chelsea across the semi-final, it had been a rare opportunity.

---

229 Allen, Kieran, interview with the author.

It would hardly have been fair to place any blame on Ivanović's shoulders, though. Now the kingpin of the Chelsea defence since Terry and Cahill had departed, with Bosingwa excelling alongside him, tidying up and covering, he had been a rock in the back line. It was an unlikely and untried partnership, but one that was serving the visitors' cause with distinction. The Chelsea players quickly scampered back to take up their defensive positions again and, seconds later, the Serb was covering a run by Sanchez and heading down to Bosingwa, who completed the clearance.

On 67 minutes, Guardiola rolled the dice and removed Cuenca. Aside from his cross that led to Busquets opening the scoring, the young wide man had been disappointingly ineffective, especially when considering that, for most of game, he had been faced by emergency right-back Ramires. In that ill-tempered press conference on the day before the the game, Guardiola had robustly defended the performance of Tello against Real Madrid. Now he was sending the young winger into the action, hoping that some dividend would be garnered from the support he had invested in him.

With 20 minutes left, the statistics of the game illustrated how Chelsea's disciplined back line had stood firm, protecting Čech, since conceding the second goal. Barcelona had fired in 14 attempts on Chelsea's goal in the 70 minutes played, but only four of them had been on target. Given that two of them were the goals and the third saved by Čech's leg before Busquets had scored, it meant that in the 25 minutes of the second period, the only attempt that Barcelona had managed to get on target was the shot from a narrow angle by Cuenca which Čech had blocked. The discipline and diligence had been laudable, but there was still plenty of time to play in which the home team could render such resistance meaningless.

Approaching the last 15 minutes, were Barcelona beginning to run out of ideas? For minutes on end they'd have control of the ball 20 or 30 metres from goal, exchanging passes as they rotated possession in front of the entire Chelsea team stacked back in defence, but hardly offering any penetration. The passing expertise of Fabregas was removed for the more directly inclined Seydou Keita. Immediately the Mali international found himself in the Chelsea area to receive a pass. Like so many probes before however, his attempt on goal was blocked and Čech collected with ease. Had the substitution meant a change of pattern, a more direct approach? Regardless, Chelsea's tactics were hardly likely to be amended.

Tello's introduction had made little difference and, after that initial flurry, Keita's looked destined for the same outcome. Only Mascherano, hovering around the centre circle to collect the long, hacked clearances from the Chelsea box and initiate another attack, was absent from that part of the pitch inside, and covering a 20-metre area around, the Chelsea penalty area. Even when a rare cross into the area caused momentary alarm, the Barcelona players snatched wildly at the chance. A weak header dropped to Busquets around the penalty spot, but he blazed over, much in the style that he had in the dying moments of the game at Stamford Bridge. On that occasion though, there was the comfort blanket of still having a full 90 minutes of the home leg to come. Now that 90 had shrunk to a mere dozen, and the hands of the remorselessly ticking clock were nagging fingers plucking at the taut, nervous tension engulfing Barcelona.

With ten minutes to play, a fully spent Drogba was offered the sanctuary of a place on the bench, with Torres sent on. Across the years, during his time with Atlético Madrid, *El Niño*, as he was known when wearing the red and white stripes of *Los Colchoneros*, had often singled out Barcelona as his most favoured opponents, as Ryan Baldi knew from bitter disappointment, 'I knew perfectly how dangerous Fernando Torres could be at the Camp Nou, because that's where he ruined my 18th birthday. It was February 2005. Barcelona were on their way to a first La Liga title since 1999 and would repeat that success and add a Champions League triumph the next season – it was the Barça of Rijkaard, Eto'o, Deco and, my idol at the time, Ronaldinho. As a birthday present, my dad got us tickets to watch them take on Atlético Madrid at the Camp Nou. Barça were unbeaten in their last 18 league games, so it was a sure thing – a Barcelona win and, hopefully, a few flashes of magic from the Brazilian enigma. Except Atlético's 20-year-old captain had other ideas. He scored in the first minute, then again in the 89th.'[230]

Upsetting the Catalan applecart was hardly an unusual achievement for Torres. In 15 appearances against Barcelona, he had scored ten goals against them, and assisted two others. It was a stunning strike record, especially considering that, for almost all of that period, Barcelona were one of the top teams in Spain, if not Europe. The boos and hoots of derision that greeted Torres on his return to a Spanish football pitch suggested that the *cules* had long enough memories to recall such exploits. A dozen minutes or so later, Torres would give the massed ranks of the Camp Nou even more reason to rage at him.

There was now just ten minutes to play and, back in England, plans were being laid. Watching with his friends, Kieran Allen was at work on his laptop at the same time. He remembered, 'As Barcelona missed chance after chance, we went online with ten minutes to go – and had flights to

230 Baldi, Ryan, interview with the author.

Germany booked but not purchased!' All that was required was to hit the 'Buy' button, but he waited. Buying now may well have jinxed the whole thing. There was no time for things like that. Fingers, arms and legs were crossed instead. Barcelona had enjoyed 72 per cent possession, but were still denied that vital goal. The Chelsea players needed all the help that good fortune, and their fans, could offer them.

With eight minutes to go, suddenly the dam was broken. Messi slid a pass to an advanced Alves, who squared for Sanchez to pass the ball into the net. All that work, all of the concentration had been undone as the Camp Nou erupted with relieved jubilation. Just as quickly it fell silent though. No Barcelona players were celebrating, their hopes dashed, ironically by a red and yellow flag. This one wasn't the quasi-national flag of Catalonia though, the Senyera, which officially carries colours of gold and blood. Instead, it was the chequered flag of the linesman on the far side of the pitch. Alves had made his run moments too soon and was snared by the disciplined Chelsea offside line. The goal was correctly ruled out, as the replays demonstrated. It had taken Barcelona a full 36 minutes of the second period to find the back of the Chelsea net, and now they only had nine, plus whatever injury time the referee deemed appropriate, to do so again, but this time legitimately.

Less than a minute later, they so nearly did. Again, possession was switched around towards the edge of Chelsea's penalty area. Passes moving the tired defenders around. The ball landed with Messi towards the right-hand side. He quickly jinked inside of Meireles, opening up the smallest of gaps. One more touch revealed a glimpse of Čech's goal. The Argentine's left-footed shot arrowed towards its target, but struck the foot of the post and cannoned clear. Chelsea fans breathed again. Later, replays revealed that, while Kieran

Allen's finger remained poised and ready over the 'Buy' button, Čech's fingers had caressed the flight of the ball slightly. What had looked like a missed chance was revealed as an outstanding save by the goalkeeper.

With five minutes of the regulation 90 to play, what had seemed an insurmountable task when Iniesta had put Barcelona in front on aggregate was now taking on the form of an irresistible inevitability. There was still time for Barcelona to prevail but there was a growing belief that, no matter what the home side did, this was going to be Chelsea's day. Messi had hit bar and post, and Barcelona's domination of possession was stretching beyond 80 per cent, but the makeshift back line with players dropped into unaccustomed roles had resisted everything that the best team in Europe had thrown at them.

The home team's pressing had, by now, passed the urgent and was veering towards the desperate. It was a time for unorthodox formations. Chelsea had, for some while, been lined up in a 4-5-0 or more often a 6-3-0 formation. Now Barcelona's urgent need for a goal saw them lining up as 3-6-1, with Barcelona players infiltrating the white lines of the Chelsea defence. On the sidelines, Guardiola slipped off his jacket, draping it over the back of his chair. On the pitch, it was the game slipping away from his team.

With 90 seconds of normal time remaining, Torres charged clear with the ball, but Mascherano brought his run to a halt. Meireles dived in to try and regain possession but, with fatigue gnawing at muscles awash with lactic acid, his challenge was a fraction of a second late. Mascherano tumbled to the ground. It looked every inch a yellow card offence, and despite the Portuguese almost hugging the referee, pleading for leniency and preventing him reaching for the card, resistance was pointless. Releasing the official from his embrace, there was no avoiding the yellow card brandished in front of him. Just as with Terry, Ramires and Ivanović, should Chelsea hold on for a famous victory Meireles, on so many occasions, not least this one, an unsung hero in Chelsea's midfield, would miss the final. The free kick was scrambled clear and now the game edged towards the final minute of normal time.

A Mascherano shot from distance was on target, but Čech seemed unruffled as he dived to his left to push the effort wide and concede a corner. Puyol's header from the corner was well over the bar, and by the time the game was restarted just a dozen seconds remained, plus three minutes of stoppage time. If much of what had passed in this game, and the one at Stamford Bridge had dripped with a drama unlikely to be matched, the game's denouement would surpass all that had gone before it.

Injury time was being played when a cross from Alves was headed away by Mikel. The ball fell to Torres who tried to run the ball clear, but lost possession to Xavi. Another ball into the area pinballed around before bouncing up to strike Cole's chest. The full-back had little in his mind other than hitting the ball as far downfield as he possibly could to eat into the seconds remaining, but it brought a reward so much greater than that. Inexplicably, after losing possession, Torres had continued to jog forward and, with Cole's clearance arcing down the pitch into what seemed acres of empty green grass – even Mascherano had, by now, joined the attack – the only player anywhere near the ball was Torres.

Racing clear from his own half of the pitch, there was no question of any offside decision. Shedding the cement overcoat that had so often dogged his play for Chelsea, this was the Torres of old, the Torres of Liverpool or, perhaps more pertinently, the Torres of Atlético Madrid who had haunted Barcelona in the past. His control of the dropping ball was sublime, coaxing it under his spell, as he ran forwards, with the nearest defender trailing some 15 metres behind him. On he went.

Seb Hutchinson remembers the moment vividly, 'For the second half all the action took place on the opposite end of the pitch to where I was and it would not be too much of an understatement to say that Chelsea never crossed into the Barça half. This is what made the Torres goal so memorable; with the match taking place a mile away, from nowhere, Torres appeared into my view, all alone with just Valdés to beat. The moment lasted a lifetime – I'm not a Chelsea supporter but it's one of those moments in football you never forget.'[231]

On another day the Torres of Chelsea, with so much time for the weight of the moment to bury him in doubt, may have hesitated and lost possession to an advancing Valdés. Not on this day, though. Back in Spain, and on a pitch where he had excelled so many times in the past, Torres never looked like missing. 'I realised it was just me against Valdés,' he remembered with a satisfied smile playing across his face. 'And I felt it was the longest pitch ever. I never could reach the goal and, when I saw Victor coming against me, I just keep the ball long and the score was ... like a relief.'[232]

Coolly easing the ball wide of the goalkeeper, he rolled it into the empty net. Gary Neville went into raptures. 'Ahhhh', climaxed the former Manchester United player, launching what would henceforth be labelled as his 'scoregasm'. The Chelsea bench exploded as a euphoric Di Matteo skipped

231 Hutchinson, Seb, interview with the author.

232 *Kings of Europe – The Chelsea Story*, Sky UK Limited, 16 September 2012.

along the sidelines, before leaping into Eddie Newton's arms, unable to contain his elation. 'Un-be-lievable,' declared Neville. 'Unbelievable!' Just in case anyone hadn't been convinced the first time. Watching, Ryan Baldi found it entirely believable, as he experienced a moment of déjà vu, 'As he raced clear and waltzed around Victor Valdés to seal Chelsea's place in the final, maybe Torres had a flashback to that night under the Camp Nou lights seven years earlier. I know I did.'[233] Just to add to the many other strange and unexpected events surrounding the semi-final, Chelsea had scored three goals across both legs, and none of them had come in the regulation time of 90 minutes. Back in west London, Drogba had scored in added time at the end of the first period, as had Ramires in the Camp Nou and, of course, the Torres goal was beyond the 90-minute mark as well. It was just one more strange statistic to add into a game that had everything – and then added even more.

The other Chelsea players swamped the celebrating Torres as the *cules* unleashed their fury behind the ecstatic group in white. In England, the celebrations were exuberantly reflected among Kieran Allen and his friends. 'As Torres scored, the house went wild,' he recalled. Fortunately, there was at least one level head to carry out the necessary action. 'Someone,' he said with relief, 'had the wherewithal to press "Buy" and we had our flights confirmed.'[234] They were going to Munich for the Champions League Final and, after the most extraordinary of semi-final ties, so too were Chelsea.

Joy for the Blues, but only sorrow for the *Blaugrana*. Guardiola took a long drink of water. Messi sank to his haunches, his body quivering with sobs before rising slowly

233 Baldi, Ryan, interview with the author.

234 Allen, Kieran, interview with the author.

to his feet. Head bowed, he pulled up the neckline of his shirt so that it covered his head, as if hiding from, what was now, an undeniable reality. After the shock of the Torres goal had waned a little, Andy West recalled the response of the Barcelona fans to the realisation that in a few short days, their dreams for the season had been torn asunder, 'Almost as soon as Fernando Torres scored, the Camp Nou erupted in a massive and prolonged chant, "Barça, Barça, Barça." It was a gesture of appreciation from the fans who knew that Torres's goal stood for much more than just a place in the Champions League Final. The team had just lost the league, now the dream of retaining the Champions League was over, and it was common knowledge that Pep Guardiola was on the brink of resigning – something he confirmed just three days later. It was the end of an era, the fans could sense that, and their reaction towards the players was one of gratitude even though they had just lost. It had been a tumultuous week for the Catalans.'[235]

Jason Pettigrove related that the defeat and elimination from the competition, especially on the back of surrendering the league title to Real Madrid, was seen in Catalonia as, '[A] complete disaster. Barcelona's supporters were in mourning for days afterwards and the Catalan sports papers went crazy. The ire appeared to be coming from the perspective of [after] scoring two relatively early goals, how on earth didn't Barça go on to win the game. It didn't help either that it was Torres who scored the clincher.'[236]

The Chelsea players, staff and fans were understandably jubilant after the game, and Alan Parry reflected on how far Di Matteo had travelled to reach this point. 'Do you

---

235 West Andy, interview with the author.

236 Pettigrove, Jason, interview with the author.

know what?' Parry asked rhetorically to any Sky viewers prepared to ponder on his query. 'Three years ago, he was in League One with MK Dons and, this very day, they lost 1-0 at home to Walsall. He's just beaten Barcelona and made a place in the Champions League Final. Well done, Di Matteo. Brilliant!' It sounded like another element of a barely believable story, and it was.

Handing back to the Sky studio, Chris Kamara's 'unbelievable' catchphrase would have been appropriate. Jeff Stelling was seldom bereft of words in moments of high drama, but the channel's popular anchorman was unusually struggling to describe what had happened. 'Magnificent. Incredible. Astonishing,' Stelling selected, thumbing through his lexicon of superlatives. 'Flabbergasted,' he tried, before giving up. 'You think of a word to describe it,' he asked of the viewing millions. 'Because I can't think of any more.'

Ian Ross remembers the match as one of the best he had watched in his long career, 'A classic game – and a totally unexpected result. I believe Barça had already scored 100 goals at the Camp Nou that season and, having moved effortlessly into a two-goal lead on the night, I feared Chelsea were going to be obliterated. I was wrong. So were the pundits and so were the bookmakers. This was a performance to lay alongside anything achieved by their Premier League contemporaries – Liverpool, Manchester United and Arsenal. There were so many memorable moments. John Terry stupidly getting himself sent off, Messi actually missing a penalty and then the much-maligned Torres sprinting clear at the death to seal the aggregate win. A magnificent performance![237]'

---

237 Ross, Ian, interview with the author.

The feeling of disbelief was flooding through Chelsea fans in the stadium and beyond. 'I still look back, to this day, and can't quite believe what happened,'[238] Alan Addicott exclaimed with a smile and shake of the head. There was plenty of media comment to confirm matters, though. The differing perspectives on the evening's events between Spanish and British newspapers, understandably, targeted their own audiences.

In Spain, most of the coverage was supportive of Barcelona; perhaps not unfairly suggesting that, although courageous in defence, Chelsea had been fortunate to reach the final. *Sport* regularly devotes more than half of its pages to the fortunes of Barcelona and, right on theme, the publication was horrified and angry in equal measure. 'Football punishes Barça with the most unfair elimination,' headlined its online summary of events. The text itself pulled few punches, 'It is difficult to explain how Barça could throw overboard a tie in which they were so infinitely better than their opponent. Chelsea at the Camp Nou was the same as the first leg at Stamford Bridge. A squalid, cowardly, miserable team. Their ultra-conservative tactics led them to defend with all their players within, or on the edge, of Čech's area … It's amazing how, by doing so little, they were able to score three goals in 180 minutes.'[239]

RTVE headed its online report with a sombre acceptance. 'Barcelona crashes into the Chelsea wall and says goodbye to the Munich final' it declared with a slight hint of irritation that was expanded upon by the text in the article, 'Chelsea … played very poor football. Di Matteo planted a defensive wall and took the game thanks to goals from Ramires, on

238 Addicott, Alan, interview with the author.

239 https://www.sport.es/es/noticias/barca/futbol-castiga-barca-eliminacion-injusta-1704907.

the brink of half-time, and from Fernando Torres, in the final added time.' The article was, understandably, skewed towards 'local' consumption, and the theme reflected that, but the summing up was still undeniably less than gracious, 'Barcelona bid farewell to the Champions [League] showing its best footballing side but showing that there are approaches that, although much less splendid, end up being more effective.'[240]

Although often more inclined to be supportive of Real Madrid, *Marca* also gave a sympathetic airing to Barcelona's cause. 'Football does not forgive Barça,' its own online report began, before going on to explain that the *Blaugrana* had been eliminated by 'an inferior team like Chelsea, who allied with the goddess Fortune to achieve a miracle'.[241] Again, although hardly gracious in defeat, it's difficult not to detect a decent measure of accuracy in the assessment.

Only *Mundo Deportivo* shifted a little away from the need to place a comforting and consoling arm around the shoulders of Barça fans, reflecting how similar the game had been to when Mourinho's Inter eliminated the club at the same stage two years previously, 'Barça fall to Chelsea, just like in Bern or against Inter'. Francesc Aguilar's online article did quote Torres, speaking after the game, and conceding that 'football is like that, the best does not always win'. 'A cliché,' Aguilar acknowledged, 'although it is true.' The journalist acknowledged that, after Terry's dismissal, Chelsea defended magnificently. There was also criticism of Barcelona, especially following Messi's penalty miss, as being too stuck in a pattern that wasn't proving effective and,

---

240 https://www.rtve.es/deportes/20120424/fc-barcelona-chelsea/518271.shtml.

241 https://www.marca.com/marcador/futbol/2011_12/champions/semifinal/vuelta/bar_che/.

despite a domination of possession, producing too few clear chances to score, 'Except for that play [the penalty], there have only been two other clear [chances]. In the first Alexis has scored but the referee has annulled Alves for offside. *Justitito*, but "offside". And then Messi, on a terrible night, [struck the frame of the goal] again, as in the penalty kick, after the giant Čech brushed the ball with his fingers (what a great goalkeeper the Czech is!) ... Barça has returned to remember in those minutes a time of the "Rijkaard Era", with excess of horizontal football and little verticality. It was of no use that Pep [sent on] Tello (to whom few balls passed) and Keita, who was an improvised battering ram, due to his theoretical ease in the passing game.'[242]

The more conservative *El Pais* offered a reflective account of how the semi-final had played out, under the headline 'Barça's most tragic monologue'. In sombre terms it reflected the fickle whims of fate, 'They assure that God takes away those things that he has given you before. It is not that Barcelona have been given the titles since the arrival of Pep Guardiola. Barça football has captivated even those who did not like football. It happens that the ball that previously ended up in the net now hits the wood and defeats are [linked] with the same speed as victories. The same rivals that Barça recently subjected with their jazz music are now collecting the outstanding victories with a game typical of a rock band, and the strikers dwarfed in their day by Messi [now] parade through the Camp Nou to collect their revenge. It already happened with Madrid on Saturday and yesterday with Chelsea. It happened with Cristiano Ronaldo and Drogba or, it does not matter, with Torres. Tormented and rickety, very unfortunate, Barça missed the Champions

242 https://www.mundodeportivo.com/20120424/barca-barcelona-chelsea-semifinales-champions-munich_54285215583.html.

League final three days after losing the League. So are the mysteries of football for teams like Barça.'[243]

Back in the UK, the press took a slightly, but again, understandably different view of events. In *The Guardian*, Daniel Taylor unashamedly focused on the heroics performed by the Chelsea players under the most intense of pressures, 'There are many emotions inspired by Chelsea's arrival in the final but, more than anything, it is sheer wonder. They refused to be cowed after John Terry's red card and deserve their place in Munich on 19 May because of the heroism that went into a night of rare achievement and glory. As triumphs in adversity go, the night they went down to ten men and knocked out Barcelona on their own ground will take some beating.'[244]

The Times had a similar take, 'Amazing, just amazing. Chelsea did more than reach the Champions League Final last night. In the most trying of circumstances, against a Barcelona team widely lauded as the best in a generation, they defied logic, somehow standing firm against wave upon wave of attacks, before Fernando Torres scored the most cathartic of goals in stoppage time. To progress to the final by any means would be an incredible feat in a turbulent season. To do so at Barcelona's expense, after John Terry's idiotic sending-off left them to play most of the game a man short, was a breathtaking achievement; a triumph of bloody-minded defiance against truly overwhelming odds.'[245]

In the *Daily Mail*, Matt Lawton took up a similar theme. 'Salute the incredibles! Terry off, 2-0 down but brave Blues

---

243 https://elpais.com/deportes/2012/04/24/actualidad/1335300665_358510.html.

244 'Torres stuns Barcelona and books Chelsea into Champions League Final', *The Guardian*, 24 April 2012.

245 'Fernando Torres adds the finishing touch to perfect ten's heroics', *The Times*, 25 April 2012.

hit back to reach final' was the opening headline. Going on to emphasise the success, he lauded Chelsea's achievement, although the closing sentence may have contained a measure of overreach, 'This was a group of players who somehow survived for 54 minutes in the absence of the dismissed John Terry and secured their passage to the Champions League Final; a team who stopped a Barcelona side that had already scored 102 goals at home this season before this semi-final began. In doing so, they joined the ranks of the European greats.'[246]

That defiance and dogged refusal to concede found a comfortable home among the red tops too. The *Daily Mirror* found it difficult to avoid reaching back into history to compare the result with heroic deeds performed under the colours, invoking military triumphs of times past. Something hardly appropriate given the cosmopolitan make-up of Chelsea's ownership, managerial setup and playing staff. Nevertheless, a 'knees-up' was suggested, 'This was the footballing equivalent of Rorke's Drift, Di Matteo's men first refusing to roll over in the face of overwhelming odds, then, almost inconceivably, dethroning the Kings of Europe on their own sacred turf.'[247] Aside from the phrasing feeling uncomfortably jingoistic, it was a strange analogy to choose, especially given there were more African – Mikel, Drogba and Kalou – than British players – Cole and Lampard – wearing Chelsea shirts on the pitch at the end of the game.

Despite the press hyperbole the reality that the game, no matter how dramatic its conclusion, was just another step on a journey not yet nearly completed was dawning on the players. Ahead of flying out to Munich for the final,

---

246 'Salute the incredibles! Terry off, 2-0 down but brave Blues hit back to reach final', *Daily Mail*, 24 April 2012.

247 'Knees-up as Torres puts Blues in final', *Daily Mirror*, 25 April 2012.

Lampard was interviewed by Barney Ronay of *The Guardian*. He responded in measured terms when asked whether the euphoria of the victory over what was widely regarded as the best team in the world might lead to a sense of anti-climax, and a drop in intensity for the final. 'It doesn't work that way,' Lampard said. 'We've enjoyed the feeling of beating the best because Barcelona certainly are the best team, or they have certainly been the best for a long time. But we're clever enough to know that if you lose the final people soon forget the semis and the quarters.'[248] For Chelsea fans who still had their eyes on the ultimate prize, it was the sort of approach that nurtured hope for the big day.

For a few of those heroes in white however, there was a price to pay for the fortune bestowed on Chelsea by the gods of football. Meireles and Ramires, who had laboured so long and hard in Chelsea's overworked midfield, had both been cautioned and would not be eligible to play in Munich. The consequence of the referee's sanctions had been all too clear to both of them during the game but, with dedication and professionalism to the fore, each had pushed the desperate disappointment to the back of their minds and concentrated on the job at hand.

Such had been the concentration of Ivanović, however, that the Serbia international was unaware of his similar fate until it was put directly to him by Sky's Geoff Shreeves in a post-match interview. After talking with Čech and Cole, Shreeves turned to Ivanović. 'Branislav, can you clear one thing up for us? Were you booked after the penalty?' The defender nodded, 'Yeah, I [was] booked.' The blow was delivered with all the empathy that the usually chirpy Shreeves could muster, 'You're know that means you're out

---

248 'Frank Lampard eager to lead Chelsea over Champions League final hurdle', *The Guardian*, 17 May 2012.

of the final now?' Reeling a little, Ivanović first looked confused, perhaps hoping he had misunderstood. 'Yeah,' he said initially, before looking at Cole for support, adding, 'I don't know.' After a moment, Shreeves confirmed, 'I'm afraid that means you don't play in the final.' A wry smile confirmed that the message had now been received, loud and clear. 'Unfortunate,'[249] Ivanović conceded with admirable understatement. Shreeves surely wasn't aware of the knife he had plunged into the Serb, but it looked heartless.

Terry, too, would be absent from the final, and a chance of redemption for that cruel moment in Moscow four years earlier was lost. While for many that consequence was entirely justified for the rash attack on Sanchez, John Helm felt sympathy for the Chelsea skipper, remembering his pain in 2008, 'John Terry's missed penalty is what still lives and must still haunt from the first all-English Champions League Final. If ever a man did not deserve that it was Chelsea's captain, leader, legend.'[250]

On top of the suspensions, there was also the question of injury weighing against Luiz and Cahill. While the Brazilian would have longer to recover, after not being involved since the FA Cup semi-final, the prognosis for his damaged hamstring was very much in sync with the diagnosis offered to Cahill after the game at the Camp Nou. Both would be extremely doubtful for the game in Munich. At that stage it was far from clear what sort of team Di Matteo could put together for the final. Before such issues had to be decided though, there was the matter to settle as to who the Blues would be facing in Munich. Would it be Real Madrid, coached by former Blues boss

249 *Kings of Europe – The Chelsea Story*, Sky UK Limited, 16 September 2012.

250 Helm, John, interview with the author.

Mourinho, or the club who called the venue for the final their home?

On the day before the meeting at Stamford Bridge, the first leg of the other semi-final had been played in Bayern Munich's Allianz Arena, in front of 66,000 fans. Franck Ribéry had ignited Bavarian dreams of playing in their own stadium for European club football's premier prize when he put the home team ahead after 17 minutes. Mesut Özil's equaliser early in the second period served to dampen expectations and gave Mourinho's team the precious asset of an away goal. It meant that, when a last-minute goal from Mario Gómez gave Bayern the slenderest of leads to take to the Spanish capital a little over two weeks later, the tie would still very much be in the balance.

While *Los Blancos* had enjoyed a fairly comfortable passage to reach this stage, in contrast, the German club had faced some tough assignments. Placed in a group with Lyon, Ajax and Dynamo Zagreb, Real Madrid had delivered the perfect programme, winning all six games, scoring 19 goals and conceding only two. Even then, those two had come in a game at the Bernabéu when they were already six goals clear against the Croatian club. Paired with CSKA Moscow in the round of 16, a 5-2 aggregate success was comfortable enough, but appeared close when compared to the 8-2 aggregate tally achieved against APOEL in the quarter-final.

Bayern's route had been much more complicated. After only finishing in third place in the 2010/11 Bundesliga, some ten points adrift of champions Borussia Dortmund, the Bavarians had needed to go through the unusual indignity of a preliminary round, facing Switzerland's FC Zurich to secure a place in the competition proper. Success took them into a group that offered substantial opposition, comprising Napoli, Manchester City and Villarreal. Despite a 2-0 defeat at the City of Manchester Stadium in their last group fixture, they managed to top the group as Napoli's results over Manchester City effectively eliminated the English club.

In the round of 16, Bayern progressed past Inter Milan on away goals, before a less taxing success over Marseille with 2-0 victories in both home and away legs. It meant that, on 25 April, with Spanish football still reeling from the unexpected elimination of Barcelona, two of the aristocratic clubs of European football, with no fewer than 14 European Cups between them, contested the second leg of the semi-final to decide who would face Chelsea in Munich on 19 May. Both sets of fans would have been thinking that this game, in effect, was the main barrier between their club and lifting the trophy. There was a feeling that Chelsea's success in removing Barcelona from the equation had merely smoothed out the way for whoever prevailed in this game to go on and become European champions. It may have given the game a little extra spice.

In pursuit of what had become the Holy Grail of their tenth title, *La Decima*, Real Madrid quickly established an ascendancy. Inside the first half-dozen minutes, David Alaba was adjudged to have handled Ángel Di María's shot. It looked both harsh and unintended, but Cristiano Ronaldo sent Manuel Neuer the wrong way and the German club's slender lead had vanished. Not long after, Arjen Robben missed a glorious chance to bring his team level on the night when he side-footed over with the goal gaping. Minutes later, it looked likely to be the most expensive of errors.

Bayern pressed, but a neat pass by Özil put Ronaldo in the clear and a cool finish had the home fans dreaming of heading to the final, with only Chelsea standing between them and *La Decima*. A dozen minutes later, those dreams were put into cold storage as Robben scored from the penalty spot following a clumsy Pepe challenge on Gómez. The scores were now mirrored across both legs and, after that frenetic opening, both teams adopted a more cautious approach. Despite chances occurring at both ends, the second leg ended 2-1 and a penalty competition was required to see who would go to Munich.

Germans and penalties. For English fans, the combination has always spelt danger, with the idealised characteristic of Teutonic efficiency suggesting a German victory was almost inevitable. This time, however, it was more Spanish fragility than German efficiency that decided the matter. Stepping up first, Alaba converted. Having already beaten the Bayern goalkeeper from the spot, Ronaldo was a 'banker' first taker for Real Madrid. His shot was low and true, but Neuer dived to parry and then grab the ball. Bayern had the lead and, should their next man score, the pressure on Madrid would be intense. Gómez converted and all eyes, and Madrid hopes, rested on the shoulders of Kaká. As the Brazilian star placed the ball, Neuer leapt up and slapped the crossbar. It was a tactic he'd repeat the following month and, if it was intended to unsettle the penalty taker, it may well have worked. Kaká aimed for the same corner where Ronaldo had targeted his penalty – with the same result. Should the next Munich player score, it would surely be all over.

Toni Kroos would later join Real Madrid but, on this occasion, it was his job to bury them. Twice, Iker Casillas had been sent the wrong way as Bayern's penalty takers delivered. Third time lucky? He guessed correctly, dived left and parried the penalty away. Real Madrid had a lifeline. They were still alive, if only just. Their next man up had to score, and Xabi Alonso coolly did so. Now Philipp Lahm had a chance to lock out the win for Bayern, but Casillas saved again.

Bayern's advantage had almost disappeared. If Sergio Ramos could convert the scores would be level with one penalty remaining each. Ronaldo aside, the centre-back would have been Madrid's choice for such a vital penalty, but the shot was blazed high over the bar, opening the door for Bayern once more, and Bastian Schweinsteiger. On the sidelines Mourinho knelt as he watched the Bavarian-born Bayern player step up. Taking precise care to ensure the penalty spot was flat and to avoid slips, and drawing deep breaths before approaching the ball, Schweinsteiger hit the ball to the left as Casillas dived in the opposite direction. Chelsea would play the Champions League Final against Bayern Munich in their own stadium.

A month or so later, the Bayern successes and failures from the penalty spot in the heat of the Bernabéu encounter would have contrasting outcomes in Munich and, as Alan Addicott had mentioned about unbelievable outcomes, 'There was more to come in the final against the might of Bayern Munich, much more!'[251] Before that game, however, there were still other games for Chelsea to play, not least an FA Cup Final.

251 Addicott, Alan, interview with the author.

8

Domestic Matters

FOUR DAYS after that dramatic game in Barcelona, Chelsea moved to strengthen their squad, agreeing a deal with Werder Bremen to bring Marko Marin to Stamford Bridge for the coming season. The wide man's time with the club would echo that of so many others who joined but never really made an impact. In four years as officially a Chelsea player, Marin would feature in just six Premier League games, scoring once. He would also spend loan periods across four different European leagues – Sevilla in Spain, Fiorentina in Italy, Anderlecht in Belgium and Trabzonspor in Turkey – before joining Greek club Olympiacos in 2016.

The new season would see Marin inherit the number 21 shirt of Salomon Kalou. The final in Munich would be the final game in Chelsea blue for the Ivorian forward, as would also be the case for his compatriot Didier Drogba, although the latter would return for a final hurrah two years later and pick up one more winner's medal for the 2014/15 League Cup triumph. Back in April 2012, however, the ecstasy of reaching the Champions League Final had to be subdued. There were four more league fixtures, plus the FA Cup Final, to complete before that.

The day after Marin agreed to join the club, Chelsea faced Queens Park Rangers at Stamford Bridge. In October, the reverse fixture at Loftus Road had been one of the low points as the Blues' season began to deteriorate. Ironically, at that time they had been third in the Premier League and now they were sixth, with little chance of any meaningful progression, but the mood around the club was now bristling with confidence.

With two cup finals coming up in the following few weeks, and the league now virtually a lost cause, Di Matteo chose a much-changed starting 11, resting many of the players who had performed so heroically in Catalonia. Petr Čech in goal was now as predictable as Chelsea playing in blue, and he maintained his position. In front of him, Paulo Ferreira was given one of his rare starts at right-back while José Bosingwa's outstanding performance as a stand-in centre-back was rewarded with the opportunity to deliver an encore, this time partnering John Terry in the middle of the back line. Ashley Cole was retained at left-back.

In midfield, the energetic Michael Essien returned, accompanied by two from the starting 11 in the Camp Nou – Frank Lampard and Juan Mata. It was a case of all change up front though as Kalou and Daniel Sturridge offered wide support to Fernando Torres. If Roberto Di Matteo had been hoping that the Spanish forward's confidence was boosted by that iconic goal in his native country, he would be richly rewarded. Some 41,000 fans packed Stamford Bridge on Sunday lunchtime to hail their heroes and were royally entertained by a sparkling performance against a team struggling to avoid a drop into the relegation zone.

The weather in the south-east of England in the previous few days had hardly been conducive to flowing football as heavy rain lashed the capital. There was even talk of the game being postponed. Fortunately, the weather relented slightly and, against a team described by Matt Lawton in the *Daily Mail* as 'abject, impotent, utterly hopeless,'[252] a buoyant Chelsea produced what may have been their most exhilarating performance of the season, crowned by a hat-trick from Torres. Given the waterlogged state of the pitch, it's tempting to say that the Blues' players were walking on water. It wasn't quite that but, to quote Lawton again from the same article, 'Chelsea were … excellent, somehow managing to play with real fluency and finesse when the pitch was so waterlogged.'

The legal proceedings involving Terry were still pending at the time, and the FA once again decided to abandon the ritual handshake ahead of kick-off to avoid any potential flashpoints. It may have been a wise move but hardly prevented sections of the home crowd giving QPR defender Anton Ferdinand rabid abuse throughout the game. Visiting fans responded in kind with their vitriol focused on the Chelsea captain. It was a distasteful element running through the game, but was merely a backdrop to some scintillating football from the home team.

Roman Abramovich had been absent at the Camp Nou a few days earlier, but was back in his usual position for this match, and his team offered up a treat for the owner. It took Chelsea less than a minute to go ahead. Cutting in from the left, a ricochet from the unfortunate Ferdinand's leg opened up a gap for Sturridge. Another step and touch saw a clear opening. The striker swept a shot wide of Paddy Kenny and into the net. The strike breached the dam, and the visitors were about to be washed away by a flood of goals.

---

252 'Chelsea 6 QPR 1: Fernando hat-trick is more proof Di Matteo has the magic touch', *Daily Mail*, 29 April 2012.

The second goal wasn't long in following along. A dozen minutes later, Lampard's shot forced Kenny to divert the ball behind for a corner. Mata crossed into the area and, with Kenny unaccountably declining to challenge for a ball around five metres from his goal, Terry towered over Clint Hill to head home from point blank range.

The skipper had used his programme notes to apologise to the Chelsea fans for his dismissal in Barcelona and express his gratitude to the team-mates who, with depleted resources, had dug out that remarkable result. For most fans, however, the most valuable of assets is a goal, and Terry ran back to the centre line after scoring, holding both of his hands up in apparent supplication before patting the badge on his chest as if emphasising his devotion to the club and regret for the events of a few days earlier.

Torres had started the game in sparkling form. Busy and eager to be involved, in sharp contrast to so many of his other performances previously, he was a constant threat to Ferdinand and centre-back partner Hill, linking play and driving forwards. With just 18 minutes on the clock he received due reward for his endeavours and effectively closed out the result.

A perceptive pass by Kalou split the visitors' defence. Torres raced forward to collect, eluded Kenny's despairing dive as easily as he had done with Víctor Valdés back in Spain and slipped the ball into the empty net. The Spaniard's performance was both pleasing and annoying in equal measure. To see the forward playing with what looked like a new-found confidence and freedom promised so much for the future, but also underscored the frustration felt by so many at the below-par performances and 'hang-dog' expressions and demeanour that had marked so much of the striker's time in Chelsea blue. For all that though, this looked like a player with a point to prove, and he would excel throughout the game, with goals to put a cherry on top of the cake.

Confidence can be a fickle mistress but, when things are running for you, it can grow exponentially. Seven minutes after his first goal, fortune dropped a second triumph into Torres's lap. A long cross-field ball on to Chelsea's left flank drifted into the visitors' penalty area. Funnelling back to clear under pressure from Torres and Sturridge, Nedum Onuoha sought the safety of Kenny's hands by nodding the ball towards his goalkeeper. Kenny, however, had been drawn towards the action, perhaps doubtful that his defender could adequately deal with the problem. The lack of coordination meant that the defender's header had only travelled a metre or so when it struck the unsuspecting Kenny, rendering a catch virtually impossible. As Kenny fell to the floor, the ball dropped perfectly for Torres to rap home his second goal. It was a gift, but as much one born of the eager confidence to pursue a seemingly lost cause as it was to mere good fortune.

Four goals clear, Chelsea were in cruise control and at half-time, containment and avoiding an embarrassing humiliation were probably uppermost in the visitors' minds. Frustration quickly came to the boil after the restart though, and Joey Barton was probably fortunate not to see a red card after leaving his foot in on Mata's ankle. Howard Webb decided that a yellow was sufficient. QPR had struggled, and largely failed, to control Chelsea's attacks with a full quota of players. Had their ranks been reduced the result could have been much worse.

Nevertheless, notwithstanding Barton's reprieve, the home team was far from finished with their early afternoon romp. Three minutes after receiving treatment following

Barton's challenge, Mata exacted his own, more cultured, form of revenge. Another astute pass from the little Spaniard found Torres running clear, with defenders vainly appealing for offside, but driven to the left and approaching Kenny's goal from a reasonably acute angle. It was anything but an easy finish but, with defenders diving back to try and block, a cool, slotted right-foot shot evaded all interventions and found the corner of the net. It was his first hat-trick since netting a treble for Liverpool against Hull City in 2009.

A beaming Torres trotted behind the goal to meet up with the celebrations of his team-mates. This was the confident Torres of Liverpool, of Atlético Madrid and of Spain in his pomp. Yes, by now the opposition were bedraggled and disorganised, struggling to cope, but the striker who had suffered so many poor performances had put them to the sword with ruthless efficiency. It was a performance to swell the heart of the club's owner sitting aloft in his seat, and perhaps thinking that £50m may not have been a mere folly after all.

Mata was withdrawn a few minutes later to rapturous applause, and replaced by Florent Malouda. On 79 minutes, the Frenchman would join the scoring party. A Kalou cross from the right was only half-blocked, leaving Malouda the easiest of tasks to bring up the half-dozen. It had been a six of the best spanking for Mark Hughes's team, and a late goal from Djibril Cissé hardly merited the appellation of being a 'consolation', despite the frenzied celebration the scorer delivered.

With the success against Barcelona fresh in the mind and this performance on top of it, to many there seemed little reason to maintain that 'interim' qualification on the front of Di Matteo's title. It was something that Matt Lawton certainly had few doubts about. 'With every game, Roberto

Di Matteo presents Roman Abramovich with another reason to give him the manager's job permanently,' the scribe suggested. 'After Tottenham at Wembley, after Barcelona at Stamford Bridge and then the Nou Camp, where victory over the best team in the world was completed, came this – proof that the Italian can draw the best out of Fernando Torres.' Warming to his theme, he later added, 'Seriously, what more does Di Matteo have to do? He has taken a team in a state of complete disarray and revived them to such an extent they are now scoring for fun, preparing for two major finals and still very much in the hunt for a top-four finish. In the 16 games that amount to his brief but brilliant tenure this was his 11th victory, his only defeat coming at Manchester City on a night when Chelsea could consider themselves a little unfortunate. Unless Pep Guardiola does suddenly decide he wants a new challenge, unless José Mourinho suddenly fancies coming back, Abramovich might struggle to come up with a reason for recruiting yet another new manager when Di Matteo seems to know how to inspire as well as organise these players. Never mind come up with contrasting tactical approaches – defensive against Barcelona, more offensive here – and still get the same end result.'[253]

Aside from the comment about a potential top-four finish that could arguably be consigned to journalistic exaggeration, it read like a compelling case. It was one echoed by fans at the game repeatedly proclaiming, 'There's only one Di Matteo.' Mark Worrall was among them and recalled, 'The dramatic upswing in Chelsea's fortunes following the sacking of Villas-Boas and the gung-ho way his replacement Di Matteo had progressed the team to FA

253 'Chelsea 6 QPR 1: Fernando hat-trick is more proof Di Matteo has the magic touch', *Daily Mail*, 29 April 2012.

Cup glory and secured a Champions League Final berth had all Blues supporters daring to dream.'[254]

That FA Cup Final appointment with Liverpool was now just a week away. Ahead of it though, Chelsea had another Premier League game to negotiate when Newcastle United visited Stamford Bridge on Wednesday, 2 May. Di Matteo's players had endured a rigorous examination of their levels of fitness and commitment over the recent weeks and, while the remaining reserves of adrenalin may have driven them on to the performance against Queens Park Rangers, a price for playing so many games in a compressed time period would have to be paid at some point.

Before a sobering and hugely unexpected 4-0 thumping at Wigan Athletic had put a stumble into their stride, Alan Pardew's team had been on a sensational run of form, driving towards one of those coveted top-four finishes. A streak of six successive victories, over Norwich City, West Bromwich Albion, Liverpool, Swansea City, Bolton Wanderers and Stoke City had delivered 13 goals with just one conceded before the Wigan reverse, and the Geordies were in the mood to put things back on track rapidly.

Newcastle hadn't enjoyed success at Stamford Bridge since 1986 but, on this occasion, they had a potent weapon. Papiss Cissé had joined in January from Bundesliga club SC Freiburg for a reported fee of £9.3m. In the 14 games he would play until the end of the season, he would score 13 goals. The final two of them came against Chelsea on that early May evening and both would be contenders in any Goal of the Season competition. A win would have lifted Chelsea above their visitors in the table and revived hopes of an unlikely scramble over the line into a Champions

---

254 Worrall, Mark, interview with the author.

League qualifying position, but the Senegalese striker's virtuoso performance at Stamford Bridge would destroy such hopes.

As well as the FA Cup Final being just three days away, Chelsea would have two more Premier League fixtures to complete, away at Liverpool and then home to Blackburn Rovers, before their date with Bayern Munich on 19 May. Di Matteo's team selection for the Newcastle game very much had Saturday's Wembley encounter with Liverpool in mind, and the result against the Geordies would colour similar decisions for those remaining league fixtures.

Aside from Ross Turnbull serving as the ever-patient understudy to Čech, the substitutes' bench was packed with regular starters. Cole was the sole defensive cover sitting alongside Di Matteo, with Mata, Lampard and Essien from midfield. Drogba and Kalou completed the seven. The starting line-up had the inevitable Čech between the posts, behind a back line of Bosingwa, Terry, Branislav Ivanović and Ryan Bertrand. No one knew it at the time, but 17 days later the inexperienced 21-year-old defender would make his European competition debut in the continent's biggest game. Ramires, Mikel John Obi and Raul Meireles formed the midfield with Malouda and Sturridge flanking Torres in attack. The Spaniard's rampant performance and goals against QPR a few days earlier demanded his inclusion, and made it easier for Di Matteo to retain Drogba on the bench, resting up for more important clashes to come.

Had Torres delivered a repeat performance of his success against the Loftus Road club, he may have given Di Matteo a decision to make for Wembley, although Drogba's record of seven goals in his nine Wembley appearances would surely have swung the balance in the Ivorian's favour. As fate would have it though, no such decision was necessary, and only four of the starting 11 against Newcastle – Ivanović, Terry, Bosingwa and Ramires – would begin the FA Cup Final.

Perhaps it was the remnants of emotional fatigue carrying over from Barcelona that had been temporarily overcome by the adrenalin still coursing through the team during the win over QPR. It may have been the imminent Wembley date at the weekend, or thoughts cast further forward towards Munich. Whatever the case however, Chelsea seemed flat, perhaps deflated by the mundane nature of the occasion, uninspired by the everyday 'meat and two veg' of domestic fare compared to the exotic feasts of memory and anticipation. In fairness to the visitors though, the goals that decided this game were anything but ordinary.

Chelsea opened the game well, with Torres looking to build on his recent success but, probably still feeling the sting of conceding four times against lowly Wigan, Newcastle's back line was in no mood to make things easy for their hosts and the early enthusiasm of the home team quickly dissipated. By the time of the first goal, Newcastle had probably claimed the ascendancy.

Approaching the 20 minutes mark, Jonás Gutiérrez attacked down the Newcastle left before feeding the ball forward to full-back Davide Santon, up in support. Cutting in, the Italian fed the ball in towards Cissé, poised on the edge of the Chelsea penalty area. With defenders closing in, the striker deftly flicked the ball up with his right foot and then crashed a volley past Čech high into the far corner of the net with his left. It was a strike of rare quality, and one that spoke of a striker enjoying a run of exquisite form. At the other end of the pitch, the player leading the line for Chelsea was having much less success.

A cross from Torres looked to have set up an equaliser for Malouda, but the Frenchman's touch sent the ball wide of Tim Krul's goal. Then a corner from Meireles found Ivanović's head but again the effort was off target. As is so often the case in teams with one striker in ebullient form and scoring freely, his partner tends to struggle in comparison – a reference to Drogba and Torres is perhaps an apposite example – with Cissé delivering in game after game, his compatriot and team-mate Demba Ba had gone more than 1,000 minutes without scoring. The Senegalese nearly halted that run just ahead of the break though, as his shot crashed against Čech's crossbar with the goalkeeper beaten. Given the heavy-legged Chelsea performance and the effervescent attack of the visitors, a second goal would hardly have flattered Pardew's team.

Looking for more creativity, Di Matteo sacrificed the running thrusts of Sturridge for the cultured creativity of Mata at the break and, just past the hour with his team still struggling to fashion a breakthrough, Drogba replaced Malouda. A few minutes later, the visitors' control of midfield was threatened when Cheick Tioté had to be removed following an accidental aerial clash with Mikel, and a prolonged period of on-field treatment. He was replaced by Ryan Taylor, but Newcastle were hardly disturbed by the change.

With time slipping away, Lampard entered the fray, as the visitors sank further back to preserve their lead. Chelsea pressed but it was more huff and puff than anything offering a real threat. They came nearest to levelling when a corner from the right was met by Terry, whose glancing header seemed destined for the far corner of the net until Santon, on sentinel duty by the post, jumped to head clear. Terry's pre-emptive celebrations were instantly cut short.

When referee Mark Halsey signalled more than eight minutes of additional time to be played, following Tiote's unfortunate injury, the home fans cheered in an attempt to rally their flagging favourites into a final effort. Another goal would follow, but at the other end of the pitch and, if Cissé's first had been spectacular, this one would be of an entirely higher order.

A couple of minutes beyond the regulation 90, with Chelsea pressing, a long clearance earned Newcastle a throw-in midway into Chelsea's half, on the Newcastle left. Taylor's throw found the chest of substitute Shola Ameobi, who cushioned the ball back towards Cissé. Eschewing the more traditional option of running the ball into the corner, and bursting with confidence, the striker unleashed a shot with the outside of his right foot. Geometry suggested that the ball would drift wide of Čech's goal. Instead, it arrowed towards the near post before the curve on the ball caused it to jag across goal, under the bar and beyond the despairing goalkeeper. To have beaten a goalkeeper of Čech's quality with such an audacious attempt only added to the lustre of the strike. The game was probably already up for Chelsea before that goal, but it crowned a superb performance by the visitors, and the bloom of the Blues' romp against QPR was blown away.

Interviewed later, Di Matteo attempted to maintain an upbeat tone, admitting disappointment at the defeat and first-half performance, but suggesting the second period had been better. It had but, realistically, only marginally so. He also suggested that as it was Chelsea's sixth game in the last 17 days, team rotation and an element of fatigue was inevitable.[255] Given that the FA Cup Final would make that seven matches in 20 days, and the Champions League Final ten in 34, the comment was hardly encouraging.

---

255 https://www.bbc.com/sport/football/17836021.

Almost beyond doubt now, a top-four place in the Premier League was out of reach, together with the consequences that carried. In *The Times*, Henry Winter gave his take on the situation, 'On a night when Papiss Cissé scored a goal for Newcastle that defied physics, Chelsea realised their chance of qualifying for the Champions League almost defies mathematics.'[256] With regard to the league opening a door to qualification, it would have been difficult to dispute the scribe's assertion. There was, however, no matter how remote the possibility seemed, another potential route into European club football's premier competition, as Shaun Custis declared in his match report for *The Sun*, 'It looks like Munich or bust for Chelsea.'[257] Three days after the defeat to Newcastle, the FA Cup Final would offer Chelsea a chance for silverware and the fall-back of a Europa League place if the Champions League spot was unattainable, should they overcome Liverpool at Wembley.

Despite rarely threatening a coveted top-four place over the previous few seasons, Liverpool had enjoyed a run of successes against Chelsea. In 2010/11 they completed a league double over the Blues, winning 2-0 at home under Roy Hodgson in November 2010 and 1-0 at Stamford Bridge the following February, after Prodigal Son Kenny Dalglish had taken charge of the team. This was despite them going on to finish sixth in the Premier League to Chelsea's runners-up spot.

It was a run of dominance that had extended into the 2011/12 season. November 2011's 2-1 victory at Stamford Bridge was followed up by expelling the Blues from the

---

256 'Papiss Cissé's moments of magic for Newcastle pile more pressure on sorry Chelsea in 2-0 home defeat', *The Times*, 3 May 2012.

257 'Papiss Cissé's sensational double kept Newcastle's Champions League fire burning', *The Sun*, 2 May 2012.

League Cup at the quarter-final stage. Again, it was a victory at Stamford Bridge, this time 2-0. It meant that on the last three occasions that Chelsea had entertained Liverpool at Stamford Bridge, the visitors had prevailed. Their form in cup matters was also franked as, following their win over Chelsea, Liverpool had already enjoyed success at Wembley, going on to win the Carling Cup by defeating Cardiff City after a penalty shoot-out. It was Liverpool's first trophy for six years, and had given the team a taste for glory.

As with Chelsea though, the Reds had also suffered a reverse in their last game ahead of the Wembley showpiece occasion, losing 1-0 at home to Fulham when a much-changed team produced a flat performance, much as had been the case in Chelsea's encounter with Newcastle. Ironically, Chelsea had been scheduled to visit Anfield for their penultimate Premier League fixture on the day of the FA Cup Final. With the Wembley date taking priority the league fixture was pushed back until 8 May. Chelsea's Premier League experience against Liverpool would have an echo three days after the final.

It came as little surprise, on the big day, that both managers had returned to what most pundits would have considered their best 11 starters. Steven Gerrard had been a slight doubt but, by only requiring a light workload over the previous few games, Dalglish had ensured his captain was fit and ready. Chelsea's skipper also had a nagging injury, with Terry suffering from those bruised ribs. He hadn't been rested from games like Gerrard had been, but there was precious little chance of him missing the final, especially with his enforced absence from the one in Munich two weeks later.

The Liverpool team had Pepe Reina in goal with a back four of former Chelsea player Glen Johnson, who had scored Liverpool's winner at Stamford Bridge in November, alongside Martin Škrtel, Daniel Agger and José Enrique. Jordan Henderson and Jay Spearing were the defensive midfield pairing while, ahead of them, Craig Bellamy, Gerrard and Stewart Downing were set up to provide the chances for Luis Suárez.

Chelsea's formation broadly matched that of Liverpool's. Čech had his perennial position in goal, with Bosingwa, Ivanović, Terry and Cole forming the back line. The midfield consisted of Mikel, Lampard and Mata with Ramires and Kalou as the nominal wide men and Drogba leading the line. The Ivorian striker had a liking for the Wembley turf with many of his strikes proving decisive in delivering trophies to Stamford Bridge. This game would follow that established pattern.

With the game under way, Drogba fired off the first shot, but it flew well over Reina's crossbar. The early minutes saw Liverpool enjoying more of the possession, but strangely their ability to attack with the ball led to them falling behind on 11 minutes. Out on the right flank, Spearing lost possession and the ball was fed to Mata, springing forward in a counter-attack. Ramires raced into the Liverpool half and an exquisite pass from the Spanish midfielder offered Enrique enough hope to jab out a foot at the ball before Ramires whisked it past him, running clear into the penalty area. Reina's pre-emptive lunge across goal, anticipating a shot towards the far post, left him exposed and the ball skewed from Ramires's foot towards the near upright. Reaching back, Reina could only flick at the ball with his left hand. It was insufficient and Chelsea were ahead as Ramires became the first Brazilian to score in an FA Cup Final.

Liverpool responded by pressing with more urgency but, for much of the time, Suárez was denied any glimpse of

Čech's goal by a defence marshalled by Terry and shielded by Mikel. Gerrard dropped deeper to try and influence the game more. It offered the Liverpool captain more time on the ball but, at the same time restricted his ability to support the increasingly isolated Suárez. A cross from Johnson that saw Ivanović first head clear, then regain his feet to block a shot from Bellamy, was the closest they came to levelling matters, and Chelsea went into the break still leading by that early goal.

Although Liverpool got the second period under way it was the Blues offering the first threat of the half, but Cole's pass to Mata was intercepted. Five minutes later, Gerrard tumbled under a challenge in the Chelsea penalty area but referee Phil Dowd was unimpressed and play continued, much to the captain's chagrin. The resulting corner brought no reward and minutes later, Chelsea were two goals clear.

Lampard scampered clear of the attentions of Spearing. Driving forwards, he pulled the Liverpool defence out of position. Drogba drifted to the left and Lampard's pass found him in space entering the penalty area. Critically, Škrtel allowed the striker a yard of space before looking to close him down. It was a costly error. Switching the ball from right to left foot, a shot through the Slovakian defender's legs deceived Reina and found the far corner of the net. It was another Drogba Wembley goal, and another for him in a final, his fourth and Chelsea were now in charge. With his contract ending in a few weeks and a move away inevitable, it would also be Drogba's final appearance at Wembley. He had signed off in style.

With little alternative, Dalglish's team pushed forwards, but Chelsea's back line looked secure. A shot from outside of the box by Suárez, comfortably turned aside by Čech, was the best they could muster and, two minutes after Drogba's strike, the Liverpool manager sent on Andy Carroll for Spearing. The former Newcastle United striker had moved to Anfield in the same January 2011 transfer window as Suárez, when Liverpool reinvested the money received from Chelsea for Torres. Ten minutes later, the substitution would bring dividends.

Covering a run by Downing, Bosingwa intercepted a pass and seemed in control of the situation. As he turned though, the Liverpool wide man slid in a challenge, directing the ball towards the muscular Carroll loitering in the area awaiting a cross. Although the control was less than dainty, Carroll managed to shift the ball, elude the block of Terry and fire powerfully into the roof of the net from ten yards or so. With more than 25 minutes to play, and Carroll looking a genuine threat, it was game on again.

Approaching the last 20 minutes, it was Carroll again causing problems for the Chelsea defence. The striker headed a cross down to his captain, but Gerrard's shot was over the bar. A couple of minutes later the changed pattern of the game was confirmed when Čech was forced to turn away an effort from Suárez. Liverpool had Chelsea under pressure, but it was hardly a novel experience for them given the games against Barcelona, and this time they had their captain to play alongside Ivanović and battle with Carroll's threat. Di Matteo freshened his midfield with 15 minutes to play as Meireles replaced Mikel. Sixty seconds later Dalglish exchanged Bellamy for Dirk Kuyt. Five minutes later came the key moment of the final.

Chelsea were being penned back into their own area and, on the rare occasions they broke forward, the eager Liverpool defence quickly regained possession and launched another attack. Inside the final ten minutes, Suárez crossed from the right. Waiting on the far post and scandalously bereft of Chelsea defenders, Carroll leapt to head powerfully on goal. Čech threw up a right hand with the ball almost past him. It cannoned up on to the bar and bounced on the line before Ivanović hacked clear. It was a save of the highest magnitude; instinctive and of vital importance.

Carroll was already wheeling away in celebration at the equaliser, convinced the ball was over the line when Čech intervened. Following in from the header Kuyt was clearly less convinced, seeking to block the clearance and force the ball over the line. The referee was of a similar mind and, as *The Guardian* reported, 'Phil Dowd let play continue, correctly as it turned out, since the immediately available replays did not establish that the ball had gone in. While from Čech's positioning it was possible to suspect it might have, there was no incontrovertible evidence, as was the case with Frank Lampard's disallowed equaliser against Germany [at the World Cup]. It was more of a goal than the Juan Mata effort that helped Chelsea past Spurs in the semi-final, though not enough of one to be awarded on the desperate pleading of Suárez and Carroll.'[258] Čech's intervention would go down as one of the greatest saves in FA Cup Final history.

Understandably, when interviewed after the game, Carroll remained convinced that Čech's efforts had been in vain, with the goalkeeper taking the opposite view, as quoted in the *Daily Mail*, 'I thought it was over the line. I thought it hit the other side of the bar. We were unlucky. We had a few chances but we couldn't put them away. It wasn't to be.' Čech, however, was adamant that was the right decision. He told ITV, 'I don't think it was over the line. If the ball

258 'Didier Drogba seals FA Cup final win for Chelsea against Liverpool', *The Guardian*, 5 May 2012.

was behind the line I couldn't have kept it out. I'm 100 per cent sure it was not in, and I felt that from the first moment.' To his credit, in the same *Mail* article, Dalglish 'refused to criticise the official's decision even though it cost his side the chance of forcing a comeback.'[259]

Liverpool continued to press, but there were no more great alarms for Chelsea and, at the final whistle, Di Matteo had won his first trophy for the club, and the Blues had their first victory over the Reds in five meetings. A goal from Drogba and outstanding goalkeeping by Čech had won the day for Chelsea. A fortnight later, in Munich, there would be glorious echoes of such heroics.

Three days later, a very different Chelsea team would fall 4-1 at Anfield in the rearranged Premier League fixture as normal service in results between the clubs was restored. In the last half-dozen meetings, Liverpool had triumphed on five occasions, but Chelsea had won the big one. Di Matteo's players now had just one more domestic fixture to fulfil before travelling to Munich.

As had become a regular feature of the Premier League, the entire final-day programme was switched to Sunday, with all games kicking off simultaneously. Ostensibly the rationale was to avoid any potential for advantages being gained by clubs playing later, knowing what they needed to achieve in order to prosper. Just as relevantly however, it also allowed the ubiquitous influence of television to oversee the dramatic denouement of the league programme, as was certainly the case on this occasion.

Entering injury time Manchester City were losing 2-1 at home to Queens Park Rangers, with the league title apparently slipping through their fingers and falling into

259 'Was it a goal? Carroll insists header should have been given but Čech says ref was right', *Daily Mail*, 6 May 2012.

the hands of their city rivals from Old Trafford. Ferguson's team had won 1-0 at Sunderland and seemed destined to snaffle the title, condemning City's title drought from 1968 to continue for a while longer.

For the first time in Premier League history however, a team going into injury time in a losing position would win a game. Edin Džeko headed an equaliser two minutes into added time. Then, with the final seconds running down, Sergio Agüero wrote his name into the annals of Premier League history by scoring the winner two minutes later. Taking his lead from Gary Neville's ecstatic climaxing in the Camp Nou a few weeks earlier, Martin Tyler delivered his own version, prolonging the final letter of the Argentinian goalscorer's name, 'Agüeroooooo!' In west London, at the same time, a more sedate ending to the league season was played out as Chelsea entertained an already relegated Blackburn Rovers team.

With the defeat to Liverpool, and other results, finally extinguishing the final flickering hopes of a fourth-place finish, and Europa League qualification already secured at worst following the FA Cup triumph, Chelsea had little to play for, and Di Matteo's team selection very much had their impending date with Bayern Munich in mind.

The German club would also be occupying Di Matteo's attention on the day before Blackburn visited Stamford Bridge. The Wembley success had given the club a lift and shown that, in the big games, with a trophy at stake, they could get over the line. On 12 May, Bayern had the opportunity to demonstrate that they had similar capabilities when they faced Jürgen Klopp's Borussia Dortmund for the DFB-Pokal, the German equivalent of the FA Cup. Bayern had enjoyed a fairly sedate ride towards the final, only conceding a single goal in the first four rounds before battling past Borussia Mönchengladbach after extra time and penalties to reach the final in Berlin.

The game didn't start well with Shinji Kagawa building the hopes of the Yellow Wall fans by giving Klopp's team an early lead with just three minutes played. Arjen Robben would equalise with a penalty on 25 minutes but, by the time Ribéry added Bayern's second goal with 15 minutes to play, Dortmund had added a further three goals with a penalty from Hummel and a brace from Robert Lewandowski. The Poland striker would complete his hat-trick inside the final ten minutes to allow Klopp to complete a domestic double triumph. The Bundesliga title was already safely in Dortmund's grasp, as they had completed their league programme a full eight points clear of Bayern, and the victory in the final was the fifth successive time that Klopp's team had triumphed over Bayern. The question was whether the loss in Berlin would demoralise the German team, or increase their determination to win the Champions League. Only time would tell. In the interim, Chelsea still had to complete their league schedule.

Ross Turnbull had taken over from Čech for the defeat at Anfield and against Blackburn would make his second league appearance of the season and only his seventh in four seasons with the club. Had there been any doubts before, and surely that hadn't been the case, Čech's performance in the FA Cup Final had merely underscored his immense value to Chelsea and their aspirations to make the 2011/12 season the greatest in the club's history. Since the Wembley game, Di Matteo had wrapped the goalkeeper in cotton wool, not even allowing him a place on the bench for the final two league games, instead preferring to use the veteran Hilário as cover for Turnbull. In front of Turnbull, the Chelsea team was packed with players either ineligible for, or unlikely to be selected to start, the Munich final.

The back four consisted of Ivanović and Terry in the centre, both of whom were suspended. Both full-backs were squad players barely into their 20s, born within two days of each other in August 1989. Sam Hutchinson, making just his second appearance of the season, was at right-back. Opposite him, Ryan Bertrand was a comparative veteran in what was his seventh league appearance of the season. No one was aware at the time, but the defender, born less than six miles from Stamford Bridge, would have one more game to play following this fairly unimportant league commitment.

In midfield, Meireles and Ramires, another two players unavailable for Munich due to suspension, combined with Essien, whose role for the final was expected to be sitting next to his manager on the bench. The front line consisted of Sturridge and Romelu Lukaku, who were likely to be alongside Essien, and Malouda. Of the 11 starters, the Frenchman was probably the only player considered to be a probable starter in Munich. As mendacious fate would have it of course, an injury and an early exit from this game, just ahead of the half-time break, placed that selection in doubt. Ferreira replaced Malouda as Di Matteo protected his other bench options.

The remaining substitutes alongside Hilário and Ferreira were Cole, Romeu, Torres, Drogba and the lesser-spotted Lucas Piazon. The highly rated Brazilian teenager had been acquired on a pre-contract by Chelsea early in 2011 after reportedly fighting off the attention of several high-profile European clubs. Following a successful period in the youth and reserve setup he signed a contract until at least 2017. Expectations slowly wilted though and he would only make a single league appearance for Chelsea, before a series of loan moves across Europe, as well as periods with Fulham and Reading, saw early promise and enthusiasm evaporate and his career drift into relative obscurity.

Perhaps as significant as those who sat on the bench were two players who were still missing. Gary Cahill and David Luiz were both working intensively to recover fitness from their respective hamstring injuries, and had there been any slight consideration of placing one or both on the bench for this game, Di Matteo had dismissed any such thoughts. There was only one game that truly mattered in the last days of Chelsea's 2011/12 season, and this league outing against Blackburn certainly was not it. Goals from Terry and Meireles in a three-minute period just past the half-hour had virtually settled the game, before a Yakubu goal on the hour offered the visitors false hope of a comeback.

Both Drogba and Torres made late substitute appearances but emerged unscathed. Concerns about Malouda's fitness for Munich would persist right up until the day beforehand, but with fingers crossed that Cahill and Luiz would make the fitness deadlines, the 40,000 fans in Stamford Bridge on 13 May, and many more scattered around the country and beyond, had their fingers crossed that there was perhaps one more miracle to come in this most dramatic of all Chelsea seasons. Mark Worrall's hopes spoke for them, 'Anything was possible given what had happened against Napoli and Barcelona and even though Bayern had home advantage it didn't dampen the belief that Chelsea could triumph in Munich.'[260]

All eyes were on Munich, as Martin Lipton asserted in the *Daily Mirror*, 'As Di Matteo paraded round SW6 at the final whistle, patting his heart in a gesture that none of the

---

260 Worrall, Mark, interview with the author.

home fans will have missed, the Italian was surely mulling over the issues and options that now confront him. Beating Bayern in their own backyard was always going to be a big ask. Probably a variant of the backs to the wall performance that defied logic and everything football is supposed to bring you in Barcelona. Beating them on Saturday, with suspensions and injuries giving Di Matteo the sort of juggling act [that] no manager would undertake with any pleasure will be even tougher.'[261]

261 'Can Roberto Di Matteo's Chelsea manage one last triumph in their extraordinary season?' *Daily Mirror*, 14 May 2012.

9

Written in the Stars

IT WAS all set. The 2011/12 Champions League Final would see Chelsea – the most unlikely of finalists – play Bayern Munich at the Allianz Arena, in front of 62,500 people on 19 May. To any Chelsea fans looking for a little portent of good fortune ahead of the game, there was a neat significance about that date. Chelsea Football Club had been formed in 1905, and now they were playing in the final of European football's premier club competition on the 19th day of the fifth month – 1905 and 19/05. If nothing else, it would ensure that no Chelsea fan would ever forget the date of the final that year, regardless of the passing seasons that would follow. There would also be other reasons to remember the game.

The Chelsea group landed in Munich just after midday on 18 May and were transferred directly to their hotel in the city centre. To allow the players to shake off the rigours of the journey, Roberto Di Matteo took the squad up on to the roof of their hotel for a stretch and general loosening up after the flight. The move also allowed the players to view the square beneath them where fans from both clubs were gathered, drinking beer in the sunshine. It was a gentle introduction to the event that was about to unfold. Chelsea had finished the Premier League programme in sixth position, 25 points behind champions Manchester City, but were now representing English football in the final of the continent's premier competition.

Later the same day, the Italian, accompanied by Frank Lampard and Didier Drogba, would hold a press conference before a brief training session at the Allianz Arena. It was a time to project a quiet confidence and determination to the assembled scribes who would pass on his words to the millions across the world who would tune in the following evening to see who would be crowned as champions of Europe.

As with Avram Grant four years earlier in Moscow, Di Matteo was now precariously balanced on a tightrope. Succeed and become a legend, fail and become unemployed. With Chelsea and their owner, there was very little latitude for any grey areas. Since taking control of the club, Roman Abramovich had employed eight men – including the incumbent – in an attempt to make Chelsea the top club in Europe, and reportedly invested more than £2bn of his personal fortune in the pursuit. If Di Matteo was under pressure, however, his beaming smile and open demeanour at the press conference did little to betray it.

'We can win it,' he declared, as if saying anything other than that was possible. 'We have to believe and have the confidence to do so.' He was, however, sensibly guarded when questioned about Abramovich's emotions ahead of the game, 'I don't know how somebody else feels. I can only guess [the owner] is excited.' It was a safe reply, very much in the manner of the way he had set his teams out to reach this stage. 'Sooner or later, it will come. We hope it's tomorrow. But with the quality that's been at this club before and will certainly come into this club again, it will happen,'[262] Di Matteo added.

In what was doubtless well-rehearsed tones, Lampard toed the company line. 'I haven't had a direct message from the owner,' he confirmed, before adding, 'The general message is always there. He has put a lot into this club. Without him, we wouldn't be sitting here now. He's always been behind us. You don't get into a final very often. We want to win it now.'[263]

For a man who, despite the outstanding turnaround in the club's fortunes since taking over from André Villas-Boas, still had the caveat of 'interim' attached to his job description, it was a polished performance and allowed many to forget that he was 90 minutes away from the termination of his contract. The Italian insisted that his future with the club was the farthest thing from his mind, and that he hadn't spoken to Abramovich about what would happen after that, win or lose. 'We haven't had time, or it wasn't relevant, to have that conversation,' he said. 'We're all focusing on being successful. I don't know what the future will hold. I'm entirely focused on this game. You make your own destiny and fate. Reaching the last stages of this competition is difficult enough and you always need a bit of luck in a cup competition.'[264]

Again, Lampard was singing from the same hymn sheet, insisting that, despite rumours to the contrary, dismissal or appointment of coaches had little to do with requests from the squad. 'People think that we ring up the owner now

262 'Now finish the job! Chelsea ready to take on Bayern in quest for Champions League glory', *Daily Mail,* 18 May 2012.

263 'Now finish the job! Chelsea ready to take on Bayern in quest for Champions League glory', *Daily Mail,* 18 May 2012.

264 'Now finish the job! Chelsea ready to take on Bayern in quest for Champions League glory', *Daily Mail,* 18 May 2012.

and again and decide who comes and who'll be sacked,' said Lampard. 'That's not how it works at this club. It shouldn't be like that at any club. A decision like that is taken out of your hands.'[265] 'It sounded earnest enough, if unconvincing to many of the more cynical tendency. He was, however, keen to voice his support for Di Matteo, lauding the positive effect he had delivered. 'You can see his importance in the results,' said Lampard. 'Roberto has been very clever managing the situation. We were struggling for confidence and rather than come in and make drastic changes, he spoke to everyone individually and created confidence in the group. We got wins – the Napoli game changed everything – and from then on quietly he's done a perfect job. If anyone deserves to win this game, it's him.'[266] Much like Di Matteo's tactics since taking control of the club, coach and players were organised, disciplined and knew their roles.

A couple of days earlier, the man who would be the stand-in skipper against Bayern had been in no doubt about the importance of the occasion, when interviewed by *The Guardian*'s Barney Ronay. His recognition of the magnitude of the final was clear. 'For Chelsea it would be the greatest achievement for sure,' Lampard said. 'It would be a huge achievement. But I think every step has been a huge achievement – the Barcelona game and the turnaround from Napoli. It would certainly be Chelsea's best ever feat.'[267]

Perhaps the only off-script line came when one member of the assembled press suggested to Drogba that he had a growing reputation for over-dramatising matters on the field,

---

265 'Now finish the job! Chelsea ready to take on Bayern in quest for Champions League glory', *Daily Mail*, 18 May 2012.

266 'Now finish the job! Chelsea ready to take on Bayern in quest for Champions League glory', *Daily Mail*, 18 May 2012.

267 'Frank Lampard eager to lead Chelsea over Champions League final hurdle', *The Guardian*, 17 May 2012.

feigning injury to break up play. Bayern's widely experienced coach Jupp Heynckes had claimed the striker occasionally 'overdoes it a bit', adding, 'Sometimes he's an outstanding actor on the pitch.'[268] Whether valid or not, the comment had caused some controversy and Bayern had quickly moved to try and defuse the situation. Claiming a mistranslation, the club asserted that the correct interpretation of the coach's words was that Drogba was an 'outstanding performer', rather than an 'outstanding actor'. It was, of course, a feasible defence but one that felt neatly convenient. The opening was there however, and the Ivorian was fed the line. An insistent denial was both predictable and forthcoming.

To the relief of all Chelsea fans, Di Matteo was also able to offer some positive news about player availability, confirming that both David Luiz and Gary Cahill were fit and available for selection. With John Terry suspended, the coach could now at least select a defence with players in their normal positions – something that had rapidly disintegrated in the second leg against Barcelona. He was less enthusiastic about the chances of Florent Malouda – yet another hamstring victim – being fit to start. That situation provoked more of a 'wait and see' assessment. At the later training session, another concern bubbled to the surface as Lampard took a less than full part in the session, concentrating instead, for much of the time, on stretching exercises. Fortunately, there was no major problem.

Ahead of the game, the bookmakers, following form and the influence of home advantage, were strongly favouring a Bayern victory. The Bavarian club was being offered at between 1/2 and 1/3, while odds of 15/8 for Chelsea lifting the trophy were widely available. While few disputed the

268 'Now finish the job! Chelsea ready to take on Bayern in quest for Champions League glory', *Daily Mail*, 18 May 2012.

logic of favouritism going to the Germans, the England manager Roy Hodgson had reservations. Talking to www.fifa.com, he suggested, 'It will be a lot closer than some of the pundits are predicting. Most people are writing Chelsea off but I don't see them as underdogs at all. They have done extremely well to get to the final, they eliminated the favourites to win the tournament with two splendid performances. If they get anywhere close to those performances, they have got every chance.'

Was there even a case for considering that Bayern could be subject to an element of over-confidence? Had defeating Real Madrid after seeing Chelsea eliminate Barcelona created a sense of destiny for the Bavarians, especially with the final being staged in their home stadium? German author and journalist Uli Hesse thought it might well be the case, 'Reaching that final was the one thing that counted. With the benefit of hindsight, and more than just a touch of kitchen sink psychology, maybe the focus should have been on winning the final, if you know what I mean. Once Bayern had actually qualified for the final, no matter whom they were going to face, there was a subconscious feeling that the really, really hard part was over and done with.'[269] Hesse's suggestion certainly contained echoes of the feelings of Bayern and Madrid fans ahead of the semi-final second leg in the Spanish capital. With Barcelona eliminated, was the second leg between the clubs, in effect, merely seen as a surrogate final, especially for Bayern fans?

In his book, *Bayern: Creating a Global Superclub*, Hesse explained how, after the disappointing loss to José Mourinho's Inter Milan in the 2010 final, 'That 2012 final – soon nicknamed *Finale dahoam* – Bavarian for "home final"

---

269 Hesse, Uli, interview with the author.

– became a target, maybe even an obsession. Since 1984, when Liverpool defeated Roma in Rome, no finalist in the European Cup or the Champions League had enjoyed home advantage.'[270] Was the fate of the final preordained, written in the stars? It's a phrase that became redolent of the game, but not how Bayern fans had anticipated.

Bayern had employed Heynckes after tiring of Louis van Gaal, and had entrusted the drive to deliver success in the *Finale dahoam* to him. The former West Germany international had already enjoyed a successful four-year spell with the club a couple of decades earlier and, with the aggressive and combative van Gaal shuffled to one side, Heynckes was seen as the ideal man to bring some stability and serenity to the club. He delivered. In *Bayern: Creating a Global Superclub,* Hesse relates, 'Heynckes's first full season back in charge produced great attacking football and at the same time brought new defensive stability – in the span of 24 days in August and September, for instance, Bayern scored 18 goals in five games against HSV, Kaiserslautern, Freiburg and FC Zurich [in the Champions League qualifiers] while conceding none. The coach also delivered, according to plan, the *Finale dahoam*; Bayern knocked out Real on penalties in the semis to reach the final at their own Allianz Arena against a surprise team, Roberto Di Matteo's Chelsea.'[271]

All that was needed now was to place the final piece into the jigsaw to complete the picture. Facing Chelsea in the final, rather than Barcelona, had made that all the more likely. Even some Chelsea fans viewed the game with some level of fatalistic resignation. 'It couldn't happen again,'

---

270 Hesse, Uli, *Bayern: Creating a Global Superclub* (London: Yellow Jersey Press, 2006).

271 Hesse, Uli, *Bayern: Creating a Global Superclub* (London: Yellow Jersey Press, 2006).

Alan Addicott recalled thinking. 'Beating Barcelona in the semi-final was reward enough, surely? It's the Champions League Final, against the mighty Bayern Munich, in their own backyard.'

A key element since Di Matteo's appointment and, in Chelsea reaching the final, had been a togetherness in the squad, a united front, almost a siege mentality that, on so many occasions, when elimination had looked inevitable, served to deliver a cussed refusal to accept defeat that had seen the team endure and prevail. It was a 'band of brothers' mentality and, ahead of the game, Di Matteo tapped into that emotion by inviting the families of the players to visit before the game. 'I needed something personal to touch the players,'[272] Di Matteo would later explain. Terry described what happened, 'He organised all the wives and the kids to speak, and for the kids to say how proud they [were] of their dads.' It was an astute move that clearly struck a chord with the players. Despite not playing, Terry remembers being moved by the meeting. 'Even talking about it now, still gets me a little bit,' he said. 'The younger players in the dressing room, they had their parents speaking … and welcoming them, wishing them good luck, and it was such a nice touch. That's one thing that will never leave me.'[273]

One of those younger players in the dressing room was Ryan Bertrand. He had played just seven Premier League games across the newly completed domestic season and, despite finding a place on the bench on occasions, across all of Chelsea's dozen games in the Champions League he had not contributed a single minute of action, and hadn't

272 *Kings of Europe – The Chelsea Story*, Sky UK Limited, 16 September 2012.

273 *Kings of Europe – The Chelsea Story*, Sky UK Limited, 16 September 2012.

even been included in the club's designated Champions League squad for the first half of the tournament. All that would change for the final. Malouda's hamstring injury had improved but, sending out the recently hamstrung Cahill and Luiz with everything crossed was already tempting fate, albeit without any feasible alternative. Had Di Matteo done so with Malouda as well, he would have been pushing his luck to the extreme. Instead, he placed the Frenchman on the bench. The question then was who should replace him in the starting 11.

Had this been a Premier League fixture, the choice may well have been to go with Sturridge. Although still only 22 himself, the Birmingham-born wide player had been much more involved throughout the season than Bertrand, and had already played a part in the majority of Chelsea's Champions League encounters. Di Matteo considered, however, that the more positive option of Sturridge ill-fitted the requirement he had in mind. With much of the possession likely to be dominated by Bayern, a more defensive-minded player looked a better option. The choice therefore came down to Paulo Ferreira, Michael Essien or Bertrand.

Although the Portuguese defender fitted the bill for the style required and he was widely experienced especially in this level of football having won the Champions League at Porto, his age, at 33 years old, plus the fact that he had only featured in nine games across all competitions in the season probably ruled him out. Similar reasons may well have counted against Essien. In the past, the Ghanaian had been Mourinho's 'go-to guy' for situations such as this, and his legendary energy would have made him an ideal fit. That was all in the past though. Although a still more than useful member of the squad, at 29 he had suffered a few knee injuries that had gnawed away at his effectiveness.

Playing him would have been a gamble in itself. In the end, Di Matteo opted to go with Bertrand.

'I was trying to find a solution on the left side to try and find a good balance,' the coach recalled. 'Eventually I selected Ryan Bertrand to start the game. It felt the right thing to do after that week's preparation to the game. He looked the best solution for the team.'[274] Whether the young defender, being aware that Malouda was struggling, had considered that he might be called upon wasn't clear. His reaction to the news that he would start in the Champions League Final, however, suggests that he hadn't. 'You know, we had a walk and a stretch just before lunch on the matchday,' Bertrand said, recalling the moment when his coach revealed the decision to him. 'He pulled me to one side and asked me if I was feeling okay, and just said, "You'll be starting tonight!"' A huge smile broke out as Bertrand bathed in the memory. 'Instantly,' he said, between grins, 'I had this reaction,' laughing nervously, before adding, 'You know, from then on that was it. I couldn't sleep in the afternoon, but I just couldn't wait then. It's everything that people, every footballer, dreams about.'[275]

Although undoubtedly a gamble, there was a sound logic to the decision. A full-back by trade, Bertrand had the advantages that Ferreira would have offered and his young legs and boundless enthusiasm provided the energy and mobility that would perhaps have been lacking had the slot been allocated to Essien. Bayern would have former Blues winger Arjen Robben operating on one flank of their attack and France international Franck Ribéry raiding from the

---

274 *Kings of Europe – The Chelsea Story*, Sky UK Limited, 16 September 2012.

275 *Kings of Europe – The Chelsea Story*, Sky UK Limited, 16 September 2012.

other. With Salomon Kalou deployed to assist José Bosingwa on the right of Chelsea's defence, Bertrand would offer similar support to Ashley Cole.

It should be noted that Bayern too had selection issues to resolve. As with Branislav Ivanović, Raul Meireles and Ramires, they too had three players yellow-carded in the semi-finals, eliminating them from the showpiece occasion: defenders David Alaba and Holger Badstuber, plus midfielder Luiz Gustavo. Badstuber had been cautioned by English referee Howard Webb in the first leg in Germany. As it was only his second caution of the tournament, that alone would not have brought the sanction. It did put him alongside Alaba and Gustavo on that perilous tightrope though, and in the return, all three players were booked by Austrian official Viktor Kassai, and Heynckes would also need to shuffle his pack to select his best 11 starters.

There had been a brief, but surely forlorn, hope for all the six players who had fallen foul of the 'yellow peril' – but not Terry – when the international players' union FIFPro appealed to UEFA to waive the suspensions until the following season. With three players from each club involved there was an equity of sorts in the proposal, and it's entirely understandable that the union would lobby for its members. The move was surely doomed to fail however and, sure enough, the governing body rejected the suggestion, dismissing the mitigation offered that the sentence, missing out on the biggest game in the club football calendar, was ill-fitting as punishment for the misdemeanours that brought about the yellow cards. Had either, or both, of the clubs voiced strong support for the move, it may have had at least a small chance of success. Neither felt inclined to do so.

UEFA did, however, confirm that, should Chelsea prevail, Terry would be allowed to lift the trophy, provided that he did so wearing a full playing kit. The same would apply to banned players collecting their medals – both winners and losers. It was a move that, as things played out, saddled the Chelsea captain with a level of opprobrium that would survive until he retired from the game in 2018 and still found opportunities to resurface years later.

The teams for the final were therefore far from the 11 that either coach would have selected had they been given a free hand – each was a compromise. Heynckes deployed his players in their regular 4-2-3-1 formation. In goal, at 26 years of age, Manuel Neuer was at the peak of his powers and one of the best goalkeepers in Europe. In front of him, skipper Philipp Lahm, Jérôme Boateng, Anatoliy Tymoshchuk and Diego Contento were experienced, if perhaps not the first-choice defensive unit. The latter two were drafted in to replace Badstuber and Alaba.

Contento was a native of Munich – as was Lahm on the opposite flank of the Bayern defence – born in the city after his family had relocated from Naples. Perhaps unsurprisingly, given that heritage, the defender's christian name was a homage to a certain Diego Armando Maradona, who had become a hero among Neapolitans. Contento had featured in the early games of the tournament, but hadn't played since the game against Manchester City, back in December 2011. He was, however, a more than adequate cover for the missing Alaba, and slotted into his natural position at full-back. Dropping Tymoshchuk into the heart of the back line was a much bigger gamble. Although the Ukrainian had appeared in a dozen of the club's Champions League encounters, several had been from the bench – and all had been in his regular position as a midfield player.

Belgian centre-back Daniel Van Buyten would have been a more obvious choice to fill the gap left by Badstuber's enforced absence but the Belgian was newly recovered from injury after breaking a foot in January, and had only played one reserve game since regaining fitness. Heynckes went with Tymoshchuk, also perhaps having in mind that, if Chelsea came to the Allianz in a similar frame of mind to that which had twice frustrated Barcelona at the semi-final stage, having a player capable of advancing into midfield would be an important asset.

In front of the defence Heynckes had Toni Kroos and Bastian Schweinsteiger to both add security and also initiate attacks. Further forward was the triple menace of Ribéry, Thomas Müller and Robben, with Mario Gómez as the focal point of the attack. The striker had scored 41 times in the season, with a dozen of those strikes coming in the Champions League. Twenty goals in his last 17 games also suggested that the forward was enjoying a rich vein of form ahead of the final.

Van Buyten was on the bench to offer Heynckes the option to replace Tymoshchuk should the situation require it. The defender would join the game late on in normal time, but not to replace the Ukrainian. Aside from substitute goalkeeper Hans-Jörg Butt, the Belgian was accompanied by Brazilian defender Rafinha, Japanese midfielder Takashi Usami, the Croatian pair of Danijel Pranjić and Ivica Olić, with German striker Nils Petersen completing a fairly cosmopolitan bench. Ten minutes after Van Buyten was summoned from the dugout to enter the game, Olić would follow him on to the pitch.

In comparison to Bayern, Chelsea were able to field four players across their defence, each of whom were in their preferred role. Bosingwa was at right-back, with Luiz and Cahill in the centre and Cole on the left. Behind them stood the imposing figure of Čech. The man in the head guard was one of the prime reasons why Chelsea had reached the final.

The midfield was arguably part of a projected 4-1-4-1 formation but, in reality that quickly proved to be more like 4-5-1. Kalou and the young Bertrand had the flanks with Mikel John Obi, Lampard and Mata in the middle. Drogba was Chelsea's lone forward and, as was much the case in the games against Barcelona, the epithet 'lone' would become most apposite. For both of the Ivorians – Kalou and Drogba – it was widely accepted that this would be their final Chelsea game. Both players had contracts that expired at the end of the season and, with no new deal agreed with the club, moves were inevitable.

Chelsea did have reasonable options on the bench to offer support to the starting 11. Turnbull returned to his regular position alongside the coaches and medical staff after his brief foray on the pitch at the end of the Premier League season. Ferreira was the sole defensive cover, with midfielders Essien, Oriol Romeu and Malouda, plus forwards Fernando Torres and Sturridge. As with Heynckes, Di Matteo would also use two players from his bench late in the game, when Malouda and later, Torres, took their bow.

Ahead of the game, as well as Bayern being widely acknowledged as the better team, the common wisdom was that home advantage for the Germans looked to be a key factor in their favour. A consideration of previous finals that had taken place in Munich, however, may have diluted that a little. This would be the fourth time that the final had been held in the city, with the three previous games taking place at the Olympiastadion. In 1979, Nottingham Forest defeated Malmö 1-0. In 1993, it was Marseille lifting the trophy as the first and so far only French club to do so, when they overcame AC Milan by the same scoreline. Finally, four years later Borussia Dortmund beat Juventus 3-1. On each of those occasions the clubs that won were lifting the trophy for the first time. Bayern Munich had a proud record of success in the tournament having already been European champions on four previous occasions. Chelsea, however, had fallen short in their only final to date. Could they maintain the run of Munich being home to first-time winners?

Some thought it possible, with Alan Addicott among them. Despite having to maintain a professional approach as he covered the game for his newspaper employers, he had a feeling that, despite the odds, it could be Chelsea's night. 'I was working the night of the final at *The Sun*, so had to have my "work" head on,' he recalled. 'Funnily enough though, I did actually feel more confident about this one before the game. I felt it was going to take a monumental performance to win it but had a far less negative attitude, which I had when we met Barça. Of course, I was also trying to be realistic. The Germans were a magnificent side, playing wonderful football. We would probably need a bit of luck to win it. Luck, destiny, fate – whatever you want to call it.'[276]

The fickle nature of fate is one thing, but so often, in such high-prestige encounters, experience of the occasion is invaluable and, weighing that factor, may have suggested an advantage for Chelsea. Only two of the 36 players across both complete squads had previously enjoyed success in the tournament, and they were both wearing blue, with Bosingwa and Ferreira part of José Mourinho's Porto team who defeated AS Monaco back in 2004.

There was also a smattering of experience from playing in previous finals across both squads, even though it was

276 Addicott, Alan, interview with the author.

when finishing as runners-up. Four players from each squad had started in their club's previous Champions League Final. Ten players from Bayern's 18 selected had been part of the squad that lost to Inter Milan in 2010, although only four figured in the starting 11 two years previously and for this final. It would surely have been five, but Ribéry had been suspended against Inter. His determination to ensure a much happier occasion in this final was clear from his performance.

There was also experience of glory in the tournament sitting on Bayern's bench. Heynckes had been coach at Real Madrid in 1998 when the Spanish club defeated Juventus during his single season in the Spanish capital. It was *Los Blancos*' seventh title and their first for more than 30 years. Gratitude to the German was, however, in short supply. The club had finished in a disappointing fourth place in the league table that season, something intensified by the fact that it was arch-rivals Barcelona taking the crown as champions of Spain. Eight days after making Real Madrid champions of Europe, Heynckes was sacked. Should Di Matteo achieve similar success in his first term in charge at Chelsea, any thoughts of dispensing with his services so swiftly would be unthinkable.

For Chelsea, eight of the players on duty at the Allianz had been selected for the squad in Moscow in 2008. As with Bayern's previous final though, only four – Čech, Cole, Lampard and Drogba – would be in the starting 11s for both finals. Again, there would have been a fifth Chelsea player to add to that number, but the price for Terry's indiscretion at the Camp Nou was now being paid in full by the Chelsea captain.

In the final tense minutes before the teams entered the pitch, with players receiving last-minute instructions in the dressing room, wearing a white shirt and blue tie, Terry stood on the edge of the pitch looking every inch the forlorn figure he must have felt. On one occasion, when the television camera sought out the man who was missing out on potentially the biggest day of his career, Terry was seen to be in deep conversation with former England manager Fabio Capello. The Italian had resigned from his post with the Three Lions in protest at the way in which the FA had dealt with his captain following the Anton Ferdinand incident. At other times, Terry appeared lost in his own thoughts, contemplating no doubt on the rash action that had led to his suspension. By any measure it had been a reckless move, but the cost now seemed high. Any chance of redemption for the slip and missed penalty back in Moscow had been denied to him.

Suspensions, team selections and how the clubs' relative problems were addressed by their coaches, experience of winning such big games and indeed of playing in them, as well as 'luck, destiny, fate – whatever you want to call it' among other factors, all have a place in deciding the outcome of games. There was even the hint of a self-inflicted curse when the teams left the sanctuary of the dressing room to enter the pitch.

Tradition demands that, ahead of any final, players shouldn't even look at the trophy being contested, let alone touch it. Someone obviously hadn't appraised Tymoshchuk of such niceties. As the players walked out for the game, filing each side of the Champions League trophy as it stood on its plinth, the Ukrainian reached out a left hand and patted it. Did that indiscretion tip the balance of the game to come? Joe Ridgeway, Danny's other son, wasn't convinced and confessed to being far less confident than Alan Addicott had been, 'I believed we were in for a pasting. Missing some key players and the likes of Bertrand playing did not fill me with confidence.'[277]

The Bayern fans in the stadium were far more upbeat about their team's chances of victory, and understandably so. Although Bayern had lost three games in their Champions League campaign, they had won all of their six played in the Allianz. Their fans had become happily accustomed to watching their team win. As the players lined up for the Champions League anthem, a huge mosaic was revealed behind the goals where the home fans were amassed. On a background of Bayern red, a huge image of a silver Champions League trophy filled the centre of the display. To the top left, in bold white lettering, the legend proclaimed 'Unsere Stadt' (Our Stadium), to the right of the trophy it read, 'Unser Stadion' (Our City). Finally, at the bottom came the claim that Chelsea were there to dispute. 'Unser Pokal' (Our Cup).

The following few hours would test the fans' prediction. At the other end of the stadium the 17,500 officially sanctioned Chelsea supporters whistled in derision. For much of the game though the drums, applause and chants of the home support would drown out those coming from Chelsea fans and the background music to the final would be German.

Roman Abramovich was also in attendance, albeit in the privileged seats, positioned between his wife Dasha Zhukova and son Arkadiy. Four years earlier, the oligarch had suffered as his dream was washed away in that Moscow downpour, struggling to contain his emotions. Although the odds were stacked against his club in this encounter, that dream had been rekindled by Chelsea's unlikely run

---

277 Ridgeway, Joe, interview with the author.

to the final. Around three hours later, 18-year-old Arkadiy would be spilling tears, much as his father had back in Moscow. This time though, those tears would be for a different reason.

The referee appointed to officiate at the game was Pedro Proença of Portugal. Given Bayern's dominant record at the Allianz, there was a strange irony that this particular referee would take control of the game. He had officiated at the stadium on two previous occasions – each time Bayern had been defeated. When he blew to start the game though any such thoughts would have been far from the minds of the German club's players and they set off at a pace as if determined to honour the faith their fans had shown in them delivering the trophy.

The early exchanges were sparky and boisterous. An early tackle – albeit a late one, as well – by Cole could have brought the first yellow card of the game inside the opening minute when he dived in on a challenge against Kroos, just after the ball had gone, but the referee merely gestured to the Bayern players, who were demanding some kind of sanction, to calm down. A minute later, where Cole had received a measure of clemency, there was no escape for Schweinsteiger when the German flung out a hand to intercept a pass and deny Chelsea a rapid counter-attack.

Moves forward for the team in blue were already looking to be a rare occasion. Other than punted clearances from Čech that Drogba won in the air, but with precious little support, the forward momentum was very much with the German team and, unsurprisingly, the first shot of the game came from Bayern. With four minutes on the clock, space opened up for Schweinsteiger to try his luck from just outside the area, but Cahill deflected the ball away from goal for a corner. When the cross came in, the ball was half-cleared towards Kroos to shoot from distance but the effort was scuffed and harmless.

Bayern were pressing and Chelsea were dropping back to defend. The pattern of the game was rapidly being established. With the Blues' back line compressing the space between them and Čech, there was the advantage of limiting the sprinting that Cahill and Luiz would need to do, as would have been the case with the defence holding a high line, and thus limiting the potential exposure to a recurrence of the hamstring problems for the central defenders.

Chelsea did have occasional thrusts upfield in the early stages, but they came to naught and were usually followed by a brisk riposte from Bayern. One such response occurred when Chelsea lost possession and Robben broke on the right but, cutting into the area, his shot was high, wide and hardly in any way handsome. The next effort came after a dozen minutes with a Ribéry cross was headed well wide by Gómez under pressure from Luiz. Chelsea had played two games against Barcelona where a backs-to-the-wall defence had ultimately prevailed. The early exchanges suggested that this game would follow a similar pattern, but Di Matteo's men could surely not expect to defy the odds once again.

Despite Chelsea being forced to defend, Čech hadn't been overly troubled by Bayern's thrusts as the initial 15 minutes came and went, but things would begin to get ramped up from there. Firstly, a corner from the left saw a Robben volley deflected by Bertrand's challenge for another corner and, as the second cross was only partially cleared, a pass cut back from the goal line found Gómez in space. Only ten yards or so from goal, a first-time effort would have caused Čech all sorts of problems but the striker hesitated, trying to feign a shot to create more space, but his control was poor and the ball ran clear.

A couple of minutes later Munich had an even better chance to go ahead. Robben and Ribéry were doubling up on their left, and the Dutch winger played a ball towards his French team-mate before regaining possession and galloping into the area. His shot was low, but Čech jabbed out a foot and diverted the ball on to the bar, before it was scrambled away for a corner. The pressure was undeniably mounting. Studied possession 30 yards or so from goal was one thing, but now the red shirts were finding gaps in the blue defence and threatening danger with worrying frequency.

Corners for Bayern were becoming a regular feature as they pressed along the flanks of the Chelsea defence and, for some periods, Neuer was the only player stationed in the Bayern half. An incisive run and pass found Kroos in space inside the area but his turn and cross found no one in support and the ball drifted harmlessly behind. With 25 minutes gone the statistics revealed that Bayern had fired in six attempts on Chelsea's goal and earned seven corners, with Chelsea's totals being stuck at zero on both counts. Unsurprisingly, Bayern had also enjoyed 64 per cent of the possession. For most people watching, and given the flow of the game, even those overwhelming figures felt understated.

On the half-hour, a clumsy challenge on Müller by Luiz – the sort of ill-disciplined play that many pundits had focused on to categorise the Brazilian as unreliable at the highest level – offered Bayern a free kick towards the edge of the penalty area, just to the right of the arc. It seemed an ideal distance and position for the left-footed Robben, but his shot was tame, cannoning into the wall and away. A third of the scheduled 90 minutes had been completed and, despite the Bayern pressure, Chelsea's back line had held firm. It was probably as much as Di Matteo could have hoped for given the pattern of the game. The remaining 15 minutes or so of the first period would bring more pressure, however.

Just a few minutes later, a break of the ball fell to Robben on the edge of the area as Müller tried to squirm free. His shot was scuffed and bounced into the welcoming arms of Čech, but the duel between the Dutch forward and the Czech goalkeeper still had plenty of time to run. On 34 minutes Chelsea earned a free kick almost mirroring the one where Robben struck the wall as Cahill ventured forward, offering and exchanging passes with Kalou before being tumbled over by Boateng. It brought a rare opportunity for Chelsea to put Neuer to the test. The goalkeeper built his wall with the precision of the fussiest of architects. It served little purpose though as Mata's shot flew well over both wall and crossbar. Chelsea's raids had been so infrequent that such profligacy was to be lamented.

Bayern's ploy of doubling up with Robben and Ribéry on one flank was a thorn in the side of Chelsea's defence – the right side in particular, where Bosingwa was often finding himself outnumbered and outgunned whenever he was left without support. Ten minutes ahead of the break the duo combined again but, as Ribéry cut into the box, he dragged his shot wide of Čech's near post. 'Mikel needs to get across quicker to help,' explained Gary Neville to the Sky Sports viewers, as he sat next to Martin Tyler in the commentary box. Chelsea would need to take note of the threat. A brief minute later Bosingwa was exposed again as Contento overlapped Ribéry to hit the goal line before crossing to Müller. The forward had found an unforgivable amount of space around the penalty spot, but his left-footed volley flew wide. The German put his hands on his head, looked to the heavens and puffed out his cheeks in exasperation. Another good chance had gone begging.

It preceded a brief, but encouraging period for the Blues. Firstly, Lampard flicked a ball on towards Drogba in the area, but an unhelpful bounce and a couple of Bayern defenders shielded him clear. Then Kalou tried to force his way into the box before being crowded out. Finally, a neat piece of interplay saw Kalou given space to fire in a shot. It was tame and Neuer collected without great discomfort, but those few minutes did show that perhaps there was still plenty in the game for Chelsea, if they could keep a clean sheet at the other end – and there was the rub.

Again, down the Bayern left, Ribéry and Robben combined, but the ball was scrambled clear after the latter failed to control effectively on the edge of the area. Cahill broke clear and fed Mata but the move broke down. With half-time approaching, there was a marked reluctance for Chelsea players to overcommit. Seconds later, justification for such caution became clear.

An attempted cross was half-blocked and ran towards Gómez on the edge of the box with his back to goal. The striker's overhead kick was blocked by Cahill, but the ball fell towards Robben in space on the edge of the box. Aware of the blue shirts charging to close him down, instead of shooting, he played the ball on towards the Bayern left, finding Ribéry in space as the defenders were drawn towards the Dutchman. With the ball bouncing up unhelpfully in front of him, Ribéry tried to hook a volley on goal, but sliced the effort terribly. Bypassing all of the Chelsea defenders in transit, the ball found its way to Gómez, lurking a few metres from goal with just Čech to beat. As with the earlier chance though, instead of going for the first-time shot which would have given the goalkeeper precious little time to react, he attempted to control the ball first, but it ran away from him and Cole hoofed it clear for a corner.

Müller's hands again found the top of his head and Ribéry looked aghast at his team-mate as Gómez found an unjustified reason to look with menace at the pitch in front of him and his colleagues' glares burnt holes in the top of his head. With each passing chance the pressure on the Bayern players seemed to be growing, unnerving them at the same time. Gómez had enjoyed a hugely successful season in the Bundesliga and in a domestic fixture would surely have buried the opportunity. Perhaps it was the occasion, perhaps the opportunities that were slipping through his team's fingers that created the tension but, with the desire to make extra sure of having the ball under his control before shooting, the opening, like others before, and more to come, slipped away. Tyler confirmed the impression. 'He's a one-touch finisher,' he declared of Gómez. 'That's his game.' Neville concurred with his commentator, 'You'd never suggest that a player of his quality, Gómez, could freeze on this stage, but he's showing the early signs of his anxiety, and not doing things [that come] naturally to him, and taking the shots early.' Robben's corner was hit too long and Chelsea fans could breathe again.

The concern identified by the commentators may have been spreading through the Bayern team. From Chelsea's throw-in, Bayern regained possession. Tymoshchuk drove forward from his own half with the ball at his feet before firing in a shot from around 40 yards. It struck Gómez in flight and bounced tamely wide but, even if it had enjoyed a clear flight, expecting to beat Čech from such distance was extravagantly optimistic at best, nervously wasteful at worst.

For the next couple of minutes Chelsea tried to defuse the growing pressure by maintaining possession. They did so but any resultant attack was driven more by hope than expectation, and easily coped with by the red-shirted defenders. It was a temporary respite.

Bayern shuffled the ball out to the right, where Robben collected before driving forcefully towards the box. He fed a pass to Müller who, challenged by Luiz, turned the ball on to Gómez, with Cahill in close attendance. The forward adroitly allowed the ball to run across his body, evading Cahill's attempted tackle and was clear on goal from around a dozen yards out. Surely this time. As Cahill recovered and threw himself to block, Gómez stretched for the ball and his shot flew high and well wide as he fell backwards. Standing in front of the Bayern bench, Heynckes threw his arms up in the air in exasperation, asking how many more chances his players would squander. In the stands, Bayern fans replicated their coach's actions and query.

The final couple of minutes of the first half were played out without any further major dramas. As the players headed towards the dressing room, Chelsea fans would have been relieved, those supporting Bayern frustrated. It was a chance for reflection and assessment ahead of the action resuming.

Joe Ridgeway took a deep breath as the half-time whistle sounded. Chelsea had been second best, and by a long way, but the scoreline was still blank and, the longer it stayed that way, the more he felt it favoured his team. 'As the game went on, the nerves were so immense as we were getting dominated,' he remembered. 'However, every chance missed made me feel like something special could happen.'[278] Having struggled to survive the first period, hope for 'something special' was probably the only refuge for Chelsea fans still clinging to dreams of glory.

278 Ridgeway, Joe, interview with the author.

He wasn't alone in harbouring such thoughts. Mark Worrall recalls having similar emotions at the time, 'As the game went on, there was a growing sense that Bayern Munich were perhaps buckling under the heavy weight of local expectation, especially given the arrogance of the pre-match banner displays proclaiming "Our City, Our Stadium, Our Cup". That said, nerves were jangling every time Bayern went forward but they kept fluffing their lines in front of goal and as long as they did that, we knew Chelsea had a puncher's chance of flooring them.'[279]

The boxing metaphor was an apt tool to describe the first period. Bayern had metaphorically 'boxed Chelsea's head off' with jabs that irritated, but hardly threatened to hurt. Each time they had thrown a haymaker punch, targeted at a knockout blow, their swing had missed the target. In boxing, the judges would have had Bayern well ahead on points, but in football points don't make prizes, only goals do, and Bayern had failed to land that big punch. Bruised and a little battered, Chelsea were still standing. Could they perform the famous Muhammad Ali 'Rope-a-Dope' trick and let their opponents punch themselves out before delivering their own sucker punch? Such hopes were pretty much all that the Chelsea fans had to cling on to.

How had the first half been perceived by the German audience? Uli Hesse's assessment was strangely familiar to that espoused by Joe Ridgeway and Mark Worrall, with Bayern fans becoming increasingly concerned with each chance that slipped by, but he still thought that Bayern would prevail. 'I'm sure Bayern fans felt that way,' he said. 'They also became increasingly aware that this "final at home" thing was maybe a burden more than a blessing. Most

279 Worrall, Mark, interview with the author.

German football fans, who as a rule support whoever Bayern happen to play, probably thought Bayern will score and win anyway, because they always do.'[280]

Neither coach made any personnel changes at the break and, as the second half got under way, it seemed like the pattern of the game would remain the same as well. Inside the first 60 seconds Ribéry rampaged down the Bayern left before hitting a low cross into the Chelsea penalty area, but Luiz hacked the ball clear. Bayern had clearly come out with a renewed intent to get the job done. If their fans had spent the 15 minutes of the half-time break pushing to the back of their minds the unpalatable possibility that the team would ultimately be punished for such wanton wastefulness in the first period, that rapid sally from Ribéry infused them with belief again, and the chants and songs were taken up once more.

Two minutes later that belief received further encouragement. This time it was Robben down Bayern's right. A favourable bounce allowed the Dutch wide man to outpace Luiz, before the ever-diligent Cole demonstrated he had the speed to live with his erstwhile team-mate and chased back to block Robben's cross, as Luiz tried to recover his position. The ball was half-cleared but fell to Kroos, who chose to chance his luck with a shot from distance. Luiz was, by now, back in his central defensive position and, as the ball arrowed on target, he flicked his curled locks at it to divert the shot over the bar for a corner. The corner was played short before Robben swung a cross into the box, but it came to nothing.

For the next few minutes Bayern were camped around the edge of Chelsea's penalty area and, each time the ball was

---

280 Hesse, Uli, interview with the author.

cleared upfield, with Drogba the only blue shirt forwards, inevitably it was returned. The period ended when another punt upfield created a brief moment of forward play for Chelsea and Drogba fired in the most optimistic of shots from distance that flew wide of Neuer's near post. The first five minutes of the second period had now passed. Chelsea still had their clean sheet and Bayern's early rapid ardour had settled back into the studied possession of the first period as they probed and pressed for an opening.

On 53 minutes, just as Chelsea were enjoying an increased portion of possession, Bayern struck. Encouraged by a new and seductive relationship with the ball, the Blues pressed further forward, but the space that the ambition created at the back was as an invite for Bayern. Ribéry set Müller free down the left, before continuing his run in an overlapping move. The midfielder shrugged off a challenge by Lampard and ploughed on to the edge of the area. Seeing only a crowd of blue shirts in the box, outnumbering the lone Gómez, he pulled the ball back to the area where Robben was waiting. The shot was well struck, low to Čech's left and may have been heading for the corner before Cole jabbed out a foot to deflect the ball wide of the far post. Instead of running behind for a corner though, the ball was directed towards Ribéry, whose support run had taken him into the box. With Čech helpless on the floor after plunging to save Robben's initial shot, it was an easy task for the Frenchman to guide the ball into the empty net. The phrase 'it had been coming' seldom felt more apt.

A goal would hardly have flattered the German team but, in his enthusiasm to support the attack, Ribéry's run had carried him well forward and, when Robben struck his shot, he was in a marginally but indisputably offside position. As the assistant referee stood with his flag in the air, the

Frenchman cursed his ill fortune and wagged a dissenting finger towards the official, insisting that he was wrong. On the sidelines, several of Bayern substitutes, warming up by the man with the flag, offered forlorn comments, supporting Ribéry's cause. It was all to no avail. On the sole occasion when Bayern had found the back of the Chelsea net they had been denied again. Chelsea fans breathed a sigh of relief. For those supporting Bayern, the confidence and belief sustained another small dent. Was there a benign fate protecting the London club?

Neville had spoken about how the outcome of some games seems to be written in the stars, and, regardless of what the players of either team do in earnest endeavour to alter things, that preordained design, conceived above, will always have its way. To many, such talk is mere nonsense. Each time similar things appear to happen, however, the case for a higher force deciding the way events play out only gathers strength. That offside flag contributed to the theory. 'The words "written" and "stars" come into a phrase coined by Gary Neville,' Tyler opined.

Ten minutes into the second half, Kroos fired in a shot from a distance and angle that all but precluded any hope of success. In the Bayern dugout Heynckes yelled out in frustration at such waste. The coach could feel that the pressure was getting to his players, causing them to abandon the disciplined professional practices that had taken them to the final. They continued to press though, and approaching the hour a chance fell to Robben inside the penalty area. His shot was struck powerfully but Cole blocked at point-blank range and the ball flew clear. 'Cole was magnificent,' commented Neville. It was a more than fair assessment. Noting the space and the ball dropping towards Robben, the full-back had darted forward from his position as others hesitated and had saved the day. The defender, widely regarded as one of the best exponents of his role, had twice been a loser in Champions League Finals, being beaten by Barcelona with Arsenal two years before Moscow. His determination to avoid an unwanted hat-trick was clear.

Entering the final 30 minutes, the Bayern fans sensed that their team needed a lift and broke out into raucous chants of 'Bayern, Bayern' accompanied by synchronised clapping. In response, chants of 'Chelsea, Chelsea' arose from behind Neuer's goal. In line with the contest on the pitch, the competition between the supporters in the stands was being stepped up as well.

Two minutes later, a run down the Bayern right and a neat wall pass with Gómez set Schweinsteiger free. Unfortunately lacking the pace of Robben or Ribéry, the midfielder was unable to exploit the opportunity to run in for a strike on goal, and his low cross was comfortably gathered by Čech, with no red-shirted forwards in attendance. Then, Ribéry charged forward on another attack down the left but, running into the blue wall on the edge of the box, possession was lost. In the previous few minutes, Bayern's attacks had lost some of their early menace. A shot dragged wide by Ribéry confirmed the trend. The Frenchman's reaction, with hands on hips and a downcast demeanour, reflected the deepening concern of all those decked in red, both on and off the pitch.

The clock was now showing less than 20 minutes of the regulation 90 remaining. Bayern were still pressing and offering waves of attacks, but increasingly looking like they were running out of ideas. For the last few minutes, thanks to tackles and blocks plus some wayward Bayern marksmanship, Čech hadn't been called on to save a shot. Chelsea even began to look like they believed that a goal on the break was possible. Superb interplay between Kalou and Mata opened up space on the Chelsea right for Bosingwa. The defender's cross arrowed towards Kalou's head as he ran into the box, but Tymoshchuk had tracked the Ivorian and just got there first to head clear. Bayern instantly responded and Robben hit a shot on target requiring intervention from Čech at last. It was almost catching practice for the goalkeeper however, as the attempt flew straight into his arms.

On 72 minutes, with Malouda standing on the sidelines awaiting his entrance, Chelsea threatened again. Bertrand had already taken a quick glance to the Chelsea bench to see the Frenchman, and probably realised that his time on the pitch was coming to an end, when he slid a ball down the touchline to Drogba. In typically muscular fashion, the forward shrugged aside the challenge of Tymoshchuk and powered into the box. Mata and Kalou were racing to get up in support but, when compelled to make his cross, Drogba's pass reached the six-yard line before either man in blue, and the danger was swept clear for a throw-in by Contento.

Before the restart, Di Matteo made his change. Bertrand walked slowly towards the sidelines, the physical efforts and mental stresses of the previous 72 minutes etched on his young face. He slapped hands with Malouda before receiving a pat from his coach and slumping down on the bench. He'd let no one down, and now Cole had Malouda's fresh legs in front of him to help repel Bayern thrusts down Chelsea's left. From the restart, a cross by Cole was only flapped at by Neuer, but Drogba's resulting shot was scuffed, speaking of understandable fatigue, and the goalkeeper gratefully gathered the ball. There was little doubt though that, with the game heading towards its final quarter-hour, Chelsea were now enjoying their best period.

At such times can matches turn. Bayern had looked less convincing in the previous few minutes but, when a ball broke to Müller inside the Chelsea penalty area, it could have been the decisive moment. Faced by the indefatigable Cole though, the Germany international pulled his shot well wide. 'If you're a Chelsea fan sitting at home,' Neville suggested, 'you must think something is happening here.' On the bench, as his coaches fell back in their chairs in frustration, Heynckes found temporary relief by straightening his tie. Müller only offered a rueful smile. It was a 'what have we got to do to score?' gesture of exasperation. The answer would come five minutes later, but Chelsea would receive advance warning first.

Inside the last ten minutes, a recovering Cole tripped Müller as the German cut back inside. The yellow card was undeniably just. From the resultant free kick, Bayern moved the ball out to their left flank and, when the cross came in towards the far post from Contento, Cole was compromised by the extra height of Müller, but the German's header was comfortably dealt with by Čech. Any aerial challenge between Cole and Müller would surely favour the German whenever Bayern could construct such an encounter. Shortly afterwards, the ploy delivered the breakthrough.

The clock had gone beyond 82 minutes when the move out on the left was repeated. This time the cross came in from Kroos. It was unclear whether he had picked out the run of the willowy Müller but, when the ball arrived at the far post, Cole was powerless to deal with the threat of the German international as he ran wide of the full-back. The header was driven down into the ground and bounced up and over the arms of Čech, who was startled by the flight of the ball as it clipped the underside of the bar before nestling in the back of the net. The clock read 83 minutes and ten seconds.

The Bayern players piled on top of the goalscorer in an untidy heap on the edge of the penalty area as the Chelsea players contemplated their fate. For the overwhelming majority of the previous 82 minutes, Bayern had been by far the better side and few could, with any justification, claim that the lead wasn't deserved. It was a crushing blow for Chelsea and while the Bayern fans celebrated with as much relief as joy, behind Neuer's goal, the crowd dressed in blue fell morosely silent.

The mood on the pitch, for those in blue, was very similar. Watching the Bayern players cavort ecstatically was difficult as Cole remembered, 'They celebrated like they'd won it. Everyone's head was down and you're thinking, "That's it." You're that close to winning the game, or going to penalties and extra time, and then you've just lost it like that. It was hard to take.'[281]

'Yep, game set and match,'[282] Joe Ridgeway remembered as he contemplated the cold, empty emotion while the Germans celebrated. Thoughts were similar in Germany as Uli Hesse recalled. After all those missed chances Bayern did what Bayern always seem to do, 'It suddenly all seemed to make sense. Which just goes to show you that humans try to find stories and patterns in whatever happens.'[283] It had been Bayern's 27th attempt on goal in the game up to that point. No one could argue about the lead being merited. As the words 'written' and 'stars' now slipped out of reality and into the realms of caprice and fancy, strangely for some, hope

---

281 *Kings of Europe – The Chelsea Story*, Sky UK Limited, 16 September 2012.

282 Ridgeway, Joe, interview with the author.

283 Hesse, Uli, interview with the author.

still sprang eternal. After all, Chelsea had scored in every Champions League tie that season.

'It was late, very late,' Mark Worrall remembered. 'I remember looking at the scoreboard, then my watch and then asking my mates how long left, even though I knew there was less than ten minutes including any stoppage time the ref might add on. We just got behind the team. "Chelsea. Chelsea. Chelsea." You have to, don't you? There's nothing else you can do. I just thought, come on, throw the kitchen sink at it, rather concede again than not try to score or give up, not that that was going to happen with Didier Drogba determined to atone for his Moscow mishap back in 2008.'[284]

Somewhat akin to Terry, Drogba felt he had a debt to repay from Moscow. A petulant slap across the face of Manchester United's Nemanja Vidić had seen the Ivorian red-carded in the final four years previously. It meant that, when the crucial penalty – the one that Chelsea needed to convert to lift the trophy – came around, Drogba was missing from the roster of takers, requiring Terry to step up in his place and bear the pain of that slip. Terry's chance of redemption had been lost with that red card in the Camp Nou. Had Drogba's fate now been similarly decided by Müller's goal?

For Chelsea now it was a case of picking up on the thread of Mark Worrall's comments. To quote from Bob Dylan, 'When you ain't got nothing, you've got nothing to lose.'[285] With around eight minutes to save the game, it was time to play all of the cards in Di Matteo's hand. Torres was sent on to replace Kalou. The much-maligned Ivorian had played his last game in Chelsea blue. From the other bench, Heynckes

---

284 Worrall, Mark, interview with the author.

285 Dylan, Bob, 'Like a Rolling Stone', *Highway 61 Revisited* (Columbia 1965).

took the opposite tack. He had plenty to lose and sought to add an extra level of protection. Before the change could be made, however, Luiz cut down Robben in what looked like a petulant foul born of the frustration and disappointment Cole had referred to. It hardly aided Chelsea's cause and the yellow card he received was entirely justified.

Before the free kick was taken Heynckes made the change, removing the goalscorer and sending on Van Buyten to bolster his defence. Given the flow of the game up to that point it looked both overly cautious and entirely understandable at one and the same time. Müller walked to the sidelines and smacked both palms of his replacement before turning to the still-celebrating crowd and offering up a double-fisted salute with arms raised in triumph. He clearly believed that his goal had won the trophy for Bayern. Few in the stadium or among the millions watching on television would have doubted his assessment.

Against a backdrop of celebrating Bayern fans bellowing support for their team with drums beating out the rhythm, the free kick was taken short and eventually Ribéry ran the ball out of play to give Chelsea a chance to launch a late attack. The clock read 86 minutes and 48 seconds as Čech struck the ball long upfield. Van Buyten headed clear above Torres and the ball ran out for a throw-in just inside the Chelsea half. The clock read 87 minutes and nine seconds as Mikel received the ball from Bosingwa.

The Nigerian midfielder strode forward towards the halfway line before being closed down by Ribéry. Seeing Mata come short to accept a pass, Mikel fed the ball on to the diminutive Spaniard who turned the ball, first time, out towards Chelsea's right flank and his compatriot Torres. On another day, the striker may have simply returned the ball and spun to seek space further forwards. There was no time for a more considered approach though; direct action was required. Torres turned and hared down the touchline towards the corner flag with Contento in pursuit. The defender slid in with a tackle, tumbling Torres, but his contact with the ball first ensured that it was a corner rather than a free kick. After 87 minutes and 22 seconds, it would be both Chelsea's first corner of the game, and probably their last chance to save it. Luiz was forward. Cahill was forward.

'Where there's life there's hope,' Tyler offered as scant encouragement to any Chelsea fans watching, as the referee separated a few pushing and shoving players in the box. Seconds ticked away. By the time he signalled for Mata to take the corner, the clock had reached 87 minutes and 49 seconds. The tension was ramped up as the ball came into the area. For Danny Ridgeway it was a moment frozen in time, 'There was ten minutes to go and we hadn't been playing particularly well [when Bayern went ahead]. Once they scored, I didn't know where the equaliser was going to come from, but then up stepped the Drogs once again!'[286]

Drogba relived the events leading up to the goal, and his message as he stood waiting in the penalty area. 'I tried to show to Juan that this is where I want the ball,' he said, lost for a moment in the memory. 'I don't know, I just went. I just saw the ball coming and I just, I just went for it.'[287] The ball's trajectory took it towards Neuer's near post, eliminating the chance of the goalkeeper coming out to collect. Lampard advanced towards the ball, but before he could make contact, the towering figure of Drogba beat him to it. The header was so powerful that, even though Neuer got his hand to the ball, he could only guide it into the roof of the net. 'Drogba!'

286 Ridgeway, Danny, interview with the author.

287 *Kings of Europe – The Chelsea Story*, Sky UK Limited, 16 September 2012.

screamed Tyler, reprising his famous Agüero moment of half a dozen days earlier. All Neville, a man rarely lost for words, could offer was an echo of his climatic exclamation of Torres's goal against Barcelona.

The clock read 87 minutes and 52 seconds. For five minutes and 42 seconds Bayern Munich's players and fans had been allowed a brief glimpse of triumph and those of Chelsea were invited to glance over the precipice and into a pit of despair. A week is a long time in politics but, in football, five minutes and 42 seconds is apparently an eternity; time enough to transform euphoria into exasperation and desolation into delirium. Watching, Ian Ross was as surprised as anyone, 'Like everyone else I thought it had gone when Thomas Müller scored late on. Few teams in Europe were better equipped than Bayern to close out a game, to defend a slender lead. But I was wrong – Drogba levelled thing up with a truly magnificent header.'[288] As Bayern fans fell into a disbelieving silence, the supporters wearing blue behind Neuer's goal exploded in rapturous delight.

In typical Drogba fashion, the striker slid on his knees towards the massed ranks of Chelsea fans, arms aloft before crossing himself in thanks to a celestial power, then climbing to his feet, arms pumping. 'Can you believe it?' Tyler asked unnecessarily. 'Chelsea will just not let go in the Champions League,' he confirmed. 'They never die,' insisted Neville. Drogba was rapidly surrounded by team-mates celebrating in joyous relief, as waves of emotion flowed down from the stands engulfing the knot of blue-shirted players in floods of emotion. 'I don't know how to explain my feelings after this goal,' Drogba later recalled, with the emotion of

288 Ross, Ian, interview with the author.

the moment clearly still etched into his memory. 'I don't know how to explain my feelings after this goal. I was on a different planet.'[289] It was the first time that Drogba had scored when Torres was on the pitch since the Spaniard had joined Chelsea. It was clearly a night for 'firsts'.

On the sidelines, Heynckes slumped back into his seat as the Chelsea bench erupted, jumping and punching the air in celebration. In contrast, Di Matteo, wearing a suit, looked every inch the stylish Italian as he stood arms aloft, but without losing an iota of composure. From the very jaws of defeat, Drogba had grabbed salvation for Chelsea. It was his sixth goal in eight matches across their Champions League campaign, and the words of Jonathan Northcroft in salute of his contribution to the cause were underscored once more.

Uli Hesse recalled how the massed German fans in the stadium were instantly stunned into disbelieving silence, seeing their cherished prize waved before their eyes, and then having it dashed away, 'Many fans in the stands felt it was poetic justice that Müller, who had missed [a] glorious chance in Madrid against Inter [in the 2010 Champions League Final], should score the winning goal. Only he didn't. With two minutes left, the Blues won their first and only corner of the night. Schweinsteiger later recalled how defender David Luiz, who had repeatedly told him, "Your team is better, but we are going to win," during the game, ran upfield for the corner and, passing him, said, "Now a goal!" Seconds later, Didier Drogba met Juan Mata's corner at the near post and equalised.'[290]

Not only were the Bayern fans stunned, so too were the players on the pitch. Heads bowed, or buried in hands,

---

289 *Kings of Europe – The Chelsea Story*, Sky UK Limited, 16 September 2012.

290 Hesse, Uli, interview with the author.

with hands on hips were the common reactions as well as minds and belief shaken. So near, and yet so far. As the game restarted, Tyler conjured up the spectre of a memory that would have been edging maliciously into the minds of any number of Bayern fans. 'Well, I don't want to mention Barcelona in 1999 to tempt fate,' he said, while doing that very thing.

In the Champions League Final of that year, Bayern had led Manchester United from the sixth minute and looked certain to lift the trophy as the clock passed 90 minutes, but goals from Teddy Sheringham and Ole Gunnar Solskjaer, one and three minutes into injury time respectively, turned the game on its head and the trophy went to Old Trafford. Surely Bayern were not going to fall foul of malevolent fate again. Drogba's equaliser hadn't quite been that late, but Tyler persisted with the analogy referring to Drogba. 'Well,' he added, 'if he's Sheringham, who's going to be the Solskjaer?'

The stadium announcer informed the crowd that there would be three minutes of additional time to play and Bayern won a late corner. It came to nothing and the dominant voices providing the backdrop to the game were now all coming from behind Neuer's goal. 'Who is writing these scripts?' Tyler asked. The answer to both of Tyler's questions nearly came seconds later, with 'Didier Drogba' looking to be the answer. The last of those extra three minutes had just ticked by when the Ivorian looked like stepping on to centre stage once more.

After Müller had scored, Luiz had conceded that petulant free kick against Robben. This time it was Bayern's tempers and frustrations leading to a lack of discipline. Mata rumbled forward with the ball and Ribéry heaved him aside, conceding a free kick some 25 yards or so from goal. It would be the last kick of the match. Bayern fans could be forgiven for thinking that this looked scarily familiar. So close to victory, conceding a late equaliser, and now, even later facing a dangerous free kick. 'Destiny. Written in the stars. Name on the cup,' intoned Tyler, grabbing at every cliche within reach as Drogba looked up to the heavens and then down at the ball. 'Last kick as a Chelsea player,' Tyler continued. 'It can't be. It can't be. Can it?' For Drogba, stranding over the ball, immortality beckoned. Three steps back, then two smaller ones to the left, before running forward for the strike.

The ball flew over the wall, but also over Neuer's bar and continued its upwards trajectory into the Chelsea fans. Proença blew for full-time. Tyler was correct. It couldn't happen. Drogba scoring the winning goal with his last kick before leaving the club? It was too fanciful for words. Well, for a while it was anyway. Immortality hadn't slipped through the striker's fingers. It had just been delayed.

After being second best for more than 88 minutes, Chelsea had enjoyed a brief period of ascendancy while Bayern players sought to clear their heads from the shuddering haymaker delivered by Drogba. Had the game continued without a break then they may well have gone on, with the momentum behind them, and scored another goal. The end of normal time, however, offered a chance for the Germans to regather themselves and concentrate on the job to come.

The experienced Heynckes moved among his players offering calm reassurance. All they needed to do was get back to playing as they had for the vast majority of 90 minutes or so just played, and surely a second goal would come their way. Bayern had faced down their 'Ghost of Final Past' when Drogba blazed that last-second free kick over the bar. Now a phantom from the dark hour of Moscow four years ago was materialising in front of the Chelsea fans. Level at 1-1 after normal time, going into an extra period and, who knows, perhaps penalties against a team in red was likely to re-open a still sore wound for fans of the London club. Had the momentum, and the force of history now swung in favour of Bayern?

Just a few minutes into the first period of extra time, it looked very much the way of things. Torres had already made an optimistic but ultimately fruitless raid into Bayern territory. Boateng's clumsy challenge inside the Bayern penalty area would have caused a few Bavarian palpitations as the Spaniard tumbled to the floor. The defender's wagging finger towards the referee suggesting he hadn't committed an offence, perhaps betrayed the concern that he had done precisely that, but the official allowed play to continue. Minutes later, Drogba would not be so fortunate. Chelsea had started brightly but events would swing violently against them after just two and a half minutes of play. Bayern had recycled possession on the edge of the Chelsea box as Contento fed the ball to Ribéry, turning to attack just inside the box. Drogba had retreated to help out his defence, but his jabbed-out foot only felled the Frenchman. This time the referee's whistle was both prompt and undeniably correct. 'Hero to zero,' confirmed Tyler as the referee pointed to the spot and then flourished a yellow card at the Ivorian.

The time between a penalty being awarded and the kick being taken is all about pressure. The goalkeeper knows the fate of his team lies in his hands and each ticking second pours more pressure on his opponent, the man with the ball in his hands, waiting to place it down and, hopefully, score. Anything other than a normal 30 seconds or so between awarding the spot kick to the penalty being struck only aids the defending team. The offence looked like a mere trip, accidental to be sure, but equally a clear penalty. As the referee called to the Bayern bench for assistance to aid the still fallen Ribéry though, the damage appeared to be more serious. Time ticked on.

The clock showed two minutes and 41 seconds when the penalty was awarded. By the time Robben had been given permission to take the shot a further 130 seconds had passed, giving Čech time to think. It was his former team-mate with the ball. Much as with the Lionel Messi spot kick in the Camp Nou, the goalkeeper had hatched a plan.

'When he took the ball, I said, "Okay, he must be as tired as everybody else." We were all tired. The pressure is huge and, if you are about to miss a penalty in the Champions League Final, you're going to shoot a proper penalty with power, and the only concern was, will he shoot in the middle or will he shoot to the left? Because he's left-footed, normally, and I'm left-footed, so if I was about to shoot really strong, it would rather go that way than on the other side. So that was what was in my mind, and I'm thinking okay, he will try to go left, and he did – luckily.'[291]

At the other end of the pitch, the experienced Schweinsteiger couldn't bear to watch. He crouched down in the arc of Bayern's penalty area, facing Neuer, hoping for some positive indication from the goalkeeper that the Dutchman had restored Bayern's lead. At the same time, behind Čech's goal, a Chelsea fan dressed in a grey t-shirt decided to take a hand in events. Having apparently inflated a large yellow beach ball in the time that Ribéry was receiving attention, as Robben approached the penalty spot he made his play. First he threw the beach ball into the air, then he slapped it forward towards the goal. If the ploy was intended to distract Robben

291 *Kings of Europe – The Chelsea Story*, Sky UK Limited, 16 September 2012.

then it failed abysmally. The Bayern player's attention never deviated from the ball. In contrast, Čech's ploy was validated as the powerfully stuck shot arrowed towards the left-hand corner of the keeper's goal. Anticipation rewarded, Čech was almost waiting for its arrival as it reached the goal line. The grey-shirted goalkeeper first blocked, then turned to gather, the ball as Robben darted after the parry forlornly. The Chelsea players rushed to both congratulate and thank their number one. But what of the beach ball?

As Čech fell on the ball covering it with his body, the beach ball rolled towards the side of the goal. With the game having the extra official running between the goalkeeper's left-hand post and the corner flag, its entry on to the pitch was hastily denied by the official. It seemed that neither referee nor Bayern players had seen the intruder's approach. Had Proença done so, he could have easily deemed it appropriate to order a retake, and that Chelsea fan in the grey t-shirt may well have cost his team dear. He didn't however, and the goal-line official deemed it unnecessary to inform him. Chelsea had escaped.

For their former player though, it was a moment that would haunt him. The winger had also missed from 12 yards in the decisive game in the Bundesliga title battle with Borussia Dortmund, but this felt worse. He lated said, 'I can't describe how I feel with words, but it's been a terrible night. Two or three times, you feel you have the cup in your hands but at the end you stand with nothing. It wasn't a good penalty. I wanted to shoot the ball hard and high in the goal, but the ball didn't go high enough. It was a terrible penalty kick. After that, I still played well but you have to change your mindset at that point.'[292]

---

292 'Arjen Robben rues penalty miss that cost Bayern Munich against Chelsea', *The Guardian*, 20 May 2012.

It felt like fate had taken a hand again, and many Chelsea fans thought so too. 'I think after Robben missed the penalty in extra time,' Danny Ridgeway recalled, 'we started to believe that it was going to be our day.'[293] His son, Joe, agreed, 'Even the Robben penalty, after that I just had this feeling he was going to miss it. [It] just felt like it was meant to be when we equalised.'[294] Neville was moved to reach a similar conclusion. 'They never die,' he repeated. 'Something is happening!'

At the other end of the pitch, Neuer urgently waved Schweinsteiger to his feet as play resumed. First there was confusion, but then the cruelty of disappointment filled the Germany international as the grim reality sank in. Heynckes had been watching and, as Čech gathered the ball protectively to his body, the Bayern coach turned and slapped the top of the dugout in dismay. It was easy to consider that Bayern's best chance had slipped away, but perhaps it hadn't. Minutes later, as Ribéry limped away, his replacement, Ivica Olić, was primed to enter the game. Inside the second period of extra time, the Croat would have an outstanding opportunity to spare Robben's blushes.

In the remaining minutes of the first period, first it was Bayern pressing again as Chelsea's defence came under examination once more. Half chances came and went. Robben fired high and wide with a shot fuelled by venomous frustration. Van Buyten had a shot blocked. Then, perhaps through fatigue, perhaps as the potential consequences of the missed penalty seeped into the Bayern players' minds, their powers, their belief, their attacking dynamism seemed to diminish.

---

293 Ridgeway, Danny, interview with the author.

294 Ridgeway, Joe, interview with the author.

The last five minutes or so were played with Chelsea achieving the sort of equality in the game that had largely eluded them across the previous 100 minutes. The substitutions of both coaches seemed to have left Chelsea stronger, and conversely Bayern weaker. While Kalou and Bertrand had worked hard to defend the flanks and support their respective full-backs, the addition of Torres and Malouda in their stead certainly bolstered Chelsea's attack.

For Bayern, when Heynckes withdrew Müller for the extra defensive solidity of Van Buyten in an attempt to see out time, it meant that the Belgian slotted in alongside Boateng at the heart of the Bayern back line with Tymoshchuk moving further forward into midfield. For all his versatility, however, the Ukrainian carried nothing like the same threat as Müller. Similarly, with Ribéry's exit, Olić was a more than decent forward with a workaholic attitude to his game but, whereas the Frenchman's darting runs had caused any number of problems for Chelsea, without him the Bayern threat was inevitably lessened. With things now more even, the outcome of the game was in the balance. The final would be decided by a battle of wills, as much as a battle of skills.

As the referee started the final 15 minutes, the Bayern fans launched into a series of raucous chants, seeking to give energy and restore the impetus that had seemed to drain away from their team as the break in extra time approached. It so nearly brought the desired result. A corner from the left began a period of Bayern pressure as Chelsea struggled to clear the ball. A couple of crosses were played into the box without success, but each time possession was recycled. Drogba took a knock and was on the floor when Lahm delivered the ball again. The defence may have been disorganised thanks to Drogba's absence, but the cross found Olić closing in on the left corner of Čech's six-yard box, with

Van Buyten, still upfield from the corner, in the middle. Both were beyond the blue back line and plaintive appeals for offside went unanswered. There were two Bayern players clear in space with just Čech to beat.

With little other option, Čech advanced to close down the angle on Olić. If the Croat had simply squared the ball it would have been a tap in to the empty net for Van Buyten. Whether Olić had decided to try for goal himself, however, or thought that his team-mate would run forward to meet his pass, is unclear, but as he stroked a gentle volley past Čech's left hand the ball neatly bisected the post and Van Buyten. Olić fell to his knees, both arms outstretched in front of him, apparently stunned that the Belgian had not taken the few steps forward, walking into the Bayern record books, and scored. Maybe it was the fact that the defender lacked a striker's natural instincts to make that desired move, or maybe it was just Olić looking for excuses as his attempt to secure personal glory slipped wide of the post. Either way, as the ball rolled behind for a goal kick Van Buyten stood rooted to the spot. Aside from Robben's missed penalty, Bayern's best chance had come and gone. As the game restarted, Drogba got to his feet, and Chelsea did much the same as fate offered them another lucky escape.

For a few minutes Bayern again looked to be shaken by another miss but they regained their composure and pushed forward once more. The game was more even now, but the Bavarians still carried the greater threat. Inside the last ten minutes, Lahm drove forward from his defensive role and exchanged passes with Robben, collecting again as he closed on Čech from the right flank. The goalkeeper advanced to narrow the already acute angle but a driven cross was arrowed towards Gómez before Cahill threw himself in front of the striker and Luiz hacked the ball clear.

The replay emphasised Cahill's heroic lunge face first towards the ball, looking for any part of his torso to take the ball away from Gómez. He fell to the floor with the agonies of cramp clawing at his left calf muscle, but his bravery had saved the day. Before the corner was taken, referee Proença sought Cahill out and instructed him to leave the field. The emotions of the moment must have clouded the official's judgement as, despite struggling with cramp, Cahill had received no outside assistance to recover and there was no reason why he should have been excluded from the play as the corner was taken. Fortunately for all concerned, Torres stretched to head clear and Cahill was allowed to return to the action. Had Bayern scored from the set piece then the repercussions could have been massive.

It was the last significant action of the game. Both teams were now spent and a penalty shoot-out looked inevitable. After allowing a mere 18 seconds of injury time, the referee blew for full time and confirmed what had become increasingly inevitable. In the course of the 120 minutes, plus additional time, Bayern had hit 35 attempts on Čech's goal compared to Chelsea's nine efforts to beat Neuer. They had also won 20 corners while Chelsea had earned a single one. That sole corner had seen the Blues equalise and brought the teams to the final whistle on level terms, but who would the supposed lottery favour? There were arguments and theories running both ways.

It was the first time that the Champions League Final had gone to penalties since Chelsea's dramatic loss to Manchester United in Moscow four years earlier, and spot kick competitions had hardly favoured the London club in the past. They had also lost out in a shoot-out at the semi-final stage of the same competition against Liverpool in 2007 and of the nine times they had been compelled to chance their arms in the Russian Roulette of a penalty shoot-out, they had prevailed on only two occasions.

Despite the widely held belief that Teutonic efficiency would always prevail in such matters, the Blues were not bereft of hope. Uli Hesse thought the matter was far from settled. There's a dread feeling in most English football fans' souls about penalty shoot-outs, especially when facing Germany, or German clubs. English fatalistic pessimism was perhaps more self-inflicted than justified by reality however, as Hesse explained: 'Confidence is the wrong word for a penalty shoot-out, because contrary to popular opinion Germans are quite aware that it's a bit of a lottery. Let's call it well-founded optimism. Bayern had beaten Real on penalties in the previous round and they had yet to lose a shoot-out against a non-German team. My guess is that most people felt they went into the shoot-out with an advantage. Let's say 60-40.'[295]

Hesse's assessment received support from a few other statistics. In the Champions League era, no English club had ever lost a penalty shoot-out to non-British opposition and, back in 1970 Heynckes had been in the Borussia Mönchengladbach team that lost the first-ever shoot-out in European competition, when his team fell to Everton. There was also, certainly among Chelsea fans, the undeniably growing belief that whatever the route taken to get there, this was their year. Mark Worrall spoke for many, 'Looking back, I thought when Didier Drogba equalised and the game dragged on through extra time to penalties that it was going to be Chelsea's night. The fact Big Pete saved former Blue Arjen Robben's penalty in extra time and it was Drogba who'd conceded it made me think, this is it. This is the night

---

295 Hesse, Uli, interview with the author.

it all comes together, upsetting the odds against a German team in their own backyard.'[296]

After the inevitable break as players sought recovery massages, fresh instructions and encouragement from coaches and support staff, the referee called the two captains together. As if facing a shoot-out in Bayern's own stadium was not enough of an advantage for the Germans, the toss of a coin to decide which end the spot kicks would be taken also fell in their favour as Lahm called correctly. The penalties would be taken with the massed ranks of Bayern fans supplying the backdrop.

Twice, once against Barcelona, and then minutes earlier in this game, Čech had relied on his forward planning when facing spot kicks to preserve Chelsea's interest in the Champions League, and he would later reveal that ahead of the game, along with the goalkeepers' coaching team he had studied videos of Bayern penalties. 'I'd seen every penalty Bayern has had since 2007,' Čech confirmed. 'So, it took me about the whole flight to Munich.'[297] This was no video game, however; it was real and, although preparation and theories had brought rewards in the past, there was no guarantee that they would do again.

Bayern would take the first penalty and captain Lahm stepped forward looking to give his team the advantage. 'In Madrid,' Tyler revealed, recalling the shoot-out in the Bernabeu, 'he went high and to the goalkeeper's right, and it was saved.' This time it was high to the goalkeeper's left but, although Čech had guessed the direction correctly, he couldn't keep it out of the net. 'I went the right way,' he recalled. 'And I touched the ball slightly, and it went in.' As

---

296 Worrall, Mark, interview with the author.

297 *Kings of Europe – The Chelsea Story*, Sky UK Limited, 16 September 2012.

it did so, Lahm went down on one knee and punched the air in celebration before rising to his feet and doing so again with both fists clenched. The fans behind the goal cheered as their team were ahead once more.

First up for Chelsea was Mata. Lahm had left the ball in the penalty area and as the little Spaniard walked forward, Neuer picked up the ball and hurled it towards him before retreating to his goal line, directed there by the referee as he sought to keep the German and Mata from any close contact. Neuer, as is so often the case with goalkeepers, is a big man and ahead of each spot kick, once on his line, he jumped up and shook the crossbar. Referees have, apparently, never sought to stop him doing this, but one is left to wonder what the officials' reactions would be if a player about to take a spot kick did this instead. It was clearly a ploy intended to unsettle the kicker, emphasising to his opponent not only the size of the man he was facing, but also the size of the task in beating him.

Despite being one of the team's most accomplished players, Mata's record from the penalty spot was less than convincing. He had converted from 12 yards against QPR in the FA Cup but missed two in the ties against Birmingham City in the following round. Walking with the ball towards the penalty area and the baying Bayern fans, Mata flipped the ball from hand to shoulder and back again a couple of times. If it was intended to project an air of nonchalant confidence then it failed to do so; the concentrated concern etched on his face was much more convincing. Questioned later as to why he had taken the first penalty, the Spaniard laughed nervously before confessing, 'Because I wanted to.' The smile then drifted away as he recalled the events. 'I was so tired after extra time, after the game, but I wanted to score because I think it's a crucial moment for the team and for [me]. And I wanted to take this responsibility.'[298]

Sometimes bravery isn't rewarded, however. Mata struck the penalty just to the left of where Neuer was standing and the goalkeeper comfortably parried the ball clear. If anything, the acclamation from the Bayern fans was even greater for the save than when Lahm had scored moments earlier. In shoot-outs saves are rarer than goals and hence their perceived value is greater. Neuer jumped to his feet and shouted towards the fans. Mata trudged slowly back towards his team-mates in the centre circle, head bowed. The memory was clearly uncomfortable. A deep sigh preceded the description of how he felt, as he searched for the right words. Later, he explained, 'You are walking like, like alone, like thinking about, just believing in Pete, believing that he can save one or two penalties.'[299] It was certainly a matter of belief now. Neuer had boxed out Bayern's lead. If they could convert their remaining four penalties, regardless of the fate of Chelsea's nominated takers, the game was up.

Perhaps there was a bit of hope as well. The next taker for Bayern was Gómez. Throughout the game the striker had been found wanting time and again as chances fell to him. Each time he had either hesitated or snatched at the opening, then looked frustrated as it passed him by. Now, he was in the ultimate pressure position. Was his confidence shaken by his misses? His walk forward was purposeful enough, betraying no signs of nerves. He rolled the ball on to the penalty spot and retreated a few steps to the edge of the area.

---

298 *Kings of Europe – The Chelsea Story*, Sky UK Limited, 16 September 2012.

299 *Kings of Europe – The Chelsea Story*, Sky UK Limited, 16 September 2012.

At the whistle, he jogged forward and drove the ball low to Čech's left, leaving the goalkeeper precious little opportunity to restore the balance of the shoot-out. 'The second one,' Čech recalled, 'I went the right way, but Gómez hit it really well, with the power, so it didn't give me a time.'[300] Chelsea faced problems. 'Gómez slides it in,' confirmed Tyler to the watching millions. The striker punched the air with left and then right fists clenched towards the Bayern fans. 'And they're getting nearer.' Two out of two converted and Chelsea having missed their one spot kick, it was difficult to dispute the assessment.

The next Chelsea player had to score, otherwise there would have been a surely unscalable mountain to climb. Up stepped David Luiz. In such circumstances confidence is key and, for all his perceived faults a lack of confidence was not a charge that could be levelled against the Brazilian with any measure of validity. The problem was that sometimes, that confidence tumbled over the line into over-confidence and, to many of his critics, that was Luiz's main problem. He had already failed to convert from 12 yards against Bayer Leverkusen in Germany, during the group stage. A similar error here could sound the death knell for Chelsea's hopes. Curly hair flopping as he strode purposefully forward, Luiz never cast a glance towards Neuer as he bounced the ball approaching the area before placing it with cool deliberation on the spot. Neuer shook the bar again. Luiz didn't notice.

Whereas Gómez had retreated the half-dozen yards from the penalty spot to the edge of the area in his run-up, Luiz's preparation took him twice that distance, and maybe a little more. It was either the most extravagant of feints, or his shot on goal would be struck with plenty of power. As the

300 *Kings of Europe – The Chelsea Story*, Sky UK Limited, 16 September 2012.

referee blew, the latter was clearly the case. 'How desperately Chelsea need this,' Tyler opined unnecessarily.

Almost reaching a sprint by the time he got to the ball, Luiz fired high into the right corner of the net as Neuer tumbled in the other direction. The power and accuracy of the strike would have negated the goalkeeper's efforts even if he had guessed correctly. Relieved of the burden, now laid down in such spectacular fashion, Luiz continued his run as it took him towards the Bayern fans, bellowing defiance. The Bayern fans booed in response. Luiz lapped it up. It was the sort of gesture that Chelsea had offered up so many times across their Champions League campaign, not as vociferous as Luiz did perhaps, but certainly with similar conviction. The Brazilian's strike had put Chelsea on the shoot-out scoreboard, restored hope, and also a little belief.

As Luiz returned to his team-mates, receiving pats of congratulation, there seemed to be some confusion in the Bayern ranks as to who would be taking their third kick. The camera remained fixated on the knot of red-shirted players gathered in the centre circle for a second, before all became clear. After Luiz's goal, Neuer had retreated to his designated position outside of the penalty area to the right of the goal. Čech approached the referee to see what was going on, but then Neuer reappeared inside the area. The message had got through to him that he was the next taker. As he had surely been told by his coach that he would be taking the third penalty, there are two main possibilities for the delay and apparent period of confusion. Either Neuer's concentration had been so intense that he had simply forgotten his place in the roster, or he was using the delay to ramp up pressure on Čech. In either instance it was a strange scenario at such a crucial stage of the shoot-out.

For Čech, it was an unexpected situation, and that may well have been part of the Bayern ploy to send Neuer forward. 'The only one I had no idea about was Neuer,' Čech revealed. 'Because you don't see keepers taking penalties.'[301] It's a fair point, but Neuer had either been practising or was confident enough to step up without doing so. The first two Bayern penalties had gone to Čech's left. Each time he had guessed correctly but was defeated by the power and accuracy of the shots. Neuer switched to the other side, hitting low to Čech's right, but the result was the same. Čech's dive was both in the correct direction, but also forlorn, for the third time.

In a shoot-out, it's almost inevitable that some players less used to converting from 12 yards are called forward to do so – Neuer was a case in point. Both of Chelsea's first two takers had been examined from the spot in the earlier parts of the season, and with a combined three misses between them during the season prior to the final, it should not have been surprising that the Blues were trailing.

In contrast to the player sent forward by Bayern for their third penalty, Chelsea's third nominated taker was very much at home. Across his long career Lampard would take 70 penalties for the Blues, successfully converting 60 of them. It was his spot kick that had ignited Chelsea's comeback against Napoli, and Lampard had also successfully converted from 12 yards in the quarter-final against Benfica. Four years ago in Moscow, facing a similar task to the one now confronting him, he had also delivered. As the stand-in captain of the team due to Terry's enforced absence, the task of keeping Chelsea's interest in the final alive fell to him.

Along with Drogba, Lampard was one of Di Matteo's prime penalty takers, and there had been some discussion

---

301 *Kings of Europe – The Chelsea Story*, Sky UK Limited, 16 September 2012.

before the shoot-out as to where in the order of takers he should be placed to maximise the benefit of his expertise. 'I was first originally. Then I was third,' Lampard remembered, and he added in a typically professional manner, 'And I didn't ask questions.'[302] For all his experiences this was the highest level of club football and, with each passing penalty, be it successful or squandered, the pressure was ramped up.

Walking slowly forward, Lampard looked drained. 'Is it going to be penalty heartache again for Chelsea?' Tyler questioned. Lampard's disdainful glance up at Neuer as he shook the bar once again both offered an answer and suggested that his demeanour was more cool detachment than something caused by nervous anxiety. The despatch from 12 yards confirmed that. The ball was driven straight and high into the roof of the net as Neuer gambled with a dive to his left, vacating the space where the ball found the back of his net. 'Well, not yet,' declared Tyler, answering his own question. The halfway point in the shoot-out had now been passed. Each team had two more attempts, and the advantage still lay with Bayern.

Despite Uli Hesse's thoughts, the English predisposition about the efficiency of Germans from the penalty spot had proved to be valid. As Bayern's next taker stepped forward though, that hoary old chestnut was put temporarily aside. It had always been likely that Schweinsteiger would be taking the final German penalty and, as Robben had been sent forward to take the spot kick when Drogba's ill-judged extra-time tackle had offered Bayern the chance to retake the lead in the game, it was assumed that he would be offered an opportunity to redeem himself in the shoot-out. As the red-shirted player emerged from the Bayern players gathered

302 *Kings of Europe – The Chelsea Story*, Sky UK Limited, 16 September 2012.

in the centre circle though, it wasn't the Dutchman, it was Olić, the Croatian substitute who had come on when Ribéry was injured. Instead, Robben stood with the remainder of the Bayern outfield players, head bowed, confidence clearly dented by the earlier miss.

It was now edging towards crisis time for Chelsea. Ever since Mata's miss, they had converted with confidence, but all of that, and their kicks to come would count for naught unless Čech could produce at least one save from Bayern's next two attempts. The goalkeeper was acutely aware of the situation. 'When Olić took the ball, I thought, "Okay, here we are. Now I'm going to get this one." Because it's impossible that I will go all the time, the right way, and not get one.'[303] In a similar situation to both Drogba and Kalou wearing Chelsea blue, this game would be Olić's last for Bayern before leaving to join VfL Wolfsburg.

He placed the ball down and stepped back. Standing square behind the ball, he paused, awaiting the referee's signal. As he did so Neville chimed in. 'I never like a straight run,' he declared. It was a pertinent point. Running on to the ball from directly behind almost betrayed the taker's intention. The Croat was left-footed and, unless he chose to strike the ball with the outside of his boot – a risky strategy – shooting to Čech's right would have been difficult. As with Robben's penalty in extra time, it suggested that he would either shoot straight or to Čech's left. Guessing right and saving the ball, however, are different things; the logic prevailed for the goalkeeper against Robben but, as Čech commented for each of the penalties so far, he had guessed correctly but was still unable to keep the shot out.

---

303 *Kings of Europe – The Chelsea Story*, Sky UK Limited, 16 September 2012.

'Chelsea fans hold their breath,' suggested Tyler as the referee blew. Olić took a step to the right and then ran forward to strike the ball. Čech's recollections again, 'So, I went again the right way and I got it.'[304] The ball was fired to the goalkeeper's left around a yard or so from the ground, but less tucked into the corner than the earlier Bayern penalties. Čech reached up a gloved right hand and pawed the ball away. 'And Čech saves!' Tyler confirmed. 'And Chelsea, yet again, are still alive.' This time the massed ranks of Bayern fans were quiet. Almost in perfect synchronicity, they reached up and put their heads in their hands, burying themselves from the fact that they may have just witnessed their lead slipping away, again. Now it was Čech's turn to celebrate as he swapped positions with Neuer. If Chelsea could convert their fourth spot kick, the scores would be level at 3-3, with each team having one more kick to come. It was, in effect, sudden death from that point forward.

Ashley Cole was an outstanding footballer, one of the best full-backs in Europe, and had hugely contributed to Chelsea's progress in their Champions League campaign. His role in the final, subduing the threats of Robben and Ribéry when they attacked down his flank, had been delivered with his usual unassuming excellence. He was not, however, a regular penalty taker. Of the five players nominated by Di Matteo – Mata, Luiz, Lampard, Cole, and Drogba to follow – he was the least experienced from 12 yards and yet now, the task of bringing his team level in the shoot-out fell to the defender. Cole had been involved in shoot-outs before, both for club and country, and had been successful in Moscow four years previously, but he was still the biggest gamble in the hand Di Matteo was playing. The coach was banking

304 *Kings of Europe – The Chelsea Story*, Sky UK Limited, 16 September 2012.

on Cole's talent and the phlegmatic way he had dealt with the challenges he had faced both on and off the pitch across his career. Cole later revealed, 'It's always nerve-wracking taking a penalty and, of course, it was in front of their fans, which is not a great situation or scenario you'd want but, you look at him and he's a massive goalie and, on every penalty, he just jumps on to the crossbar, and shakes the crossbar so you're like, "This guy is massive! How am I going to put it past him?" But, so, you've just got to be confident and, with penalties, anything can happen and, luckily, I was one of the ones that scored.'[305]

Cole's description is as self-deprecating as his penalty was efficient. He drilled the ball towards the same area where Olić had seen his kick parried by Čech. The Chelsea player's shot was struck with both more power and more accuracy than the earlier one and there was little chance of Neuer reprising Čech's feat. The ball arrowed into the inside of the side netting and Chelsea were level.

'It's a magnificent penalty,' Tyler exclaimed. Cole turned away, trotting back towards the centre circle portraying a nonchalant indifference that served as a less than totally convincing camouflage for the relief and elation he must have been feeling. Lampard and Cole had both been successful from the spot in the shoot-out but this wasn't the first time they'd faced this pressure from 12 yards in a Champions League final. Both men had also scored in the defeat to Manchester United in Moscow four years earlier, and they joined Carlos Mozer for Benfica in 1988 and Marseille three years later as the only players to score in two different final shoot-outs.

---

305 *Kings of Europe – The Chelsea Story*, Sky UK Limited, 16 September 2012.

Nearing the collection of blue-shirted players, Cole reached up with his right-hand and patted the Chelsea badge on his shirt a few times. Bosingwa advanced to meet and congratulate his fellow defender. Behind him though, and unseen by many, Drogba was on his knees offering up prayers. Whatever happened with the next penalty, there was no possibility of the Ivorian not being involved in a crucial moment. His kick would either be to keep Chelsea alive or to deliver them to the very top table of European club football. Penalty novice Cole had probably delivered the best spot kick of the night among his team-mates and set up a denouement for the evening that had looked a distant dream on any number of occasions across the previous few hours.

Before Drogba's ordeal, Bayern sent Schweinsteiger forward. Saving your most accomplished penalty taker until the final moments of a shoot-out can be seen as a risk. Sometimes the issue is decided even before it reaches that stage, meaning that you lost out with your best card still in your hand. There's always the comfort of having a reliable option available when the heat is at it hottest though and, despite Di Matteo sending first-choice penalty taker Lampard in at number three, both coaches had kept a trusted ace in their hand until the fifth penalties.

Schweinsteiger is almost the epitome of the ideal Bayern Munich player. Born in Kolbermoor in the district of Rosenheim, less than an hour's travel from Munich, he is well and truly a Bavarian, joining the club's youth setup in 1998, precisely one month short of his 14th birthday, and progressing through the ranks until his first team debut in 2002. In a career stretching across 13 seasons with Bayern, he would appear exactly 500 times for the club, winning multiple domestic league and cup titles.

When the critical moment arrived in the semi-final shoot-out in Madrid, it was Schweinsteiger who converted the fifth penalty to send Bayern through to the final. Seconds earlier, with the scores tied, Sergio Ramos's nerve had let him down as he blazed his penalty over the bar. In contrast, Schweinsteiger had looked cool and calm. Striding purposefully forward, he spent what seemed an interminable time patting down the penalty spot with the bottom of his boot to ensure the surface was smooth. He seemed in no hurry, oblivious to his surroundings, as the hoots and baying of the *Madrilenos* washed over him. When ready, and only then, he addressed the ball, advancing and firing to the right of Iker Casillas as the goalkeeper committed himself in the opposite direction. Trusting him to deliver in the final was not only an act of faith for Heynckes but also one of confidence.

Čech had already thwarted Robben from 12 yards in extra time and then saved Olić's spot kick in the shoot-out to bring Chelsea level after Mata's early miss. Now the onus fell on him again. If he could repeat the feat against Schweinsteiger, he could set up the chance for Drogba to dismiss all those sad Moscow memories, and regrets about what might have been. The next couple of minutes would be pivotal in the history of Chelsea Football Club. 'I knew that this was the last two pens,' Čech recalled, looking back on those crucial moments. 'And it would be Schweinsteiger and Didier. So, I was like, "Okay, we can give Didier a happy ending."'[306]

'You get the feeling something is happening,' Neville suggested as Schweinsteiger paced forward from the centre circle, stroking his chin in exaggerated nonchalance. 'Something is happening,' Neville persisted. As had been

---

306 *Kings of Europe – The Chelsea Story*, Sky UK Limited, 16 September 2012.

the case in Madrid, the Bavarian patted down on the penalty spot with his boot before carefully placing the ball down. 'He has the nerve. He has the temperament,' Tyler predicted.

Watching him intently, Čech stood on his line, swaying gently from side to side, arms spread and raised in the air, as some bird of prey about to plunge on to its quarry. 'The Bavarian, with all of Bavaria's hopes resting on him here,' Tyler unnecessarily hyped up the tension as Schweinsteiger paced forwards, paused, and then struck the ball. Čech lunged. Ian Ross remembered the moment, 'Bayern [had still been] the favourites, especially after Juan Mata missed Chelsea's first kick. Astonishingly it was a miss by one of football's coolest players, Bastian Schweinsteiger, which left Drogba with one kick to win the trophy and so realise Abramovich's dream.'[307]

'I knew he was going to wait,' Čech revealed. 'So, when he slowed down, I was still not moving. And then, when he slowed down, you know that he can't get, or generate, enough power to shoot strong. So, my guess was that he would go there again [as Olić had]. So, I went to the left and, as I touched the ball, I was sure it was not going in, but my concern was that it was going to hit me on the back, so I tried to lie as still as I could.' A nervous laugh spread across Čech's face as the memory of his concerns drifted away, much as the ball did from the goal, 'And it passed my heels by about two inches.'[308] A couple of inches may have been an entirely understandable exaggeration, but whatever the gap, it was sufficient.

'He's hit the post! And Chelsea are one penalty away,' Tyler confirmed as Čech's fingertips finessed the flight of

---

307 Ross, Ian, interview with the author.

308 *Kings of Europe – The Chelsea Story*, Sky UK Limited, 16 September 2012.

the ball, causing it to strike the upright and bounce clear behind the goalkeeper's back. 'But that's what they were in Moscow,' he added, injecting a note of caution. Čech sprang to his feet, and punched the air in celebration. Fearing the worst was to come, Schweinsteiger pulled his shirt up to cover his face, but nothing could hide him from the reality of the moment. Lahm and another Bayern player came forward to escort their devastated team-mate back towards the centre circle.

Halfway there, they passed Drogba heading in the other direction – in more ways than one. 'It is written in the stars!' predicted Mystic Nev. Many Chelsea players felt the same way. Standing to the right of the goal, Čech had few, if any doubts. 'So, here we are,' he remembered thinking. 'Because I couldn't imagine Drogba missing a penalty … I was sure it was the last kick of the game.'[309] With the remainder of his team-mates around him, Lampard was as convinced as Čech. 'I couldn't see him missing,' he said.[310] Terry shook his head slightly, beaming at the memory of Drogba's penalty, 'Not one single doubt. Not one doubt.'[311]

There was certainly a steely, determined look on Drogba's face as he paced slowly forwards, although later he would admit that, even at that stage, he wasn't sure how to take the spot kick. He even contemplated attempting a Panenka-style shot, but dismissed the thought. He had noticed how Neuer had carefully watched the run-up of each of the Chelsea penalty takers, as if trying to discern some hint of their intentions by the angle and speed of their approach. He

---

309 *Kings of Europe – The Chelsea Story*, Sky UK Limited, 16 September 2012.

310 *Kings of Europe – The Chelsea Story*, Sky UK Limited, 16 September 2012.

311 *Kings of Europe – The Chelsea Story*, Sky UK Limited, 16 September 2012.

decided to annul this concern by taking merely two strides before shooting.

In the centre circle the Chelsea players stood, for the main with arms around shoulders in a solid line of support. Only Luiz and Mata were apart. The former, his penalty miss still haunting him, sat on the floor, with the Brazilian crouching behind him, leaning on his shoulders. On the Chelsea bench the scene was replicated. Terry looked up to the heavens, asking for the support of the celestial powers that had deserted the club during that vital moment in Moscow.

Placing the ball carefully on the spot, Drogba raised himself back up again, pulling his socks up, hitching up his shorts and straightening out his shirt. If he was going to light the blue touchpaper for a Chelsea celebration, he was going to look the part. Taking three careful steps back, he still hadn't looked at Neuer since he had entered the penalty area. Seeing him poised over the ball, just steps away, Cole felt pangs of unrest, 'Just please score. So, when you looked at him, and he didn't take a massive run-up, you're thinking, Didier, what are you doing?'[312] He needn't have worried.

The referee ushered the goalkeeper back to his line and Neuer jumped up and shook the crossbar. Drogba looked like he hadn't noticed. If he delivered the penalty correctly, there would be little that Neuer could do; his presence would be an irrelevance. This moment was about Drogba and Chelsea. It was his only thought. 'I can be a Champions League winner,' he remembered thinking to himself. 'This my chance. This is my chance and it's happening.'[313]

---

312 *Kings of Europe – The Chelsea Story*, Sky UK Limited, 16 September 2012.

313 *Kings of Europe – The Chelsea Story*, Sky UK Limited, 16 September 2012.

The whistle sounded and Drogba stepped forward. One step, then a second before the sweep of his right foot sent the ball towards the bottom-right corner of Neuer's net. Such was the accuracy of the strike that, even if the goalkeeper had guessed correctly, reaching the ball in time would have been difficult. As he fell away to his left, Neuer looked back over his shoulder to see the ball rolling over the line and into the net.

Also watching but from the stand was Abramovich with his wife and son. As they saw the ball go in they jumped to their feet. The owner hesitantly rose first, perhaps doubting that the day had at last arrived. He clapped a little, then punched the air. His dream had been delivered. Spouse Dasha, who had been covering her face as Drogba approached the ball, now waved her hands in the air in celebration. Son Arkadiy also celebrated, two fists raised before embracing his father. There were already traces of tears in the teenager's eyes. They would be given full flow minutes later.

For the only time in the entire contest, Bayern were behind. That scenario lasted for a split second before Pedro Proença's whistle confirmed it as the final result. 'He's done it!' acclaimed Tyler. 'The greatest moment in the history of Chelsea Football Club. European champions.' Abramovich couldn't hear Tyler's words, but he may well have been saying precisely the same thing to himself anyway.

Drogba turned away, wheeling first to his left, arms aloft, drowning in a sea of delirium. Then he turned back towards Čech, the man whose two saves had made his moment of destiny possible. The goalkeeper was almost rooted to the spot. 'I didn't know what to do,' Čech recalled. 'It was just amazing.'[314] As the ball hit the back of the net, that line of

314 *Kings of Europe – The Chelsea Story*, Sky UK Limited, 16 September 2012.

blue in the centre circle exploded as if someone had shot a million volts through each of the players. Mata was the only exception. His team-mates raced off to all corners of the ground, not knowing where to run, but suddenly infused with new energy and the irresistible urge to spend it. The little Spaniard rolled forward, flat on to the ground, lost in tears. 'When Didier scored, I was just falling on the pitch, and crying, and …' Mata remembered, before being lost for words for a second or two. 'Suddenly, all of the supporters were crying as well, so [it] was one of the best moments in my life.'[315]

'The emotion was like nothing I've ever had before,'[316] Cole confessed. Within seconds, goalkeeper and penalty scorer had been engulfed by a tide of blue. Drogba laughs at the memory of him embracing Čech. 'Then blackout. Boom. Boom. Boom. People jumping, the players jumping on us.' The smile was broad. 'It was a great moment, a great feeling,'[317] he recalled.

Climbing to his feet as the mountain of blue finally cleared from over him, Drogba suddenly set off, running away from the end where he had scored that winning penalty, away from the Bayern fans, and towards those rejoicing, decked in blue behind the opposite goal. On he went, arms outstretched as some Christ the Redeemer, from atop Sugar Loaf Mountain looking down on Rio de Janeiro, now come to life. The strides were fuelled not by energy, that had all been spent minutes ago, but by pure adrenalin. Entering the penalty area, he peeled off his shirt and whirled it around

---

315 *Kings of Europe – The Chelsea Story*, Sky UK Limited, 16 September 2012.

316 *Kings of Europe – The Chelsea Story*, Sky UK Limited, 16 September 2012.

317 *Kings of Europe – The Chelsea Story*, Sky UK Limited, 16 September 2012.

in the air, before finally hurling it to the floor by the corner flag. Later, he stood around the penalty spot in front of the Chelsea fans, celebrating with them, before raising his hands to his face as if in disbelief at what had just happened.

Di Matteo was also lost in the moment, 'It was just an immense feeling of pride and satisfaction.' The pitch was suddenly full of blue-shirted players either on their knees or flat out on the floor as a handful of fans spilled on to the grass to share in the moment. 'They've found a Holy Grail after an adventure fraught with danger,' declared Tyler with a line that had surely been prepared beforehand.

Across the Atlantic Ocean, US President Barack Obama was hosting a G8 Summit at Camp David, but the meetings came to a temporary halt as the final drama was played out. UK Prime Minister David Cameron stood alongside Angela Merkel, the German chancellor, as the assembled dignitaries watched Drogba deliver the final act. Cameron, a noted Aston Villa – or was it West Ham United? – fan beamed as Drogba rolled the ball into the net, celebrating as Merkel looked downcast. Negotiations may have been trickier from that moment, but no Chelsea supporter had any care for such lofty matters. Alan Addicott was among their number, 'To be honest, it was another miracle. The Germans played Chelsea off the park. But, if your name's on the cup as they say. Were Chelsea worthy champions? A resounding yes. They showed character, resilience and a never-say-die attitude.'[318]

Peeling off a tracksuit quicker than you can say 'You weren't even playing!', Terry appeared in full kit to join in the celebrations. Ian Ross confesses to being less than impressed by the suspended captain's actions, 'The only sour note for

---

318 Addicott, Alan, interview with the author.

me (and for millions of non-Chelsea supporters) was the ridiculous sight of the suspended Terry holding aloft the cup in full kit. He was widely (and rightly) ridiculed and I hope he now regrets his actions that night.'[319]

As Ross commented, it was a view that found common cause among many non-Chelsea fans, and there was certainly a lot of comment about Terry afterwards, many of it driven by opprobrium. There may be at least a measure of inequity in them though. Terry later revealed, 'UEFA sent the club an email that they wanted the players in their full kits,' he explained. 'Shin-pads, I didn't have, regardless of what people have said.' He then confessed, 'I must have changed super quick, once we won, and the bottoms were off, the top was off, and [in effect] I made out I was playing.'[320]

Neither was the Chelsea captain the only suspended player or substitute to follow the instructions laid out in UEFA's missive for the celebrations. Branislav Ivanović and Raul Meireles – banned along with Ramires and Terry – were seen celebrating in their full kit immediately after the shoot-out, joined moments later by the Brazilian. None of those players drew anything like the criticism aimed at Terry.

When the pandemonium had calmed a little the Chelsea players were corralled into some kind of order to climb the stairs and collect their prize. Led by Di Matteo and walking through a forest of congratulatory pats and slaps, they ascended to where the gleaming trophy was waiting. The stairs would go up and then into the stadium, on to a short platform, before emerging again into view then, one final turn, for the final flight to touch the sky.

Beaming smiles were impossible to suppress and, as

---

319 Ross, Ian, interview with the author.

320 *Kings of Europe – The Chelsea Story*, Sky UK Limited, 16 September 2012.

Di Matteo reached the final platform, he was confronted by an emotional owner. Embraces were exchanged before Di Matteo stepped back a little and, clenching both fists, shouted, 'I won it! I won it!' He moved on and, as each player followed their coach on to the broad platform where the trophy and medals were waiting, they all received congratulations from Abramovich. The last two players to reach the platform were Terry and then Lampard. A special long embrace was reserved for the suspended captain and, by this time, Arkadiy Abramovich's tears had the better of any sense of restrained decorum. Lampard received similar acclaim. The teenager also exchanged embraces with Terry.

As he walked towards the place where the trophy stood, Di Matteo reached across and placed his right hand on his heart before puffing out his cheeks. It was a hugely emotional moment for a man who had, so recently, been dismissed by West Bromwich Albion, and had now climbed to the highest point in European club football. That beating heart must have been racing. A few short months ago he had inherited a club spiralling downwards and seemingly set for a season as poor as any since Abramovich had taken control. In that short period though, the renaissance had been nothing short of incredible, a story that if penned by a fiction writer would have stretched credulity to breaking point.

The blue line snaked forward, filling the platform until all of the party were assembled and Lampard was called forward to raise the trophy. It wasn't a task he would have to complete on his own as Terry explained, 'It was one of those things that myself and Frank had done. In the last two or three years we've done it. When we've won FA Cups, I've said to Frank that I want him to lift it with me, captain and vice-captain, you know. And then it comes to that and he turns to me and says, you know, the night before, that if we do go and win it, he wants me to lift it with him, which was a nice touch. It was a nice feeling to go up there and lift the trophy, and get my medal.'[321] The potential distaste of others at the event was not even a consideration.

Among a sea of blue shirts, and a few assorted national flags as well, partly obscured by celebrating team-mates, Terry and Lampard lifted the Champions League trophy that confirmed Tyler's earlier words. It was indeed the greatest night in the history of Chelsea Football Club. They were champions of Europe. There was one more special moment to come though.

The trophy was passed around the group, giving each player a chance to raise it in the air. When it came to Drogba's turn, instead he carried the gleaming prize across to the edge of the platform, where Abramovich stood, smiling broadly, a Chelsea flag twirling in his hands. Drogba passed the trophy to the owner before standing back and smiling broadly. Abramovich then elicited one of the biggest cheers of the evening as he raised the cup above his head and brandished it in the direction of the Chelsea fans.

For every celebration though, for every tear spilt in joy, there are many others shed in disappointment. As the dust settled, and perhaps even before Chelsea fans truly had the chance to fully comprehend what had happened, for Bayern Munich and their supporters there was the dawning sad reality that the home final, the fated victory, had eluded them. The prize had slipped through their fingers and, as Chelsea scampered away to celebrate, there was only regret and lament.

Uli Hesse recalled the situation as invoking an unusual emotion for non-Bayern fans in Germany, 'There aren't

---

321 *Kings of Europe – The Chelsea Story*, Sky UK Limited, 16 September 2012.

many moments when Germans feel sorry for Bayern, but this was one of them. The other being the 1999 final [when Bayern lost the Champions League Final to Manchester United after two late goals]. There was a general sense that this had been the last chance for the Lahm/Schweinsteiger generation to win a major trophy. Also, by 2012, a lot of people had come to feel a lot of sympathy for Jupp Heynckes, who had reinvented himself as an elder statesman of the coaching profession. There was little sense of *Schadenfreude* going around.'[322]

Most fans freely acknowledged that it had been a cruel defeat for Bayern. In *Bayern: Creating a Global Superclub*, Uli Hesse related how the final had been lost, not once but three times. '[Bayern] first won it seven minutes from time, when Thomas Müller scored … Bayern won the game for the second time when Drogba brought down Ribéry with [that] reckless challenge and conceded a penalty just three minutes into extra time. Former Chelsea player Arjen Robben confidently stepped up, but goalkeeper Petr Čech guessed the right corner, plunged to his left and denied the Dutch winger. The Reds then won the final for the third time when Mata missed Chelsea's first spot kick in the penalty shoot-out. But even this lead wasn't enough. Čech saved from Ivica Olić and then pushed Bastian Schweinsteiger's penalty against the post with his fingertips. When Drogba converted the last penalty of the night, you had to fear for some of the Bayern players. Schweinsteiger in particular looked so devastated that you wondered if he would ever recover from what is now widely known as the *Fiasko dahoam*. And no prize for guessing what that means, either.'[323]

---

322 Hesse, Uli, interview with the author.

323 Hesse, Uli, *Bayern: Creating a Global Superclub* (London: Yellow Jersey Press, 2006).

In contrast, Chelsea had only won it once, with the last kick of the game. That single triumph had eclipsed Bayern's three 'wins', however. It seemed to reflect the game as a whole. Despite their disappointment, Joe Ridgeway particularly recalled the behaviour and attitude of the Bayern supporters at the stadium, 'The Munich fans were top notch and it was a great day to be a part of. All my years following the Blues, a very close call between that night and winning the league at Bolton [in 2005]. Very lucky to be at both matches!'[324]

Of course, as well as those supporting Bayern, not all English football fans were delighted with the outcome. 'Chelsea's gain is Tottenham's pain,' explained Tyler as the worst fears of the Spurs faithful were realised. Despite finishing in fourth position, the miraculous victory for their London neighbours denied Spurs a place in the following season's Champions League. Harry Redknapp, who in any other season would surely have taken the White Hart Lane club into European club football's premier tournament, lost his job a month later, reportedly over a failure to agree a new contract.

At the time, Mike Collett was Reuters' global soccer editor, a position he held for 25 years until retiring in 2016. He's also a Spurs fan, 'I've been lucky enough to be at 28 Champions League/European Cup finals as either a fan or journalist since I saw my first one aged 15 in 1968 when Manchester United beat Benfica at Wembley. I saw Chelsea play six times during their successful 2012 campaign, and I can't explain it, but I had this "sixth sense" feeling from the day they lost 3-1 to Napoli in the first leg of the round of 16 in the February of 2012 that they were going to go all the way in the competition.

---

324 Ridgeway, Joe, interview with the author.

'The match against Napoli at the Bridge was the first tangible evidence it was on. AVB had been sacked ten days before the match after two wins in their previous nine matches, and in his two games in charge, interim manager Roberto Di Matteo had seen them win 2-0 at Birmingham and 1-0 at home to Stoke. Once Drogba scored in the first half against Napoli to make it 2-3 on aggregate, and with an unbelievable atmosphere at Stamford Bridge, there was only going to be one winner and with Terry and Lampard also scoring to seal extra time, it was almost symbolic!

'Chelsea were jittery against Benfica in the home second leg of the quarter-final at the beginning of April. Almost exactly 50 years to the day since Bill Nicholson's Spurs beat Benfica 2-1 in a European Cup semi-final second leg in London, but went out to the Portuguese club 4-3 on aggregate, Benfica were back in London, and were again beaten 2-1 but this time Chelsea succeeded where Spurs failed all those years earlier by going through to the semis 3-1 on aggregate.

'Although Benfica played most of the match with ten men after stand-in skipper Maxi Pereira was sent off, Chelsea were ponderous and at 1-1 on the night survived a late scare when a Benfica goal would have knocked them out. Instead, Raul Meireles's stoppage-time winner kept their dream alive.

'Whether or not their name was on the trophy, they survived against all the odds against the reigning champions and favourites Barcelona in the semi. With Terry off and trailing 2-0 [in the second leg], Ramires' goal just before the break was just the first of several times that night they came back from the dead. Barcelona had so many chances, but when even Messi misses a penalty you just know the gods are smiling down on you.

'Nailing my colours to the mast, as a lifelong Spurs fan, I was desperate for Chelsea to prove me wrong and for Bayern to win the final. Spurs had qualified for the following season's Champions League – as long as Chelsea, who finished sixth in the Premier League, did not beat Bayern. But throughout the evening I could not shake off the sense I had carried with me since February that Chelsea's name was on the trophy. There had been too many turning points, all in Chelsea's favour. There seemed no way they were going to run out of luck now. No way that fate was about to desert them. I allowed myself a moment of hope when Müller put Bayern ahead so late in the game, but as soon as Chelsea won that corner with two minutes left, I knew, I just knew, they were going to equalise. Why did no one challenge Drogba? Bayern don't make mistakes like that – but they did.

'People forget that Chelsea were both 2-0 down and 3-1 down as the shoot-out progressed, but for me the crucial miss was Ivica Olić's. If he'd have scored Bayern would have led 4-3 going into the final kicks after Cole converted his. Bastian Schweinsteiger would then have gone up to take the kick that would have won the cup making it five out of five for Bayern – but of course that never happened. A German missing a penalty in Germany? In a final? No chance. But he did, leaving Drogba to wrap it all up. You're not a fan when you're a professional journalist. You're a professional journalist. But once I'd finished work at about 3am, I turned back into being a Spurs fan and hated the fact I'd been right all along!'[325]

At the end of the day, what did the victory mean to Chelsea, did it elevate them to the level of one of Europe's elite clubs? Jonathan Northcroft is less than convinced, 'In all

---

325 Collet, Mike, interview with the author.

honesty, I would say that it didn't raise them to the level of say Barcelona, or Real Madrid, Bayern Munich or Liverpool or Manchester United in European terms. I think, to do that, Chelsea would have to go and repeat the triumph. But what it did do, was that it ended that perception of Chelsea as a "nearly club", as a kind of "wannabe" club. It kind of took them out of the limbo that I think Paris Saint-Germain and Manchester City are probably in now [2020]. Limbo being a club known for its ambition, and its quality, but which hasn't fully arrived. I think Chelsea did arrive in that triumph in Munich.

'I was there in Moscow in 2008, when the finest of margins denied Abramovich and Chelsea the dream. I was there at Anfield in 2005 when, again, a game of incredibly fine margins denied Chelsea the chance to go to the Champions League Final. And, I was there when Barcelona put Chelsea out, very much against the dynamics of the tie with the great Iniesta goal [in 2009]. So, I'd seen Chelsea and, in fact, I was there at Highbury when Chelsea put Arsenal out, all those years ago [in 2004], but then cocked up in the semi-final. So, I'd seen the near misses, and I was there in Munich that night, and for Chelsea to win finally, and win so much against the odds was a real moment of catharsis and, I think, a sort of completing the circle for the football club.'[326]

It's an astute assessment of the events of that Champions League campaign and Chelsea's progress throughout the 2011/12 season. Their success in becoming champions of Europe was, on so many levels, unexpected. The decline in the club's fortunes in the latter months of André Villas-Boas's troubled tenure at the club, a disillusioned squad, the

326 Northcroft, Jonathan, interview with the author.

appointment of an 'interim head coach' clearly with the plan to just see the season out before a permanent appointment, the multiple occasions when the club were heading towards the exit door before a cussed refusal to bend the knee saw them through, all point towards a bleak and discouraging end to the season.

Instead, they scaled unprecedented heights, with that will to win – 'They never die,' as Gary Neville observed – seeing them not only to FA Cup but also Champions League success. It may not have been the most glorious run to securing European club football's premier trophy; in so many ways, it fell far short of that mark. It was, however, surely one of the most extraordinary. It was a victory full of triumph over adversity, remarkable comebacks, and glorious redemption. It was truly a triumph that came out of the blue.

SAMSUNG
MUNICH FINAL 2012